THE INDIVIDUAL IN THE COMMUNITY
Fourth Edition

Timothy Dansdill
Seán Duffy
Quinnipiac University

(Obama 15)

Aristotle "Selections from Politics" in
The Individual in the Community, 4th Edition, Edited by
Timothy Dansdill and Sean Duffy. New York:
Learning Solutions; 2010. 5-14.

Jaimie—
800-222-3872
x 2062

Learning Solutions
New York   Boston   San Francisco
London   Toronto   Sydney   Tokyo   Singapore   Madrid
Mexico City   Munich   Paris   Cape Town   Hong Kong   Montreal

Front cover image courtesy of John Hassett.
Back cover image courtesy of Google Earth.

Previously published as:
The Individual in the Community, Second Edition
by Seán Duffy
Copyright © 2006, 2005 by Sean Duffy
Published by Kendall/Hunt Publishing Company
Dubuque, Iowa 52002

Grateful acknowledgment is made to the following sources for permission to reprint material copyrighted or controlled by them:

"Individual and Social Narcissism," from chapter four, in *The Heart of Man*. First published in 1964 by Harper & Row, Publishers, New York, as volume XII of the "Religious Perspectives" planned and edited by Ruth Nanda Anshen. Copyright © 1964 by Erich Fromm. American Mental Health Foundation Books edition 2010.

Pearson Learning Solutions, 501 Boylston Street, Suite 900, Boston, MA 02116
A Pearson Education Company
www.pearsoned.com

Printed in the United States of America

1 2 3 4 5 6 7 8 9 10 V3DZ 15 14 13 12 11 10

000200010270582089

CY/JS

ISBN 10: 0-558-71538-9
ISBN 13: 978-0-558-71538-0

CONTENTS

PREFACE

In September 2002, the Quinnipiac University curriculum committee asked the faculty to consider two questions as part of the review of general education goals and structure: what do the faculty want students to gain from their general education at Quinnipiac University and what common set of educational philosophies unites us as a learning community? In August 2004, the first ten sections of the freshman seminar, QU101: "The Individual in the Community," were piloted. The first of three interdisciplinary seminars at the heart of our innovative general education curriculum, it introduces our freshmen to the core value that most fully encompasses Quinnipiac's stated mission as a university: community. Accordingly, the course introduces students to academic perspectives that address human nature, individuality, and the goals of community, while easing their transition into a new community—Hamden, Connecticut—and a new *type* of community—Quinnipiac University. By challenging students with an academically rigorous experience within a supportive environment, we hope to produce intentional learners who confidently take control of their own educational decisions and success. Finally the general subjects of individual and community examined throughout this first seminar provide the base for the university seminar series which will further explore the concept of community but at the national and global levels.

This volume brings together selected writings intended to facilitate the exploration of important ideas regarding the dialectical tensions between the individual and the community. It is a work in progress, but has already benefited from the positive contributions of many members of Quinnipiac's faculty and staff.

We would be negligent if we failed to acknowledge the superior efforts of the ten "pioneers" who designed and offered the first ten sections of QU101: Cheryl Barnard, Crystal Brian, Eric Bronson, Debbie Clark, Ray Foery, Jill Martin, Scott McLean, Bruce Saulnier, Bob Smart, and Allison Stratton. Their contributions can never be surpassed. In addition, we would like to thank Walter Mullen, Quinnipiac's former Coordinator of Assessment and Academic Research, who was a part of the planning process for QU101 from the beginning. We also thank Linda Broker, former Director of Academic Programs, for her organizational genius in helping to start up and sustain QU101. Their contributions in building QU101 went farther than their "official" roles. Both kept us mindful of whether the objectives we intend are being met.

The course, and the readings included in this volume, continues to reflect the contributions of the faculty who have taught the course and shared their ideas with their colleagues—both formally and informally. Their numbers are too great to thank them each individually; nevertheless, this volume is a testament to their continued support and generosity.

We recognize below a true, continuing community of collaborating faculty, students, and administrators, who, together with ourselves, have undertaken the review of the materials and methods featured in this new 2010 edition of *The Individual in the Community.* We also recognize in this group acknowledgment faculty who assisted in the 2009 Faculty Training. Finally, we recognize three students who participated in the Fall 2009 pilot initiative of the "Peer Catalyst Initiative" (conceived and administered by Mark Hoffman and Andrew Delohery). This initiative will expand from three faculty-student cohorts to nine cohorts during the Fall, 2010 semester. We have placed in bold type the names of faculty and staff who have played multiple roles in helping to advance the quality of the QU101 Seminars since 2009.

Kevin Basmadjian, Ewa Callahan, Sam Chaney (student), Deborah Clark, **Andrew Delohery**, Daniel Dempsey (student), **Aileen Dever**, Thomas Gallo (student), **Bernie Grindel**, **Raymond Foery**, **Mark Hoffman**, Tanya Huggler (student), **Melissa Kaplan**, Keith Kerr, **Joan Kreiger**, **Penny Leisring, Linda Lindroth**, Michele Moore, **Scott McLean**, Rebecca Muller (student), **Siggy Nystrom**, **Gary Pandolfi**, John Paton, Andrea Rogers (student), Jennifer Sacco, Jill Shahverdian, Travis Weisse (student), Joseph Woods.

We thank John Hassett, Quinnipiac University photographer, for the cover photo of graduating Quinnipiac students.

We thank Wendy Nelson, publishing representative of Pearson Custom Publishing for her intelligence, efficiency, humor, and astute editorial suggestions.

Finally, we extend special thanks to three members of Administrative Affairs: Angela Skyers, Director of Academic Programs: for her always calm and wise counsel; Edward Kavanagh, Associate Vice President for Academic Affairs: for his provocative assessments of QU101's role in student engagement and retention; and Mark Thompson, Senior Vice President for Academic Affairs: for his steady determination and clear vision that QU101, and the entire QU Seminar series, shall remain the center of the University Curriculum, and will play a central role in advancing the goals of the "New Synthesis Initiative" for building greater Intellectual Community at Quinnipiac University.

INTRODUCTION TO THE 4TH EDITION OF THE QU101 ANTHOLOGY "THE INDIVIDUAL IN THE COMMUNITY" A PRIMER FOR INSTRUCTORS AND STUDENTS

Welcome once again to QU101: "The Individual in the Community." Although you have long since read and discussed your individual instructor's course syllabus, including its rationale and learning objectives, we thought it worthwhile to review and underscore QU101's ultimate purpose. Following our rationale, we provide an overview of some new working features of this new, 2010 edition of the QU101 Common Reader. We also provide a detailed review of the common methods of critical reading, discussion, and writing that will help instructors and students model and achieve a number of "Essential Learning Proficiencies" that motivate Quinnipiac University's *New Synthesis for Undergraduate Education*. Using words from the mission statement of Quinnipiac University's "Essential Learning Proficiencies for the 21st Century," we believe this new edition of the QU101 Reader will challenge faculty and prepare our students to "…examine the forces that have shaped and continue to shape our world and use this knowledge to integrate their specific interests into the broader context of the local, national, and global community."

QU101: A RATIONALE AND A REVIEW

QU101 is the first of three required University Seminars designed to introduce all Quinnipiac students to the learning proficiencies and intellectual habits of mind that are essential to the life of an informed, educated citizen—one who bears a collective responsibility for the well-being of our increasingly interdependent communities—whether local, national, or global. QU101 is a humanities-based, cross-disciplinary seminar that features close, creative reading, open, involved discussion, and critical, evidence-based writing about some of the enduring questions and inevitable tensions that arise between individual rights and communal responsibilities.

QU101's six common course questions help students and instructors focus their discussions and pursue their answers together—as "colleagues"—on a series of common course readings. These common readings explore and explain the apparent separateness, divergence, and difference implied in the concept of the "Individual," as well as the apparent unity, convergence, and sameness implied in the concept of "Community." The tensions and conflicts that arise, both in our conceptualizations and lived experiences of individuality, community, and their continuous interaction, are by turns obvious and elusive, mundane and mysterious.

"Annotated" Reading and the focused discussions that flow from it in QU101 are intended to make first semester students more intentional in answering the six Common Course questions, and in doing so, achieve the set of "Essential Learning Proficiencies" which Quinnipiac University associates with both academic and lifelong professional excellence. All QU101 instructors and students will need therefore to need to work together in our reading, discussion, and writing in response to this new QU101 Common Reader. We also understand that the realization of these essential proficiencies depends on particular methods of intellectual analysis and synthesis—namely: "Annotation," "Dialectical Reasoning," and "Thematic Triangulation."

ESSENTIAL LEARNING PROFICIENCIES FOR THE 21ST CENTURY

Of the nine "Essential Learning Proficiencies," four are specified as "Interpersonal" and five as "Intellectual." We believe that six of the nine proficiencies are tied to the common learning methods and outcomes of QU101.

INTERPERSONAL PROFICIENCIES

Written and Oral Communication – An ability to think critically, clearly, and creatively in both written and oral expression….

Responsible Citizenship – An ability to recognize, analyze and influence decisions and actions at the local, national and global community, and to engage with these communities as responsible citizens.

Diversity Awareness and Sensitivity – An understanding of, and respect for, the similarities and differences among human communities. This includes a recognition and appreciation for the unique talents and contributions of all individuals.

Social Intelligence – An ability to work effectively with others, to understand and manage interactions, and to act ethically, constructively, and responsibly to achieve individual and common goals.

INTELLECTUAL PROFICIENCIES

Critical Thinking and Reasoning – An ability to recognize problems, and to acquire, assess and synthesize information in order to derive creative and appropriate solutions.

Creative Thinking and Visual Literacy – An ability to imagine, create, and communicate fresh ideas and approaches that connect to, and expand upon, knowledge through an understanding of the visual, literary, and performing arts.

As you absorb the intention of each of these proficiencies, it should be obvious that a reading, discussion, and writing based seminar is designed explicitly to help you achieve greater "Oral and Written Communication," and "Critical Thinking and Reasoning." Given the extraordinary theme of QU101 and the entire QU Seminar series, it should also be obvious that a focus on the individual's relation to Community in its Local, National, and Global contexts will sensitize and challenge you toward a deeper understanding of "Social Intelligence," "Diversity Awareness," and "Responsible

Citizenship." Less obvious is how QU101 will help you achieve proficiency in "Creative Thinking and Visual Literacy." As we review and exemplify two of the common course methods for analysis and synthesis—"Dialectical Reasoning" and "Thematic Triangulation"—we believe this proficiency will also be exercised in your discussions of QU101's common readings and films.

We trust that as you read through these proficiencies—particularly the "Interpersonal Proficiencies"—you have also recognized some of the key words that distinguish QU101's six Common Questions. The cross-referencing between course questions and the essential interpersonal proficiencies is not accidental, but fully intentional. Navigating the course of Quinnipiac's University Curriculum through seminar-based common questions, readings, and discussion writing opens the way toward realizing these essential proficiencies in the name of greater intellectual community.

THREE NEW FEATURES OF THE 2010 QU101 READER

The 2010 edition of the QU101 Common Reader features three important innovations that will affect how all QU101 instructors, will approach and realize these commonly held learning proficiencies and outcomes with their students. The first major innovation to note about this new edition is the number and content of new readings and how they shakeup and enliven the readings we have retained from previous editions of the reader. The second innovation involves how the readings are organized. The third innovation involves how the pages of text are formatted to foster *Annotation*, which in turn enables *Dialectical Reasoning* and *Thematic Triangulation*. Following the sections that describe the new features of this new edition are in-depth descriptions of these common methods for evoking and ensuring consistent, rigorous acts of critical reading, discussion, and writing in QU101.

FIRST INNOVATION: A REMIX OF "OLD" AND "NEW" READINGS

While all of the readings in this new edition will be "new" to all students of QU101, and to those faculty teaching QU101 for the first time, many instructors of long experience with the course will discover that roughly half of the readings are new. In fact, seventeen readings that were part of past editions have been replaced with seventeen new readings. We selected these new readings for various reasons.

- to provide more opportunity for ideological contrast and "dialectical" tension in our acts of reading, discussion, and writing in QU101;
- to acknowledge some recent trends in social and intellectual development;
- to exercise more "creative" thinking through literary representations of QU101's course questions and themes;
- to shake up and refresh our modes of common reading, discussion and thinking in light of the changes expressed in such new institutional

mission statements as the "Essential Learning Proficiencies for the 21st Century."

We therefore think it useful for all instructors and their students to preview some of the new readings in relation to some of the "old" core readings we have retained. The groupings we cite in each preview are not meant to serve as a final, definitive selection. Because individual instructors bring a diversity of intellectual views and understandings of a seminar that is dedicated to achieving a series of common, humanities-based proficiencies, there are, potentially, an unlimited number of possibilities for organizing annotated readings and focused discussions that draw in common from QU101's six Course Questions. We organize these previews in light of the Six Common Course Questions and offer some very brief extensions of the annotative, dialectical, and thematic possibilities for class discussion, our common writing assignments, and for the achievement of the various "Essential Learning Proficiencies" outlined above.

We also should note that, as students and instructors have become conversant with the course questions in their annotated discussions of Obama's memoir, they now recognize that these questions are neither meant to be self-contained, nor can they be. Instead, they are interrelated and interactive—all the more so as we move into the QU101 Common Reader. We suggest some few of the many possible cross-question and cross-textual connections in our previews. Individual instructions may well—and are encouraged to—organize this new edition's readings in light of particular course questions according to their own intellectual and curricular sensibilities. Similarly, students are strongly encouraged in their reading of a particular set of texts, especially if formally tied to a specific course question, to note and mark passages that correspond to other course questions. As we will detail below, the course questions are connected, and so too are the texts in this new reader, by a dialectical view of reading and learning.

PREVIEW OF READINGS FOR COURSE QUESTION 1: WHAT DEFINES AND LOCATES AN INDIVIDUAL?

Maalouf, Amin. Selections from *In the Name of Identity*
Levinas, Emmanuel. "The Face and Responsibility for the Other"
Tatum, Beverly Daniel. "The Development of White Identity"
Machan, Tibor. Selections from *Classical Individualism*
Fromm, Erich. "Individual and Social Narcissism"

In the Name of Identity has been a core text for QU101 since the course was first conceived. We have integrated selections from the entire book into the new edition of this reader to better reinforce his conceptions of personal, ethnic, and national "identity." Students will recognize in this selection Maalouf's conception of "two heritages"—the "Vertical" and "Horizontal." It was featured in the prompt for your "Directed Self-Placement" essay, and graces the back of the "QU101 Questions" bookmark.

The Levinas interview might as have been titled, "In the Face of Identity," because his philosophical and ethical view of the human face can be read as the interactive complement to the Proper Name that signifies Self and Other. Though very brief, Levinas is difficult reading that will initially resist comprehension. Still, all students will literally recognize what he is claiming about the face and face-to-face encounters: Even before the act of self-identification through the birthright of our Proper Name, we recognize our face. This principle of first personal encounter holds even greater visual sway when face-to-face with an Other. The face-to-face encounter not only secures a sense of individual identity; it is the threshold across which we form and sustain—or disavow—a sense of community.

Tatum's "The Development of White Identity" is another text retained for this new edition. Not unlike Maalouf, Tatum's study of "white" identity argues that identity is not given once and for all, or "inherited," but rather, is earned over time in our encounters with Others—in our yearning, if not learning, to look past either/or oppositional notions of "Sameness" and "Difference." As students annotate these three readings, we believe the cross-references to their annotations of Obama's text will come fast and furious, depending on their instructor's openness to a circling or "recursive" approach to a fully animated and "annotated" discussion.

Machan's historical analysis of the idea of "Individualism" is new to this edition, and a much needed counter-narrative to Rousseau's notion of "the general will" in *The Social Contract*. His arguments for the sustainability of a pure individual freedom will challenge students and instructors as they turn later in the reader to Hardin's "The Tragedy of the Commons."

Fromm's analysis of the nature of "narcissism" not only deepens our view of the psychological sources and pitfalls of individual and social identity, but opens the way to understanding some of the questions of QU201: Is a sense of "National Identity and National Community" symptomatic of a narcissistic mindset? Like the six course questions, this is a question that carries no single, simple answer. The answers we entertain in our discussions open onto other new questions that anticipate and connect to other texts in the reader. Most certainly, when students read and discuss Bauerlein's text, they will want to review their annotations of Fromm.

READINGS FOR COURSE QUESTION 2: HOW IS INDIVIDUAL IDENTITY FORMED AND SUSTAINED?

McElroy, Wendy.   "Individualism: A New View Of Feminism"
Pinker, Steven. "The Moral Instinct"
Gilligan, Carol. "Moral Orientation and Moral Development"
Zimbardo, Philip G. "A Situationist Perspective on the Psychology of Evil"

Because of the sheer complexity of moral questions—their origins, developmental schemes, and real world outcomes—we will be err on the side of brevity in this preview. Like Maalouf's, Zimbardo's text has anchored QU101's curriculum from its beginning. By posing the presence and progression of "evil" as an essential part of and challenge to all individual identity development, Zimbardo's case studies align well with Fromm's analysis of "narcissism." Zimbardo, Pinker, and Gilligan are all psychologists of moral development, but their analyses are start from different research premises, and end with very different implications for what it means to be a "Moral" individual. In effect, annotations of all three will "triangulate" richly. The "moral" terms, situations, and "effects" they illustrate and summarize, (Zimbardo's "bystander effect" is one of many), should engage students at the level of their own personal and social experience. Gilligan's distinctions between an ethic of "caring" and one of "justice" pairs well with McElroy's view of "individualism." We also note that Gilligan's "care" ethic triangulates well when McElroy's feminist view of "individualism" is read against the grain of Machan's decidedly more "masculinist" views. (We also believe Stanton's "The Solitude of Self" would work with this course question in mind, but prefer to place her under question four because of the conflict she raises between a woman's place in the male-dominated world of her time.)

COURSE QUESTION 3: WHAT DEFINES AND LOCATES A COMMUNITY?

Plato. Selections from *The Republic*
Aristotle. Selections from *Politics*
Boyer, Ernest. Two Essential Goals
Mills, Andrew P. "What's So Good About a College Education?"
Bauerlein, Mark. "The Betrayal of the Mentors"
Putnam, Robert. "Thinking About Social Change in America"
Subdivided (film)
Malls R Us (film)

Plato's *Republic* has not only been at the core of the QU101 seminars from its conception and inception. Plato, perhaps the most influential of "Western" philosophers, founded the first "Academy." His *Republic* remains as one of the core texts for understanding the history of what we mean by an educated "community" and "citizenry" which pursues "Justice" or a balanced life. We have added to this new edition selections from the *Politics* of Aristotle, (Plato's student, and equally influential as a founding figure of Western Philosophy). These selections comment on and directly criticize his teacher's conception of the ideal communal justice and the individuals who are best fit to inhabit and sustain it. Boyer, Mills and Bauerlein all address the ultimate importance of education—of how to best draw forth, preserve, but also to adapt, those social and intellectual habits of mind that every new generation must manifest if our communities of local, national and global purpose are to prosper. The two films, *Subdivided* and *Malls R Us*, provide both visual and creative commentary on what defines and how we locate— and literally, educate—ourselves (or not) in community values. Putnam's text triangulates well with these two films, especially with his concepts of "social capital" and our local and national responsibilities for "bridging and bonding." We should point out that these readings could very well fit with Course Question 4, as those under four could fulfill Question 3. These two questions are truly in "dialectical" tension and interaction, and we encourage instructors and students to make cross-connections between questions and texts through repeated considerations of their evolving annotations. Questions 3 and four represent the conceptual and thematic pivot point for QU101, and so open-endedness and adaptation on the part of instructors and students is encouraged.

COURSE QUESTION 4: HOW IS A SENSE OF COMMUNITY FORMED AND SUSTAINED?

Macintyre, Alasdair. "The Virtues, the Unity of a Human Life and the Concept of a Tradition"
Rousseau, Jean-Jacques. Selections from *The Social Contract*
Quinnipiac Student Handbook (selections)
"The Constitution of the United States" (selections)
Hardin, Garrett. "The Tragedy of the Commons"
Hampton, Keith. Selections from "Social Isolation and New Technology"
Digital Nation (film)

Rousseau's *Social Contract*, like Plato's *Republic*, is broadly accepted by the QU Seminars Community to be a founding core text not only for successive editions of our Common Reader, but for generations of university-educated individuals who come to understand that the notion and application of a "contract" literally *underwrites* virtually every system of social, economic, ethical and political community human beings have experienced throughout history. When read as a theoretical treatment of our civilized obligations in dialectical contrast to the historically lived policy document and legal roadmap that is our "Constitution," *The Social Contract* takes on ever-renewable relevance. When we then look to a "local" social contract such as the "Quinnipiac Student Handbook," we begin to understand that contracts, constitutions, and covenants are the foundations—often unread or recognized—of why we form, and how we can sustain, any organization of community life. Macintyre's idea of "unity" and "virtue" are deeply linked to what we decide value in the individuals who participate in various communities. Arguing against the claims of extreme "individualism," Hardin's sense of "tragedy" is that without some "coerced" a sense of "common" purpose, some renewed conscience as to the virtue of self-sacrifice, none of our most pressing problems of sustainability can be resolved. The dialectical findings that can emerge from within and across these readings—such as Freedom/Authority or Alienation/Obligation, to name just two of many—set up a turn toward the issues raised in Hampton's research survey of how we are adapting to digital technologies and new social media. Hampton's findings play well and provocatively with the questions of social distraction and civic dislocation raised by the documentary film, *Digital Nation*.

COURSE QUESTION 5: HOW DO INDIVIDUALS DEAL WITH TENSIONS AND CONFLICTS BETWEEN PERSONAL INTERESTS AND COMMUNITY INTERESTS?

Stanton, Elizabeth Cady. "The Solitude of Self"
Bradbury, Ray. "All Summer in a Day"
Kaminer, Wendy. "Bullying and the Phoebe Prince Case"
Jaggar, Alison. "Caring as a Feminist Practice of Moral Reason"
Holtz, Jeff. "A Student Editor Finds Himself at the Center of the News"
New York Times, Editorial. "Curbing Speech at Quinnipiac"
Three QU *Chronicle* Articles on *Blackboard*

Stanton's early "feminist" cry from the heart for both solitude and solidarity, addressed to a vastly more sexist culture that had not yet accepted the equality of women in all modes of being and becoming, pairs well with Jaggar's review and recapitulation of the gender differences in moral development raised by Gilligan. Jaggar more explicitly juxtaposes "care reasoning" from "justice reasoning," and analyzes their imbalance in Gilligan. In doing so, her call for a dialectical equilibrium, and the emergence perhaps of a third kind of reasoning for dealing with the conflicts underscored in question 5, points back to Plato's monolithic focus on the meaning and end of "Justice" in *The Republic*. Stanton's sense of solitude in tension with a need for solidarity also pairs well with Bradbury's very short story about social stigma and literal as well as emotional isolation. Likewise, Kaminer's early short reporting on the "Phoebe Prince Case" draws a bright line on face to face versus "virtual" bullying, and should stimulate discussion in its own right on "crowd behavior" and the role played by the "guardians"—parental and educational—in monitoring and preventing what Zimbardo might understand as an act of "scapegoating" that meets with the "bystander effect." We assume students will be aware of this case and instructors are encouraged to add more recent reflections and reports on the issues of care and justice that surround Prince's death. The final three short pieces involve our local community of Quinnipiac administrators and students in a conflict over "freedom of the press" and the "freedom to associate." The two *New York Times* articles cover two distinct, but related events that placed two Quinnipiac students—Jason Braff and Jaclyn Hirsch—who were associated with Quinnipiac's student newspaper, *The Chronicle*, and with the "underground" WEB-based newpaper, the *QUAD*. They found themselves at the center of a perennial conflict that pits the rights of individuals when they act on what they believed to be "guaranteed rights" whose public status do not hold in a private institutional realm.

COURSE QUESTION 6: HOW DO PERCEPTIONS OF INDIVIDUAL DIFFERENCE AND DIVERSITY AFFECT COMMUNITY?

McIntosh, Peggy. "White Privilege and Male Privilege"
"A Statement from Eight Alabama Clergymen"
King, Martin Luther. "Letter from Birmingham Jail"

O'Connor, Flannery. "The Artificial Nigger"
Wells, H.G. "The Country of the Blind"

It would be easy yet careless to characterize this group of readings as dealing exclusively with "identity politics"—race and racism, sex and sexism, class and class-based prejudice. King's now classic letter of response to eight Alabama clergy who used their religious status and power in the community to reinforce their racism is much more than an eloquent anti-racist classic. It is a thoroughgoing argument for how we can alter our perceptions of difference, knowing that we are all the same at the core of our human being and becoming. For King, there really is no "white" or "black" identity, to take one of the most potent and poisonous of binary oppositions. As he declares in his letter, "We are caught in an inescapable network of mutuality, tied in a single garment of destiny. Whatever affects one directly, affects all indirectly." Students will see many instances in these readings that this confident ideal is not universally agreed upon or shared in common. When we read McIntosh's personal narrative and institutional catalogue of how blind we all can be to the "invisible" operations of privilege and power historically determined and maintained, we not only see that the tensions she reviews and raises are backlit by the King/Clergymen texts.

We also see that Obama's memoir can be brought back into play when considering these two texts—not only because he is the living embodiment of "blackness" and "whiteness" in dialectical play. Recall that the subtitle to his memoir is "A Story of Race and Inheritance." Obama's sense of his own international inheritance offers a return to what Maalouf means by this in his axis of the vertical and horizontal heritages. While we often, and stubbornly, believe we are each uniquely "individual," we do so by remaining blind to the essential *sameness* (the literal meaning of "identity") of ourselves.

This allegorical sense of "blindness," and its dialectical partner, *insight* come into play in Wells' "The Country of the Blind." Wells plays up the ironies of such well-worn adages as "The Blind leading the blind" when we come to consider who is the individual most qualified to be the "Leader" of a given community, and what are those qualities? He can be profitably read in cross-annotated reference to Plato and Aristotle. Wells' story combines themes of alienation, isolation, and escape from the conformist requirements of one kind of communal existence into another. The conflicting needs for the power of love and for the love of power also run through this story. The careful reader and class participant is led to ask the question: "Where do we belong and not belong?" This question runs through the heart of O'Connor's still tense, provocative tale of the "white/black" binary opposition, with particular and surprising focus on "white" alienation and trepidation within "black" community, rather than the reverse scenario. We will not belabor its relevance to this particular course question, as the main characters, and their locations within and between distinct identity and community enclaves, will create connections and comparisons that take us back not only to Obama and Maalouf, but to Tatum and Putnam, to name only a few.

SECOND INNOVATION: WIDER MARGINS AND NOTE PAGES TO FOSTER ANNOTATION

The second important change to note in this new edition is a new page format with wider margins to support the common, critical method of reading—*aka* Annotation—that was introduced in Fall 2009. This edition also offers several blank pages at the end of each reading, and at the end of the book. These pages for "Notes" allow students and instructors to collect and synthesize specific annotations from the margins of the given text, or to record notable remarks made by fellow annotators during large and small group discussions. At its most basic, annotation is what happens to a book's margins when a reader forms the habit of reading with a pen or pencil—not a highlighter!—in his or her hand. Known more formally as *marginalia*, *annotations* began to appear long before the birth of printed books. The word "note" is at the center of annotation, and according to the *Oxford English Dictionary* (more on this reference site below), annotation appears in the 12th century as: "to notice, pay attention to, to perceive, to indicate, to put down in writing, to mention" (*OED*). The QU101 students now reading about the origins of annotation will also be taking English 101, and if they read the very first page of the common anthology of readings for that course—*Ways of Reading*—they will in fact recognize a similar argument on the very first page of the Introduction in the section title itself: "*Making a Mark*." The authors first offer one rather vague form of re-reading: "A reader can go back and scan …to find passages…that might be worth reconsidering." They follow with this alternative:

> Or a reader can construct a personal index, making marks in the margin….A mark is a way of saying, "This is something I might want to work on later." If you mark the sentences in this book as you read them, you will give yourself a working record of what, at the first moment of reading, you felt might be worth a second reading (Bartholomae7).[i]

Here is evidence of annotation as a common academic method or habit of mind that a student at any level of knowledge or professional achievement would do well to practice across his or her disciplinary subjects. What the authors of *Ways of Reading* do not appear to share with QU101's transformative sense of constructing a "personal index," of "making marks in the margin," of giving oneself "a working record," is that annotation, as the act of noting something important in one's reading, can serve as a continued, communal act of speaking—an action for *discussion* with one's fellow annotators.

Thus, this act of speaking through annotation is not only addressed to the First Year-at-University Self, nor to the Self of the Author, nor even to some imagined Future Reader of an Annotated QU101 Common Reader. In QU101, our annotations, when based on both a "personal index" and on a communal set of questions that all students and teachers are interested to consider, become part of a much longer, older interactive history of reading, writing, and discussion.

Our annotations are more than random (re)marks in the margins. They impose speaking cues, become imposing scripts for performing our part in our QU101 class discussions. H.J. Jackson's *Marginalia: Readers Writing in Books* speaks to this act of imposition on our sense of time, space, and ownership in the dialectical act of reading to annotate and annotating to read. She first examines the history of arguments *against* writing in books—particularly those that don't belong to us—(such as those owned by libraries and school systems for use by all individuals in a given community.) We think the following passage important to our argument in favor of annotation because writing down our thinking is always a major imposition on our time, and it imposes a focus and change upon the space of our thinking, when compared, say, to speaking our thoughts. So the added imposition to write down our thinking—to annotate—in relation to our reading, will also radically refocus and change how we locate ourselves as readers pursuing answers to the common questions at the heart of QU101.

> Renaissance scholars have long been aware that...marginal annotation can radically alter a reader's perception of the centered text....They introduce other facts and contrary opinions, the facts and opinions themselves being less significant than the demonstrated possibility of alternatives and opinions. They impose not just criticism but a critical attitude upon all the following readers. Naturally book producers resent them....[For many] readers [who come to a book filled with a previous reader's annotations] however, the core objection is not so much an insult to the book, author, or publisher as the imposition upon the reader [expecting clean margins]. This is a complicated affair (Jackson 241).

We agree that annotation—both as a practice and found artifact—indeed remains a "complicated affair." The vast majority of modern readers have all been trained to view writing in books, particularly community-owned books, and even our own privately held volumes, as a kind of assault, vandalism or defilement. The simplest way in here as an argument for why students and instructors should annotate their own, freshly published books, is that our own annotations "impose...a critical attitude" upon our own proficiencies of Oral and Written Communication and of "Critical Thinking and Reasoning." They impose upon, and leave a record of, our individual minds at work. A blank book, or even one highlighted, by contrast, leaves no identity trace that your "I", that reader identified by your name on the inside cover, was ever there conversing with the author or the self you once were, in your first semester of college. As long time readers, as we look back and reread our own annotations in books from our college or graduate school years, we can assure you that our intellectual identities have most assuredly changed over the course of our own lifelong learning. The practical "proficiency" outcomes for a weekly seminar are clear and present, but to then read over one's own annotations from years past is to recognize and to impose upon one's self a sometimes a barely familiar stranger.

On Jackson's notion of "resentment" over "annotation," we thought it appropriate to share a moment in during the first week of discussion of Obama's text in a QU101 course in the fall semester of 2009. After asking students how annotation affected their reading of Obama's text, one student was quite resentful, complaining that it "slowed down my reading; it is very annoying." A tense silence ensued until another student replied: "But that is the point. It makes you slow down and re-think what you're reading using the Course Questions." Many students also asked why they just can't highlight their texts. The question was posed to the class, and one student responded: "Highlights have no words to go back to." Still other students begged for the alternative of using narrow slips or normal squares of "stickies." Last fall, many instructors compromised with students on this point. This semester, we don't think they should— especially given the new format of wider margins and blank pages following each reading for transferring and synthesizing marginal comments.

Resentment and resistance against writing in the margin's of one's own purchased book remains strong, and not mainly for reasons of acculturation by public schools and libraries that writing in books is selfish, destructive and an imposition upon future readers of a text paid for by public funds and held in common trust. Behaving like book sellers, rather than working intellectuals, college students now cultivate the preservation of a clean, pristine—and often unread—book to ensure a high resale value to the market in "used books." We very well understand that the cost of books is high. (So are cell phone and texting plans.) We also realize that in the new age of digital technology, of WEB pages and of ebooks that many students—and not a few cultural theorists— foretell and welcome the Beginning of the End of the Printed Book. Given the goals of QU101, our claim is that, having made your mark on this book, your active ownerships of it lends to it a use value that transcends any resale value.

The University bookstore will not, in any case, repurchase your reader. Nor will online bookstores be interested in a book so thoroughly annotated; its resale value will be, in a word, $0. As you progress in your personal and professional lives, consider your very own marked up reader to be a valuable historical record of your maturing intellectual identity and individuality. Consider it a gift to the individual you will become. Given the trends in book use in libraries— declining—and the resale trends of college texts—expanding—your QU101 Reader might well be the only book that you will retain from your college years.

You might well consider this book an educational legacy for your own future family. Imagine sitting down with your own college-bound son or daughter and showing them what you were thinking about as you read and annotated to discover some of the answers to these lasting questions of Individuality and Community. You might hear yourself saying to them: "I held this very book in my hands, along with my fellow first semester college students, and just look at what I wrote in the margins. Why, I hardly *recognize* the person I was who was thinking in these ways!" Most essentially, your annotations are a lasting record of your own mind at work no longer at the margins of your entrance into the University

Curriculum, but one that will represent a center of your becoming an individual proficient in a lifelong quest of intellectual community.

DIALECTICAL REASONING: CONCEPT AND METHOD

In her book on marginalia, Jackson informs us that there are samples from over 2000 thousand years ago. Older than the act of annotation is the art of *Dialectic*, which appeared in Greece over 2500 years ago. For Socrates, (who never wrote anything down—his student Plato did that—and who believed writing would destroy memory), *dialectic* was the learned art of focused *conversation*; it was the *discussion* of the most important enduring questions for being human and for human becoming. Most simply, the art of *dialectic* can be equated with conducting a *dialogue*. In keeping with the strongly implied need in our Common Course Questions 1 and 3 to "define" the two words that are at the dialectical and dialogical heart of QU101, we reference *The Oxford English Dictionary*, the most comprehensive dictionary in the history of the language.[1] Following are some pertinent sections on the definition of "dialectic": "...conversation, way of speaking, language of a country or district, from: to discourse, converse; originally: through, across + to speak."

We can now recognize that, given the original meaning of dialectic of to "speak through" or "speak across," it is no connotative stretch to insist that the annotation-based discussions at the heart of every QU101 class qualify them as deeply and originally "dialectical." Why? Because we need to speak through and across our annotations, and across the discussion circles we form throughout the semester if we are to come close to achieving the essential learning proficiency of "Oral Communication." Let's continue to unpack some of the *OED*'s entry information, and in doing so, illustrate that we are in fact performing an annotation of these selected texts.

> The art of critical examination into the truth of an opinion; the investigation of truth by discussion: scientifically developed by Plato, by whom the term was used in two senses, (*a*) the art of definition or discrimination of 'ideas', (*b*) the science which views the inter-relation of the ideas in the light of a single principle— 'the good' (*OED Online*).

We can see that the design of the QU101 seminar is in full accord with the Platonic "art" and "science" of the dialectic in so far as we privilege discussion dedicated to the definition and interrelation of ideas. We have already previewed Plato's most crucial question in *The Republic*: how to achieve "Justice" through

---

[1] The online version of the OED is available to all QU students through the Arnold Bernhard Library. Type this URL into your browser: https://myq.quinnipiac.edu/IT%20%20Libraries/ABL/Pages/GeneralReference.aspx and look for the link to Oxford English Dictionary. We encourage all QU instructors and their students to engage and integrate the use of this great reference work in the course of their common learning. They could do no better than to start with the entries on "Individual" and "Community." Defining and deepening our knowledge of key words and concepts with the *OED* is an essential first step toward realizing the "Essential Learning Outcome" of "Critical Thinking and Reasoning."

the proper education of an individual in harmony with the community. In *The Republic* Plato elevates "Dialectic" to the most important of the studies one must undertake to become a "Guardian"—if not a "Ruler"—in his ideal community. A responsible "Individual in the Community" was required to learn how to speak with others about the most important questions of the best way to form and sustain a community of informed, justice-seeking citizens.

Ironically, most of the "discussion" in Plato's so-called "dialogues" feature his mouth-piece Socrates engaged in a lecturing *monologue*, with a few "yes men" to move the prescribed resolution of the debated question to an end. In QU101, we do not endorse teacher monologues, or one "Socratic" questioner. We are more attuned to the original notion of a "Local Discussion", of learning "to speak from and across" one's individual annotations so as to connect with those of one's fellow thinkers in intellectual community.

We will annotate one more section from the *OED*'s entry on "dialectic." This meaning should remind the careful reader that Plato's notion of "justice" was derived from Greek philosophers who lived long before Socrates and Plato: Heraclitus and Empedocles. Empedocles, for example, believed that all of existence was derived from the two motives or forces—"Love and Strife." One of the surviving fragments of Heraclitus states: "It is wise to agree that all things are one. In differing it agrees with itself, a backward-turning connection....The path up and down is one and the same." These dialectically driven conceptions of justice persist in the *OED*'s contemporary sense of the dialectic: "In more general use, the existence or working of opposing forces, tendencies." Following all of its historically evolved definitions, the *OED* then supplies examples from across the disciplinary spectrum to illustrate a given definition. Here are the supporting references for its contemporary definition of dialectic.

> 1965 *Listener* 25 Nov. 837/2 Schofield presents only one half of the dialectic and virtually ignores the other half, namely the counter-pressures which parents, and adult society in general, must bring to bear on rebellious youth.
> 1967 J. K. Galbraith suggested that for every apparently dominant force in modern capitalism, an equal and opposite force existed or could be conjured up: big trade unions to oppose monopolies, the state to oppose both, and so on, in an endless dialectic (*OED Online*).

These more recent examples of how the dialectic has been contextualized for our students' understanding might lead them to believe that dialectical reasoning is a reductive, counter-productive, even destructive game of either/or, absolute "yes or no", or "black and white" oppositions. They might be reminded of the format of *Fox News* interviews that deliberately preempts careful critical reasoning and civil, consensus-seeking discussion in favor of "last word" shouting matches that end as they begin: in polarized, divided viewpoints from the "liberal left" and the "conservative right." There is never an attempt to reach a consensus or some constructive *synthesis* of the two contending positions. In his comprehensive history, *Dialectical Thinking and Adult Development*, the psychologist Michael Basseches reminds that dialectical reasoning is a movement of mature thought that features three phases:

> The first phase involves reflection upon a thought—the *thesis*—to a new thought—the *antithesis*. A thesis is any idea of element of thought. An antithesis is not necessarily the opposite of the thesis; it is any idea or element of thought exluded from, outside of, or contrary to the thesis.
>
> The second phase involves movement from reflection upon both thesis and antithesis to a third thought—the *synthesis*—in which the thesis and the antithesis (or some aspect of each) are related to each other. The synthesis usually has a more complex form than either the thesis of the antithesis, since it includes aspects of thesis and antithesis within itself and binds those aspects together, (that is, it is both more differentiated and integrated at once).
>
> The overall movement may be *cyclical* in that the synthesis can become *a new thesis*, reflection upon which can then lead to a thought which is alternative to or omitted from it, (that is, a *new antithesis*). This, in turn, can then lead to an idea with an even more complex form than the first synthesis, (that is, a second synthesis) (Basseches 77-78, emphasis added).

A careful look back at the second example from the OED regarding the author's characterization of Galbraith's analysis of capitalism's historical movement "in an endless dialectic" both confirms Basseches' three phase description, yet undermines it with the sense that dialectical thinking and action is inevitably aggressive—that any new synthesis is a "winner take all" outcome. As an intellectual method for tracking our annotations, sharing them in focused, caring discussions, and analyzing them in formal writing assignments, we are keen to dispel this sense of a *negative* dialectical approach to the enduring questions and problems posed by the QU101 seminar and its readings. While we acknowledge that force, aggression, domination are a fact of existence, and that the six Common Course Questions are themselves charged with oppositions, tensions, and conflicts, we also charge our fellow instructors and students new to the university learning community to work in their discussions toward open-ended, consensual, and collaborative solutions and answers to these course questions.

Since QU101 students are just out of high school, we thought it apt to share how Joe Greenwald, high school teacher who teaches dialectical reasoning to his students, defines the *dialectic*: "a method of reasoning that compares and contrasts opposing points of view in order to find a new point of view that will incorporate whatever is true in the originals "Greenwald".[2] Whatever is true in the original course questions is itself a matter of informed personal opinion in dialectical interplay with the ideas and views of our common course readings. With any working definition we offer, we trust that instructors and their students will adapt and apply it in their quest to achieve the essential learning outcomes.

What is very important to understand is that the conception and practice of the *Dialectic* that we have been reviewing up this point—from Socrates and Plato, to the *Oxford English Dictionary's* examples, to a clinical psychologist and high school teacher—is the *Western* philosophical and methodological view. That is, the *Dialectic* is itself a cyclical movement of two aspects or alternatives. In short, there is an *Eastern* philosophical and methodological view of the *Dialectic*. Using a table of "binary oppositions," we will transition from the *Western* to this *Eastern* conception, and thus illustrate that there is always a "third" list of "opposing" terms. Look at this stack of juxtaposed boxes divided by an apparently impassable vertical line.

Binary Oppositions	
Male	Female
Brightness	Darkness
Good	Evil
Master	Apprentice
Knowledge	Ignorance
Self	Other
Right	Responsibility
Citizen	Alien
Voluntary	Mandatory
Life	Death
Zero	One

No one would argue that this rectilinear grid, built from horizontal and vertical lines, is not a powerful visual, organizational, and teaching aid for distinguishing and understanding the dual nature of things, processes, and ideas. Another representation of these binary oppositions has them separated by a *back slash*—as with *feminine/masculine; black/white; homo/heterosexual; poor/rich*. We can imagine that the hard and fast, rigid rectilinear line relaxing, falling toward the horizontal, into the *horizon* of the more natural curvilinear flow of relationships, as in land§sea.

Lao-Tzu, a Chinese philosopher who lived at the same time as the pre-Socratic philosopher, Heraclitus—nearly two centuries before Socrates and Plato—conceived of duality in much the same way as his "western" counterpart. Recall that Heraclitus declares that, "The path up and down is one and the same." In his philosophy of Taosim, Lao-Tzu declares: "Life and death are one thread, the same line viewed from different sides." What if we are to re-

---

[2] http://ablemedia.com/ctcweb/showcase/greenwaldgreece11.html

imagine this table of binary opposites, focusing particularly on the line of separation as a curving "thread"—or as "curvilinear" (defined as: "A relationship between two or more variables which is depicted graphically by anything other than a straight line"(Gordon[3])? What we might visualize is the figure of a circle not so much divided, as united by that curving thread which binds not conflicting, but rather, complementary opposites within the greater whole of that circle—the Yin and Yang. In the Eastern view of dialectical interaction, the principle of polarity does not mean opposites are not "polar opposites" or a "polarized debate." Alan Watts, the great American purveyor and interpreter of Eastern philosophies and religions for popular Western understanding collaborated with a Chinese scholar, Al Chung-liang, on the final book completed just before his death. They explain "the principle of polarity" as represented in the figure of the Yin and Yang this way:

The principle of polarity is not to be confused with the ideas of opposition or conflict. In the metaphors of other cultures, light is at war with darkness, life with death, good with evil, and the positive with the negative, and thus an idealism to cultivate the former and be rid of the latter flourishes throughout much of the world. To the traditional way of Taoist thinking, this is as incomprehensible as an electric current with both positive and negative poles, for polarity is the principle that ± and —, north and south, are different aspects of one and the same system, and that the disappearance of either one of them would be the disappearance of the system. People who have been brought up in the aura of Christian and Hebrew aspirations find this principle frustrating, even threatening, because it seems to deny any possibility of progress, an ideal which flows from their linear (as distinct from cyclic) view of time and history (Watts 19-20).[4]

Watts and Huang are actually proposing a counter-narrative of the all too often unseen Other side of any great and enduring question. They are proposing an "opposable" (as in the evolution of the thumb and finger) to better grasp a *method* for understanding the predicament of human progress and the progress of the human predicament. In quoting their reading of Judeo-Christian tradition, it is important to note that we are neither espousing nor endorsing any particular religious or philosophical system. In a course such as QU101, dedicated to cross-disciplinary consideration of human identity

[3] Marshall, Gordon. "curvilinear relationship." *A Dictionary of Sociology*. 1998. http://www.encyclopedia.com/doc/1O88-curvilinearrelationship.html

[4] Watts, Alan. *Tao: The Watercourse Way.* Pantheon: New York, 1975.

[5] Campbell, Joseph. *Myths to Live By*. Viking: New York, 1972.

and community at a secular, liberal arts university, we are interested in presenting at least two sides, two ways of seeing, two methods for visualizing and advancing every idea and question that QU101 raises.

In *Myths to Live By*, the great scholar of World Mythology, Joseph Campbell characterizes Taoist philosophy and the metaphorical figure of the *yang* and *yin* reminds us that our western tendency to polarize, moralize and politicize along rigid lines of binary opposition do not travel well along the curvilinear "thread", up and down the "stream" of Taoist dialectical reasoning.

> The light and dark side of this system of thought are named respectively *yang* and *yin*, which are words referring to the sunny (*yang*) and shady (*yin*) sides of a stream…Dark, cool, and moist; light, hot, and dry: earth and sun in counteraction. These are associated, further, with the female and the male as passive and active principles. There is no *moral* verdict here intended; neither principle is "better" than the other, neither "stronger" than the other. They are two equally potent grounding principles on which all the world rests, and in their interaction they inform, constitute, and decompose all things (Campbell 116, author's emphasis).[5]

Campbell's ultimate aim as a "mythologist," one who wrote dozens of books attempting marry the "Eastern" and "Western" edges of their narratives and plots, was to rectify and restore the rightful meaning and purpose of *myth*. Here is the Oxford English Dictionary's reference on the original meaning of the word: "a speech, narrative…plot." We believe that the mastery of dialectical reasoning is a universally "mythic" method to live and learn by—an essential learning proficiency, more simply known as "Oral and Written Communication."

Of course, if we wanted to begin populating the *Yin-Yang* figure with explicitly "Western" terms, or even "American" ideas or systems, then we can draw a series of circles on or classroom's whiteboard, or on a blank page in our notebooks, add the curvilinear thread whose up and down are one and the same, and write in whatever is most pressing for consideration. Here is an example from the "Patriot Resistance" website, which espouses radical American Individualism, Capitalism, and Exceptionalism.[6]

(Patriotic Resistance)

So aside from practicing a series of quotation and commentary exercises— brief "writing-to-learn" from our annotated readings—exercises that draw on a dialectical frame of mind in selecting passages and developing our marginal comments—the question arises as to how we can exercise the essential learning proficiency of "Creative Thinking and Visual Literacy." We believe that instructors and students in QU101 must not only freely discuss their anno-tations under the influence of dialectical reasoning, but should freely experi-ment with the figurative and visual metaphors that are the "western" dialec-tical grids, and "eastern" circles by populating them with the theses, antitheses, and new syntheses that emerge from their critical and creative encounters with the QU101 curriculum. In doing so, we will travel some way toward exercising this often neglected, or under-imagined proficiency. One of us has taken to drawing a series of large circles on the board that stu-dents then populate with interdependent "binaries." Then, instead of insert-ing the "S" into the center of the circle, the curve is widened to accommo-date a sentence or more that students work on individually or in small groups. The carefully revised statement is then written into the curving space and looks more like a "mythic" stream flowing between the "eastern" and "western" banks of not so much opposing, as reversible, concepts.

The ever (re)turning dialectical circle also reminds us that the way we populate and activate the space of our thinking and discussion in our class-rooms matter deeply. We want students to think and discuss in circles. We urge teachers and students to level, and to literally, *circulate* their selves, inside and across the space of a discussion circle—if the classroom configu-ration permits. We don't believe that critical, intimate, creative discussion for all will happen within the box-like grid of classroom space set in rows and columns. In fact, we don't believe that a seminar can conduct itself inside or "outside the box" of such a classroom. Lecture lends itself to one person—the teacher—talking and thinking "outside this box." Seminar discussion, by dialectical contrast, lends itself to the circle—and the art of focused conver-sation should meet and retreat, open and close, spin within, without and beyond… and swirl, as represented by these three figures.

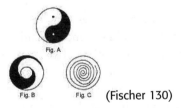

(Fischer 130)

Having designated the Dialectic as the foundational method for con-ducting our common practices of reading and discussion in QU101, we turn now to a new kind of "thirdness" or "new synthesis": The Art of Thematic *Triangulation*.

THIRD INNOVATION: THE INTELLECTUAL OPPORTUNITIES OF THE THEMATIC TRIANGULATION

Sociologist Norman K. Denzin's, *The Research Act*, remains an essential read for all professors and students in any discipline who are interested to refine more self-consciously intellectual methods and habits of mind in the service of the essential learning proficiencies and of making new knowledge. The two key innovations in his book which are particularly relevant to QU101 are what he calls the "sensitizing concept" and "the logic of triangulation" (from "triangle," meaning, "three-cornered.") The triangle, like the square, might appear to be a constricting geometric shape, but as a "sensitizing concept" it is no less powerful for visualizing and activating critical and creative thinking then is the dialectical grid or circle. Note Denzin's synthesis of the circle and the triangle to convey the convergence of "the research act" and "new realms of observation."

Denzin has enabled us to recognize QU101's concept, method, and intellectual outcome in his "conceptual sensitizers," in how these simultaneously open up and close off "new realms of observation," and in his call for a "logic of triangulation" (which is, most simply, the inevitable logic of "dialectical thirdness" cast in new conceptual and methodological clothing.) Here is how he sets the table for "the logic of triangulation."

> Thus, both concepts and research methods act as *sensitizers* of scientific observation. [While] concepts and methods open new realms of observation, they close others. Two important consequences follow: If each leads to different features of empirical reality, then no single method can ever completely capture all the relevant features of that reality; consequently, sociologists must learn to employ multiple methods in the analysis of the same empirical events (Denzin 13, author's emphasis).

Among Denzin's "multiple methods" is one type of Triangulation— "Data Triangulation"—that is especially relevant for QU101's students and instructors. For Denzin, who is concerned to improve the research acts of social scientists, *DT* is at the heart of "[a]ll sociological observations [and] relates to activities of socially situated *persons*—whether they are in groups, or organizations, or aggregately distributed over some social area or community. A focus on *time* and *space* as observational units recognizes their relationship to the observations of persons" (Denzin 301-302, author's emphasis). So how does *DT* as a social scientific method, involving the observation of *persons* in *time* and *space*, transfer to what we do in QU101 as a general educational principle for building intellectual community?

TRIANGULATION IN PRINCIPLE

First, note the shared importance of "observation" for sociological research and for annotation; then recall that the original meaning of annotation is "to observe" one's own act of reading, which is itself, formally in time and space, an act of research. Second, we can't emphasize enough that each of the six Common Course Questions guiding our reading, discussion and writing in QU101, contains at least one "sensitizing concept" or larger "sensitizing theme" that will inform how, what, and why we annotate a given passage in a given text. Remember also that each individual reading in our Common Reader presents to each individual annotator a potentially endless and diverse number of sensitizing concepts and themes. Third, we must understand that we must spend *quality time* to read a text closely as an annotator. The annotating reader is a mono-tasker, not a multi-tasker, one who focuses attention on the space of the text and re-searches that space to remark on what has been read in the open space of the margins. Or rather, the annotator is multitasking in the triple research action that triangulates eye-hand-brain. This, focused, undistracted intellectual *time*, spent annotating the marginal *space* of our Common Reader with our Common Course Questions in mind, binds us together as individual *persons* who will then come together in groups with our teachers where we are intellectually situated to build our learning communities.

PRACTICING THEMATIC TRIANGULATION IN QU101

Now that we understand the meaning and purpose of "data triangulation" in principle, let us focus on its importance in academic practice. When, as an individual reader we annotate a particular passage in our common reader, we are noting, observing, recognizing a piece or strand of "data" that we deem critical to answering or advancing the sensitizing concepts that inform both the course questions and the overarching dialectical significance of *The Individual in the Community*. As we add to and accumulate the record of our active dialogue and participation with a given text, we begin to recognize repeating conceptual codes and thematic patterns of meaning *across* the texts we've annotated previously. Also, remember that our annotated texts have already been shared and discussed in relation to those of our fellow annotators in class as we continue to share in the work of building a learning community through informal and formal writing assignments. This visual metaphor of the triangulation between writer, reader, and subject matter is a worth a thousand more words on the who, what, and why we writing is an essential learning proficiency.

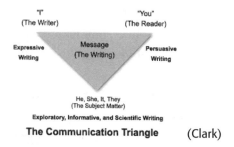

"I" (The Writer)   "You" (The Reader)

Expressive Writing   Message (The Writing)   Persuasive Writing

He, She, It, They (The Subject Matter)

Exploratory, Informative, and Scientific Writing

The Communication Triangle   (Clark)

There are many ways to "triangulate" your annotated readings. Count on your instructor to adopt or adapt from the two we summarize here. The first method simply re-searches and re-cognizes the "conceptual thirdness" that emerges from thinking like a *Dialectician*— one who, as we have seen above, is always counter-posing any important question or assertion that comes across in reading or discussion with its conceptual or situational opposite. Thus, annotators will review their marginal comments either within a single reading or between two different readings, and then select two annotated passages that strike them as holding some meaningful tension or energy that when juxta-posed and analyzed according to their dominant, conceptual sensitizers, will produce a new, or "third" way of understanding a course question or theme.

The second method differs only in that the review and re-search of one's record of annotations now includes *three* annotated passages in a single read-ing, or from *three* different readings. With any of these two approaches and all imaginable options, the next step is to isolate the samples from the bulk of our common reader and place them into a working Word document. Once isolated in their own new reading and writing space, the reader-annotator now must take some quality, focused *time* to explain the thematic connections, oppositions, and most important, the new knowledge that has emerged from his or her selection, relocation, and re-search of the original reading and annotation. If annotation is an act of "Reading to Learn," this act of *thematic triangulation* is an act of "*Writing-to-Learn*"—part of a sequence of "Low Stakes," usually ungraded, assignments that all QU instructors have been trained to employ and are required to assign.

THE NEW READER, THE KNOWING ANNOTATOR, AND THE-MATIC TRIANGULATION

We have already designated Dialectic as QU101's foundational, "sensitizing concept," one whose methods and lines action are no better represented than in our course title and theme—*The Individual in the Community*. We also now understand that "thirdness" is always present and runs like an alternating cur-rent, sensitizing all forms of lived social, aesthetic and intellectual experience. We now designate "*Thematic Triangulation*" as the logical advance of the dialectical method. Following Denzin's argument in *The Research Act*, we ask that all trained QU101 teachers underscore with their students that *Dialecti-cal Opposition* and *Thematic Triangulation* are inseparable, cooperative, and required acts of research of the methodical observations we will make as reader-annotators in QU101. All students will be asking questions of their teachers about *Annotation, Dialectics, and Triangulation*.

English department Chair, and Director of Writing Across the Curriculum, Robert Smart, has proposed that *Thematic Triangulation* will advance writing across the University Curriculum, and enliven the humanities-based proficiencies and goals that the "New Synthesis for Undergraduate Education QU101 aims to achieve in its first year seminars. Along with Andrew Delohery, Director of the University Learning Center, Smart has refined Thematic Triangulation over some seven years of training faculty in "Writing Across the Curriculum" (WAC) methods. The two of us have been trained in this method and have trained many faculty as members of Quinnipiac University's WAC program.

In keeping with the original spirit of the word, *Thematic* (originally,"*to put down, to place*") *Triangulation* asks that critical and creative annotators imagine themselves as geographers, and the pages of their books—along with their margins—as territories, as locations, in which they variously explore, occupy, and even "lose themselves" as readers discovering where they are. Smart originally described the three steps in thematic triangulation by analogy to the geographic procedure for locating the position of an object in space and time in relation to the person who is seeking that object (as with "Data Triangulation"). He and Delohery have since proposed a model of *Thematic* Triangulation that they believe will yield greater critical and creative thinking and reasoning among students as they are annotating. The three steps are to: *Prioritize, Translate, and Analogize*. Here are the definitions of each step.

> *Prioritization*: being able to figure out what's most important in any given text, and being able to articulate why;
> *Translation*: students are asked to turn difficult language in their reading into language of their own. This process, it should be noted, will reveal the student's "field of comprehension:" how much they do know and understand, and (more importantly) what they don't yet know;
> *Analogization*: being able to see how one part of a discussion or text or idea is like another, not as a result of simple comparison, but based on the student's understanding of pattern similarity (*or, in dialectical terms, patterns of* conceptual tension or opposition—editors' addition).

Students in QU101 will notice that when they perform a second reading of their texts—as they, literally, *re-search* the content of their annotations—they will need to *Prioritize* those passages that they want to feature in their "Writing-to-Learn" assignments devoted to *Thematic* Triangulation. And, as they explain or articulate why their three selections have been prioritized, they will need to *Translate* the author's language, or central "sensitizing concept," into their own language and experience, yet always in light of one or more of the six course questions. Finally, the *Analogies* they create from their three prioritized and translated annotations will come from the act of re-search, the yet to be seen findings that will emerge from the process of triangulation itself. The analogy—or imagery—to suggest this yet to be conceived connection between three texts and their thematic angles is the empty, yet very active thematic inner space of the triangle itself.

With the new open-ended organizing principle of this new edition of the QU101 Reader, students and their teachers will have much greater freedom in how they will read, (and re-read) the texts in light of the six course questions. The alphabetical *order* of this new edition is no order at all. The order that needs to be brought to the common course reader is not unlike that question mark inhabiting the triangle. The order that is needed—that will be answered—can only be initiated by students and teachers collaborating freely on their shared annotations, dialectical actions, and triangulations of texts. With that greater freedom—without the prescribed thematic organization that set and sequenced past editions—students are invited to assume a much greater measure of individual and communal responsibility for how they will conduct *Thematic Triangulations* of particular annotations across the common texts.

In the deepest *dialectical* sense, intellectual freedom is inseparable from intellectual responsibility. QU101 is your initiation into a common learning community that will help you, but also expects you, to build our "New Synthesis for Undergraduate Education." As your fellow teachers of QU101, but most importantly, as your colleagues in quest of intellectual community at Quinnipiac University, we urge you to exercise your academic freedom and responsibility in equal, energetic measure. Mark Thompson, our Senior Vice-President for Academic and Student Affairs, has written about how we can all work together toward "developing a culture of intellectual vitality" to achieve a "New Synthesis."

> The New Synthesis seeks to fully engage students, faculty and staff in a synergistic partnership that achieves demonstrable progress toward the attainment of clearly defined, well articulated and purposeful learning outcomes. This will transform students from academic consumers into engaged participants. Everyone must understand their role and readily recognize how their individual efforts contribute to the common purpose of excellence in education. All members of our community must speak with one reinforcing voice that shows a broad, common understanding of what we are attempting to accomplish.

As students and teachers together, we ask that you take ownership of this, your Common Reader, and of QU101, a course we hold in common obligation as critical and creative thinkers, and as engaged citizens responsible for our local, national, and global communities of the 21st century.

WORKS CITED

Bartholomae, David and Anthony Petrosky. New York: Bedford/ St. Martin's, 7th edition, 2004.

Basseches, Michael. *Dialectical Thinking and Adult Development*, Ablex, NJ: 1984

Campbell, Joseph. *Myths to Live By*. Viking: New York, 1972.

Clark, L.   http://legacy.lclark.edu/~krauss/russiaweb2005/wrworkshop/ images/triangle.gif

Denzin, Norman. *The Research Act*. Butterworths: London, 1970.

Fischer-Schreiber, Ingrid. Shambhala Dictionary of Taoism

Greenwald, Joe.http://ablemedia.com/ctcweb/showcase/ greenwaldgreece11.html

Marshall, Gordon. "curvilinear relationship." A Dictionary of Sociology. 1998. http://www.encyclopedia.com/doc/1O88-curvilinearrelation-ship.html

Oxford English Dictionary Online, Oxford University Press. http://dictionary.oed.com/cgi/entry/50063108?query_type=word&queryword=dialectic
http://dictionary.oed.com/cgi/entry/00320492?query_type=word&queryword=myth

"Patriotic Resistance" http://www.satoridesign.biz/freemarket.php

Watts, Alan. *Tao: The Watercourse Way*. Pantheon: New York, 1975.

A STATEMENT FROM EIGHT ALABAMA CLERGYMEN

We the undersigned clergymen are among those who, in January, issued "an appeal for law and order and common sense," in dealing with racial problems in Alabama. We expressed understanding that honest convictions in racial matters could properly be pursued in the courts, but urged that decisions of those courts should in the meantime be peacefully obeyed.

Since that time there had been some evidence of increased forbearance and a willingness to face facts. Responsible citizens have undertaken to work on various problems which cause racial friction and unrest. In Birmingham, recent public events have given indication that we all have opportunity for a new constructive and realistic approach to racial problems.

However, we are now confronted by a series of demonstrations by some of our Negro citizens, directed and led in part by outsiders. We recognize the natural impatience of people who feel that their hopes are slow in being realized. But we are convinced that these demonstrations are unwise and untimely.

We agree rather with certain local Negro leadership which has called for honest and open negotiation of racial issues in our area. And we believe this kind of facing of issues can best be accomplished by citizens of our own metropolitan area, white and Negro, meeting with their knowledge and experience of the local situation. All of us need to face that responsibility and find proper channels for its accomplishment.

Just as we formerly pointed out that "hatred and violence have no sanction in our religious and political traditions," we also point out that such actions as incite to hatred and violence, however technically peaceful those actions may be, have not contributed to the resolution of our local problems. We do not believe that these days of new hope are days when extreme measures are justified in Birmingham.

We commend the community as a whole, and the local news media and law enforcement officials in particular, on the calm manner in which these demonstrations have been handled. We urge the public to continue to show restraint should the demonstrations continue, and the law enforcement officials to remain calm and continue to protect our city from violence.

We further strongly urge our own Negro community to withdraw support from these demonstrations, and to unite locally in working peacefully for a better Birmingham. When rights are consistently denied, a cause should be pressed in the courts and in negotiations among local leaders, and not in the streets. We appeal to both our white and Negro citizenry to observe the principles of law and order and common sense.

Reprinted by permission of Writers House.

Bishop C.C.J. Carpenter, D.D., LL.D., Episcopalian Bishop of Alabama

40   Bishop Joseph A. Durick, D.D., Auxiliary Bishop, Roman Catholic Diocese of Mobile, Birmingham

Rabbi Milton L. Grafman, Temple Emanu-El, Birmingham, Alabama

Bishop Paul Hardin, Methodist Bishop of the Alabama-West Florida Conference

Bishop Nolan B. Harmon, Bishop of the North Alabama Conference of the Methodist Church

Rev. George M. Murray, D.D., LL.D, Bishop Coadjutor, Episcopal Diocese of Alabama

Rev. Edward V. Ramage, Moderator, Synod of the Alabama Presbyterian

50   Church in the United States

Rev. Earl Stallings, Pastor, First Baptist Church, Birmingham, Alabama

NOTES

FROM *POLITICS*
Aristotle

BOOK ONE

I

Every state is a community of some kind, and every community is   1
established with a view to some good; for mankind always act in order
to obtain that which they think good. But, if all communities aim at some
good, the state or political community, which is the highest of all, and which
embraces all the rest, aims at good in a greater degree than any other, and at
the highest good.

Some people think that the qualifications of a statesman, king, householder,
and master are the same, and that they differ, not in kind, but only in the
number of their subjects. For example, the ruler over a few is called a master;
over more, the manager of a household; over a still larger number, a statesman   10
or king, as if there were no difference between a great household and a small
state. The distinction which is made between the king and the statesman is
as follows: When the government is personal, the ruler is a king; when,
according to the rules of the political science, the citizens rule and are ruled
in turn, then he is called a statesman.

But all this is a mistake; for governments differ in kind, as will be evident
to any one who considers the matter according to the method which has
hitherto guided us. As in other departments of science, so in politics, the
compound should always be resolved into the simple elements or least parts
of the whole. We must therefore look at the elements of which the state is   20
composed, in order that we may see in what the different kinds of rule differ
from one another, and whether any scientific result can be attained about each
one of them.

II

He who thus considers things in their first growth and origin, whether a state
or anything else, will obtain the clearest view of them. In the first place
there must be a union of those who cannot exist without each other; namely,
of male and female, that the race may continue (and this is a union which
is formed, not of deliberate purpose, but because, in common with other
animals and with plants, mankind have a natural desire to leave behind them
an image of themselves), and of natural ruler and subject, that both may be   30
preserved. . . . The family is the association established by nature for the
supply of men's everyday wants. . . . The family is the association established
by nature for the supply of men's everyday wants, and the members of it are

Reprinted from *Politics*, translated by Benjamin Jowett (1885).

called by Charondas 'companions of the cupboard,' and by Epimenides the Cretan, 'companions of the manger.' But when several families are united, and the association aims at something more than the supply of daily needs, the first society to be formed is the village. And the most natural form of the village appears to be that of a colony from the family, composed of the children and grandchildren, who are said to be suckled 'with the same milk'. . . .

40   When several villages are united in a single complete community, large enough to be nearly or quite self-sufficing, the state comes into existence, originating in the bare needs of life, and continuing in existence for the sake of a good life. And therefore, if the earlier forms of society are natural, so is the state, for it is the end of them, and the nature of a thing is its end. For what each thing is when fully developed, we call its nature, whether we are speaking of a man, a horse, or a family. Besides, the final cause and end of a thing is the best, and to be self-sufficing is the end and the best.

    Hence it is evident that the state is a creation of nature, and that man is by nature a political animal. And he who by nature and not by mere accident
50 is without a state, is either a bad man or above humanity; he is like the
    Tribeless, lawless, heartless one,
whom Homer denounces—the natural outcast is forthwith a lover of war; he may be compared to an isolated piece at draughts.

    Now, that man is more of a political animal than bees or any other gregarious animals is evident. Nature, as we often say, makes nothing in vain, and man is the only animal whom she has endowed with the gift of speech. And whereas mere voice is but an indication of pleasure or pain, and is therefore found in other animals (for their nature attains to the perception of pleasure and pain and the intimation of them to one another, and no further), the
60 power of speech is intended to set forth the expedient and inexpedient, and therefore likewise the just and the unjust. And it is a characteristic of man that he alone has any sense of good and evil, of just and unjust, and the like, and the association of living beings who have this sense makes a family and a state.

    Further, the state is by nature clearly prior to the family and to the individual, since the whole is of necessity prior to the part; for example, if the whole body be destroyed, there will be no foot or hand, except in an equivocal sense, as we might speak of a stone hand; for when destroyed the hand will be no better than that. But things are defined by their working and power; and we ought not to say that they are the same when they no
70 longer have their proper quality, but only that they have the same name. The proof that the state is a creation of nature and prior to the individual is that the individual, when isolated, is not self-sufficing; and therefore he is like a part in relation to the whole. But he who is unable to live in society, or who has no need because he is sufficient for himself, must be either a beast or a god: he is no part of a state. A social instinct is implanted in all men by nature, and yet he who first founded the state was the greatest of benefactors. For man, when perfected, is the best of animals, but, when separated from law and justice, he is the worst of all; since armed injustice is the more dangerous,

and he is equipped at birth with arms, meant to be used by intelligence and virtue, which he may use for the worst ends. Wherefore, if he have not virtue, he is the most unholy and the most savage of animals, and the most full of lust and gluttony. But justice is the bond of men in states, for the administration of justice, which is the determination of what is just, is the principle of order in political society. . . .

FROM BOOK TWO

I

Our purpose is to consider what form of political community is best of all for those who are most able to realize their ideal of life. We must therefore examine not only this but other constitutions, both such as actually exist in well-governed states, and any theoretical forms which are held in esteem; that what is good and useful may be brought to light. And let no one suppose that in seeking for something beyond them we are anxious to make a sophistical display at any cost; we only undertake this inquiry because all the constitutions with which we are acquainted are faulty.

[margin note: Hypothetical systems of govt.]

We will begin with the natural beginning of the subject. Three alternatives are conceivable: The members of a state must either have (1) all things or (2) nothing in common, or (3) some things in common and some not. That they should have nothing in common is clearly impossible, for the constitution is a community, and must at any rate have a common place—one city will be in one place, and the citizens are those who share in that one city. But should a well ordered state have all things, as far as may be, in common, or some only and not others? For the citizens might conceivably have wives and children and property in common, as Socrates proposes in the Republic of Plato. Which is better, our present condition, or the proposed new order of society?

II

There are many difficulties in the community of women. And the principle on which Socrates rests the necessity of such an institution evidently is not established by his arguments. Further, as a means to the end which he ascribes to the state, the scheme, taken literally is impracticable, and how we are to interpret it is nowhere precisely stated. I am speaking of the premise from which the argument of Socrates proceeds, 'that the greater the unity of the state the better.' Is it not obvious that a state may at length attain such a degree of unity as to be no longer a state? Since the nature of a state is to be a plurality, and in tending to greater unity, from being a state, it becomes a family, and from being a family, an individual; for the family may be said to be more than the state, and the individual than the family. So that we ought not to attain this greatest unity even if we could, for it would be the destruction of the state.

Again, a state is not made up only of so many men, but of different kinds of men; for similars do not constitute a state. . . .

. . . Hence it is evident that a city is not by nature one in that sense which some persons affirm; and that what is said to be the greatest good of cities is in reality their destruction; but surely the good of things must be that which preserves them. Again, in another point of view, this extreme unification of the state is clearly not good; for a family is more self-sufficing than an individual, and a city than a family, and a city only comes into being when the community is large enough to be self-sufficing. If then self-sufficiency is to be desired, the lesser degree of unity is more desirable than the greater.

FROM BOOK III

But, even supposing that it were best for the community to have the greatest degree of unity, this unity is by no means proved to follow from the fact 'of all men saying "mine" and "not mine" at the same instant of time,' which, according to Socrates, is the sign of perfect unity in a state. For the word 'all' is ambiguous. If the meaning be that every individual says 'mine' and 'not mine' at the same time, then perhaps the result at which Socrates aims may be in some degree accomplished; each man will call the same person his own son and the same person his wife, and so of his property and of all that falls to his lot. This, however, is not the way in which people would speak who had their had their wives and children in common; they would say 'all' but not 'each.' In like manner their property would be described as belonging to them, not severally but collectively. There is an obvious fallacy in the term 'all': like some other words, 'both,' 'odd,' 'even,' it is ambiguous, and even in abstract argument becomes a source of logical puzzles. That all persons call the same thing mine in the sense in which each does so may be a fine thing, but it is impracticable; or if the words are taken in the other sense, such a unity in no way conduces to harmony. And there is another objection to the proposal. For that which is common to the greatest number has the least care bestowed upon it. Every one thinks chiefly of his own, hardly at all of the common interest; and only when he is himself concerned as an individual. For besides other considerations, everybody is more inclined to neglect the duty which he expects another to fulfill; as in families many attendants are often less useful than a few. Each citizen will have a thousand sons who will not be his sons individually but anybody will be equally the son of anybody, and will therefore be neglected by all alike. Further, upon this principle, every one will use the word 'mine' of one who is prospering or the reverse, however small a fraction he may himself be of the whole number; the same boy will be 'so and so's son,' the son of each of the thousand, or whatever be the number of the citizens; and even about this he will not be positive; for it is impossible to know who chanced to have a child, or whether, if one came into existence, it has survived. But which is better—for each to say 'mine' in this way, making a man the same relation to two thousand or ten thousand

citizens, or to use the word 'mine' in the ordinary and more restricted sense?
For usually the same person is called by one man his own son whom another
calls his own brother or cousin or kinsman—blood relation or connection   160
by marriage either of himself or of some relation of his, and yet another his
clansman or tribesman; and how much better is it to be the real cousin of
somebody than to be a son after Plato's fashion! Nor is there any way of
preventing brothers and children and fathers and mothers from sometimes
recognizing one another; for children are born like their parents, and they will
necessarily be finding indications of their relationship to one another.

V

Next let us consider what should be our arrangements about property: should
the citizens of the perfect state have their possessions in common or not?
This question may be discussed separately from the enactments about women
and children. Even supposing that the women and children belong to   170
individuals, according to the custom which is at present universal, may there
not be an advantage in having and using possessions in common? Three cases
are possible: (1) the soil may be appropriated, but the produce may be thrown
for consumption into the common stock; and this is the practice of some
nations. Or (2), the soil may be common, and may be cultivated in common,
but the produce divided among individuals for their private use; this is a form
of common property which is said to exist among certain barbarians. Or (3),
the soil and the produce may be alike common.

When the husbandmen are not the owners, the case will be different and
easier to deal with; but when they till the ground for themselves the question   180
of ownership will give a world of trouble. If they do not share equally
enjoyments and toils, those who labor much and get little will necessarily
complain of those who labor little and receive or consume much. But indeed
there is always a difficulty in men living together and having all human relations
in common, but especially in their having common property. The partnerships
of fellow-travelers are an example to the point; for they generally fall out
over everyday matters and quarrel about any trifle which turns up. So with
servants: we are most able to take offense at those with whom we most we
most frequently come into contact in daily life.

These are only some of the disadvantages which attend the community   190
of property; the present arrangement, if improved as it might be by good
customs and laws, would be far better, and would have the advantages of both
systems. Property should be in a certain sense common, but, as a general
rule, private; for, when everyone has a distinct interest, men will not complain
of one another, and they will make more progress, because every one will be
attending to his own business. And yet by reason of goodness, and in respect
of use, 'Friends,' as the proverb says, 'will have all things common.' Even
now there are traces of such a principle, showing that it is not impracticable,
but, in well-ordered states, exists already to a certain extent and may be carried

200 further. For, although every man has his own property, some things he will place at the disposal of his friends, while of others he shares the use with them. The Lacedaemonians, for example, use one another's slaves, and horses, and dogs, as if they were their own; and when they lack provisions on a journey, they appropriate what they find in the fields throughout the country. It is clearly better that property should be private, but the use of it common; and the special business of the legislator is to create in men this benevolent disposition. Again, how immeasurably greater is the pleasure, when a man feels a thing to be his own; for surely the love of self is a feeling implanted by nature and not given in vain, although selfishness is rightly censured; this,

210 however, is not the mere love of self, but the love of self in excess, like the miser's love of money; for all, or almost all, men, love money and other such objects in a measure. And further, there is the greatest pleasure in doing a kindness or service to friends or guests or companions, which can only be rendered when a man has private property. These advantages are lost by excessive unification of the state. The exhibition of two virtues, besides, is visibly annihilated in such a state: first, temperance towards women (for it is an honorable action to abstain from another's wife for temperance' sake); secondly, liberality in the matter of property. No one, when men have all things in common, will any longer set an example of liberality or do any liberal action;

220 for liberality consists in the use which is made of property.

Such legislation may have a specious appearance of benevolence; men readily listen to it, and are easily induced to believe that in some wonderful manner everybody will become everybody's friend, especially when some one is heard denouncing the evils now existing in states, suits about contracts, convictions for perjury, flatteries of rich men and the like, which are said to arise out of the possession of private property. These evils, however, are due to a very different cause—the wickedness of human nature. Indeed, we see that there is much more quarrelling among those who have all things in common, though there are not many of them when compared with the vast

230 numbers who have private property.

Again, we ought to reckon, not only the evils from which the citizens will be saved, but also the advantages which they will lose. The life which they are to lead appears to be quite impracticable. The error of Socrates must be attributed to the false notion of unity from which he starts. Unity there should be, both of the family and of the state, but in some respects only. For there is a point at which a state may attain such a degree of unity as to be no longer a state, or at which, without actually ceasing to exist, it will become an inferior state, like harmony passing into unison, or rhythm which has been reduced to a single foot. The state, as I was saying, is a plurality which should be united

240 and made into a community by education; and it is strange that the author of a system of education which he thinks will make the state virtuous, should expect to improve his citizens by regulations of this sort, and not by philosophy or by customs and laws, like those which prevail at Sparta and Crete respecting common meals, whereby the legislator has made property common. Let us

[margin annotations:]
Private Property but shared use

love of self vs selfishness

who will be left out?

forced generosity can't be felt

where were his examples?

unity not a state

harmony

remember that we should not disregard the experience of ages; in the multitude of years these things, if they were good, would certainly not have been unknown; for almost everything has been found out, although sometimes they are not put together; in other cases men do not use the knowledge which they have. Great light would be thrown on this subject if we could see such a form of government in the actual process of construction; for the legislator could not form a state at all without distributing and dividing its constituents into associations for common meals, and into phratries and tribes. But all this legislation ends only in forbidding agriculture to the guardians, a prohibition which the Lacedaemonians try to enforce already.

But, indeed, Socrates has not said, nor is it easy to decide, what in such a community will be the general form of the state. The citizens who are not guardians are the majority, and about them nothing has been determined: are the husbandmen, too, to have their property in common? Or is each individual to have his own? And are the wives and children to be individual or common? If, like the guardians, they are to have all things in common, what do they differ from them, or what will they gain by submitting to their government? Or, upon what principle would they submit, unless indeed the governing class adopt the ingenious policy of the Cretans, who give their slaves the same institutions as their own, but forbid them gymnastic exercises and the possession of arms. If, on the other hand, the inferior classes are to be like other cities in respect of marriage and property, what will be the form of the community? Must it not contain two states in one, each hostile to the other? He makes the guardians into a mere occupying garrison, while the husbandmen and artisans and the rest are the real citizens. But if so the suits and quarrels, and all the evils which Socrates affirms to exist in other states, will exist equally among them. He says indeed that, having so good an education, the citizens will not need many laws, for example laws about the city or about the markets; but then he confines his education to the guardians. Again, he makes the husbandmen owners of the property upon condition of their paying a tribute. But in that case they are likely to be much more unmanageable and conceited than the Helots, or Penestae, or slaves in general. And whether community of wives and property be necessary for the lower equally with the higher class or not, and the questions akin to this, what will be the education, form of government, laws of the lower class, Socrates has nowhere determined: neither is it easy to discover this, nor is their character of small importance if the common life of the guardians is to be maintained.

Again, if Socrates makes the women common, and retains private property, the men will see to the fields, but who will see to the house? And who will do so if the agricultural class have both their property and their wives in common? Once more: it is absurd to argue, from the analogy of the animals, that men and women should follow the same pursuits, for animals have not to manage a household. The government, too, as constituted by Socrates, contains elements of danger; for he makes the same persons always rule. And if this is often a cause of disturbance among the meaner sort, how much

290   more among high-spirited warriors? But that the persons whom he makes rulers must be the same is evident; for the gold which the God mingles in the souls of men is not at one time given to one, at another time to another, but always to the same: as he says, 'God mingles gold in some, and silver in others, from their very birth; but brass and iron in those who are meant to be artisans and husbandmen.' Again, he deprives the guardians even of happiness, and says that the legislator ought to make the whole state happy. But the whole cannot be happy unless most, or all, or some of its parts enjoy happiness. In this respect happiness is not like the even principle in numbers, which may exist only in the whole, but in neither of the parts; not so happiness.

300   And if the guardians are not happy, who are? Surely not the artisans, or the common people. The Republic of which Socrates discourses has all these difficulties, and others quite as great.

Ancient
  Sparta
  Crete
  Athens
  Thebes

Modern

  The Diggers
  Brook Farm
  Hutterites
  Amish
  Shakers
  Kibbutzim Israel
  Harmony Society - Harmony PA
  Fruitlands - Harvard, MA
  Oneida - Oneida NY
  Mondern Times - Long Island
  Amana - Iowa
  Twin Oaks Community
  Ganas - Staten Island
  Home Colony - WA, Key Peninsula
  Ejido - modern + history in Mexico
  Sieben Linden Ecovillage
  Oakland Morehouse

Role of Women
            Slaves
Arrangements Property
          re:
Religious or Non-Religious

THE BETRAYAL OF THE MENTORS
Mark Bauerlein

It is the nature of adolescents to believe that authentic reality begins with themselves, and that what long preceded them is irrelevant. For 15-year-olds in the United States in the twenty-first century, the yardstick of pertinence is personal contact, immediate effects. Space and time extend not much further than their circumstances, and what does Holbein's portrait of Sir Thomas More have to say to a kid who works at Wendy's, struggles with algebra, and can't find a girlfriend? The attitude marks one of the signal changes of the twentieth century in the United States. It insists that a successful adolescence and rightful education entail growing comfortable with yourself, with who you are age 17. Many generations ago, adolescent years meant preparation for something beyond adolescence, not authentic selfhood but serious work, civic duty, and family responsibility, with parents, teachers, ministers, and employers training teens in grown-up conduct. Adolescence formed a tenuous middle ground between the needs of childhood and the duties of adulthood, and the acquisition of the virtues of manhood and womanhood was an uncertain progress. It did not terminate with an acceptance and approval of the late-teen identity. The shrewdest approach was not to prize the interval but to escape it as efficiently as possible.

Not anymore. For a long time now, adolescence has claimed an independent value, an integrity all its own. The rise of adolescence is too long a story to tell, but the stance of teachers and researchers that fostered it may be indicated by a few highlights. In one of its first authoritative expressions, Professor G. Stanley Hall, president of Clark University and head of the American Psychological Association, composed a massive volume outlining the uniqueness of the stage. In *Adolescence: Its Psychology and Its Relations to Physiology* . . . (1904), he observed in glorious cadences, "Self-feeling and ambition are increased, and every trait and faculty is liable to exaggeration and excess. It is all a marvelous new birth, and those who believe that nothing is so worthy of love, reverence, and service as the body and soul of youth, and who hold that the best test of every human institution is how much it contributes to bring youth to the ever fullest possible development, may well review themselves and the civilization in which we live to see how far it satisfies this supreme test."

A cover story in *Time* magazine exemplifies it well (24 Jan 2005). The article profiles a new youth phenomenon, an unforeseen generational sub-cohort termed the "Twixters." This curious social outcropping rests in a novel cluster of demographic traits. Twixters:

- are 22 to 30 years old;
- have a college degree, or substantial college coursework;

Reprinted from *The Dumbest Generation: How the Digital Age Stupefies Young Americans and Jeopardizes Our Future* (2008), Penguin Group.

40   • come from middle-class families; and
    • reside in cities and large suburban centers.

These features embody nothing unusual, certainly, but where they lead is surprising. What makes the Twixters different from other people with the same demographics from the past is the lifestyle they pursue after college.

Despite their circumstances, Twixters aren't marginal youngsters sinking into the underclass. They drift through their twenties, stalled at work and saving no money, but they like it that way. They congregate just as they did before college, hopping bar to bar on Friday night and watching movies on Saturday. They have achieved little, but they feel good about themselves. Indeed,

50   precisely along the lines of Reich's understanding, they justify their aimless lifestyle as a journey of self-discovery. Yes, they put off the ordinary decisions of adulthood (career, marriage), but with a tough job market and so many divorced parents, their delays mark a thoughtful desire to "search their souls and choose their life paths," to find a livelihood right for their "identity." So Lev Grossman, the author of the story, phrases it. Social scientists quoted in the article, too, ennoble the lifestyles, judging Twixter habits (in Grossman's paraphrase) "important work to get themselves ready for adulthood." These young people take adulthood "so seriously, they're spending years carefully choosing the right path into it." University of Maryland psychologist Jeffrey

60   Arnett dislikes the "Twixter" label, preferring "emerging adulthood." They assume no responsibilities for or to anyone else, he concedes, but that only permits them "this wonderful freedom to really focus on their own lives and work on becoming the kind of person they want to be." Sociologist James Côté blames their delay on the economy: "What we're looking at really began with the collapse of the youth labor market," he says, which persists today and means that young people simply can't afford to settle down until their late twenties. Marshall Heskovitz, creator of the television shows *thirtysomething* and *My So-Called Life*, gives the problem a social/emotional angle: "it's a result of the world not being particularly welcoming when they come into it. Lots

70   of people have a difficult time dealing with it, and they try to stay kids as long as they can because they don't know how to make sense of all this. We're interested in this process of finding courage and one's self." And a Dartmouth neuroscientist backs the economic and social resistances with brain chemistry: "We as a society deem an individual at the age of 18 ready for adult responsibility. Yet recent evidence suggests that our neuropsychological development is many years from being complete."

Their comments apply a positive spin to what less sympathetic elders would call slacker ways. But even if we accept the characterizations—their brains aren't ready, the cost of living is high, they take marriage too seriously to plunge

80   into it—there is something missing from the expert observations in the article, an extraordinary absence in the diagnosis. In casting Twixter lifestyle as genuine exploration and struggle, neither the author nor the researchers nor

the Twixters themselves whisper a single word about intellectual labor. Not one of the Twixters or youth observers mentions an idea that stirs them, a book that influenced them, a class that inspired them, or a mentor who guides them. Nobody ties maturity to formal or informal learning, reading or studying, novels or paintings or histories or syllogisms. For all the talk about life concerns and finding a calling, none of them regard history, literature, art, civics, philosophy, or politics a helpful undertaking. Grossman speaks of Twixter years as "a chance to build castles and knock them down," but these castles haven't a grain of intellectual sand in them. As these young people forge their personalities in an uncertain world, they skirt one of the customary means of doing so—that is, acquainting themselves with the words and images, the truths and beauties of the past—and nobody tells them they have overlooked anything. Social psychologists don't tell them so, nor do youth experts and educators, but the anti-intellectual banality of their choices is stark. What is the role of books in the Twixter's world? Negligible. How has their education shaped their lives? Not at all. This is what the Twixters themselves report. One of them remarks, "Kids used to go to college to get educated. That's what I did, which I think now was a bit naïve. Being smart after college doesn't really mean anything."

In a word, the Twixter vision aligns perfectly with that of their wired younger brothers and sisters. It's all social, all peer-oriented. Twixters don't read, tour museums, travel, follow politics, or listen to any music but pop and rap, much less do something such as lay out a personal reading list or learn a foreign language. Rather, they do what we expect an average 19-year-old to do. They meet for poker, buy stuff at the mall, and jump from job to job and bed to bed. The maturity they envision has nothing to do with learning and wisdom, and the formative efforts that social scientists highlight don't include books, artworks, ideologies, or Venn diagrams. For the Twixters, mature identity is entirely a social matter developed with and through their friends. The intellectual and artistic products of the past aren't stepping-stones for growing up. They are the fading materials of meaningless schooling.

Does tradition have to retire so conspicuously in order for the adolescent self to come into its own?

Spend some hours in school zones and you see that the indulgent attitude toward youth, along with the downplaying of tradition, has reached the point of dogma among teachers, reporters, researchers, and creators in arts and humanities fields, and pro-knowledge, pro-tradition conceptions strike them as bluntly unpleasant, if not reactionary and out of touch. Indeed, the particular mode of sympathy for the kids has taken such a firm hold that offering education as a fruitful dialectic of tradition and individuality looks downright smothering. Uttered so rarely in education circles, a modest opinion in favor of tradition comes across to experts and mentors as an aggression against the students, a curmudgeon's grievance. For many of them, the power of cultural tradition sounds authoritarian and retrograde, or aligned with a Eurocentric, white male

lineage, their view recalling the Culture Wars of the 1980s when conservative activists battled liberal professors over the content of the curriculum in English classes. In truth, however, the indulgence crosses ideological boundaries,
130 touching generational feelings that mix widely among liberals and conservatives alike. It's not a political conflict. It's a cultural condition, a normative sentiment positioning young people in relation to a past and a future, the cultural inheritance and their prospective adulthood. Instead of charting as Left or Right, it charts as traditionalist or self-centered (or youth-centered, present-fixated, individualist). And while traditionalists lean toward conservative opinion, many liberals feel a similar respect for the past and impatience with youth self-absorption, and many conservatives no longer set their moral values, religious faith, and civic pride under the long shadow of great books and thoughts and artworks.

140 What makes someone say to an adolescent, "Before you sally forth into the world, heed the insight of people long dead who possessed a lot more talent and wisdom than you," is more a personal ethic than a political creed. The ethic has seeped down to the level of etiquette, so that when a dissenting voice calls for more traditional knowledge, it sounds not just wrong, but wrongheaded, mean-spirited, bad form. The intellectual force of the call is obscured by its impropriety. This is the natural course of a norm. It begins as a fresh and unusual idea, then passes through the stages of argument, clarification, revision, and acceptance. It may have been radical or controversial once, but over time, adopted by more and more people, it turns into com-
150 mon sense and its distinctiveness dims. When an idea becomes a habit, it stops sparking thought. When everybody accepts it, it abides without evidence. At that point, the idea acts as a tacit premise, like travel directions you print out from Mapquest when taking a trip for the first time. You follow the route and arrive at Point B. You don't ponder alternatives. In a traditional classroom from way back when, a youth-centered approach might have appeared iconoclastic and provocative, triggering disputes over learning, maturity, and selfhood. Now it passes without a murmur.

The sentimentality justifies mentors in downgrading their mentoring task. They can't produce much solid evidence of youth brilliance and drive, and
160 so they resort to lofty and flushed language to make the case. "Young adults are fiercely individualistic. . . . They are still incredibly open to new ideas and they want to dabble and experiment." So enthuses a report from the Advertising Council (with funding from MTV and the Pew Research Center), though providing little evidence of the good of their "dabbling." The *Philadelphia Inquirer*'s columnist Jane Eisner acknowledges the embarrassing voting rates of 18- to 29-year-olds, but shifts the issue: "Only if we address the structural reasons that young people don't vote can we begin to count on them to infuse our democracy with the ideas and idealism for which young Americans have always been prized" (Sept 2004). "Always been prized" for their "ideas
170 and idealism"? Since 1965, perhaps, but not before.

Young people pick up these rationalizations and run with them. For a study of news consumption entitled *Tuned Out: Why Americans Under 40 Don't Follow the News* (2005), journalist David Mindich interviewed hundreds of young adults who told him that "the political process is both morally bankrupt and completely insulated from public pressure," a sentiment whose truth is doubtful—how do *they* know?—but that saves them the trouble of civic action. In a 1999 survey by Northwestern University's Medill School of Journalism ("Y Vote 2000: Politics of a New Generation"), 69 percent of 15- to 24-year-olds concurred with the statement "Our generation has an important voice, but no one seems to hear it." The cliché is so hollow it could rank with the statement "Our generation has sexual desires, but no one satisfies them," but it has acquired a seriousness that 50 years ago would have been inconceivable. It is normal for young people, temporarily, to act disaffected and feel unheard, but for the mentors to turn this condition into an injustice is to downgrade their position, with youths only too eager to play along. No matter how benevolent the rhetoric of the mentors, though, the thing it bestows—intellectual independence—does the majority of youths no favors. And this isn't only because most youths aren't ready to exercise it wisely, to their long-term benefit. It's also because, while the indulgence emancipates the young mind, it sends an implicit and far-reaching message, too, one the kids handily discern. It sabotages something that may, perhaps, be more fragile than the transmission of knowledge from old to young, namely, the simple, sturdy conviction that knowledge itself is worth receiving, the conviction that traditions remote from their daily circumstances have any bearing.

When teachers stand before the young and assure them of the integrity and autonomy of what adolescents think and say and write, teachers expect the young to respond affirmatively, to seek out knowledge and truth on their own. And maybe that works for the upper-crust students, those contending zealously for a place at Yale or an internship on the Hill. But beyond that talented tenth or twentieth student, something different happens. All of them expect the mentors to enter the room with credentialed authority, some know-how that justifies their position, even if some of the kids begrudge and reject it. When the mentors disavow their authority, when they let their discipline slacken, when they, in the language of the educators, slide from the "sage on the stage" to the "guide on the side," the kids wonder what goes. They don't consider the equalizing instructor a caring liberator, and they aren't motivated to learn on their own. They draw another, immobilizing lesson. If mentors are so keen to recant their expertise, why should students strain to acquire it themselves?

The opposite of what the indulgers intend sets in. Knowledge and tradition are emptied of authority. Ronald Reagan once declared, "Freedom is never more than one generation away from extinction," but a more elemental rule may be, "Knowledge is never more than one generation away from oblivion." If the guardians of tradition claim that the young, though ignorant, have

a special perspective on the past, or if teachers prize the impulses of tenth-graders more than the thoughts of the wise and the works of the masters, learning loses its point. The thread of intellectual inheritance snaps. The young man from Boston who announces with pride that he cares nothing about Rembrandt and Picasso typifies the outcome. His disregard follows from the men-
220   tors' disregard, their own infidelity to tradition, and the transfer affects all students more or less, the best and brightest as well as the dropouts. The indulgers assume that their approval will bring teachers and students closer together, throwing students further into academic inquiry, inspiring them to learn and study, but the evidence shows that this does not happen.

One pertinent measure of the trend appears as an item on the *National Survey of Student Engagement* (NSSE). The question tallies how many first-year and senior undergraduates "Discussed ideas from your readings or classes with faculty members outside of class." The activity goes beyond course requirements, the tests and papers, and thus charts how many students are
230   inspired by lectures and homework to confer with the instructor on their own. The numbers are disappointing. In 2003, fully 40 percent of the first-year respondents "Never" exchanged a word with a teacher beyond the classroom. Seniors that year displayed more engagement—only 25 percent responded "Never"—although that is still too high a figure after three years of coursework. Normally, as students proceed, they pursue more specialization in a major and form shared interests and career concerns with teachers. Nevertheless, one quarter of all seniors ignore their professors outside the classroom. Worse, three years later, both ranks increased their disengagement. In 2006, first-year students raised the "Never talk to my teacher"
240   rate to 43 percent, and seniors to 28 percent. More students tune their professors out once the hour is up, and the engagement score gap between seniors and freshmen still stands at only 15 points—a sign that the curriculum hasn't improved.

Notwithstanding the disengagement numbers, however, researchers summarizing the 2003 NSSE survey commend precisely the pedagogical methods of the indulgers. The report observes,

> One of the pleasant surprises from the first few years of NSSE findings was the substantial number of students engaged in various forms of active and collaborative learning activities. This shift from passive,
250   > instructor-dominated pedagogy to active, learner-centered activities promises to have desirable effects on learning.

A nice prediction, but wholly without support. As "instructor domination" dwindles, as "learner-centered" classrooms multiply, then students should feel empowered to hunt down their profs at other times and places. But while "active, learner-centered" pedagogies have proliferated, more student-teacher contact hasn't happened, as subsequent NSSE reports show. In a "passive" mode, with an authoritative teacher before them, students may feel more secure and encouraged to consult one-on-one. Once "activated" by power-sharing profs, though, students head elsewhere. A paradox may have set in: the more equal and accessible the teachers, the less accessed they are by the students. Nonetheless, NSSE researchers buy the "learner-centered" assumption. They assert that youth-approving teaching strategies "take students to deeper levels of understanding and meaning," but if deeper understanding entails closer engagement with instructors, their own data don't correlate with the theory.

The researchers could find other noncorrelations elsewhere, too. For instance, *Your First College Year*, a survey of first-year students, sponsored by the Higher Education Research Institute at UCLA, provided the following summary in 2005:

> Although most respondents studied and discussed their courses with other students during the first year, findings suggest that many remain disengaged from their coursework: over half "frequently" or "occasionally" came late to class; almost half turned in course assignments that did not reflect their best work or felt bored in class; and approximately one-third skipped class at least "occasionally" in the first year.

College delinquency of this kind says nothing about these students' intelligence. It marks an attitude, a sign of disrespect, and we may blame several influences for its spread. When colleges treat students as consumers and clients, they encourage it, as does pop culture when it elevates hooky-playing tricksters such as Ferris Bueller into heroes. College professors complain all the time about it, but they have their own part in the students' negligence, for they pass it along whenever they esteem the students' knowledge and deauthorize their own.

That isn't what they think they do, of course, but the effect is the same. Many indulgers believe that teacher-centered instruction bores the kids into diffidence or proves too difficult to handle, and that student-centered instruction will inspire the lesser-caliber students to work harder and stay in school, but in fact those lesser students say otherwise. In a National Governors Association poll of 10,378 teenagers (reported in July 2005), nearly 90 percent intended to graduate, and more than one-third of them stated that high school has been "easy" (less than 10 percent called it "very hard"). Surprisingly, the future dropouts scored similarly on the "hardness" index. Of the 11 percent who admitted that they didn't intend to graduate from high school, only one in nine gave as a reason, "schoolwork is too hard." At the top, at 36 percent, was the claim that they were "not learning anything," 12 points higher than sheer "hate" for the school they attend. The reactions of delinquent college students are less extreme than that, but they echo the high school dropouts' motives. When "instructor-domination" decreases, a few students step up

[handwritten margin note: Students as consumers — has to be hard to be worth what you're paying for]

[handwritten margin note: What does Bauerlein mean by "indulgers"]

their learning, but most of them cut their discipline, now and then blowing
300   off in-class duties and all the time ignoring their teachers out of class. A 2005
report sponsored by Achieve, Inc., on college and workplace readiness heard
less than one-quarter of high school graduates say that they were "significantly challenged and faced high expectations" (*Rising to the Challenge: Are
High School Graduates Prepared for College and Work?*). In the *First-Year* study,
only 30 percent of students studied 11 or more hours per week, and 39 percent did six hours or less. Only 24 percent "frequently" felt that their courses
inspired them "to think in new ways." Half the students (49 percent) visited an instructor's office hours a sorry two times or fewer per term. Let the
students guide themselves, and they'll do so happily.

310   As they glide through their courses, they seem unaware of the long-term
disadvantages. Here, too, the abnegation of the mentors plays a role, for in
releasing students from the collective past they deny students a resource to
foster a healthy and prosperous future. Dissociated from tradition, with nobody
telling them that sometimes they must mute the voices inside them and heed
instead the voices of distant greatness, young people miss one of the sanative,
humbling mechanisms of maturity. This is the benefit of tradition, the result
of a reliable weeding-out process. At any present moment, a culture spills over
with ideas and images, sayings and symbols and styles, and they mingle promis-
cuously. Many of them arise passing only a commercial standard, not a criti-
320   cal or moral one, and in the rush of daily life it's hard to discriminate them,
the significant from the insignificant, trendy from lasting, tasteful from vulgar. As time goes by, though, the transient, superficial, fashionable, and hack-
neyed show up more clearly and fall away, and a firmer, nobler continuity forms.
We think of jazz, for instance, as the tradition of Armstrong, Ellington, Parker,
Monk, Fitzgerald, Getz, and the rest, but at the time when they recorded their
signature pieces, jazz looked much different. The cream hadn't fully risen to
the top, and "Parker's Mood" and "Blue 7" appeared amid a thousand other,
now forgotten songs in the jazz landscape. Only with the passage of time does
the field refine and settle into its superior creations.

330   The tradition-making process, then, somewhat distorts the actual historical
genesis of its ingredients. But it serves a crucial moral and intellectual function.
Tradition provides a surer standard, a basis for judgment more solid than present comparisons, than political, practical, and commercial grounds. Young Americans exist amidst an avalanche of input, and the combination overwhelms their
shaky critical sense. Tradition provides grounding against and refuge from the
mercurial ebb and flow of youth culture, the nonstop marketing of youth products to youths. The great nineteenth-century critic Matthew Arnold explained
the benefits of connecting to "the ancients" in precisely these "steadying" terms:

The present age makes great claims upon us: we owe it service, it will
340   not be satisfied without our admiration. I know not how it is, but their
commerce with the ancients appears to me to produce, in those who

constantly practice it, a steadying and composing effect upon their judgment, not of literary works only, but of men and events in general.

Contact with the past steadies and composes judgment of the present. That's the formula. People who read Thucydides and Caesar on war, and Seneca and Ovid on love, are less inclined to construe passing fads as durable outlooks, to fall into the maelstrom of celebrity culture, to presume that the circumstances of their own life are worth a Web page. They distinguish long-term meanings in the sequence of "men and events," and they gamble on the lasting stakes of life, not the meretricious ones.   350

Nobody likes a scold, but the critical filter has never been more needed. The rush of the "present age" noted by Arnold in 1853 has cascaded into a deluge. Digital technology has compounded the incoming flow, and young adults flounder in it the most. Their grandparents watch them at the keyboard, on the cell phone, with the BlackBerry, etc., and it looks like delirium. All the more reason, then, to impart the unchanging and uncompromising examples, in Arnold's words, the "best that is known and thought in the world." Without the anchor of wise and talented men and women long gone, of thoughts and works that have stood the test of time, adolescents fall back upon the meager, anarchic resources of their sole selves. They watch a   360   *fellshort?* movie—say, *Pretty Woman*—and see it in the light of real and imagined high school romances instead of, in this case, fairy tales and 1980s finance wizards. Asked for a political opinion, they recall the images they catch on television, not the models of Washington, Churchill, and Pope John Paul II. Instead of understanding the young adult roller coaster of courtship and rejection with the help of novels by Jane Austen, they process their miasmic feelings by themselves or with sympathetic friends. And why should they do otherwise when the counsel of mentors, not to mention the avalanche of movies, music, and the rest, upholds the sovereignty of youth perspective? The   370 currents of social life press upon them hourly, while the pages within *The Decline and Fall of the Roman Empire* and *Wuthering Heights* seem like another, irrelevant universe. They don't know much about history and literature, but they have feelings and needs, and casualty figures from Shiloh and lines from Donne don't help.

No wonder psychological assessments show rising currents of narcissism among Americans who haven't yet joined the workforce. In one study publicized in early 2007, researchers analyzed the responses of more than 16,000 college students on the Narcissistic Personality Inventory going back to the early 1980s. Undergraduates in 2006, it turned out, scored 30 percent higher than students in 1982 on the narcissism scale, with two-thirds of them reaching above-average levels. The researchers traced the rise directly to self-esteem   380 orientations in the schoolroom, and lead author Jean Twenge groused, "We need to stop endlessly repeating, 'You're special,' and having children repeat that back. Kids are self-centered enough already."

The behavioral features of narcissism are bad enough, but a set of other studies demonstrates just how disabling it proves, particularly with school-work. One consequence of narcissism is that it prevents young people from weighing their own talents and competencies accurately. Narcissists can't take criticism, they hate to hand power over to others, and they turn disappoint-
390   ments into the world's fault, not their own. These are the normal hurdles of growing up, but for narcissists they represent a hostile front advancing against them. It's a distorted and destroying mirror, as Narcissus himself showed when he fixed upon his own reflection in the pool and snubbed the calls of love and caution he'd heard before, unable to leave his lovely countenance until the end. Education requires the opposite, a modicum of self-doubt, a capac-ity for self-criticism, precisely what the narcissist can't bear.

The attitude is even more harmful than the knowledge deficiencies we've seen earlier. An ignorant but willing mind can overcome ignorance through steady work and shrewd guidance. Read a few more books, visit a museum,
400   take some classes, and knowledge will come. An unwilling mind can't, or won't. It already knows enough, and history, civics, philosophy, and literature have too little direct application to satisfy. For many young Americans, that trans-lates into a demoralizing perception problem, a mismatch of expectation and ability. An October 2005 report by the U.S. Department of Education drew the distinction in gloomy forecasts. Titled *A Profile of the American High School Senior in 2004: A First Look,* it culled four traits out, of the academic lives of more than 13,000 students from across the country. They were: tested achieve-ment, educational intentions, reasons for choosing a particular college, and life goals. Set alongside each other, the first two characteristics settled so far
410   apart as to signal a national pathology. The study focused on student achieve-ment ratings on math scores and derived the usual abysmal picture. Only "a third (35 percent) showed an understanding of intermediate-level mathe-matical concepts," and 21 percent of them could not perform "simple oper-ations with decimals, fractions, powers, and roots." More than one-third of high school seniors (37.6 percent) could not complete "simple problem solv-ing, requiring the understanding of low-level mathematical concepts," and a tiny 3.9 percent reached proficiency in "complex multistep word problems."

A troubling outcome, but no shocker. The surprise comes with the second trait, the students' expectations. The survey asked high school seniors how
420   much education they expected to complete—not *wanted* to complete, but would successfully complete—and their answers bounded far beyond trait #1. Fully 69 percent of the respondents "expected to complete college with a 4-year degree," and of that group 35 percent believed that they would pro-ceed further to earn a professional or postbaccalaureate degree. Of the oth-ers, 18 percent predicted that they would earn a two-year degree or attend college for some period of time. That left 8 percent who had no prediction, and only 5 percent who admitted that they would never attend college.

Broken down by proficiency, the expectations looked downright heart-breaking. Nearly one-third (31.7 percent) of the students who expected to grad-

uate from college could handle, at best, simple problem solving, and one-fifth   430
of those anticipating an advanced degree could do no better. Only 7.6 percent of the I-expect-an-advanced-degree group reached advanced proficiency
in mathematics, while 9.4 percent of graduate-degree intenders compiled a
transcript with the highest mathematics coursework as pre-algebra or lower.

In the National Governors Association poll cited on page 21, similar mis-
estimations came up. When asked "How well do you think your high school
prepares you in each of the following areas?" 80 percent replied "Excellent/Good"
in basic reading skills and math skills—a number far exceeding the actual percentage. Three-quarters of them claimed "Ability to read at a high level," and
71 percent boasted excellent/good algebra talents. Furthermore, they demanded   440
more courses in senior year "related to the kind of job I want," not realizing that
they can't proceed to more specialized courses until they improve their basic proficiencies in standard subjects.

Indeed, when comparing the self-image of the students and the knowledge/
skill deficits that emerge whenever they undergo objective tests, one has to
wonder: What are they thinking? Optimism is nice, but not when it reaches
delusional limits. Soon enough, the faulty combo of aptitude and ambition
will explode, and the teenagers won't understand why. Michael Petrilli of the
Fordham Foundation terms it "the reality gap between students' expectations and their skills" (see McCluskey), and the illusion gets punctured all too   450
readily not long after high school graduation. General education requirements
in college include a math course, and any degree in the sciences entails more
than that. One week in calculus sends them scurrying to drop/add, and many
end up in remediation or disappear altogether. It doesn't make sense. The math
skills they lack are requisite for the degrees they expect, but they don't make
the connection. They must get their college readiness conceits from somewhere besides test scores and coursework, partly, no doubt, from teachers who,
with the best intentions, tell middling students that they're doing great, that
they should follow their dreams, be all they can be . . .

All too often, the mentors don't see the results of their indulgence, which   460
emerge only after students leave their class, leaving teachers unaware of how
the approach misleads their charges. A recent study of teachers' expectations
touches one of the significant thresholds in a person's educational life: graduation. When a student graduates from high school, the diploma is supposed to signify a certain level of skill and knowledge, but the teachers
who have graded them don't seem to realize the levels actually expected of
students at the next stage. Instead, high school teachers consistently assess
the skills of their graduating students much more highly than college teachers assess the skills of their entering students. That's the finding of companion surveys sponsored by the *Chronicle of Higher Education* in 2006, one   470
of them directed at high school teachers, the other at college professors
(see *Chronicle of Higher Education*, "What Professors and Teachers Think").
Researchers asked 746 high school teachers and 1,098 college professors
specifically about the college readiness of the kids they instructed, and the

variance was huge. On the general question "How well prepared are your students for college-level work?" 31 percent of the teachers stated "Very well," while only 13 percent of professors stated "Very well." In the "Not well" category, professors doubled the teacher score, 24 percent to 12 percent, meaning that while only one in eight high school teachers found among
480 the students "large gaps in preparation" that left them "struggling," one in four college teachers found them. In certain subject areas, the discrepancy between high school and college perceptions increased to a ratio of nine to one. In mathematics, fully 37 percent of teachers estimated that the students were "Very well prepared," while a meager 4 percent of professors agreed. For science, 38 percent of teachers gave them "Very well prepared," but only 5 percent of professors did. In writing, nearly half the professors (44 percent) rated the freshman class "Not well prepared," while only 10 percent of teachers were equally judgmental. Interestingly, for motivational traits the discrepancy shrank significantly, for example, with teach-
490 ers and professors differing by only three points in judging students "Very well prepared" to "work hard." The decrease indicates that the problem lies not in the students' diligence but in their intellectual tool kits, and that the energy students devote to schoolwork (and leisure play) often dodges activities that build college-level knowledge and skills.

One of the most precious tools they lack does not appear in predominant education philosophies, however, nor does it shape training programs for teachers and professors, nor does it arise in discussions of American competitiveness and innovation among business leaders and politicians interested in education. When foundation personnel talk of school improvement and
500 education officers announce academic outcomes, they cite test scores, retention rates, school choice plans, technology, and a dozen other topics, but not this one. And if it were posed to intellectuals, academics, educators, and journalists, a few might seize it as crucial but most would give it a limp nod of approval, or stare blankly, or reject it outright. It sounds fainthearted to them, or outmoded, moralistic, or irrelevant. The tool is precisely what has been lost in the shifting attitude in favor of youth: self-criticism in the light of tradition.

Adolescents are painfully self-conscious, to be sure, and they feel their being intensely, agonizing over a blemish on the cheek and a misstep in the lunch-
510 room. But the yardstick of their judgment comes not from the past but from the present, not from wise men and women but from cool classmates, not from art and thought through the ages but from pop culture of the moment. They pass through school and home ever aware of inadequacy, but the ideals they honor raise them only to the condition of peer respect. Their idols are peer idols, their triumphs the envy of friends, not adults. Their self-criticism isn't enlightened and forward-looking, nor is it backward-looking. It's social and shortsighted.

What young Americans need isn't more relevance in the classroom, but less. A June 2006 op-ed in *Education Week* on student disengagement in class, "The Small World of Classroom Boredom," concludes, "Instead of responding to our students as individuals with their own interests and knowledge, the school curriculum is, by and large, remote, providing little connection between the classroom and students' lives" (see Schultz). Yes, the coursework is remote, but instead of blaming the curriculum and offering more blather about sparking "intellectual curiosity" and "independent thinking," as the author does, let's blame "students' lives" for stretching the divide. Young people need mentors not to go with the youth flow, but to stand staunchly against it, to represent something smarter and finer than the cacophony of social life. They don't need more pop culture and youth perspectives in the classroom. They get enough of those on their own. Young Americans need someone somewhere in their lives to reveal to them bigger and better human stories than the sagas of summer parties and dormitory diversions and Facebook sites.

In slighting the worth of tradition, in allowing teenagers to set their own concerns before the civilization of their forebears, mentors have only opened more minutes to youth contact and youth media. And not just school time, but leisure time, too, for the betrayal of the mentors ripples far beyond the campus. In the past, as long as teachers, parents, journalists, and other authorities insisted that young people respect knowledge and great works, young people devoted a portion of out-of-class hours to activities that complement in-class work. These include the habits we've already charted: books for fun, museums, "art music," dance and theater, politics.

The more mentors have engaged youth in youth terms, though, the more youth have disengaged from the mentors themselves and from the culture they are supposed to represent. To take one more example: in 1982, 18- to 24-year-olds made up 18.5 percent of the performing arts attendance. In 2002, the portion fell to 11.2 percent, a massive slide in audience makeup, and an ominous sign for the future of arts presenters (National Endowment for the Arts, *Survey of Public Participation in the Arts*).

The decline of school-supporting leisure habits—lower reading rates, fewer museum visits, etc.—created a vacuum in leisure time that the stuff of youth filled all too readily, and it doesn't want to give any of it back. Digital technology has fostered a segregated social reality, peer pressure gone wild, distributing youth content in an instant, across continents, 24/7. Television watching holds steady, while more screens mean more screen time. What passes through them locks young Americans ever more firmly into themselves and one another, and whatever doesn't pass through them appears irrelevant and profitless. Inside the classroom, they learn a little about the historical past and civic affairs, but once the lesson ends they swerve back to the youthfull, peer-bound present. Cell phones, personal pages, and the rest unleash persistent and simmering forces of adolescence, the volatile mix of cliques and loners, rebelliousness and conformity, ambition and self-destruction, idol-atry and irreverence, know-nothing-ness and know-it-all-ness, all of which tra-dition and knowledge had helped to contain. The impulses were always there, but the stern shadow of moral and cultural canons at home and in class man-aged now and then to keep them in check. But the guideposts are now unmanned, and the pushback of mentors has dwindled to the sober objections of a faithful few who don't mind sounding unfashionable and insensitive.

The ingredients come together into an annihilating recipe. Adolescent urg-
570   ings, a teen world cranked up by technology, a knowledge world cranked down by abdicating mentors . . . they commingle and produce young Americans whose wits are just as keen as ever, but who waste them on screen diversions; kids whose ambitions may even exceed their forebears', but whose aims merge on career and consumer goals, not higher learning; youths who experience a typical stage of alienation from the adult world, but whose alienation doesn't stem from countercultural ideas and radical mentors (Karl Marx, Herbert Mar-cuse, Michel Foucault, etc.), but from an enveloping immersion in peer stuff. Their lengthening independence has shortened their mental horizon. Teen material floods their hours and mentors esteem them, believing the kids more
580   knowledgeable and skilled than they really are, or, perhaps, thinking that assur-ance will make them that way.

Few things are worse for adolescent minds than overblown appraisals of their merits. They rob them of constructive self-criticism, and obscure the les-sons of tradition. They steer their competitive instincts toward peer triumphs, not civic duty. They make them mistrust their guides, and interpret cynically both praise and censure. They set them up for failure, a kind of Peter Princi-ple in young people's lives whereby they proceed in school and in social cir-cles without receiving correctives requisite to adult duties and citizenship. They reach a level of incompetence, hit a wall in college or the workplace, and never
590   understand what happened. The rising cohort of Americans is not "The Next Great Generation," as Strauss and Howe name them in their hagiographic book *Millennials Rising*. We wish they were, but it isn't so. The twenty-first-century teen, connected and multitasked, autonomous yet peer-mindful, marks no great leap forward in human intelligence, global thinking, or "netizen"-ship. Young users have learned a thousand new things, no doubt. They upload and download, surf and chat, post and design, but they haven't learned to ana-lyze a complex text, store facts in their heads, comprehend a foreign policy decision, take lessons from history, or spell correctly. Never having recognized their responsibility to the past, they have opened a fissure in our civic foun-
600   dations, and it shows in their halting passage into adulthood and citizenship. They leave school, but peer fixations continue and social habits stay the same. They join the workforce only to realize that self-esteem lessons of home and class, as well as the behaviors that made them popular, no longer apply, and it takes them years to adjust. They grab snatches of news and sometimes vote, but they regard the civic realm as another planet. And wherever they end up, whomever they marry, however high they land in their careers, most of

them never acquire the intellectual tools they should have as teenagers and young adults. Perhaps during their twenties they adapt, acquiring smarter work and finance habits. But the knowledge and culture traits never catch up.

A few years of seasoning in the American workplace may secure their income and inculcate maturity in private life, but it won't sustain the best civic and cultural traditions in American history. If young people don't read, they shut themselves out of public affairs. Without a knowledge formation in younger years, adults function as more or less partial citizens. Reading and knowledge have to enter their leisure lives, at their own initiative. Analyzing Pew Research data from 2002 and 2004, political scientists Stephen and Linda Bennett lay out the simple fact: "People who read books for pleasure are more likely than non-readers to report voting, being registered to vote, 'always' voting, to pay greater attention to news stories about national, international, and local politics, and to be better informed."

As the rising generation reaches middle age, it won't re-create the citizenship of its precursors, nor will its ranks produce a set of committed intellectuals ready to trade in ideas, steer public policy, and espouse social values on the basis of learning, eloquence, and a historical sense of human endeavor. This is one damaging consequence of the betrayal of the mentors that is often overlooked. When people warn of America's future, they usually talk about competitiveness in science, technology, and productivity, not in ideas and values. But the current domestic and geopolitical situation demands that we generate not only more engineers, biochemists, nanophysicists, and entrepreneurs, but also men and women experienced in the ways of culture, prepared for contest in the marketplace of ideas. Knowledge-workers, wordsmiths, policy wonks . . . they don't emerge from nowhere. They need a long foreground of reading and writing, a home and school environment open to their development, a pipeline ahead and behind them. They need mentors to commend them when they're right and rebuke them when they're wrong. They need parents to remind them that social life isn't everything, and they need peers to respect their intelligence, not scrunch up their eyes at big words. It takes a home, and a schoolhouse, and a village, and a market to make a great public intellectual and policy maker. The formula is flexible, but with the Dumbest Generation its breakdown is under way, and with it the vitality of democracy in the United States.

TWO ESSENTIAL GOALS
Ernest L. Boyer

An effective college has a clear and vital mission. Administrators, faculty, and students share a vision of what the institution is seeking to accomplish. The goals at such an institution flow from the needs of society and also from the needs of the persons seeking education.

Both not one

But can the modern college, with all its separations and divisions, be guided by a common vision? And can the search for goals be something more than a diversion?

America's first colleges were guided by a vision of coherence. The goal was to train not only the clergy, but a new civic leadership as well. These struggling institutions sought "to develop a sense of unity where, in a society created from many of the nations of Europe, there might otherwise be aimlessness and uncontrolled diversity" [said Frederick Rudolph in *The American College and University*].

The confidence of professors and their students in this era "owed much to their membership in an established middle class, a commitment to European learning, and a Christian conception of character and culture." Within that framework, bitter disputes sometimes did rage, but from today's perspective the colonial college seems stiflingly monolithic.

The first students at tiny Harvard College advanced in lockstep fashion, studied a common curriculum, one subject a day, from 8:00 A.M. until 5:00 P.M., Monday through Friday, and a half day on Saturday. In the first year, there was logic, Greek and Hebrew, rhetoric, divinity catechetical, history, and the nature of plants. The second year included ethics and politics, Aramaic, and further studies in rhetoric and divinity catechetical. The final year of college was capped by arithmetic, astronomy, Syriac, more Greek, rhetoric, and, of course, divinity catechetical.

This academic core was considered absolute and immutable, to be accepted, not criticized or questioned. The goal was to discipline the mind and, through such training, graduates were to move comfortably into prestigious professions—the clergy, business, medicine, law, and civic leadership.

Our present academic world would be unrecognizable to the men who founded Harvard College in 1636. The fixed curriculum of the colonial era is as much an anachronism today as the stocks in the village square. Separations and divisions, not unity, mark the undergraduate program. Narrow departmentalization divides the campus. So distinctive are the different disciplines in method and content, the argument goes, that there is no way to connect them in the minds of students. Knowledge is so vast and specialization so persistent that shared goals cannot be defined.

Reprinted from *College: The Undergraduate Experience in America* (1987), by permission of the Carnegie Foundation for the Advancement of Teaching.

There is, we believe, a way out of our dilemma. While preparing this report
40 we repeatedly were reminded that two powerful traditions—*individuality*
and *community*—have been at the heart of the undergraduate experiences.
These two priorities have defined throughout the years the boundaries of the
collegiate debate about purposes and goals and within these traditions there
is, perhaps, sufficient common ground on which a vital academic program
can be built.

The focus on individuality, on the personal benefits and the utility of
education, has a rich tradition in American higher education. Throughout
the years, students have come to college to pursue their own goals, to follow
their own aptitudes, to become productive, self-reliant human beings, and,
50 with new knowledge, to continue learning after college days are over. Serving
individual interests has been a top priority in higher education.

But amidst diversity, the claims of community must be vigorously affirmed.
By community we mean an undergraduate experience that helps students go
beyond their own private interests, learn about the world around them,
develop a sense of civic and social responsibility, and discover how they, as individuals, can contribute to the larger society of which they are a part.

Robert Bellah, co-author of *Habits of the Heart,* observes that "since
World War II, the traditions of atomistic individualism have grown stronger,
while the traditions of the individual in society have grown weaker. The sense
60 of cohesive community is lost." In an era when an emphasis on narrow voca-
tionalism dominates many campuses, the challenge is to help students relate
what they have learned to concerns beyond themselves.

Individuals should become empowered [or enabled] to live productive,
independent lives. They also should be helped to go beyond private interests
and place their own lives in larger context. When the observant Frenchman
Alexis de Tocqueville visited the United States in the 1830s, he warned that
"as individualism grows, people forget their ancestors and form the habit of
thinking of themselves in isolation and imagine their whole destiny is in their
hands." To counter this cultural disintegration, Tocqueville argued, "Citizens
70 must turn from the private inlets and occasionally take a look at something
other than themselves."

We suggest, then, that within the traditions of individuality and community, educational and social purposes for the undergraduate experience can be
defined. The individual preferences of each student must be served. But
beyond diversity, the college has an obligation to give students a sense of passage toward a more coherent view of knowledge and a more integrated life.

Individualism is necessary for a free and creative society, and the historic
strength of our democracy lies in its commitment to personal improvement
and fulfillment. We need individualism but, at the same time, we must be
80 mindful of the consequences of selfishness. It is appropriate, therefore, for
educational institutions that are preparing students to be citizens in a partic-
ipatory democracy to understand the dilemmas and paradoxes of individualistic culture.

Just as we search culturally to maintain the necessary balance between private and public obligations, in education we seek the same end. The college, at its best, recognizes that, although we live alone, we also are deeply dependent on each other. Through an effective college education, students should become personally empowered and also committed to the common good.

ALL SUMMER IN A DAY
Ray Bradbury

No one in the class could remember
a time when there wasn't rain.

"Ready?"   1

"Ready."

"Now?"

"Soon."

"Do the scientists really know? Will it happen today, will it?"

"Look, look; see for yourself!"

The children pressed to each other like so many roses, so many weeds, intermixed, peering out for a look at the hidden sun.

It rained.   10

It had been raining for seven years; thousand upon thousands of days compounded and filled from one end to the other with rain, with the drum and gush of water, with the sweet crystal fall of showers and the concussion of storms so heavy they were tidal waves come over the islands. A thousand forests had been crushed under the rain and grown up a thousand times to be crushed again. And this was the way life was forever on the planet Venus, and this was the schoolroom of the children of the rocket men and women who had come to a raining world to set up civilization and live out their lives.

"It's stopping, it's stopping!"

"Yes, yes!"   20

Margot stood apart from these children who could never remember a time when there wasn't rain and rain and rain. They were all nine years old, and if there had been a day, seven years ago, when the sun came out for an hour and showed its face to the stunned world, they could not recall. Sometimes, at night, she heard them stir, in remembrance, and she knew they were dreaming and remembering and gold or a yellow crayon or a coin large enough to buy the world with. She knew they thought they remembered a warmness, like a blushing in the face, in the body, in the arms and legs and trembling hands. But then they always awoke to the tatting drum, the endless shaking down of clear bead necklaces upon the roof, the walk, the gardens, the forests, and their dreams were gone.   30

All day yesterday they had read in class about the sun. About how like a lemon it was, and how hot. And they had written small stories or essays or poems about it:

I think the sun is a flower,
That blooms for just one hour.

Reprinted from *Bradbury Stories* (2003), William Morrow & Co., Inc.

That was Margot's poem, read in a quiet voice in the still classroom while the rain was falling outside.

"Aw, you didn't write that!" protested one of the boys.

"I did," said Margot. "I *did.*"

40   "William!" said the teacher.

But that was yesterday. Now the rain was slackening, and the children were crushed in the great thick windows.

"Where's teacher?"

"She'll be back."

"She'd better hurry, we'll miss it!"

They turned on themselves, like a feverish wheel, all tumbling spokes.

Margot stood alone. She was a very frail girl who looked as if she had been lost in the rain for years and the rain had washed out the blue from her eyes and the red from her mouth and the yellow from her hair. She was an old

50   photograph dusted from an album, whitened away, and if she spoke at all her voice would be a ghost. Now she stood, separate, staring at the rain and the loud wet world beyond the huge glass.

"What're *you* looking at?" said William.

Margot said nothing.

"Speak when you're spoken to." He gave her a shove. But she did not move; rather she let herself be moved only by him and nothing else.

They edged away from her, they would not look at her. She felt them go away. And this was because she would play no games with them in the echoing tunnels of the underground city. If they tagged her and ran, she stood

60   blinking after them and did not follow. When the class sang songs about happiness and life and games her lips barely moved. Only when they sang about the sun and the summer did her lips move as she watched the drenched windows.

And then, of course, the biggest crime of all was that she had come here only five years ago from Earth, and she remembered the sun and the way the sun was and the sky was when she was four in Ohio. And they, they had been on Venus all their lives, and they had been only two years old when last the sun came out and had long since forgotten the color and heat of it and the way it really was. But Margot remembered.

70   "It's like a penny," she said once, eyes closed.

"No it's not!" the children cried.

"It's like a fire," she said, "in the stove."

"You're lying, you don't remember!" cried the children.

But she remembered and stood quietly apart from all of them and watched the patterning windows. And once, a month ago, she had refused to shower in the school shower rooms, had clutched her hands to her ears and over her head, screaming the water mustn't touch her head. So after that, dimly, dimly, she sensed it, she was different and they knew her difference and kept away.

There was talk that her father and mother were taking her back to Earth   80
next year; it seemed vital to her that they do so, though it would mean the
loss of thousands of dollars to her family. And so, the children hated her for
all these reasons of big and little consequence. They hated her pale snow face,
her waiting silence, her thinness, and her possible future.

"Get away!" The boy gave her another push. "What're you waiting for?"

Then, for the first time, she turned and looked at him. And what she was
waiting for was in her eyes.

"Well, don't wait around here!" cried the boy savagely. "You won't see
nothing!"

Her lips moved.   90

"Nothing!" he cried. "It was all a joke, wasn't it?" He turned to the other
children. "Nothing's happening today. *Is* it?"

They all blinked at him and then, understanding, laughed and shook
their heads. "Nothing, nothing!"

"Oh, but," Margot whispered, her eyes helpless. "But this is the day, the
scientists predict, they say, they *know*, the sun. . . ."

"All a joke!" said the boy, and seized her roughly. "Hey, everyone, let's put
her in a closet before teacher comes!"

"No," said Margot, falling back.

They surged about her, caught her up and bore her, protesting, and then   100
pleading, and then crying, back into a tunnel, a room, a closet, where they
slammed and locked the door. They stood looking at the door and saw it
tremble from her beating and throwing herself against it. They heard her
muffled cries. Then, smiling, they turned and went out and back down the
tunnel, just as the teacher arrived.

"Ready, children?" she glanced at her watch.

"Yes!" said everyone.

"Are we all here?"

"Yes!"

The rain slackened still more.   110

They crowded to the huge door.

The rain stopped.

It was as if, in the midst of a film, concerning an avalanche, a tornado, a
hurricane, a volcanic eruption, something had, first, gone wrong with the
sound apparatus, thus muffling and finally cutting off all noise, all of the
blasts and repercussions and thunders, and then, second, ripped the film
from the projector and inserted in its place a peaceful tropical slide which did
not move or tremor. The world ground to a standstill. The silence was so
immense and unbelievable that you felt your ears had been stuffed or you had
lost your hearing altogether. The children put their hands to their ears. They   120
stood apart. The door slid back and the smell of the silent, waiting world
came in to them.

The sun came out.

It was the color of flaming bronze and it was very large. And the sky around it was a blazing blue tile color. And the jungle burned with sunlight as the children, released from their spell, rushed out, yelling, into the springtime.

"Now don't go too far," called the teacher after them. "You've only two hours, you know. You wouldn't want to get caught out!"

130　But they were running and turning their faces up to the sky and feeling the sun on their cheeks like a warm iron; they were taking off their jackets and letting the sun burn their arms.

"Oh, it's better than the sun lamps, isn't it?"

"Much, much better!"

They stopped running and stood in the great jungle that covered Venus, that grew and never stopped growing, tumultuously, even as you watched it. It was a nest of octopi, clustering up great arms of flesh-like weed, wavering, flowering this brief spring. It was the color of rubber and ash, this jungle, from the many years without sun. It was the color of stones and white cheeses

140　and ink, and it was the color of the moon.

The children lay out, laughing, on the jungle mattress, and heard it sigh and squeak under them, resilient and alive. They ran among the trees, they slipped and fell, they pushed each other, they played hide-and-seek and tag, but most of all they squinted at the sun until the tears ran down their faces, they put their hands up to that yellowness and that amazing blueness and they breathed of the fresh, fresh air and listened and listened to the silence which suspended them in a blessed sea of no sound and no motion. They looked at everything and savored everything. Then, wildly, like animals escaped from their caves, they ran and ran in shouting circles. They ran for

150　an hour and did not stop running.

And then—

In the midst of their running one of the girls wailed.

Everyone stopped.

The girl, standing in the open, held out her hand.

"Oh, look, look," she said, trembling.

They came slowly to look at her opened palm.

In the center of it, cupped and huge, was a single raindrop.

She began to cry, looking at it.

They glanced quietly at the sky.

160　"Oh. Oh."

A few cold drops fell on their noses and their cheeks and their mouths. The sun faded behind a stir of mist. A wind blew cool around them. They turned and started to walk back toward the underground house, their hands at their sides, their smiles vanishing away.

A boom of thunder startled them and like leaves before a new hurricane, they tumbled upon each other and ran. Lightening struck ten miles away, five miles away, a mile, a half mile. The sky darkened into midnight in a flash.

They stood in the doorway of the underground for a moment until it was raining hard. Then they closed the door and heard the gigantic sound of the rain falling in tons and avalanches, everywhere and forever.   170

"Will it be seven more years?"

"Yes. Seven."

Then one of them gave a little cry.

"Margot!"

"What?"

"She's still in the closet where we locked her."

"Margot."

They stood as if someone had driven them, like so many stakes, into the floor. They looked at each other and then looked away. They glanced out at the world that was raining now and raining and raining steadily. They could   180 not meet each other's glances. Their faces were solemn and pale. They looked at their hands and feet, their faces down.

"Margot."

One of the girls said, "Well . . . ?"

No one moved.

"Go on," whispered the girl.

They walked slowly down the hall in the sound of the cold rain. They turned through the doorway to the room in the sound of the storm and thunder, lightening on their faces, blue and terrible. They walked over to the closet door slowly and stood by it.   190

Behind the closed door was only silence.

They unlocked the door, even more slowly, and let Margot out.

1900 – 1980
German Social Psychologist

INDIVIDUAL AND SOCIAL NARCISSISM
Erich Fromm

One of the most fruitful and far-reaching of Freud's discoveries is his concept of narcissism. Freud himself considered it to be one of his most important findings, and employed it for the understanding of such distinct phenomena as psychosis ("narcissistic neurosis"), love, castration fear, jealousy, sadism, and also for the understanding of mass phenomena, such as the readiness of the suppressed classes to be loyal to their rulers. In this chapter I want to continue along Freud's line of thought and examine the role of narcissism for the understanding of nationalism, national hatred, and the psychological motivations for destructiveness and war . . . 1

. . . What is the development of narcissism in the "normal" person? Freud sketched the main lines of this development, and the following paragraph is a short summary of his findings. 10

The fetus in the womb still lives in a state of absolute narcissism. "By being born", says Freud, "we have made the step from an absolutely self-sufficient narcissism to the perception of a changing external world and the beginning of the discovery of objects,"[1] It takes months before the infant can even perceive objects outside as such, as being part of the "not me." By many blows to the child's narcissism, his ever increasing acquaintance with the outside world and its laws, thus of "necessity," man develops his original narcissism into "object love." But, says Freud, "a human being remains to some 20 extent narcissistic even after he has found external objects for his libido."[2] Indeed, the development of the individual can be defined in Freud's term as the evolution from absolute narcissism to a capacity for objective reasoning and object love, a capacity, however, which does not transcend definite limitations. The "normal," "mature" person is one whose narcissism has been reduced to the socially accepted minimum without ever disappearing completely. Freud's observation is confirmed by everyday experience. It seems that in most people one can find a narcissistic core which is not accessible and which defies any attempt at complete dissolution.

Those not sufficiently acquainted with Freud's technical language will 30 probably not obtain a distinct idea of the reality and power of narcissism, unless some more concrete description of the phenomenon is forthcoming. This I shall try to give in the following pages. Before I do so, however, I wish to clarify something about the terminology. Freud's views on narcissism are based on his concept of sexual libido. As I have already indicated, this mechanistic libido concept proved more to block than to further the development of the concept of narcissism. I believe that the possibilities of bringing it to its full fruition are much greater if one uses a concept of psychic energy which is not identical with the energy of the *sexual* drive. This was done by Jung; it even found some initial recognition in Freud's idea of desexualized 40

From chapter 4, "Individual and Social Narcissism," in *The Heart of Man*. First published in 1964 by Harper & Row, Publishers, New York, as volume XII of the "Religious Perspectives" planned and edited by Ruth Nanda Anshen. Copyright © 1964 by Erich Fromm. American Mental Health Foundation Books edition 2010.

libido. But although nonsexual psychic energy differs from Freud's libido it is, like libido an *energy* concept; it deals with psychic forces, visible only through their manifestations, which have a certain intensity and a certain direction. This energy binds, unifies, and holds together the individual within himself as well as the individual in his relationship to the world outside. Even if one does not agree with Freud in his earlier view that aside from the drive for survival, the energy of the sexual instinct (libido) is the only important motive power for human conduct, and if one uses instead a general concept of psychic energy, the difference is not as great as many who

50   think in dogmatic terms are prone to believe. The essential point on which any theory or therapy which could be called psychoanalysis depends, is the *dynamic* concept of human behavior; that is, the assumption that highly charged forces motivate behavior, and that behavior can be understood and predicted only by understanding these forces. This dynamic concept of human behavior is the center of Freud's system. How these forces are theoretically conceived, whether in terms of a mechanistic-materialistic philosophy or in terms of humanistic realism, is an important question, but one which is secondary to the central issue of the dynamic interpretation of human behavior.

60   Let us begin our description of narcissism with two extreme examples: the "primary narcissism" of the newborn infant, and the narcissism of the insane person. The infant is not yet related to the outside world (in Freudian terminology his libido has not yet cathexed outside objects). Another way of putting it is to say that the outside world does not exist for the infant, and this to such a degree that it is not able to distinguish between the "I" and the "not I". We might also say that the infant is not "interested" (inter-esse) = "to be in") in the world outside. The only reality that exists for the infant is itself: its body, its physical sensations of cold and warmth, thirst, need for sleep and bodily contact.

70   The insane person is in a situation not essentially different from that of the infant. But while for the infant the world outside has *not yet emerged* as real, for the insane person it *has ceased* to be real. In the case of hallucinations, for instance, the senses have lost their function of registering outside events—they register subjective experience in categories of sensory response to objects outside. In the paranoid delusion the same mechanism operates. Fear or suspicion, for instance, which are subjective emotions, become objectified in such a way that the paranoid person is convinced that others are conspiring against him; this is precisely the difference to the neurotic person: the latter may be constantly afraid of being hated, persecuted, etc., but he still knows that this is

80   what he *fears*. For the paranoid person the fear has been transformed into a fact.

A particular instance of narcissism which lies on the borderline between sanity and insanity can be found in some men who have reached an extraordinary degree of power. The Egyptian pharaohs, the Roman Caesars, the Borgias, Hitler, Stalin, Trujillo—they all show certain similar features. They have attained absolute power; their word is the ultimate judgment of every-

thing, including life and death; there seems to be no limit to their capacity to do what they want. They are gods, limited only by illness, age and death. They try to find a solution to the problem of human existence by the desperate attempt to transcend the limitation of human existence. They try to pretend that there is no limit to their lust and to their power, so they sleep   90
with countless women, they kill numberless men, they build castles everywhere, they "want the moon," they "want the impossible."3 This is madness, even though it is an attempt to solve the problem of existence by pretending that one is not human. It is a madness which tends to grow in the lifetime of the afflicted person. The more he tries to be god, the more he isolates himself from the human race; this isolation makes him more frightened, everybody becomes his enemy, and in order to stand the resulting fright he has to increase his power, his ruthlessness, and his narcissism. This Caesarian madness would be nothing but plain insanity were it not for one factor: by his power Caesar has bent reality to his narcissistic fantasies. He has forced every-   100
body to agree that he is god, the most powerful and the wisest of men—hence his own megalomania seems to be a reasonable feeling. On the other hand, many will hate him, try to overthrow and kill him—hence his pathological suspicions are also backed by a nucleus of reality. As a result he does not feel disconnected from reality—hence he can keep a modicum of sanity, even though in a precarious state.

Psychosis is a state of absolute narcissism, one in which the person has broken all connection with reality outside, and has made his own person the substitute for reality. He is entirely filled with himself, he has become "god and the world" to himself. It is precisely this insight by which Freud for the first   110
time opened the way to the dynamic understanding of the nature of psychosis.

However, for those who are not familiar with psychosis it is necessary to give a picture of narcissism as it is found in neurotic or "normal" persons. One of the most elementary examples of narcissism can be found in the average person's attitude toward his own body. Most people like their own body, their face, their figure, and when asked whether they would want to change with another perhaps more handsome person, very definitely say no. Even more telling is the fact that most people do not mind at all the sight or smell of their own feces (in fact, some like them), while they have a definite aversion for those of other people. Quite obviously there is no aesthetic or other judgment   120
involved here; the same thing which when connected with one's own body is pleasant, is unpleasant when connected with somebody else's . . .

. . . Let us look at two phenomena which are apparently extremely different, and yet both of which are narcissistic. A woman spends many hours every day before the mirror to fix her hair and face. It is not simply that she is vain. She is obsessed with her body and her beauty, and her body is the only important reality she knows. She comes perhaps nearest to the Greek legend which speaks of Narcissus, a beautiful lad who rejected the love of the nymph Echo, who died of a broken heart. Nemesis punished him by making him fall in love with the reflection of his own image in the water of the lake; in self-admiration   130 he fell into the lake and died. The Greek legend indicates clearly that this kind of "self-love" is a curse, and that in its extreme form it ends in self-destruction.[4] Another woman (and it could well be the same one some years later) suffers from hypochondriasis. She is also constantly preoccupied with her body although not in the sense of making it beautiful, but in fearing illness. Why the positive, or the negative, image is chosen has, of course, its reasons; however, we need not deal with these here. What matters is that behind both phenomena lies the same narcissistic preoccupation with oneself, with little interest left for the outside world . . .

140   . . . How does one recognize the narcissistic person? There is one type which is easily recognized. That is the kind of person who shows all the signs of self-satisfaction; one can see that when he says some trivial words he feels as if he has said something of great importance. He usually does not listen to what others say, nor is he really interested. (If he is clever, he will try to hide this fact by asking questions and making it a point to seem interested.) One can also recognize the narcissistic person by his sensitivity to any kind of criticism. This sensitivity can be expressed by denying the validity of any criticism, or by reacting with anger or depression. In many instances the narcissistic orientation may be hidden behind an attitude of modesty and humility;

150 in fact, it is not rare for a person's narcissistic orientation to take his humility as the object of his self-admiration. Whatever the different manifestations of narcissism are, a lack of genuine interest in the outside world is common to all forms of narcissism.[5]

     Sometimes the narcissistic person can also be recognized by his facial expression. Often we find a kind of glow or smile, which gives the impression of smugness to some, of beatific, trusting, childlikeness to others. Often the narcissism, especially in its most extreme forms, manifests itself in a peculiar glitter in the eyes, taken by some as a symptom of half-saintliness, by others of half-craziness. Many very narcissistic persons talk incessantly—often at

160 a meal, where they forget to eat and thus make everyone else wait. Company or food are less important than their "ego."

     The narcissistic person has not even necessarily taken his whole person as the object of his narcissism. Often he has cathexed a partial aspect of his personality with his narcissism; for instance, his honor, his intelligence, his physical prowess, his wit, his good looks (sometimes even narrowed down to such details as his hair or his nose). Sometimes his narcissism refers to qualities about which normally a person would not be proud, such as his capacity to be afraid and thus to foretell danger. "He" becomes identified with a partial aspect of himself. If we ask who "he" is, the proper answer would be that "he"

170 is his brain, his fame, his wealth, his penis, his conscience, and so on. All the idols of the various religions represent so many partial aspects of man. In the narcissistic person the object of his narcissism is any one of these partial qualities which constitute for him his self. The one whose self is represented by his property can take very well a threat to his dignity, but a threat to his property is like a threat to his life. On the other hand, for the one whose self is

represented by his intelligence, the fact of having said something stupid is so painful that it may result in a mood of serious depression. However, the more intense the narcissism is, the less will the narcissistic person accept the fact of failure on his side, or any legitimate criticism from others. He will just feel outraged by the insulting behavior of the other person, or believe that the other person is too insensitive, uneducated, etc., to have proper judgment. (I think, in this connection, of a brilliant, yet highly narcissistic man who, when confronted with the results of a Rorschach test he had taken and which fell short of the ideal picture he had of himself, said, "I am sorry for the psychologist who did this test: he must be very paranoid.")

We must now mention one other factor which complicates the phenomenon of narcissism. Just as the narcissistic person has made his "self-image" the object of his narcissistic attachment, he does the same with everything connected with him. *His* ideas, *his* knowledge, *his* house, but also people in *his* "sphere of interest" become objects of his narcissistic attachment. As Freud pointed out, the most frequent example is probably the narcissistic attachment to one's children. Many parents believe that their own children are the most beautiful, intelligent, etc., in comparison with other children. It seems that the younger the children are, the more intense is this narcissistic bias. The parents' love, and especially the mother's love for the infant, is to a considerable extent love for the infant as an extension of oneself. Adult love between man and woman also has often a narcissistic quality. The man who is in love with a woman may transfer his narcissism to her once she has become "his." He admires and worships her for qualities which he has conferred upon her; precisely because of her being part of him, she becomes the bearer of extraordinary qualities. Such a man will often also think that all things he possesses are extraordinarily wonderful, and he will be "in love" with them.

Narcissism is a passion the intensity of which in many individuals can only be compared with sexual desire and the desire to stay alive. In fact, many times it proves to be stronger than either. Even in the average individual in whom it does not reach such intensity, there remains a narcissistic core which appears to be almost indestructible. This being so we might suspect that like sex and survival, the narcissistic passion also has an important *biological function*. Once we raise this question the answer comes readily. How could the individual survive unless his bodily needs, his interests, his desires, were charged with much energy? Biologically, from the standpoint of survival, man must attribute to himself an importance far above what he gives to anybody else. If he did not do so, from where would he take the energy and interest to defend himself against other, to work for his subsistence, to fight for his survival, to press his claims against those of others? Without narcissism he might be a saint—but do saints have a high survival rate? What from a spiritual standpoint would be most desirable—absence of narcissism—would be most dangerous from the mundane standpoint of survival. Speaking teleologically, we can say that nature had to endow man with a great amount of narcissism to enable him to do what is necessary for survival. This is true especially because nature has not endowed man with well-developed instincts such as the animal has. The animal has no "problems" of survival in the sense that its built-in instinctive nature takes care of survival in such a way that the animal does not have to consider or decide whether or not it wants to make an effort. In man the instinctive apparatus has lost most of its efficacy—hence narcissism assumes a very necessary biological function.

However, once we recognize that narcissism fulfills an important biological function, we are confronted with another question. Does not extreme narcissism have the function of making man indifferent to others, incapable of giving second place to his own needs when this is necessary for co-operation with others? Does not narcissism make man asocial and, in fact, when it reaches an extreme degree, insane? There can be no doubt that extreme individual narcissism would be a severe obstacle to all social life. But if this is so, narcissism must be said to be in *conflict* with the principle of survival, for the individual can survive only if he organizes himself in groups; hardly anyone would be able to protect himself all alone against the dangers of nature, nor would he be able to do many kinds of work which can only be done in groups.

We arrive then at the paradoxical result that narcissism is necessary for survival, and at the same time that it is a threat to survival. The solution of this paradox lies in two directions. One is that *optimal* rather than *maximal* narcissism serves survival; that is to say, the biologically necessary degree of narcissism is reduced to the degree of narcissism that is compatible with social co-operation. The other lies in the fact that individual narcissism is transformed into group narcissism, that the clan, nation, religion, race, etc., become the objects of narcissistic passion instead of the individual. Thus, narcissistic energy is maintained but used in the interests of the survival of the group rather than for the survival of the individual . . .

. . . There is, however, still another solution to the threat to narcissism which is more satisfactory to the individual, although more dangerous to others. This solution consists in the attempt to transform reality in such a way as to make it conform, to some extent, with his narcissistic self-image. An example of this is the narcissistic inventor who believes he has invented a *perpetuum mobile*, and who in the process has made a minor discovery of some significance. A more important solution consists in getting the consensus of one other person, and, if possible, in obtaining the consensus of millions. The former case is that of a *folie à deux* (some marriages and friendships rest on this basis), while the latter is that of public figures who prevent the open outbreak of their potential psychosis by gaining the acclaim and consensus of millions of people. The best-known example for this latter case is Hitler. Here was an extremely narcissistic person who probably could have suffered a manifest psychosis had he not succeeded in making millions believe in his won self-image, take his grandiose fantasies regarding the millennium of the "Third Reich" seriously, and even transforming reality in such a way that it seemed proved to his followers that he was right. (After he had failed he had to kill himself, since otherwise the collapse of his narcissistic image would have been truly unbearable.)

There are other examples in history of megalomaniac leaders who "cured" their narcissism by transforming the world to fit it; such people must also try to destroy all critics, since they cannot tolerate the threat which the voice of sanity constitutes for them. From Caligula and Nero to Stalin and Hitler we see that their need to find believers, to transform reality so that it fits their narcissism, and to destroy all critics, is so intense and so desperate precisely because it is an attempt to prevent the outbreak of insanity. Paradoxically, the element of insanity in such leaders makes them also successful. It gives them that certainty and freedom from doubt which is so impressive to the average person. Needless to say, this need to change the world and to win others to share in one's ideas and delusions requires also talents and gifts which the average person, psychotic or nonpsychotic, lacks.

In discussing the pathology of narcissism it is important to distinguish between two forms of narcissism—one *benign*, the other *malignant*. In the benign form, the object of narcissism is the result of a person's effort. Thus, for instance, a person may have a narcissistic pride in his work as a carpenter, as a scientist, or as a farmer. Inasmuch as the object of his narcissism is something he has to work for, his exclusive interest in what is *his* work and *his* achievement is constantly balanced by his interest in the process of work itself, and the material he is working with. The dynamics of this benign narcissism thus are self-checking. The energy which propels the work is, to a large extent, of a narcissistic nature, but the very fact that the work itself makes it necessary to be related to reality, constantly curbs the narcissism and keeps it within bounds. This mechanism may explain why we find so many narcissistic people who are at the same time highly creative.

In the case of malignant narcissism, the object of narcissism is not anything the person does or produces, but something he *has;* for instance, his body, his looks, his health, his wealth, etc. The malignant nature of this type of narcissism lies in the fact that it lacks the corrective element which we find in the benign form. If I am "great" because of some quality I *have*, and not because of something I *achieve*, I do not need to be related to anybody or anything; I need not make any effort. In maintaining the picture of my greatness I remove myself more and more from reality and I have to increase the narcissistic charge in order to be better protected from the danger that my narcissistically inflated ego might be revealed as the product of my empty imagination. Malignant narcissism, thus, is not self-limiting, and in consequence it is crudely solipsistic as well as xenophobic. One who has learned to achieve cannot help acknowledging that others have achieved similar things in similar ways—even if his narcissism may persuade him that his own achievement is greater than that of others. One who has achieved nothing will find it difficult to appreciate the achievements of others, and thus he will be forced to isolate himself increasingly in narcissistic splendor.

We have so far described the dynamics of individual narcissism: the phenomenon, its biological function, and its pathology. This description ought to enable us now to understand the phenomenon of *social narcissism* and the role it plays as a source of violence and war.

The central point of the following discussion is the phenomenon of the transformation of personal into group narcissism. We can start with an observation about the sociological function of group narcissism which parallels the biological function of individual narcissism. From the standpoint of any organized group which wants to survive, it is important that the group be
320 invested by its members with narcissistic energy. The survival of a group depends to some extent on the fact that its members consider its importance as great as or greater than that of their own lives, and furthermore that they believe in the righteousness, or even superiority, of their group as compared with others. Without such narcissistic cathexis of the group, the energy necessary for serving the group, or even making severe sacrifices for it, would be greatly diminished.

In the dynamics of group narcissism we find phenomena similar to those we discussed already in connection with individual narcissism. Here too we can distinguish between benign and malignant forms of narcissism. If the
330 object of group narcissism is an achievement, the same dialectical process takes place which we discussed above. The very need to achieve something creative makes it necessary to leave the closed circle of group solipsism and to be interested in the object it wants to achieve. (If the achievement which a group seeks is conquest, the beneficial effect of truly productive effort will of course be largely absent.) If, on the other hand, group narcissism has as its object the group as it is, its splendor, its past achievements, the physique of its members, then the countertendencies mentioned above will not develop, and the narcissistic orientation and subsequent dangers will steadily increase. In reality, of course, both elements are often blended.

340 There is another sociological function of group narcissism which has not been discussed so far. A society which lacks the means to provide adequately for the majority of its members, or a large proportion of them, must provide these members with a narcissistic satisfaction of the malignant type if it wants to prevent dissatisfaction among them. For those who are economically and culturally poor, narcissistic pride in belonging to the group is the only—and often a very effective—source of satisfaction. Precisely because life is not "interesting" to them, and does not offer them possibilities for developing interests, they may develop an extreme form of narcissism. Good examples of this phenomenon in recent years are the racial narcissism which existed in
350 Hitler's Germany, and which is found in the American South today. In both instances the core of the racial superiority feeling was, and still is, the lower middle class; this backward class, which in Germany as well as in the American South has been economically and culturally deprived, without any realistic hope of changing its situation (because they are the remnants of an older and dying form of society) has only one satisfaction: the inflated image of

Examples?

itself as the most admirable group in the world, and of being superior to another racial group that is singled out as inferior. The member of such a backward group feels: "Even though I am poor and uncultured I am somebody important because I belong to the most admirable group in the world—I am white"; or, "I am an Aryan."   360

Group narcissism is less easy to recognize than individual narcissism. Assuming a person tells others, "I (and my family) are the most admirable people in the world; we alone are clean, intelligent, good, decent; all others are dirty, stupid, dishonest and irresponsible," most people would think him crude, unbalanced, or even insane. If, however, a fanatical speaker addresses a mass audience, substituting the nation (or race, religion, political party, etc.) for the "I" and "my family," he will be praised and admired by many for his love of country, love of God, etc. Other nations and religions, however, will resent such a speech for the obvious reason that they are held in contempt. *Within* the favored group, however, everybody's personal narcissism is flat-   370 tered and the fact that millions of people agree with the statements makes them appear as reasonable. (What the majority of people consider to be "reasonable" is that about which there is agreement, if not among all, at least among a substantial number of people; "reasonable," for most people, has nothing to do with reason, but with consensus.) Inasmuch as the group as a whole requires group narcissism for its survival, it will further narcissistic attitudes and confer upon them the qualification of being particularly virtuous.

The group to which the narcissistic attitude is extended has varied in structure and size throughout history. In the primitive tribe or clan it may comprise only a few hundred members; here the individual is not yet an   380 "individual" but is still united to the blood group by "primary bonds"[6] which have not yet been broken. The narcissistic involvement with the clan is thus strengthened by the fact that its members emotionally have still no existence of their own outside of the clan.

In the development of the human race we find an ever increasing range of socialization; the original small group based on blood affinity gives way to ever larger groups based on a common language, a common social order, a common faith. The larger size of the group does not necessarily mean that the pathological qualities of narcissism are reduced. As was remarked earlier, the group narcissism of the "whites" or the "Aryans" is as malignant as the   390 extreme narcissism of a single person can be. Yet in general we find that in the process of socialization which leads to the formation of larger groups, the need for co-operation with many other and different people not connected among themselves by ties of blood, tends to counteract the narcissistic charge within the group. The same holds true in another respect, which we have discussed in connection with benign individual narcissism: Inasmuch as the large group (nation, state, or religion) makes it an object of its narcissistic pride to achieve something valuable in the fields of material, intellectual, or artistic production, the very process of work in such fields tends to lessen the narcissistic charge. The history of the Roman Catholic Church is one of   400 many examples of the peculiar mixture of narcissism and the counteracting forces within a large group. The elements counteracting narcissism within the Catholic Church are, first of all, the concept of the universality of man and of a "catholic" religion which is no longer the religion of one particular tribe or nation. Second, the idea of personal humility which follows from the idea of God and the denial of idols. The existence of God implies that no man can be God, that no individual can be omniscient or omnipotent. It thus sets a definite limit to man's narcissistic self-idolatry. But at the same time the Church has nourished an intense narcissism; believing that the Church is the only chance of salvation and that the Pope is the Vicar of Christ, its members were able to develop an intense narcissism inasmuch as they were members of such an extraordinary institution. The same occurred in relation to God; while the omniscience and omnipotence of God should have led to man's humility, often the individual identified himself with God and thus developed an extraordinary degree of narcissism in this process of identification.

This same ambiguity between a narcissistic or an antinarcissistic function has occurred in all the other great religions, for example, in Buddhism, Judaism, Islam, and Protestantism. I have mentioned the Catholic religion not only because it is a well-known example, but mainly because the Roman Catholic religion was the basis both for humanism and for violent and fanatical religious narcissism at one and the same historical period: the fifteenth and sixteenth centuries. The humanists within the Church and those outside spoke in the name of a humanism which was the fountainhead of Christianity . . .

. . . Looking back to the religious hatred of the sixteenth and seventeenth centuries, its irrationalities are clear. Both sides spoke in the name of God, of Christ, of love, and they differed only in points which, if compared with the general principles, were of secondary importance. Yet they hated each other, and each was passionately convinced that humanity ended at the frontiers of his own religious faith. The essence of this over-estimation of ones' own position and the hate for all who differ from it is narcissism. "We" are admirable; "they" are despicable. "We" are good; "they" are evil. Any criticism of one's own doctrine is a vicious and unbearable attack; criticism of the others' position is a well-meant attempt to help them to return to the truth.

From the Renaissance onward, the two great contradictory forces, group narcissism and humanism, have each developed in its own way. Unfortunately the development of group narcissism has vastly outstripped that of humanism. While it seemed possible in the late Middle Ages and at the time of the Renaissance that Europe was prepared for the emergence of a political and religious humanism, this promise failed to materialize. New forms of group narcissism emerged, and dominated the following centuries. This group narcissism assumed manifold forms: religious, national, racial, political. Protestants against Catholics, French against Germans, whites against blacks, Aryans against non-Aryans, Communists against capitalists; different as the contents are, psychologically we deal with the same narcissistic phenomenon and its resulting fanaticism and destructiveness.[7]

While group narcissism grew, its counterpart—humanism—also developed. In the eighteenth and nineteenth centuries—from Spinoza, Leibniz, Rousseau, Herder, Kant, to Goethe and Marx—the thought developed that mankind is one, that each individual carries within himself all of humanity, that there must be no privileged groups claiming that their privileges are based on their intrinsic superiority . . .   450

. . . As a reaction to this threat to humanity, a renaissance of humanism can be observed today in all countries and among the representatives of diverse ideologies; there are radical humanists among Catholic and Protestant theologians, among socialist and nonsocialist philosophers. Whether the danger of total destruction, the ideas of the neohumanists and the bonds created between all men by the new means of communication will be sufficient to stop the effects of group narcissism is a question which may determine the fate of mankind . . .   460

ENDNOTES

1. Freud, *Group Psychology* (Standard Edition), Vol. XVIII, p. 130.
2. Freud, *Totem and Taboo* (Standard Edition), Vol. XIII, p. 89.
3. Camus, in his drama *Caligula*, has portrayed this madness of power most accurately.
4. Cf. my discussion of self-love in *Man for Himself*. I try to show there that true love for self is not different from love for others; that "self-love" in the sense of egoistic, narcissistic love is to be found in those who can love neither others nor themselves.
5. Sometimes it is not easy to distinguish between the vain, narcissistic person and one with a low self-evaluation; the latter often is in need of praise and admiration, not because he is not interested in anyone else, but because of his self-doubts and low self-evaluation. There is another important distinction which is also not always easy to make: that between narcissism and egotism. Intense narcissism implies an inability to experience reality in its fullness; intense egotism implies to have little concern, love or sympathy for others but it does not necessarily imply the overevaluation of one's subjective processes. In other words the extreme egotist is not necessarily extremely narcissistic; selfishness is not necessarily blindness to objective reality.
6. Cf. the discussion of primary bonds in E. Fromm, *Escape From Freedom* (New York: Holt, Rinehart & Winston, 1941).
7. There are other more harmless forms of group narcissism directed toward small groups like lodges, small religious sects, "the old school tie," etc. While the degree of narcissism in these cases may not be less than in those of the larger groups, the narcissism is less dangerous simply because the groups involved have little power, and hence little capacity to cause harm.

NOTES

MORAL ORIENTATION AND MORAL DEVELOPMENT
Carol Gilligan

When one looks at an ambiguous figure like the drawing that can be 1
seen as a young or old woman, or the image of the vase and the faces,
one initially sees it in only one way. Yet even after seeing it in both ways, one
way often seems more compelling. This phenomenon reflects the laws of perceptual organization that favor certain modes of visual grouping. But it also
suggests a tendency to view reality as unequivocal and thus to argue that
there is one right or better way of seeing.

The experiments of the Gestalt psychologists on perceptual organization
provide a series of demonstrations that the same proximal pattern can be
organized in different ways so that, for example, the same figure can be seen 10
as a square or a diamond, depending on its orientation in relation to a surrounding frame. Subsequent studies show that the context influencing which
of two possible organizations will be chosen may depend not only on the features of the array presented but also on the perceiver's past experience or
expectation. Thus, a bird watcher and a rabbit-keeper are likely to see the
duck-rabbit figure in different ways; yet this difference does not imply that
one way is better or a higher form of perceptual organization. It does, however, call attention to the fact that the rabbit-keeper, perceiving the rabbit,
may not see the ambiguity of the figure until someone points out that it can
also be seen as a duck. 20

This paper presents a similar phenomenon with respect to moral judgment, describing two moral perspectives that organize thinking in different
ways. The analogy to ambiguous figure perception arises from the observation that although people are aware of both perspectives, they tend to adopt
one or the other in defining and resolving moral conflict. Since moral judgments organize thinking about choice in difficult situations, the adoption of
a single perspective may facilitate clarity of decision. But the wish for clarity
may also imply a compelling human need for resolution or closure, especially
in the face of decisions that give rise to discomfort or unease. Thus, the
search for clarity in seeing may blend with a search for justification, encour- 30
aging the position that there is one right or better way to think about moral
problems. This question, which has been the subject of intense theological
and philosophical debate, becomes of interest to the psychologist not only
because of its psychological dimensions—the tendency to focus on one perspective and the wish for justification—but also because one moral perspective currently dominates psychological thinking and is embedded in the most
widely used measure for assessing the maturity of moral reasoning.

In describing an alternative standpoint, I will reconstruct the account of
moral development around two moral perspectives, grounded in different

Reprinted from *Women and Moral Theory*, edited by Eva Feder Kittay and Diana Meyers (1987),
by permission of Rowman & Littlefield Publishers, Inc.

*Justice
vs
care*

40   dimensions of relationship that give rise to moral concern. The justice perspective, often equated with moral reasoning, is recast as one way of seeing
moral problems and a care perspective is brought forward as an alternate
vision or frame. The distinction between justice and care as alternative perspectives or moral orientations is based empirically on the observation that a
shift in the focus of attention from concerns about justice to concerns about
care changes the definition of what constitutes a moral problem, and leads
the same situation to be seen in different ways. Theoretically, the distinction
between justice and care cuts across the familiar divisions between thinking
and feeling, egoism and altruism, theoretical and practical reasoning. It calls
50   attention to the fact that all human relationships, public and private, can be
characterized *both* in terms of equality and in terms of attachment, and that
both inequality and detachment constitute grounds for moral concern. Since
everyone is vulnerable both to oppression and to abandonment, two moral
visions—one of justice and one of care—recur in human experience. The
moral injunctions not to act unfairly toward others, and not to turn away
from someone in need, capture these different concerns.

The conception of the moral domain as [comprising] at least two moral
orientations raises new questions about observed differences in moral judgment and the disagreements to which they give rise. Key to this revision is
60   the distinction between differences in developmental stage (more or less adequate positions within a single orientation) and differences in orientation
(alternative perspectives or frameworks). The findings reported in this paper
of an association between moral orientation and gender speak directly to the
continuing controversy over sex differences in moral reasoning. In doing so,
however, they also offer an empirical explanation for why previous thinking
about moral development has been organized largely within the justice
framework.

My research on moral orientation derives from an observation made in
the course of studying the relationship between moral judgment and action.
70   Two studies, one of college students describing their experiences of moral
conflict and choice and one of pregnant women who were considering abortion, shifted the focus of attention from the ways people reason about hypothetical dilemmas to the ways people construct moral conflicts and choices
in their lives. This change in approach made it possible to see what experiences people define in moral terms, and to explore the relationship between
the understanding of moral problems and the reasoning strategies used and
the actions taken in attempting to resolve them. In this context, I observed
that women, especially when speaking about their own experiences of moral
conflict and choice, often define moral problems in a way that eludes the cat-
80   egories of moral theory and is at odds with the assumptions that shape psychological thinking about morality and about the self.[1] This discovery, that a
different voice often guides the moral judgments and the actions of women,
*design
problem*   called attention to a major design problem in previous moral judgment
research: namely, the use of all-male samples as the empirical basis for theory
construction.

The selection of an all-male sample as the basis for generalizations that are applied to both males and females is logically inconsistent. As a research strategy, the decision to begin with a single-sex sample is inherently problematic, since the categories of analysis will tend to be defined on the basis of the initial data gathered and subsequent studies will tend to be restricted to these categories. Piaget's work on the moral judgment of the child illustrates these problems since he defined the evolution of children's consciousness and practice of rules on the basis of his study of boys playing marbles, and then undertook a study of girls to assess the generality of his findings. Observing a series of differences both in the structure of girls' games and "in the actual mentality of little girls," he deemed these differences not of interest because "it was not this contrast which we proposed to study." Girls, Piaget found, "rather complicated our interrogatory in relation to what we know about boys," since the changes in their conception of rules, although following the same sequence observed in boys, did not stand in the same relation to social experience. Nevertheless, he concluded that "in spite of these differences in the structure of the game and apparently in the players' mentality, we find the same process at work as in the evolution of the game of marbles."[2]

Thus, girls were of interest insofar as they were similar to boys and confirmed the generality of Piaget's findings. The differences noted, which included a greater tolerance, a greater tendency toward innovation in solving conflicts, a greater willingness to make exceptions to rules, and a lesser concern with legal elaboration, were not seen as germane to "the psychology of rules," and therefore were regarded as insignificant for the study of children's moral judgment. Given the confusion that currently surrounds the discussion of sex differences in moral judgment, it is important to emphasize that the differences observed by Piaget did not pertain to girls' understanding of rules *per se* or to the development of the idea of justice in their thinking, but rather to the way girls structured their games and their approach to conflict resolution—that is, to their use rather than their understanding of the logic of rules and justice.

Kohlberg, in his research on moral development, did not encounter these problems since he equated moral development with the development of justice reasoning and initially used an all-male sample as the basis for theory and test construction. In response to his critics, Kohlberg has recently modified his claims, renaming his test a measure of "justice reasoning" rather than of "moral maturity" and acknowledging the presence of a care perspective in people's moral thinking.[3] But the widespread use of Kohlberg's measure as a measure of moral development together with his own continuing tendency to equate justice reasoning with moral judgment leaves the problem of orientation differences unsolved. More specifically, Kohlberg's efforts to assimilate thinking about care to the six-stage developmental sequence he derived and refined by analyzing changes in justice reasoning (relying centrally on his all-male longitudinal sample), underscores the continuing importance of the points raised in this paper concerning (1) the distinction between differences in developmental stage within a single orientation and differences in orientation, and (2) the fact that the moral thinking of girls and women was not examined in establishing either the meaning or the measurement of moral judgment within contemporary psychology.

An analysis of the language and logic of men's and women's moral reasoning about a range of hypothetical and real dilemmas underlies the distinction elaborated in this paper between a justice and a care perspective. The empirical association of care reasoning with women suggests that discrepancies observed between moral theory and the moral judgments of girls and
140   women may reflect a shift in perspective, a change in moral orientation. Like the figure-ground shift in ambiguous figure perception, justice and care as moral perspectives are not opposites or mirror-images of one another, with justice uncaring and care unjust. Instead, these perspectives denote different ways of organizing the basic elements of moral judgment: self, others, and the relationship between them. With the shift in perspective from justice to care, the organizing dimension of relationship changes from inequality/equality to attachment/detachment, reorganizing thoughts, feelings, and language so that words connoting relationship like "dependence" or "responsibility" or even moral terms such as "fairness" and "care" take on different meanings. To
150   organize relationships in terms of attachment rather than in terms of equality changes the way human connection is imagined, so that the images or metaphors of relationship shift from hierarchy or balance to network or web. In addition, each organizing framework leads to a different way of imagining the self as a moral agent.

From a justice perspective, the self as moral agent stands as the figure against a ground of social relationships, judging the conflicting claims of self and others against a standard of equality or equal respect (the Categorical Imperative, the Golden Rule). From a care perspective, the relationship becomes the figure, defining self and others. Within the context of relation-
160   ship, the self as a moral agent perceives and responds to the perception of need. The shift in moral perspective is manifest by a change in the moral question from "What is just?" to "How to respond?"

For example, adolescents asked to describe a moral dilemma often speak about peer or family pressure in which case the moral question becomes how to maintain moral principles or standards and resist the influence of one's parents or friends. "I have a right to my religious opinions," one teenager explains, referring to a religious difference with his parents. Yet, he adds, "I respect their views." The same dilemma, however, is also construed by adolescents as a problem of attachment, in which case the moral question
170   becomes: how to respond both to oneself and to one's friends or one's parents, how to maintain or strengthen connection in the face of differences in belief. "I understand their fear of my new religious ideas," one teenager explains, referring to her religious disagreement with her parents, "but they really ought to listen to me and try to understand my beliefs."

One can see these two statements as two versions of essentially the same thing. Both teenagers present self-justifying arguments about religious disagreement; both address the claims of self and of others in a way that honors both. Yet each frames the problem in different terms, and the use of moral language points to different concerns. The first speaker casts the problem in terms of individual rights that must be respected within the relationship. In other words, the figure of the considering is the self looking on the disagreeing selves in relationship, and the aim is to get the other selves to acknowledge the right to disagree. In the case of the second speaker, figure and ground shift. The relationship becomes the figure of the considering, and relationships are seen to require listening and efforts at understanding differences in belief. Rather than the right to disagree, the speaker focuses on caring to hear and to be heard. Attention shifts from the grounds for agreement (rights and respect) to the grounds for understanding (listening and speaking, hearing and being heard). This shift is marked by a change in moral language from the stating of separate claims to rights and respect ("I have a right . . . I respect their views.") to the activities of relationship—the injunction to listen and try to understand ("I understand . . . they ought to listen . . . and try to understand."). The metaphor of moral voice itself carries the terms of the care perspective and reveals how the language chosen for moral theory is not orientation neutral.

The language of the public abortion debate, for example, reveals a justice perspective. Whether the abortion dilemma is cast as a conflict of rights or in terms of respect for human life, the claims of the fetus and of the pregnant woman are balanced or placed in opposition. The morality of abortion decisions thus construed hinges on the scholastic or metaphysical question as to whether the fetus is a life or a person, and whether its claims take precedence over those of the pregnant woman. Framed as a problem of care, the dilemma posed by abortion shifts. The connection between the fetus and the pregnant woman becomes the focus of attention and the question becomes whether it is responsible or irresponsible, caring or careless, to extend or to end this connection. In this construction, the abortion dilemma arises because there is no way not to act, and no way of acting that does not alter the connection between self and others. To ask what actions constitute care or are more caring directs attention to the parameters of connection and the costs of detachment, which become subjects of moral concern.

Finally, two medical students, each reporting a decision not to turn in someone who has violated the school rules against drinking, cast their decision in different terms. One student constructs the decision as an act of mercy, a decision to override justice in light of the fact that the violator has shown "the proper degrees of contrition." In addition, this student raises the question as to whether or not the alcohol policy is just, i.e., whether the school has the right to prohibit drinking. The other student explains the decision not to turn in a proctor who was drinking on the basis that turning him in is not a good way to respond to this problem, since it would dissolve the relationship between them and thus cut off an avenue for help. In addition, this student raises the question as to whether the proctor sees his drinking as a problem.

This example points to an important distinction, between care as understood or construed within a justice framework and care as a framework or a perspective on moral decision. Within a justice construction, care becomes the mercy that tempers justice; or connotes the special obligations or supererogatory duties that arise in personal relationships; or signifies altruism freely chosen—a decision to modulate the strict demands of justice by considering equity or showing forgiveness; or characterizes a choice to sacrifice the claims of the self. All of these interpretations of care leave the basic assumptions of a justice framework intact: the division between the self and others, the logic of reciprocity or equal respect.

As a moral perspective, care is less well elaborated, and there is no ready vocabulary in moral theory to describe its terms. As a framework for moral decision, care is grounded in the assumption that self and other are interdependent, an assumption reflected in a view of action as responsive and, therefore, as arising in relationship rather than the view of action as emanating from within the self and, therefore, "self governed." Seen as responsive, the self is by definition connected to others, responding to perceptions, interpreting events, and governed by the organizing tendencies of human interaction and human language. Within this framework, detachment, whether from self or from others, is morally problematic, since it breeds moral blindness or indifference—a failure to discern or respond to need. The question of what responses constitute care and what responses lead to hurt draws attention to the fact that one's own terms may differ from those of others. Justice in this context becomes understood as respect for people in their own terms.

The medical student's decision not to turn in the proctor for drinking reflects a judgment that turning him in is not the best way to respond to the drinking problem, itself seen as a sign of detachment or lack of concern. Caring for the proctor thus raises the question of what actions are most likely to ameliorate this problem, a decision that leads to the question of what are the proctor's terms.

The shift in organizing perspective here is marked by the fact that the first student does not consider the terms of the other as potentially different but instead assumes one set of terms. Thus the student alone becomes the arbiter of what is *the* proper degree of contrition. The second student, in turn, does not attend to the question of whether the alcohol policy itself is just or fair. Thus each student discusses an aspect of the problem that the other does not mention.

These examples are intended to illustrate two cross-cutting perspectives that do not negate one another but focus attention on different dimensions of the situation, creating a sense of ambiguity around the question of what is the problem to be solved. Systematic research on moral orientation as a dimension of moral judgment and action initially addressed three questions: (1) Do people articulate concerns about justice and concerns about care in discussing a moral dilemma? (2) Do people tend to focus their attention on one set of concerns and minimally represent the other? and (3) Is there an association between moral orientation and gender? Evidence from studies that included a common set of questions about actual experiences of moral conflict and matched samples of males and females provides affirmative answers to all three questions.

When asked to describe a moral conflict they had faced, 55 out of 80 (69 percent) educationally advantaged North American adolescents and adults raised considerations of both justice and care. Two-thirds (54 out of 80) however, focused their attention on one set of concerns, with focus defined as 75 percent or more of the considerations raised pertaining either to justice or to care. Thus the person who presented, say, two care considerations in discussing a moral conflict was more likely to give a third, fourth, and fifth than to balance care and justice concerns—a finding consonant with the assumption that justice and care constitute organizing frameworks for moral decision. The men and the women involved in this study (high school students, college students, medical students, and adult professionals) were equally likely to demonstrate the focus phenomenon (two-thirds of both sexes fell into the outlying focus categories). There were, however, sex differences in the direction of focus. With one exception, all of the men who focused, focused on justice. The women divided, with roughly one third focusing on justice and one third on care.[4]

These findings clarify the different voice phenomenon and its implications for moral theory and for women. First, it is notable that if women were eliminated from the research sample, care focus in moral reasoning would virtually disappear. Although care focus was by no means characteristic of all women, it was almost exclusively a female phenomenon in this sample of educationally advantaged North Americans. Second, the fact that the women were advantaged means that the focus on care cannot readily be attributed to educational deficit or occupational disadvantage—the explanation Kohlberg and others have given for findings of lower levels of justice reasoning in women.[5] Instead, the focus on care in women's moral reasoning draws attention to the limitations of a justice-focused moral theory and highlights the presence of care concerns in the moral thinking of both women and men. In this light, the Care/Justice group composed of one third of the women and one third of the men becomes of particular interest, pointing to the need for further research that attends to the way people organize justice and care in relation to one another—whether, for example, people alternate perspectives, like seeing the rabbit and the duck in the rabbit-duck figure, or integrate the two perspectives in a way that resolves or sustains ambiguity.

Third, if the moral domain is [composed] of at least two moral orientations, the focus phenomenon suggests that people have a tendency to lose sight of one moral perspective in arriving at a moral decision—a liability equally shared by both sexes. The present findings further suggest that men and women tend to lose sight of different perspectives. The most striking

310   result is the virtual absence of care-focus reasoning among the men. Since the men raised concerns about care in discussing moral conflicts and thus presented care concerns as morally relevant, a question is why they did not elaborate these concerns to a greater extent.

In summary, it becomes clear why attention to women's moral thinking led to the identification of a different voice and raised questions about the place of justice and care within a comprehensive moral theory. It also is clear how the selection of an all-male sample for research on moral judgment fosters an equation of morality with justice, providing little data discrepant with this view. In the present study, data discrepant with a justice-focused moral
320   theory comes from a third of the women. Previously, such women were seen as having a problem understanding "morality." Yet these women may also be seen as exposing the problem in a justice-focused moral theory. This may explain the decision of researchers to exclude girls and women at the initial stage of moral judgment research. If one begins with the premise that "all morality consists in respect for rules,"[6] or "virtue is one and its name is justice,"[7] then women are likely to appear problematic within moral theory. If one begins with women's moral judgments, the problem becomes how to construct a theory that encompasses care as a focus of moral attention rather than as a subsidiary moral concern.

330   The implications of moral orientation for moral theory and for research on moral development are extended by a study designed and conducted by Kay Johnston.[8] Johnston set out to explore the relationship between moral orientation and problem-solving strategies, creating a standard method using fables for assessing spontaneous moral orientation and orientation preference. She asked 60 eleven- and fifteen-year-olds to state and to solve the moral problem posed by the fable. Then she asked: "Is there another way to solve this problem?" Most of the children initially constructed the fable problems either in terms of justice or in terms of care; either they stood back from the situation and appealed to a rule or principle for adjudicating the con-
340   flicting claims or they entered the situation in an effort to discover or create a way of responding to all of the needs. About half of the children, slightly more fifteen- than eleven-year-olds, spontaneously switched moral orientation when asked whether there was another way to solve the problem. Others did so following an interviewer's cue as to the form such a switch might take. Finally, the children were asked which of the solutions they described was the best solution. Most of the children answered the question and explained why one way was preferable.

Johnston found gender differences parallel to those previously reported, with boys more often spontaneously using and preferring justice solutions
350   and girls more often spontaneously using and preferring care solutions. In addition, she found differences between the two fables she used, confirming Langdale's finding that moral orientation is associated both with the gender of the reasoner and with the dilemma considered.[9] Finally, the fact that children, at least by the age of eleven, are able to shift moral orientation and can

explain the logic of two moral perspectives, each associated with a different problem-solving strategy, heightens the analogy to ambiguous figure perception and further supports the conception of justice and care as organizing frameworks for moral decision.

The demonstration that children know both orientations and can frame and solve moral problems in at least two different ways means that the choice   360 of moral standpoint is an element of moral decision. The role of the self in moral judgment thus includes the choice of moral standpoint, and this decision, whether implicit or explicit, may become linked with self-respect and self-definition. Especially in adolescence, when choice becomes more self-conscious and self-reflective, moral standpoint may become entwined with identity and self-esteem. Johnston's finding that spontaneous moral orientation and preferred orientation are not always the same raises a number of questions as to why and under what conditions a person may adopt a problem-solving strategy that he or she sees as not the best way to solve the problem.

The way people choose to frame or solve a moral problem is clearly not the   370 only way in which they can think about the problem, and is not necessarily the way they deem preferable. Moral judgments thus do not reveal *the* structure of moral thinking, since there are at least two ways in which people can structure moral problems. Johnston's demonstration of orientation-switch poses a serious challenge to the methods that have been used in moral judgment and moral development research, introducing a major interpretive caution. The fact that boys and girls at eleven and fifteen understand and distinguish the logics of justice and care reasoning directs attention to the origins and the development of both ways of thinking. In addition, the tendency for boys and girls to use and prefer different orientations when solving the same problem raises a number of   380 questions about the relationship between these orientations and the factors influencing their representation. The different patterns of orientation use and preference, as well as the different conceptions of justice and of care implied or elaborated in the fable judgments, suggest that moral development cannot be mapped along a single linear stage sequence.

One way of explaining these findings, suggested by Johnston, joins Vygotsky's theory of cognitive development with Chodorow's analysis of sex differences in early childhood experiences of relationship.[10] Vygotsky posits that all of the higher cognitive functions originate as actual relations between individuals. Justice and care as moral ideas and as reasoning strategies thus   390 would originate as relationships with others—an idea consonant with the derivation of justice and care reasoning from experiences of inequality and attachment in early childhood. All children are born into a situation of inequality in that they are less capable than the adults and older children around them and, in this sense, more helpless and less powerful. In addition, no child survives in the absence of some kind of adult attachment—or care, and through this experience of relationship children discover the responsiveness of human connection including their ability to move and affect one another.

400   Through the experience of inequality, of being in the less powerful position, children learn what it means to depend on the authority and the good will of others. As a result, they tend to strive for equality of greater power, and for freedom. Through the experience of attachment, children discover the ways in which people are able to care for and to hurt one another. The child's vulnerability to oppression and to abandonment thus can be seen to lay the groundwork for the moral visions of justice and care, conceived as ideals of human relationship and defining the ways in which people "should" act toward one another.

     Chodorow's work then provides a way of explaining why care concerns
410 tend to be minimally represented by men and why such concerns are less frequently elaborated in moral theory. Chodorow joins the dynamics of gender identity formation (the identification of oneself as male or female) to an analysis of early childhood relationships and examines the effects of maternal child care on the inner structuring of self in relation to others. Further, she differentiates a positional sense of self from a personal sense of self, contrasting a self defined in terms of role or position from a self known through the experience of connection. Her point is that maternal child care fosters the continuation of a relational sense of self in girls, since female gender identity is consonant with feeling connected with one's mother. For boys, gender
420 identity is in tension with mother-child connection, unless that connection is structured in terms of sexual opposition (e.g., as an Oedipal drama). Thus, although boys experience responsiveness or care in relationships, knowledge of care or the need for care, when associated with mothers, pose a threat to masculine identity.[11]

     Chodorow's work is limited by her reliance on object relations theory and problematic on that count. Object relations theory ties the formation of the self to the experience of separation, joining separation with individuation and thus counterposing the experience of self to the experience of connection with others. This is the line that Chodorow traces in explicating male devel-
430 opment. Within this framework, girls' connections with their mothers can only be seen as problematic. Connection with others or the capacity to feel and think *with* others is, by definition, in tension with self-development when self-development or individuation is linked to separation. Thus, object-relations theory sustains a series of oppositions that have been central in Western thought and moral theory, including the opposition between thought and feelings, self and relationship, reason and compassion, justice and love. Object relations theory also continues the conventional division of psychological labor between women and men. Since the idea of a self, experienced in the context of attachment with others, is theoretically impossible,
440 mothers, described as objects, are viewed as selfless, without a self. This view is essentially problematic for women, divorcing the activity of mothering from desire, knowledge, and agency, and implying that insofar as a mother experiences herself as a subject rather than as an object (a mirror reflecting

her child), she is "selfish" and not a good mother. Winnicott's phrase "good-enough mother" represents an effort to temper this judgment.

Thus, psychologists and philosophers, aligning the self and morality with separation and autonomy—the ability to be self-governing—have associated care with self-sacrifice, or with feelings—a view at odds with the current position that care represents a way of knowing and a coherent moral perspective. This position, however, is well represented in literature written by women. For example the short story "A Jury of Her Peers," written by Susan Glaspell in 1917, a time when women ordinarily did not serve on juries, contrasts two ways of knowing that underlie two ways of interpreting and solving a crime.[12] The story centers on a murder; Minnie Foster is suspected of killing her husband.

A neighbor woman and the sheriff's wife accompany the sheriff and the prosecutor to the house of the accused woman. The men, representing the law, seek evidence that will convince a jury to convict the suspect. The women, collecting things to bring Minnie Foster in jail, enter in this way into the lives lived in the house. Taking in rather than taking apart, they begin to assemble observations and impressions, connecting them to past experience and observations until suddenly they compose a familiar pattern, like the log-cabin pattern they recognize in the quilt Minnie Foster was making. "Why do we *know*—what we know this minute?" one woman asks the other, but she also offers the following explanation:

> We live close together, and we live far apart. We all go through the same things—it's all just a different kind of the same thing! If it weren't—why do you and I *understand*.[13]

The activity of quilt-making—collecting odd scraps and piecing them together until they form a pattern—becomes the metaphor for this way of knowing. Discovering a strangled canary buried under pieces of quilting, the women make a series of connections that lead them to understand what happened.

The logic that says you don't kill a man because he has killed a bird, the judgment that finds these acts wildly incommensurate, is counterposed to the logic that sees both events as part of a larger pattern—a pattern of detachment and abandonment that led finally to the strangling. "I *wish* I'd come over here once in a while," Mrs. Hale, the neighbor, exclaims. "That was a crime! Who's going to punish that?" Mrs. Peters, the sheriff's wife, recalls that when she was a girl and a boy killed her cat, "If they hadn't held me back I would have—" and realizes that there had been no one to restrain Minnie Foster. John Foster was known as "a good man . . . He didn't drink, and he kept his word as well as most, I guess, and paid his debts." But he also was "a hard man," Mrs. Hale explains, "like a raw wind that gets to the bone."

Seeing detachment as the crime with murder as its ultimate extension, implicating themselves and also seeing the connection between their own and Minnie Foster's actions, the women solve the crime by attachment—by joining together, like the "knotting" that joins pieces of a quilt. In the decision to remove rather than to reveal the evidence, they separate themselves from a legal system in which they have no voice but also no way of voicing what they have come to understand. In choosing to connect themselves with one another and with Minnie, they separate themselves from the law that would use their understanding and their knowledge as grounds for further separation and killing.

490

In a law school class where a film-version of this story was shown, the students were divided in their assessment of the moral problem and in their evaluation of the various characters and actions. Some focused on the murder, the strangling of the husband. Some focused on the evidence of abandonment or indifference to others. Responses to a questionnaire showed a bimodal distribution, indicating two ways of viewing the film. These different perspectives led to different ways of evaluating both the act of murder and the women's decision to remove the evidence. Responses to the film were not aligned with the sex of the viewer in an absolute way, thus dispelling any implication of biological determinism or of a stark division between the way women and men know or judge events. The knowledge gained inductively by the women in the film, however, was also gained more readily by women watching the film, who came in this way to see a logic in the women's actions and to articulate a rationale for their silence.

500

The analogy to ambiguous figure perception is useful here in several ways. First, it suggests that people can see a situation in more than one way, and even alternate ways of seeing, combining them without reducing them—like designating the rabbit-duck figure as both duck and rabbit. Second, the analogy argues against the tendency to construe justice and care as opposites or mirror-images and also against the implication that these two perspectives are readily integrated or fused. The ambiguous figure directs attention to the way in which a change in perspective can reorganize perception and change understanding, without implying an underlying reality or pure form. What makes seeing both moral perspectives so difficult is precisely that the orientations are not opposites or mirror images or better and worse representations of a single moral truth. The terms of one perspective do not contain the terms of the other. Instead, a shift in orientation denotes a restructuring of moral perception, changing the meaning of moral language and thus the definition of moral conflict and moral action. For example, detachment is considered the hallmark of mature moral thinking within a justice perspective, signifying the ability to judge dispassionately, to weigh evidence in an even-handed manner, balancing the claims of others and self. From a care perspective, detachment is *the* moral problem.

510

520

> "I could've come," retorted Mrs. Hale . . . "I wish I had come over to see Minnie Foster sometimes. I can see now . . . If there had been years and years of—nothing, then a bird to sing to you, it would be awful—still—after the bird was still. . . . I know what stillness is."

530

The difference between agreement and understanding captures the different logics of justice and care reasoning, one seeking grounds for agreement, one seeking grounds for understanding, one assuming separation and thus the need for some external structure of connection, one assuming connection and thus the potential for understanding. These assumptions run deep, generating and reflecting different views of human nature and the human condition. They also point to different vulnerabilities and different sources of error. The potential error in justice reasoning lies in its latent egocentrism, the tendency to confuse one's perspective with an objective standpoint or truth, the temptation to define others in one's own terms by putting oneself in their place.   540
The potential error in care reasoning lies in the tendency to forget that one has terms, creating a tendency to enter into another's perspective and to see oneself as "selfless" by defining oneself in other's terms. These two types of error underlie two common equations that signify distortions or deformations of justice and care: the equation of human with male, unjust in its omission of women; and the equation of care with self-sacrifice, uncaring in its failure to represent the activity and the agency of care.

The equation of human with male was assumed in the Platonic and in the Enlightenment tradition as well as by psychologists who saw all-male samples as "representative" of human experience. The equation of care with self-   550
sacrifice is in some ways more complex. The premise of self-interest assumes a conflict of interest between self and other manifest in the opposition of egoism and altruism. Together, the equations of male with human and of care with self-sacrifice form a circle that has had a powerful hold on moral philosophy and psychology. The conjunction of women and moral theory thus challenges the traditional definition of human and calls for a reconsideration of what is meant by both justice and care.

To trace moral development along two distinct although intersecting dimensions of relationship suggests the possibility of different permutations of justice and care reasoning, different ways these two moral perspectives can   560
be understood and represented in relation to one another. For example, one perspective may overshadow or eclipse the other, so that one is brightly illuminated while the other is dimly remembered, familiar but for the most part forgotten. The way in which one story about relationship obscures another was evident in high school girls' definitions of dependence. These definitions highlighted two meanings—one arising from the opposition between dependence and independence, and one from the opposition of dependence to isolation ("No woman," one student observed, "is an island.") As the word "dependence" connotes the experience of relationship, this shift in the implied opposite of dependence indicates how the valence of relationship   570
changes, when connection with others is experienced as an impediment to autonomy or independence, and when it is experienced as a source of comfort and pleasure, and as a protection against isolation. This essential ambivalence of human connection provides a powerful emotional grounding for two moral perspectives, and also may indicate what is at stake in the effort to reduce morality to a single perspective.

It is easy to understand the ascendance of justice reasoning and of justice-focused moral theories in a society where care is associated with personal vulnerability in the form of economic disadvantage. But another way of thinking about the ascendance of justice reasoning and also about sex differences in moral development is suggested in the novel *Masks*, written by Fumiko Enchi, a Japanese woman.[14] The subject is spirit possession, and the novel dramatizes what it means to be possessed by the spirits of others. Writing about the Rokujo lady in *Tales of Genji*, Enchi's central character notes that

> her soul alternates uncertainly between lyricism and spirit possession, making no philosophical distinction between the self alone and in relation to others, and is unable to achieve the solace of a religious indifference.[15]

The option of transcendence, of a religious indifference or a philosophical detachment, may be less available to women because women are more likely to be possessed by the spirits and the stories of others. The strength of women's moral perceptions lies in the refusal of detachment and depersonalization, and insistence on making connections that can lead to seeing the person killed in war or living in poverty as someone's son or father or brother or sister, or mother, or daughter, or friend. But the liability of women's development is also underscored by Enchi's novel in that women, possessed by the spirits of others, also are more likely to be caught in a chain of false attachments. If women are at the present time the custodians of a story about human attachment and interdependence, not only within the family but also in the world at large, then questions arise as to how this story can be kept alive and how moral theory can sustain this story. In this sense, the relationship between women and moral theory itself becomes one of interdependence.

By rendering a care perspective more coherent and making its terms explicit, moral theory may facilitate women's ability to speak about their experiences and perceptions and may foster the ability of others to listen and to understand. At the same time, the evidence of care focus in women's moral thinking suggests that the study of women's development may provide a natural history of moral development in which care is ascendant, revealing the ways in which creating and sustaining responsive connection with others becomes or remains a central moral concern. The promise in joining women and moral theory lies in the fact that human survival, in the late twentieth century, may depend less on formal agreement than on human connection.

ENDNOTES

1. Gilligan, C. (1977). "In a Different Voice: Women's Conceptions of Self and of Morality." *Harvard Educational Review* 47 (1982): 481–517; *In a Different Voice: Psychological Theory and Women's Development.* Cambridge, Mass.: Harvard University Press.
2. Piaget, J. (1965). *The Moral Judgment of the Child.* New York: N.Y.: The Free Press Paperback Edition, pp. 76–84.
3. Kohlberg, L. (1984). *The Psychology of Moral Development.* San Francisco, Calif.: Harper & Row Publishers, Inc.
4. Gilligan, C. and J. Attanucci. (1986). *Two Moral Orientations.* Harvard University, unpublished manuscript.
5. See Kohlberg, L. *op. cit.*, also Walker, L. (1984). "Sex Differences in the Development of Moral Reasoning: A Critical Review of the Literature." *Child Development* 55 (3):677–91.
6. Piaget, J., *op. cit.*
7. Kohlberg, L., *op. cit.*
8. Johnston, K. (1985). *Two Moral Orientations—Two Problem-solving Strategies: Adolescents' Solutions to Dilemmas in Fables.* Harvard University, unpublished doctoral dissertation.
9. Langdale, C. (1983). *Moral Orientation and Moral Development: The Analysis of Care and Justice Reasoning Across Different Dilemmas in Females and Males from Childhood through Adulthood.* Harvard University, unpublished doctoral dissertation.
10. Johnston, K., *op. cit.;* Vygotsky, L. (1978). *Mind in Society.* Cambridge, Mass.: Harvard University Press; Chodorow, N. (1974). "Family Structure and Feminine Personality" in *Women, Culture and Society*, L. M. Rosaldo and L. Lamphere, eds., Stanford, Calif.: Stanford University Press; see also Chodorow, N. (1978). *The Reproduction of Mothering: Psychoanalysis and the Sociology of Gender*, Berkeley, Calif.: University of California Press.
11. Chodorow, N., *op. cit.*
12. Glaspell, S. (1927). *A Jury of Her Peers*, London: E. Benn.
13. *Ibid.*
14. Fumiko, E. (1983). *Masks.* New York: Random House.
15. Ibid. p. 54.

SOCIAL ISOLATION AND NEW TECHNOLOGY: HOW THE INTERNET AND MOBILE PHONES IMPACT AMERICANS' SOCIAL NETWORKS
Keith Hampton; Lauren Sessions; Eun Ja Her; Lee Rainie

The following is the Overview of the full Pew Internet and American Life Project Study, found at http://www.pewinternet.org/ Reports/2009/18—Social-Isolation-and-New-Technology.aspx

ARE AMERICANS MORE SOCIALLY ISOLATED?

Our survey results challenge the finding that an increasing number of Americans have no one with whom they can discuss important matters. However, our findings support existing research that suggests that the average size and diversity of core discussion networks have declined. Our findings show:　1

- Compared to 1985, there has been small-to-modest change, rather than a large drop in the number of people who report that they have no one with whom they can discuss important matters. 12% of Americans have no discussion confidants.
- Few Americans are truly socially isolated. Only 6% of the adult population has no one with whom they can discuss important matters or　10 who they consider to be "especially significant" in their life.
- The average size of Americans' core discussion networks has declined since 1985; the mean network size has dropped by about one-third or a loss of approximately one confidant.
- The diversity of core discussion networks has markedly declined; discussion networks are less likely to contain non-kin—that is, people who are not relatives by blood or marriage; although the decline is not as steep as has been previously reported.

IS INTERNET OR MOBILE PHONE USE RELATED TO SMALLER OR LESS DIVERSE CORE NETWORKS?

Use of newer information and communication technologies (ICTs), such as the internet and mobile phones, is not the social change responsible for the　20 restructuring of Americans' core networks. We found that ownership of a mobile phone and participation in a variety of internet activities were associated with larger and more diverse core discussion networks:

- Larger core discussion networks are associated with owning a cell phone, and use of the internet for sharing digital photos and instant messaging. On average, the size of core discussion networks is 12% larger amongst cell phone users, 9% larger for those who share photos online, and 9% bigger for those who use instant messaging.

- Whereas only 45% of Americans discuss important matters with someone who is not a family member, internet users are 55% more likely to have a non-kin discussion partner.
- Internet users are 38% less likely to rely exclusively on their spouses/partners as discussion confidants. Those who use instant messaging are even less likely, 36% less likely than other internet users, or 59% less likely than non-internet users to rely exclusively on their spouses/partners for important matters.
- Those who use the internet to upload photos to share online are 61% more likely to have discussion partners that cross political lines.
- Maintaining a blog is associated with a 95% higher likelihood of having a cross-race discussion confidant. Frequent at home internet users are also 53% more likely to have a confidant of a different race.

When we explored the size and diversity of people's core networks—their strongest social ties that include both those with whom they "discuss important matters" and those they consider "especially significant" in their life—there continued to be a strong, positive relationship between the size and diversity of people's closest social ties, mobile phone use, and participation in a range of internet activities.

- Mobile phone users and those who go online to use instant messaging have larger core networks. Mobile phone users' core networks tend to be 12% larger than nonusers, and those who use instant messaging have core networks that are an average of 11% larger than those who do not.
- Mobile phone users, general internet users, and especially internet users who go Pew Internet & American Life Project Social Isolation and New Technology.
- Mobile phone users and those who go online to use instant messaging have larger core networks. Mobile phone users' core networks tend to be 12% larger than nonusers, and those who use instant messaging have core networks that are an average of 11% larger than those who do not.
- Mobile phone users, general internet users, and especially internet users who go online at home more than once per day, share digital photos online, or exchange instant messages have more non-kin in their core networks. The diversity of core networks tends to be 25% larger for mobile phone users and 15% larger for internet users. However, some internet activities are associated with having even larger non-kin core networks. Compared to other internet users, those who frequently use the internet at home tend to have an additional 17%

non-kin, those who share photos average 12% more non-kin, and those who use instant messaging tend to have 19% more non-kin.   70

IS INTERNET USE LEADING TO LESS FACE-TO-FACE CONTACT WITH OUR CLOSEST SOCIAL TIES OR WITH LOCAL SOCIAL TIES?

Whereas most studies of core social networks focus exclusively on face-to-face contact, this analysis looked at the many ways that people maintain social networks using communication media. When those other kinds of interactions are taken into account, we find:

- In-person contact remains the dominant means of communication with core network members. On average, there is face-to-face contact with each tie on 210 out of 365 days per year.
- Mobile phone use has replaced the landline telephone as the most frequently mediated form of communication—195 days per year.
- Text messaging has tied the landline telephone as the third most popular means of contact between core ties—125 days per year.   80
- Cards and letters are the least frequent means of social contact—8 letters or cards per year.
- When available, other ICTs supplement these dominant modes of communication: email (72 days per year), instant messaging (55 days per year), and social networking websites (39 days per year).

Contrary to the assumption that internet use encourages social contact across vast distances, we found that many internet technologies are used as much for local contact as they are for distant communication.

- When available, other ICTs supplement these dominant modes of communication: email (72 days per year), instant messaging (55 days per year), and social networking websites (39 days per year).   90
- In-person contact, landline telephones, mobile phones, and text messaging (SMS) are used most frequently for contact with local social ties.
- Cards and letters are used most extensively with distant social ties.
- Email, social networking services, and instant messaging promote "glocalization" that is, they are used as frequently to maintain nearby core social ties as they are used to maintain ties at a distance.

ARE CORE NETWORK MEMBERS ALSO OUR "FRIENDS" ON SOCIAL NETWORKING SERVICES SUCH AS FACEBOOK, MYSPACE, LINKEDIN?

Social networking services, such as Facebook, provide new opportunities for users to maintain core social networks. Core ties can be highly influential in decision making and exposure to ideas, issues, and opinion. This makes core   100 network members prime targets for marketers and interest groups who may want to use social networking services to influence decision making about consumer products or political opinion.

- A majority—71%—of all users of social networking services have listed at least one member of their core network of influentials as a "friend" on a social networking service.
- The use of social networking services to maintain core networks is highest among 18–22-year-olds. Thirty percent of 18–22-year-olds use a social networking service to maintain contact with 90% or more of their core influentials.

110

IS INTERNET USE RELATED TO LESS INTERACTION WITH NEIGHBORS OR LOWER LEVELS OF PARTICIPATION IN LOCAL VOLUNTARY ASSOCIATIONS?

Contrary to the argument that internet use limits people's participation in the local community, local institutions, and local spaces, our findings show that most internet activities are associated with higher levels of local activity. However, we find some evidence that use of social networking services (e.g., Facebook, MySpace, LinkedIn) substitutes for some level of neighborhood involvement.

- With the exception of those who use social networking services, internet users are no more or less likely than non-users to know at least some of their neighbors. Users of social networking services are 30% less likely to know at least some neighbors.

120

- Internet and mobile phone users are as likely as non-users to talk to their neighbors in-person at least once per month. And, they supplement their local contact with email. 10% of internet users send emails to their neighbors.
- Users of social networking services are 26% less likely to use their neighbors as a source of companionship, but they remain as likely as other people to provide companionship to their neighbors.
- Internet users are 40% less likely to rely on neighbors for help in caring for themselves or a family member. Those who use social networking services are even less likely to rely on neighbors for family care, they are 39% less likely than other internet users, or 64% less likely than non-internet users, to rely on neighbors for help in caring for themselves or a family member.
- Internet users are 26% less likely to rely on their neighbors for help with small services, such as household chores, repairs, and lending tools, but they remain as likely to help their neighbors with the same activities.

130

- Owners of a mobile phone, frequent internet users at work, and bloggers are more likely to belong to a local voluntary group, such as a neighborhood association, sports league, youth group, church, or social club.   140

When the internet is used as a medium for neighborhood social contact, such as a neighborhood email list or community forum (e.g., i-neighbors.org), participants tend to have very high levels of local engagement.

- 60% of those who use an online neighborhood discussion forum know "all or most" of their neighbors, compared to 40% of Americans.
- 79% who use an online neighborhood discussion forum talk with neighbors in person at least once a month, compared to 61% of the general population.
- When the internet is used as a medium for neighborhood social contact, such as a neighborhood email list or community forum (e.g., i-neighbors.org), participants tend to have very high levels of local engagement.   150
- 43% of those on a neighborhood discussion forum talk to neighbors on the telephone at least once a month, compared to the average of 25%.   *wow!*
- 70% on a neighborhood discussion forum listened to a neighbor's problems in the previous six months, and 63% received similar support from neighbors, compared to 49% who gave and 36% who received this support in the general population.   160

IS INTERNET USE ASSOCIATED WITH "COCOONING," OR A WITHDRAWAL FROM PUBLIC AND SEMIPUBLIC SPACES?

Public spaces, such as parks, libraries, and community centers, as well as "third places" highlighted by analyst Ray Oldenburg, such as cafés and restaurants, are an important source of exposure to diverse ideas, issues, and opinions—as well as meeting places for interacting with social ties. Contrary to concerns that internet use leads to withdrawal from public spaces, we generally found that interest use is associated with engagement in such places.   *"Third Places" idea*   *internet*

- Compared to those who do not use the internet, internet users are 42% more likely to visit a public park or plaza and 45% more likely to visit a coffee shop or café.   170
- Bloggers are 61% more likely to visit a public park than internet users who do not maintain a blog, or about 2.3 times more likely than non-internet users.

The findings also show that internet access has become a common component of people's experiences within many public spaces. We asked respondents who had visited public spaces whether they had access to the internet there in the past month. Examining all visits to public and semipublic spaces, we found that a significant proportion of people accessed the internet either through a cell phone, wifi network, or some other means at these locales:

180
- 36% of library patrons.
- 18% of those in cafés or coffee shops.
- 14% who visited a community center.
- 11% of people who frequented a bar.
- 8% of visitors to public parks and plazas.
- 6% of customers at fast food restaurants.
- 7% of customers at other restaurants.
- 5% of people who visited a church, synagogue, mosque, or temple.

ARE INTERNET AND MOBILE PHONE USE ASSOCIATED WITH MORE OR LESS DIVERSE PERSONAL NETWORKS?

When the diversity of people's full social network was measured, we found the expected: that participation in traditional social milieus, such as neigh-
190 borhoods, voluntary groups, and public spaces, accounts for much of the diversity in people's social networks. However, we also discovered that internet use, and in particular the use of social networking services, are independently associated with higher levels of network diversity.

- Compared to those who do not use the internet, most people who use the internet and use a social networking service, such as Facebook, MySpace, or LinkedIn, have social networks that are about 20% more diverse.

Newer information and communication technologies provide new settings and a means of communication that independently contribute to the diver-
200 sity of people's social networks. . . .

. . . . In addition, while participation in traditional social settings—neighborhoods, voluntary associations, and public spaces—remain the strongest predictors of a diverse social network, internet use, and in particular use of social networking services, has emerged as a new social setting that is directly linked with having a more diverse personal network. . . . For this reason, our survey results suggest that people's lives are likely to be enhanced by participation with new communication technologies, rather than by fearing that their use of new technology will send them into a spiral of isolation.

Conclusion ✗

Technology is good/evil.

We are becoming more
~~so~~ cut off/ more connected
to one another.

~~Being in Society~~ forces
Social ~~pressures~~ make us
better/worse

Acceptance of racial and gender
Diversity ~~~~ is / is not
~~~~
increasing

Bauerlein - Digital Nation
▽
Hampton

Putnam - Subdivided
▽
Hampton

Kaminer - Zimbardo
▽
Hampton

Tatum Gilligan use as
▽ example
Hampton

THE TRAGEDY OF THE COMMONS
Garrett Hardin

At the end of a thoughtful article on the future of nuclear war, Wiesner and York[1] concluded that: "Both sides in the arms race are . . . confronted by the dilemma of steadily increasing military power and steadily decreasing national security. *It is our considered professional judgment that this dilemma has no technical solution.* If the great powers continue to look for solutions in the area of science and technology only, the result will be to worsen the situation."

I would like to focus your attention not on the subject of the article (national security in a nuclear world) but on the kind of conclusion they reached, namely that there is no technical solution to the problem. An implicit and almost universal assumption of discussions published in professional and semipopular scientific journals is that the problem under discussion has a technical solution. A technical solution may be defined as one that requires a change only in the techniques of the natural sciences, demanding little or nothing in the way of change in human values or ideas of morality.

In our day (though not in earlier times) technical solutions are always welcome. Because of previous failures in prophecy, it takes courage to assert that a desired technical solution is not possible. Wiesner and York exhibited this courage; publishing in a science journal, they insisted that the solution to the problem was not to be found in the natural sciences. They cautiously qualified their statement with the phrase, "It is our considered professional judgment. . . ." Whether they were right or not is not the concern of the present article. Rather, the concern here is with the important concept of a class of human problems which can be called "no technical solution problems," and, more specifically, with the identification and discussion of one of these.

It is easy to show that the class is not a null class. Recall the game of tick-tack-toe. Consider the problem, "How can I win the game of tick-tack-toe?" It is well known that I cannot, if I assume (in keeping with the conventions of game theory) that my opponent understands the game perfectly. Put another way, there is no "technical solution" to the problem. I can win only by giving a radical meaning to the word "win." I can hit my opponent over the head; or I can drug him; or I can falsify the records. Every way in which I "win" involves, in some sense, an abandonment of the game, as we intuitively understand it. (I can also, of course, openly abandon the game—refuse to play it. This is what most adults do.)

The class of "No technical solution problems" has members. My thesis is that the "population problem," as conventionally conceived, is a member of this class. How it is conventionally conceived needs some comment. It is fair

Reprinted from *Science Magazine*, December 1968, American Association for the Advancement of Science.

40 to say that most people who anguish over the population problem are trying to find a way to avoid the evils of overpopulation without relinquishing any of the privileges they now enjoy. They think that farming the seas or developing new strains of wheat will solve the problem—technologically. I try to show here that the solution they seek cannot be found. The population problem cannot be solved in a technical way, any more than can the problem of winning the game of tick-tack-toe.

WHAT SHALL WE MAXIMIZE?

Population, as Malthus said, naturally tends to grow "geometrically," or, as we would now say, exponentially. In a finite world this means that the per capita share of the world's goods must steadily decrease. Is ours a finite world?

50 A fair defense can be put forward for the view that the world is infinite; or that we do not know that it is not. But, in terms of the practical problems that we must face in the next few generations with the foreseeable technology, it is clear that we will greatly increase human misery if we do not, during the immediate future, assume that the world available to the terrestrial human population is finite. "Space" is no escape.[2]

A finite world can support only a finite population; therefore, population growth must eventually equal zero. (The case of perpetual wide fluctuations above and below zero is a trivial variant that need not be discussed.) When this condition is met, what will be the situation of mankind? Specifically, can Bentham's goal of "the greatest good for the greatest number" be realized?

60 No—for two reasons, each sufficient by itself. The first is a theoretical one. It is not mathematically possible to maximize for two (or more) variables at the same time. This was clearly stated by von Neumann and Morgenstern,[3] but the principle is implicit in the theory of partial differential equations, dating back at least to D'Alembert (1717–1783).

The second reason springs directly from biological facts. To live, any organism must have a source of energy (for example, food). This energy is utilized for two purposes: mere maintenance and work. For man, maintenance of life requires about 1600 kilocalories a day ("maintenance calories"). Anything that he does over and above merely staying alive will be defined as

70 work, and is supported by "work calories" which he takes in. Work calories are used not only for what we call work in common speech; they are also required for all forms of enjoyment, from swimming and automobile racing to playing music and writing poetry. If our goal is to maximize population it is obvious what we must do: We must make the work calories per person approach as close to zero as possible. No gourmet meals, no vacations, no sports, no music, no literature, no art. . . . I think that everyone will grant, without argument or proof, that maximizing population does not maximize goods. Bentham's goal is impossible.

In reaching this conclusion I have made the usual assumption that it is

80 the acquisition of energy that is the problem. The appearance of atomic

energy has led some to question this assumption. However, given an infinite source of energy, population growth still produces an inescapable problem. The problem of the acquisition of energy is replaced by the problem of its dissipation, as J. H. Fremlin has so wittily shown.[4] The arithmetic signs in the analysis are, as it were, reversed; but Bentham's goal is still unobtainable.

The optimum population is, then, less than the maximum. The difficulty of defining the optimum is enormous; so far as I know, no one has seriously tackled this problem. Reaching an acceptable and stable solution will surely require more than one generation of hard analytical work—and much persuasion.

We want the maximum good per person; but what is good? To one person it is wilderness, to another it is ski lodges for thousands. To one it is estuaries to nourish ducks for hunters to shoot; to another it is factory land. Comparing one good with another is, we usually say, impossible because goods are incommensurable. Incommensurables cannot be compared.

Theoretically this may be true; but in real life incommensurables are commensurable. Only a criterion of judgment and a system of weighting are needed. In nature the criterion is survival. Is it better for a species to be small and hideable, or large and powerful? Natural selection commensurates the incommensurables. The compromise achieved depends on a natural weighting of the values of the variables.

Man must imitate this process. There is no doubt that in fact he already does, but unconsciously. It is when the hidden decisions are made explicit that the arguments begin. The problem for the years ahead is to work out an acceptable theory of weighting. Synergistic effects, nonlinear variation, and difficulties in discounting the future make the intellectual problem difficult, but not (in principle) insoluble.

Has any cultural group solved this practical problem at the present time, even on an intuitive level? One simple fact proves that none has: there is no prosperous population in the world today that has, and has had for some time, a growth rate of zero. Any people that has intuitively identified its optimum point will soon reach it, after which its growth rate becomes and remains zero.

Of course, a positive growth rate might be taken as evidence that a population is below its optimum. However, by any reasonable standards, the most rapidly growing populations on earth today are (in general) the most miserable. This association (which need not be invariable) casts doubt on the optimistic assumption that the positive growth rate of a population is evidence that it has yet to reach its optimum.

We can make little progress in working toward optimum population size until we explicitly exorcize the spirit of Adam Smith in the field of practical demography. In economic affairs, *The Wealth of Nations* (1776) popularized the "invisible hand," the idea that an individual who "intends only his own gain," is, as it were, "led by an invisible hand to promote . . . the public interest."[5] Adam Smith did not assert that this was invariably true, and perhaps neither did any of his followers. But he contributed to a dominant tendency of thought that has ever since interfered with positive action based on rational analysis, namely, the tendency to assume that decisions reached individually will, in fact, be the best decisions for an entire society. If this assumption is correct it justifies the continuance of our present policy of laissez-faire in reproduction. If it is correct we can assume that men will control their individual fecundity so as to produce the optimum population. If the assumption is not correct, we need to reexamine our individual freedoms to see which ones are defensible.

TRAGEDY OF FREEDOM IN A COMMONS

The rebuttal to the invisible hand in population control is to be found in a scenario first sketched in a little-known pamphlet[6] in 1833 by a mathematical amateur named William Forster Lloyd (1794–1852). We may well call it "the tragedy of the commons," using the word "tragedy" as the philosopher Whitehead used it:[7] "The essence of dramatic tragedy is not unhappiness. It resides in the solemnity of the remorseless working of things." He then goes on to say, "This inevitableness of destiny can only be illustrated in terms of human life by incidents which in fact involve unhappiness. For it is only by them that the futility of escape can be made evident in the drama."

The tragedy of the commons develops in this way. Picture a pasture open to all. It is to be expected that each herdsman will try to keep as many cattle as possible on the commons. Such an arrangement may work reasonably satisfactorily for centuries because tribal wars, poaching, and disease keep the numbers of both man and beast well below the carrying capacity of the land. Finally, however, comes the day of reckoning, that is, the day when the long-desired goal of social stability becomes a reality. At this point, the inherent logic of the commons remorselessly generates tragedy.

As a rational being, each herdsman seeks to maximize his gain. Explicitly or implicitly, more or less consciously, he asks, "What is the utility *to me* of adding one more animal to my herd?" This utility has one negative and one positive component.

1) The positive component is a function of the increment of one animal. Since the herdsman receives all the proceeds from the sale of the additional animal, the positive utility is nearly +1.

2) The negative component is a function of the additional overgrazing created by one more animal. Since, however, the effects of overgrazing are shared by all the herdsmen, the negative utility for any particular decision-making herdsman is only a fraction of −1.

Adding together the component partial utilities, the rational herdsman concludes that the only sensible course for him to pursue is to add another animal to his herd. And another; and another. . . . But this is the conclusion reached by each and every rational herdsman sharing a commons. Therein is the tragedy. Each man is locked into a system that compels him to increase his herd without limit—in a world that is limited. Ruin is the destination toward which all men rush, each pursuing his own best interest in a society that believes in the freedom of the commons. Freedom in a commons brings ruin to all.

Some would say that this is a platitude. Would that it were! In a sense, it was learned thousands of years ago, but natural selection favors the forces of psychological denial.[8] The individual benefits as an individual from his ability to deny the truth even though society as a whole, of which he is a part, suffers.

Education can counteract the natural tendency to do the wrong thing, but the inexorable succession of generations requires that the basis for this knowledge be constantly refreshed.

A simple incident that occurred a few years ago in Leominster, Massachusetts, shows how perishable the knowledge is. During the Christmas shopping season the parking meters downtown were covered with plastic bags that bore tags reading: "Do not open until after Christmas. Free parking courtesy of the mayor and city council." In other words, facing the prospect of an increased demand for already scarce space, the city fathers reinstituted the system of the commons. (Cynically, we suspect that they gained more votes than they lost by this retrogressive act.)

In an approximate way, the logic of the commons has been understood for a long time, perhaps since the discovery of agriculture or the invention of private property in real estate. But it is understood mostly only in special cases which are not sufficiently generalized. Even at this late date, cattlemen leasing national land on the western ranges demonstrate no more than an ambivalent understanding, in constantly pressuring federal authorities to increase the head count to the point where overgrazing produces erosion and weed-dominance. Likewise, the oceans of the world continue to suffer from the survival of the philosophy of the commons. Maritime nations still respond automatically to the shibboleth of the "freedom of the seas." Professing to believe in the "inexhaustible resources of the oceans," they bring species after species of fish and whales closer to extinction.[9]

The National Parks present another instance of the working out of the tragedy of the commons. At present, they are open to all, without limit. The parks themselves are limited in extent—there is only one Yosemite Valley— whereas population seems to grow without limit. The values that visitors seek in the parks are steadily eroded. Plainly, we must soon cease to treat the parks as commons or they will be of no value to anyone.

What shall we do? We have several options. We might sell them off as private property. We might keep them as public property, but allocate the right to enter them. The allocation might be on the basis of wealth, by the use of an auction system. It might be on the basis of merit, as defined by some agreed-upon standards. It might be by lottery. Or it might be on a first-come, first-served basis, administered to long queues. These, I think, are all the reasonable possibilities. They are all objectionable. But we must choose—or acquiesce in the destruction of the commons that we call our National Parks.

POLLUTION

In a reverse way, the tragedy of the commons reappears in problems of pollution. Here it is not a question of taking something out of the commons, but of putting something in—sewage, or chemical, radioactive, and heat wastes into water; noxious and dangerous fumes into the air, and distracting and unpleasant advertising signs into the line of sight. The calculations of utility are much the same as before. The rational man finds that his share of the cost of the wastes he discharges into the commons is less than the cost of purifying his
220 wastes before releasing them. Since this is true for everyone, we are locked into a system of "fouling our own nest," so long as we behave only as independent, rational, free-enterprisers.

The tragedy of the commons as a food basket is averted by private property, or something formally like it. But the air and waters surrounding us cannot readily be fenced, and so the tragedy of the commons as a cesspool must be prevented by different means, by coercive laws or taxing devices that make it cheaper for the polluter to treat his pollutants than to discharge them untreated. We have not progressed as far with the solution of this problem as we have with the first. Indeed, our particular concept of private property,
230 which deters us from exhausting the positive resources of the earth, favors pollution. The owner of a factory on the bank of a stream—whose property extends to the middle of the stream, often has difficulty seeing why it is not his natural right to muddy the waters flowing past his door. The law, always behind the times, requires elaborate stitching and fitting to adapt it to this newly perceived aspect of the commons.

The pollution problem is a consequence of population. It did not much matter how a lonely American frontiersman disposed of his waste. "Flowing water purifies itself every 10 miles," my grandfather used to say, and the myth was near enough to the truth when he was a boy, for there were not too many
240 people. But as population became denser, the natural chemical and biological recycling processes became overloaded, calling for a redefinition of property rights.

HOW TO LEGISLATE TEMPERANCE?

Analysis of the pollution problem as a function of population density uncovers a not generally recognized principle of morality, namely: *the morality of an act is a function of the state of the system at the time it is performed.*[10] Using the commons as a cesspool does not harm the general public under frontier conditions, because there is no public, the same behavior in a metropolis is unbearable. A hundred and fifty years ago a plainsman could kill an American bison, cut only the tongue for his dinner, and discard the rest of the ani-
250 mal. He was not in any important sense being wasteful. Today, with only a few thousand bison left, we would be appalled at such behavior.

In passing, it is worth noting that the morality of an act cannot be determined from a photograph. One does not know whether a man killing an elephant or setting fire to the grassland is harming others until one knows the total system in which his act appears. "One picture is worth a thousand words," said an ancient Chinese; but it may take 10,000 words to validate it. It is as tempting to ecologists as it is to reformers in general to try to persuade others by way of the photographic shortcut. But the essence of an argument cannot be photographed: it must be presented rationally—in words.   260

That morality is system-sensitive escaped the attention of most codifiers of ethics in the past. "Thou shalt not . . ." is the form of traditional ethical directives which make no allowance for particular circumstances. The laws of our society follow the pattern of ancient ethics, and therefore are poorly suited to governing a complex, crowded, changeable world. Our epicyclic solution is to augment statutory law with administrative law. Since it is practically impossible to spell out all the conditions under which it is safe to burn trash in the back yard or to run an automobile without smog-control, by law we delegate the details to bureaus. The result is administrative law, which is rightly feared for an ancient reason—*Quis custodiet ipsos custodes?*—"Who   270 shall watch the watchers themselves?" John Adams said that we must have "a government of laws and not men." Bureau administrators, trying to evaluate the morality of acts in the total system, are singularly liable to corruption, producing a government by men, not laws.

Prohibition is easy to legislate (though not necessarily to enforce); but how do we legislate temperance? Experience indicates that it can be accomplished best through the mediation of administrative law. We limit possibilities unnecessarily if we suppose that the sentiment of *Quis custodiet* denies us the use of administrative law. We should rather retain the phrase as a perpetual reminder of fearful dangers we cannot avoid. The great challenge facing us now is to invent the corrective feedbacks that are needed to keep cus-   280 todians honest. We must find ways to legitimate the needed authority of both the custodians and the corrective feedbacks.

FREEDOM TO BREED IS INTOLERABLE

The tragedy of the commons is involved in population problems in another way. In a world governed solely by the principle of "dog eat dog"—if indeed there ever was such a world—how many children a family had would not be a matter of public concern. Parents who bred too exuberantly would leave fewer descendants, not more, because they would be unable to care adequately for their children. David Lack and others have found that such a negative feedback demonstrably controls the fecundity of birds.[11] But men are   290 not birds, and have not acted like them for millenniums, at least.

If each human family were dependent only on its own resources; if the children of improvident parents starved to death; *if,* thus, overbreeding brought its own "punishment" to the germ line—*then* there would be no public interest in controlling the breeding of families. But our society is deeply committed to the welfare state,[12] and hence is confronted with another aspect of the tragedy of the commons.

300 In a welfare state, how shall we deal with the family, the religion, the race, or the class (or indeed any distinguishable and cohesive group) that adopts overbreeding as a policy to secure its own aggrandizement?[13] To couple the concept of freedom to breed with the belief that everyone born has an equal right to the commons is to lock the world into a tragic course of action.

Unfortunately this is just the course of action that is being pursued by the United Nations. In late 1967, some 30 nations agreed to the following:[14]

> The Universal Declaration of Human Rights describes the family as the natural and fundamental unit of society. It follows that any choice and decision with regard to the size of the family must irrevocably rest with the family itself, and cannot be made by anyone else.

It is painful to have to deny categorically the validity of this right; deny-310 ing it, one feels as uncomfortable as a resident of Salem, Massachusetts, who denied the reality of witches in the 17th century. At the present time, in liberal quarter, something like a taboo acts to inhibit criticism of the United States. There is a feeling that the United States is "our last and best hope," that we shouldn't find fault with it; we shouldn't play into the hands of arch-conservatives. However, let us not forget what Robert Louis Stevenson said: "The truth that is suppressed by friends is the readiest weapon of the enemy." If we love the truth, we must openly deny the validity of the Universal Declaration of Human Rights, even though it is promoted by the United Nations. We should also join with Kingsley Davis[15] in attempting to get 320 Planned Parenthood-World Population to see the error of its ways in embracing the same tragic ideal.

CONSCIENCE IS SELF-ELIMINATING

It is a mistake to think that we can control the breeding of mankind in the long run by an appeal to conscience. Charles Galton Darwin made this point when he spoke on the centennial of the publication of his grandfather's great book. The argument is straightforward and Darwinian.

People vary. Confronted with appeals to limit breeding, some people will undoubtedly respond to the plea more than others. Those who have more children will produce a larger fraction of the next generation than those with more susceptible consciences. The difference will be accentuated, generation 330 by generation.

In C. G. Darwin's words: "It may well be that it would take hundreds of generations for the progenitive instinct to develop in this way, but if it should do so, nature would have taken her revenge, and the variety *Homo contracipiens* would become extinct and would be replaced by the variety *Homo progenitivus.*"[16]

The argument assumes that conscience or the desire for children (no matter which) is hereditary—but hereditary only in the most general formal sense. The result will be the same whether the attitude is transmitted through germ cells, or exosomatically, to use A. J. Lotka's term. (If one denies the latter possibility as well as the former, then what's the point of education?) The argument has here been stated in the context of the population problem, but it applies equally well to any instance in which society appeals to an individual exploiting a commons to restrain himself for the general good—by means of his conscience. To make such an appeal is to set up a selective system that works toward the elimination of conscience from the race.

PATHOGENIC EFFECTS OF CONSCIENCE

The long-term disadvantage of an appeal to conscience should be enough to condemn it; but has serious short-term disadvantages as well. If we ask a man who is exploiting a commons to desist "in the name of conscience," what are we saying to him? What does he hear?—not only at the moment but also in the wee small hours of the night when, half asleep, he remembers not merely the words we used but also the nonverbal communication cues we gave him unawares? Sooner or later, consciously or subconsciously, he senses that he has received two communications, and that they are contradictory: (i) (intended communication) "If you don't do as we ask, we will openly condemn you for not acting like a responsible citizen"; (ii) (the unintended communication) "If you do behave as we ask, we will secretly condemn you for a simpleton who can be shamed into standing aside while the rest of us exploit the commons."

Everyman then is caught in what Bateson has called a "double bind." Bateson and his co-workers have made a plausible case for viewing the double bind as an important causative factor in the genesis of schizophrenia.[17] The double bind may not always be so damaging, but it always endangers the mental health of anyone to whom it is applied. "A bad conscience," said Nietzsche, "is a kind of illness."

To conjure up a conscience in others is tempting to anyone who wishes to extend his control beyond the legal limits. Leaders at the highest level succumb to this temptation. Has any President during the past generation failed to call on labor unions to moderate voluntarily their demands for higher wages, or to steel companies to honor voluntary guidelines on prices? I can recall none. The rhetoric used on such occasions is designed to produce feelings of guilt in noncooperators.

For centuries it was assumed without proof that guilt was a valuable, perhaps even an indispensable, ingredient of the civilized life. Now, in this post-Freudian world, we doubt it.

Paul Goodman speaks from the modern point of view when he says: "No good has ever come from feeling guilty, neither intelligence, policy, nor compassion. The guilty do not pay attention to the object but only to themselves, and not even to their own interests, which might make sense, but to their anxieties."[18]

guilt not of utility

380   One does not have to be a professional psychiatrist to see the consequences of anxiety. We in the Western world are just emerging from a dreadful two-centuries-long Dark Ages of Eros that was sustained partly by prohibition laws, but perhaps more effectively by the anxiety-generating mechanism of education. Alex Comfort has told the story well in *The Anxiety Makers;*[19] it is not a pretty one.

Since proof is difficult, we may even concede that the results of anxiety may sometimes, from certain points of view, be desirable. The larger question we should ask is whether, as a matter of policy, we should ever encourage the use of a technique the tendency (if not the intention) of which is psycholog-

390   ically pathogenic. We hear much talk these days of responsible parenthood; the coupled words are incorporated into the titles of some organizations devoted to birth control. Some people have proposed massive propaganda campaigns to instill responsibility into the nation's (or the world's) breeders. But what is the meaning of the word responsibility in this context? Is it not merely a synonym for the word conscience? When we use the word responsibility in the absence of substantial sanctions are we not trying to browbeat a free man in a commons into acting against his own interest? Responsibility is a verbal counterfeit for a substantial *quid pro quo.* It is an attempt to get something for nothing.

400   If the word responsibility is to be used at all, I suggest that it be in the sense Charles Frankel uses it.[20] "Responsibility," says this philosopher, "is the product of definite social arrangements." Notice that Frankel calls for social arrangements—not propaganda.

MUTUAL COERCION MUTUALLY AGREED UPON

The social arrangements that produce responsibility are arrangements that create coercion, of some sort. Consider bank-robbing. The man who takes money from a bank acts as if the bank were a commons. How do we prevent such action? Certainly not by trying to control his behavior solely by a verbal appeal to his sense of responsibility. Rather than rely on propaganda we follow Frankel's lead and insist that a bank is not a commons; we seek the

410   definite social arrangements that will keep it from becoming a commons. That we thereby infringe on the freedom of would-be robbers we neither deny nor regret.

The morality of bank-robbing is particularly easy to understand because we accept complete prohibition of this activity. We are willing to say "Thou shalt not rob banks," without providing for exceptions. But temperance also can be created by coercion. Taxing is a good coercive device. To keep downtown shoppers temperate in their use of parking space we introduce parking meters for short periods, and traffic fines for longer ones. We need not actually forbid a citizen to park as long as he wants to; we need merely make it increasingly expensive for him to do so. Not prohibition, but carefully biased options are what we offer him. A Madison Avenue man might call this persuasion; I prefer the greater candor of the word coercion.

Coercion is a dirty word to most liberals now, but it need not forever be so. As with the four-letter words, its dirtiness can be cleansed away by exposure to the light, by saying it over and over without apology or embarrassment. To many, the word coercion implies arbitrary decisions of distant and irresponsible bureaucrats; but this is not a necessary part of its meaning. The only kind of coercion I recommend is mutual coercion, mutually agreed upon by the majority of the people affected.

To say that we mutually agree to coercion is not to say that we are required to enjoy it, or even to pretend we enjoy it. Who enjoys taxes? We all grumble about them. But we accept compulsory taxes because we recognize that voluntary taxes would favor the conscienceless. We institute and (grumblingly) support taxes and other coercive devices to escape the horror of the commons.

An alternative to the commons need not be perfectly just to be preferable. With real estate and other material goods, the alternative we have chosen is the institution of private property coupled with legal inheritance. Is this system perfectly just? As a genetically trained biologist I deny that it is. It seems to me that, if there are to be differences in individual inheritance, legal possession should be perfectly correlated with biological inheritance—that those who are biologically more fit to be the custodians of property and power should legally inherit more. But genetic recombination continually makes a mockery of the doctrine of "like father, like son" implicit in our laws of legal inheritance. An idiot can inherit millions, and a trust fund can keep his estate intact. We must admit that our legal system of private property plus inheritance is unjust—but we put up with it because we are not convinced, at the moment, that anyone has invented a better system. The alternative of the commons is too horrifying to contemplate. Injustice is preferable to total ruin.

It is one of the peculiarities of the warfare between reform and the status quo that it is thoughtlessly governed by a double standard. Whenever a reform measure is proposed it is often defeated when its opponents triumphantly discover a flaw in it. As Kingsley Davis has pointed out,[21] worshippers of the status quo sometimes imply that no reform is possible without unanimous agreement, an implication contrary to historical fact. As nearly as I can make out, automatic rejection of proposed reforms is based

on one of two unconscious assumptions: (i) that the status quo is perfect; or
(ii) that the choice we face is between reform and no action; if the proposed
reform is imperfect, we presumably should take no action at all, while we
460   wait for a perfect proposal.

But we can never do nothing. That which we have done for thousands of
years is also action. It also produces evils. Once we are aware that the status
quo is action, we can then compare its discoverable advantages and disadvantages with the predicted advantages and disadvantages of the proposed
reform, discounting as best we can for our lack of experience. On the basis
of such a comparison, we can make a rational decision which will not involve
the unworkable assumption that only perfect systems are tolerable.

RECOGNITION OF NECESSITY

Perhaps the simplest summary of this analysis of man's population problems
is this: the commons, if justifiable at all, is justifiable only under conditions
470   of low-population density. As the human population has increased, the commons has had to be abandoned in one aspect after another.

First we abandoned the commons in food gathering, enclosing farm land
and restricting pastures and hunting and fishing areas. These restrictions are
still not complete throughout the world.

Somewhat later we saw that the commons as a place for waste disposal
would also have to be abandoned. Restrictions on the disposal of domestic
sewage are widely accepted in the Western world; we are still struggling to
close the commons to pollution by automobiles, factories, insecticide
sprayers, fertilizing operations, and atomic energy installations.

480   In a still more embryonic state is our recognition of the evils of the commons in matters of pleasure. There is almost no restriction on the propaga-
tion of sound waves in the public medium. The shopping public is assaulted
with mindless music, without its consent. Our government is paying out billions of dollars to create supersonic transport which will disturb 50,000 people for every one person who is whisked from coast to coast 3 hours faster.
Advertisers muddy the airwaves of radio and television and pollute the view
of travelers. We are a long way from outlawing the commons in matters of
pleasure. Is this because our Puritan inheritance makes us view pleasure as
something of a sin, and pain (that is, the pollution of advertising) as the sign
490   of virtue?

Every new enclosure of the commons involves the infringement of somebody's personal liberty. Infringements made in the distant past are accepted
because no contemporary complains of a loss. It is the newly proposed infringements that we vigorously oppose; cries of "rights" and "freedom" fill the air. But
what does "freedom" mean? When men mutually agreed to pass laws against
robbing, mankind became more free, not less so. Individuals locked into the
logic of the commons are free only to bring on universal ruin once they see the

necessity of mutual coercion, they become free to pursue other goals. I believe it was Hegel who said, "Freedom is the recognition of necessity."

The most important aspect of necessity that we must now recognize, is   500 the necessity of abandoning the commons in breeding. No technical solution can rescue us from the misery of overpopulation. Freedom to breed will bring ruin to all. At the moment, to avoid hard decisions many of us are tempted to propagandize for conscience and responsible parenthood. The temptation must be resisted, because an appeal to independently acting consciences selects for the disappearance of all conscience in the long run, and an increase in anxiety in the short.

The only way we can preserve and nurture other and more precious freedoms is by relinquishing the freedom to breed, and that very soon. "Freedom is the recognition of necessity"—and it is the role of education to reveal to all   510 the necessity of abandoning the freedom to breed. Only so, can we put an end to this aspect of the tragedy of the commons.

ENDNOTES

1. J. B. Wiesner and H. F. York, *Sci. Amer.* **211** (No. 4), 27 (1964).
2. G. Hardin, *J. Hered.* **50,** 68 (1959); S. von Hoernor, *Science* **137,** 18 (1962).
3. J. von Neumann and O. Morgenstern, *Theory of Games and Economic Behavior* (Princeton Univ. Press, Princeton, N.J., 1947), p. 11.
4. J. H. Fremlin, *New Sci.,* No. 415 (1964), p. 285.
5. A. Smith, *The Wealth of Nations* (Modern Library, New York, 1937), p. 423.
6. W. F. Lloyd, *Two Lectures on the Checks to Population* (Oxford Univ. Press, Oxford, England, 1833), reprinted (in part) in *Population, Evolution, and Birth Control,* G. Hardin, Ed. (Freeman, San Francisco, 1964), p. 37.
7. A. N. Whitehead, *Science and the Modern World* (Mentor, New York, 1948), p. 17.
8. G. Hardin, Ed. *Population, Evolution, and Birth Control* (Freeman, San Francisco, 1964), p. 56.
9. S. McVay, *Sci. Amer.* **216** (No. 8), 13 (1966).
10. J. Fletcher, *Situation Ethics* (Westminster, Philadelphia, 1966).
11. D. Lack, *The Natural Regulation of Animal Numbers* (Clarendon Press, Oxford, 1954).
12. H. Girvetz, *From Wealth to Welfare* (Stanford Univ. Press, Stanford, Calif., 1950).
13. G. Hardin, *Perspec. Biol. Med.* **6,** 366 (1963).
14. U. Thant, *Int. Planned Parenthood News,* No. 168 (February 1968), p. 3.
15. K. Davis, *Science* **158,** 730 (1967).

16. S. Tax, Ed., *Evolution after Darwin* (Univ. of Chicago Press, Chicago, 1960), vol. 2, p. 469.
17. G. Bateson, D. D. Jackson, J. Haley, J. Weakland, *Behav. Sci.* **1,** 251 (1956).
18. P. Goodman, *New York Rev. Books* 10(8), 22 (23 May 1968).
19. A. Comfort, *The Anxiety Makers* (Nelson, London, 1967).
20. C. Frankel, *The Case for Modern Man* (Harper, New York, 1955), p. 203.
21. J. D. Roslansky, *Genetics and the Future of Man* (Appleton-Century-Crofts, New York, 1966), p. 177.

A STUDENT EDITOR FINDS HIMSELF
AT THE CENTER OF THE NEWS
Jeff Holtz

Some day, Jason Braff, now a junior at Quinnipiac University in Hamden, could join Tom Brokaw, Ted Koppel, Peter Jennings and Leslie Stahl as a recipient of the college's Fred Friendly Award—named for the former CBS News president and bestowed for showing courage in preserving free speech. But for now, Mr. Braff, in his first year as editor of the student newspaper, *The Chronicle,* is in a battle with the administration over what he and others say is his right, and that of the paper's, to criticize the university.

Mr. Braff, 20, a print journalism major, said that his difficulties began this year, when, in an editorial for the paper and in an interview he later gave to The Waterbury Republican-American on free speech issues for students, he criticized a policy that bans *The Chronicle* from posting articles on its Web site before the weekly print version comes out.

The policy was established the previous school year, after the paper reported a story, about an off-the-court incident involving players on the men's basketball team, first online.

Mr. Braff said that while the paper had adhered to the online policy, the policy prevented the paper from reporting breaking news. He said that the administration had threatened to fire him for speaking out against the policy. Lynn Bushnell, the school's vice president for public affairs, denied that such a threat had been made.

"We do not discipline students who criticize the university or its policies," she said in a statement. "We do discipline students who fail to follow clearly established policies. However, student leaders, especially those in paid positions, are expected to generally be supportive of university policies. If they disagree with established policies, we expect them to go through normal administrative channels to try to change policies."

Ms. Bushnell said that she "seriously doubted" that a student would be fired for publicly disagreeing with a policy.

But Mr. Braff said that a letter from the university's vice president and dean of students, Manuel C. Carreiro, on Nov. 2 said otherwise. It read: "Please understand that any disregard for university or Student Center policies, or any public statement by you expressing disagreement with such policies, will seriously place your position and organization at risk with the university."

Mr. Braff said last week that the administration had agreed to discuss changes to the online policy and that he was less concerned about losing his job, which comes with an $8,000 stipend, similar to a scholarship. "At the same time, I feel that I and every other student shouldn't have to worry about expressing our opinions publicly, whether it is favorable or not, about the school," he said.

40   As for the online policy, Ms. Bushnell said it had been put in place to protect the university and its students, not infringe on their right of free speech. "The policy is intended to reduce the potential for serious error in light of a student's enthusiasm to release 'breaking news,'" she said. Ms. Bushnell added that such an error could result in libel, or a violation of a student's privacy rights.

However, Margarita E. Diaz, an assistant professor of journalism and the faculty adviser for *The Chronicle,* said that she agreed with Mr. Braff, that not allowing him to speak against the university's policies was a violation of his rights. "Any attempt by the university to control the statements by any stu-
50   dent leader, whether it is about university policies, or anything else going on on campus, I see as an attack on freedom of speech on campus," she said.

Ms. Diaz also said that the student journalists have had difficulty gaining access to the administration. "A university that prides itself on its journalism program is putting up barriers to the exercise of journalism on campus," Ms. Diaz said. "Having an administration that appears to not support the mission of our program is totally disheartening for all of us."

Mr. Braff said last week that the administration was also considering changes to how much access student reporters have to administration officials. (The administration required that questions for this article be submit-
60   ted to Ms. Bushnell by e-mail, and she responded by e-mail.)

The Chronicle, which is completely funded by the university, prints about 2,500 copies each edition and has 10 to 15 student reporters.

Mr. Braff said he was pleased that he and the administration were talking, but realized that no changes in policy had been promised.

"No matter what comes out of this, *The Chronicle* wants to see change," he said. "We're not very happy right now. These policies are not fair."

CARING AS A FEMINIST PRACTICE OF MORAL REASON
Alison M. Jaggar

In less than two decades, the ethics of care has achieved a spectacular rise to fame and fortune, at least in North America.[1] Almost unheard of in 1980, today caring is widely regarded as a moral perspective that is both distinctively feminine and peculiarly appropriate for feminists; it has even been institutionalized in establishments such as the Center for Human Caring, run by the School of Nursing at my own University of Colorado.[2] Although the ethics of care has been variously described, it is typically portrayed as a moral orientation that not only produces assessments of action different from those provided by traditional Western moralities, especially the ethics associated with the European Enlightenment, but that also arrives at those assessments through an alternative process of moral thinking.[3] My present interest is not in care as a moral ideal or value or virtue but rather in the potential of care thinking as a feminist mode or "style" of practical moral reasoning (Hacking 1985).

Practical moral reasoning is intended to identify morally desirable, or at least morally permissible, actions and practices, although it cannot, of course, be expected to do so infallibly. Since feminism, by definition, revolves around moral opposition to women's subordination, a mode of moral reasoning adequate for feminism should be capable of critiquing conventionally accepted practices of male dominance and identifying actions and practices that promote feminist ideals and values. Since male dominance is manifested in both institutional arrangements and personal relationships and in both the so-called public and private domains, feminist moral reasoning must be able to address all these aspects of social life. In addition, since feminist thought and action occur by definition in a world that is morally imperfect, a feminist mode of moral reasoning must be applicable to circumstances that are less than morally ideal.

This chapter discusses what I find to be two limitations of care thinking as a practice of moral reasoning suitable for feminism. My arguments suggest that although care thinking may have considerable utility for feminists, feminist practical ethics cannot rely exclusively on care but must supplement it with other modes of moral reasoning.

DISTINCTIVE FEATURES OF CARE REASONING

As a practice of moral thinking, care involves a distinctive moral orientation toward another person or persons. This orientation has both affective and cognitive dimensions: the caring individual is simultaneously concerned about the other's welfare and perceives acutely and insightfully how it is with

Reprinted from *Justice and Care: Essential Readings in Feminist Ethics*, edited by Virginia Held (1995).

the other. The carer recognizes and takes pleasure in the other's happiness and identifies and is concerned about her needs (Blum 1992). Descriptions of care thinking often take as paradigmatic situations in which the other is in 40 need, but Sara Ruddick notes that participants in caring relations also strive to delight and empower each other (Ruddick, personal correspondence).

Care thinking is generally explained by contrasting it with so-called justice thinking. One contrast lies in the structure of moral reasoning attributed to each mode of thinking. Justice thinking is portrayed as appealing to rational and universalizable moral principles, applied impartially, whereas accounts of care thinking emphasize its responsiveness to particular situations whose morally salient features are perceived with an acuteness thought to be made possible by the carer's emotional posture of empathy, openness, and receptiveness (Blum 1992). Care theorists' emphasis on moral perception is 50 sometimes taken to imply that care is immediate rather than deliberate, but several authors assert that it may be thoughtful and reflective (Blum 1991:706). However, rather than validating its responses by reference to general principles, care reasoning is likely to take the form of a narrative in which the concrete details of specific situations become intelligible in the context of people's ongoing lives and relationships (Walker 1992:167).

Perhaps the most distinctive and controversial feature attributed to care thinking is its particularity, which means not only that it addresses the needs of others in their concrete specificity but that it is unmediated by general principles. Addressing the needs of others in their concrete specificity is 60 understood as responding to them as unique, irreplaceable individuals rather than as "generalized" others regarded simply as representatives of a common humanity (Benhabib 1986). Such responsiveness requires paying as much moral attention to the ways in which people differ from each other as to the ways in which they are the same (Dillon 1992). Care's intense focus on particular others is taken to entail the denial that it is impartial in the sense of universalizable; thus, asserting the moral propriety of a particular caring response is claimed to carry no implication that someone else in a similar situation should do something similar (Walker 1987).

Care and justice thinking have sometimes been portrayed by contrasting 70 allegedly dispassionate justice with supposedly nonrational care, but in fact such portrayals caricature both justice and care. Although traditional accounts of moral reason often neglected or disparaged the moral significance of emotion, recent accounts increasingly acknowledge that even justice involves characteristic emotions such as respect and indignation. Similarly, theorists of care resist reducing it to a simple feeling, insisting that its cognitive elements be recognized. They consider care not simply as a motivation to right action, itself conceived as established through a process of rational calculation, but also as a distinct moral capacity with cognitive dimensions, necessary to determining what actions are morally appropriate (Blum 80 1992:125). The significant contrast seems to be not that care is emotional whereas justice is rational but rather that, as Virginia Held points out, the emotions play a different epistemic role in each perspective: the justice perspective limits the role of emotion to that of motivating actions whose moral permissibility must be determined by reason; the care perspective regards emotions as having "an important function in developing moral understanding itself, in helping us decide what the recommendations of morality themselves ought to be." Specifically, caring "involves feelings and requires high degrees of empathy to enable us to discern what morality recommends in our caring activities" (Held 1993:30).

Care is not rational in the senses of being purely intellectual, deductive, or even egoistic, but Nel Noddings asserts that "rationality and reasoning involve more than the identification of principles and their deductive application" (Noddings 1990a:27). Proponents of care thinking regard it as rational in a broader, honorific sense of being a distinctively human way of engaging with others that produces morally appropriate action.

WOMEN AND THE ETHICS OF CARE

There is nothing new in the assertion that women are uninterested in—often, indeed, neglectful of—justice. This claim has been made not only by antifeminists, such as Sigmund Freud, who thought that lack of concern for justice was inherent in women's nature (Freud 1933), but also by feminists, such as John Stuart Mill, who thought that women would develop a greater concern for justice if they were allowed to extend their sphere of activity beyond the home (Mill 1980). Until the 1970s, antifeminists and feminists alike assumed that to establish women's lack of concern about justice would be tantamount to demonstrating that women were morally inferior to men. The contemporary feminist counterclaim, that an exclusive preoccupation with *justice* reflects a moral sensibility that is also defective, is quite uncharacteristic of modern Western moral philosophy—although we shall see that it is not entirely unprecedented in it.

Even though the ethics of care is widely associated with women, some critics contend that the alleged connection between women and caring cannot be validated empirically. Some studies have found no sex differences emerging on tests of moral development when subjects are matched for education and occupation: with the exception of women who work in the home, males and females are said to achieve almost identical scores on Kohlbergian tests (Walker 1984:677–691). Moreover, many men as well as women have been asserted to employ care thinking, including members of traditional African societies (Harding 1987), African Americans migrating back from the northern to the southern United States (Stack 1986:321–324), and the members of some Native American cultures—not to mention so-called new age men.

Even within male-dominated Western philosophy, the themes that define the ethics of care are not entirely novel. Apart from Christ's injunction to love our neighbors, we may think of Aristotle's remark in Book VIII of his *Nicomachean Ethics* that "when we have justice, we also need friendship but when we have friends, we no longer need justice" echoed by Aquinas's assertion in

his ethics commentaries that "a moralist should be more profoundly concerned with friendship than justice." Annette Baier regards David Hume's moral thought as congenial with Gilligan's account of the ethics of care (Baier 1987b), and Joan Tronto finds caring themes in the work of two other Scot-
130 tish Enlightenment thinkers, Francis Hutcheson and Adam Smith (Tronto 1993).[4] Such examples are more than sufficient to discredit any simple claims that the ethics of justice and care reflect invariable differences between the moral thinking of men and women.

None of the major theorists of care makes any such simple claim, though many have been misread as doing so. Even in her early work, Carol Gilligan[5] asserted that as men and women age, their moral thinking converges, and in a later study of "educationally advantaged Americans" she found that a third of the women focused on justice, a third on care, and a third raised considerations of both justice and care (Gilligan 1987:25–26). Even though men
140 thought about situations almost exclusively in terms of justice and failed to raise concerns of care spontaneously, both sexes were able to recognize both moral orientations when these were suggested to them. Virginia Held and Sara Ruddick both associate care thinking with mothering, but Ruddick asserts that men as well as women are able to mother and Held speaks of "mothering persons" with pointed gender neutrality. Noddings attributes care thinking to those who saved Jews during the Holocaust, people who certainly included men as well as women (Noddings 1990a:27–28).

Although feminist proponents of the ethics of care recognize that some women think in terms of justice and some men think in terms of care, they
150 still associate caring with women because they believe that the care perspective emerges from forms of socialization and experience that, in contemporary Western society, are predominantly feminine. Gilligan suggests that women's affinity for the ethics of care and men's preference for the ethics of justice may be explained at least partly in terms of Nancy Chodorow's version of neo-Freudian object relations theory, which claims that because children are reared primarily by women, girls' gender identity is defined through connection with others whereas boys' gender identity must be established through separation from others (Gilligan 1987:28). Although Held and Ruddick both assert that mothering may be performed by men, they are clear
160 that male mothering is the exception rather than the rule. Noddings connects care with the feminine work of raising children, tending to the elderly, maintaining a supportive home environment, nursing, and teaching (Noddings 1990a:26).

Joan Tronto argues that in contemporary Western society, care is linked not only with gender but also with race and class. Defining care as those practices aimed at "maintaining, continuing and repairing the world," she associates the moral perspective of care with the work of cleaning up after bodily functions, tasks that in Western history have been relegated primarily to women, but not to women exclusively and not to all women (Tronto
170 1993:104). Tronto asserts that in "modern industrial societies, these tasks of

caring continue to be disproportionately carried out by the lowest ranks of society: by women, the working class, and in most of the West, by people of color" (Tronto 1993:113). She argues, therefore, that it is misleading to associate care with femininity *simpliciter:* the ethics of care reflects primarily the experience of women of certain races and classes—as well as of some racial/ethnic men of those classes (Tronto 1993:112). Tronto's analysis of the social genesis of care thinking fits well with Lawrence Blum's characterization of two prominent versions of the ethics of justice, the moral rationalisms of Kant and Hegel, as expressing a juridical-administrative perspective that, in modern Western societies, is typically masculine (Blum 1982). Blum's view   180
suggests that the justice orientation does not reflect the moral perspective of men universally, but only the perspective of men from the professional, administrative, and managerial classes—leaving open the possibility that the ethics of justice may well be adopted by the increasing numbers of women currently entering professional and administrative occupations. Tronto's and Blum's work suggests several reasons that caring themes are recessive rather than dominant in modern Western moral philosophy; such themes appear to characterize the thinking not only of women but also of people in premodern societies and of lower-class people, including people of color—none of whom are well represented among modern Western philosophers.   190

In addition to reflecting a social experience that is usually but not invariably or inevitably feminine, care may also be feminine in a symbolic or normative sense. Marilyn Friedman asserts that the genders are "moralized" in that

> specific moral ideals, values, virtues, and practices are culturally conceived as the special projects or domains of specific genders. These conceptions determine which commitments and behaviors are to be considered normal, appropriate, and expected of each gender, which commitments and behaviors are to be considered remarkable or heroic, and which commitments and behaviors are to be considered   200
> deviant, improper, outrageous, and intolerable. (Friedman 1993:123)

Friedman reports that the moralization of gender is commonplace at the level of popular perception in contemporary Western societies. Both men and women expect women to be more empathic and altruistic, to display concern for the welfare of others, to be caring and nurturant and, to a lesser extent, to be interpersonally sensitive, emotionally expressive, and gentle in personal style. By contrast, men are expected to be assertive, dominant, independent, self-confident, personally efficacious, and direct and adventurous in personal style (Friedman 1993:124). Friedman concludes that the ethics of care is feminine not simply in springing from types of labor assigned gener-   210
ally to women but also in reflecting moral ideals that are culturally feminine.

That the ethics of care is in some plausible senses feminine does not of course establish it as a mode of moral reasoning that is especially appropriate

for feminism. Although Western feminists in both the nineteenth and twentieth centuries have occasionally attempted to reclaim the culturally feminine, including the domestic and the emotional,[6] most feminists, and certainly most Western philosophers who have promoted women's equality, such as Plato, Marx, and Mill, have been concerned to challenge and even reject the feminine (Coole 1988). Developing the ethics of care is clearly one
220   means of reappropriating the feminine in the area of moral philosophy, but to evaluate the possibilities for the success of this project requires a critical examination of the strengths and weaknesses of care reasoning for feminist purposes.

ARE CARE AND JUSTICE THINKING COMPATIBLE?

In her early accounts of the ethics of care, Gilligan spoke of the need to marry care with justice, but she did not explain how this might be possible (Gilligan 1982:174). Several philosophers have explored how such a marriage might be consummated, suggesting ways in which care and justice might not only coexist but even presuppose each other. Susan Okin, for instance, argues both that justice is needed to frame caring relationships and that care for oth-
230   ers is the value implicit in impartiality (Okin 1989). Friedman argues both that being just is one form of caring and that caring should be done justly so that, for instance, one partner does not bear most of the burden of sustaining the personal relationship or accomplishing the family or parenting labor (Friedman 1993:127–130).

If care and justice are construed as values or ideals, there seems no reason to doubt that both may be part of the same value system and compatibility in this sense is not threatened by occasional uncertainty over which ideal should take precedence, just as liberty and equality may both be part of a single value system even though there may be occasional tension between them.
240   But when care and justice are construed as alternative modes of moral thinking or reasoning, it is harder to see how they may be compatible. As Friedman expresses the opposition between them, care thinking emphasizes moral commitments to particular individuals and justice thinking, to general principles (Friedman 1993:136). Although Friedman asserts that the two modes of thinking may be integrated, her own argument, which recognizes the difficulty of choosing between them, suggests that they are compatible only in the sense that a moral agent may elect at one time to use one mode of thinking, at another time, the other (Friedman 1993:138–139). Friedman does not show that care and justice thinking are compatible in that both may be
250   used on the same occasion, let alone that each implies the other.

Some philosophers have attempted to make precisely such an argument, suggesting that care and justice reasoning be interpreted not as independent practices of moral thinking but rather as aspects of a single practice. With such an interpretation, the ethics of care would not identify a different voice, new at least to philosophy, but would rather present a somewhat different way of listening to a familiar voice, emphasizing elements previously ignored by moral philosophers.

Various suggestions have been offered for construing care as one aspect of a complex practice of moral reasoning. Some Kantian feminists have suggested that care might be interpreted as a moral motive operating within a 260 framework of morally permissible action determined by the Categorical Imperative (Herman 1983; Baron 1984; O'Neill 1984). Other philosophers have suggested that care be equated with the faculty that Kant calls judgment, which is a direct and non-rule-governed but nonetheless moral assessment of the nature of the situation (Kant 1965:177). Still other moral theorists redescribe care reasoning as universalizable, whether or not agents appeal consciously to the Categorical Imperative, arguing that it involves a suppressed major premise (Kohlberg 1982:513–528; Sher 1987:187–188). If accounts of care thinking do not designate a hitherto unrecognized mode or practice of moral reasoning but instead highlight unremarked aspects of a familiar prac- 270 tice, it is plausible to suppose that both aspects must be included in a complete account of moral reasoning and thus that justice and care are not only logically compatible with but even logically indispensable to each other.

Suggesting that justice and care ethics each represent different aspects of moral reasoning is not the only way of arguing for their compatibility. Another approach is to recognize them as distinct practices of moral thinking but, assuming that they originate in the experience of public and private life respectively, to suggest that they complement each other in the sense of being appropriate for different domains. Not only Kohlberg and his colleagues (Kohlberg, Levine, and Hewer 1983) but also Blum (1992:126) have 280 suggested that care is especially appropriate for intimate relations or one-to-one encounters.

A third strategy for viewing care and justice as compatible and even complementary is to construe each as addressing a different set of issues. Jürgen Habermas suggests that care thinking is concerned with "evaluative questions of the good life" and "the evaluation of personality types and modes of action." He regards these as "personal" issues of self-realization, not truly moral, unlike the questions of universal obligation, which he takes to be the subject of justice thinking. For Habermas, care is distinguished from justice in reflecting *Sittlichkeit* rather than *Moralitaet* and addressing questions of 290 the good rather than the right, the content of morality rather than its form (Habermas 1990:178–180).

Although compatibility claims are accepted by some advocates of the ethics of care, they are made more frequently by those committed to the primacy of justice. Often compatibility claims are presented in a way that is deflationary, minimizing the moral and theoretical significance of care by reducing it to one aspect of a morality whose essential constituents are the impartiality and universalizability thought to be defining characteristics of the ethics of justice. George Sher, for instance, denies firmly that the articulation of the ethics of care provides any reason to suppose that moral theory 300 needs radical revision; he states that "far from being novel, this approach [making moral decisions on the basis of care and sympathy] . . . is central to the existing tradition" (Sher 1987:184).

Advocates of care thinking are especially resistant to compatibility proposals that trivialize the concerns raised by the ethics of care, proposals that Barbara Houston has diagnosed as expressing a "politics of dismissal" (Houston 1988). Blum, for instance, has objected to several attempts to assimilate caring to one aspect of justice thinking. He insists that care cannot be reconstructed in terms of rules that are in principle universalizable (Blum

310 1987:326–327), and he distinguishes moral perception from the Kantian notion of moral judgment on the grounds that its task is not to apply moral principles but rather to individuate the situations in which moral judgment operates (Blum 1991:708–714). Margaret Walker argues that some moral reasoning is irreducibly particular and nonuniversalizable because those practicing it assign a discretionary weight, rank, or value to moral particulars, in the process defining their own moral personae, the kind of persons they are (Walker 1987).

Many care advocates reject also the suggestion that care and justice are each appropriate for a different domain. Apart from Noddings's attempt to extend

320 care thinking to handle all moral concerns in all domains (Noddings 1991:97), some argue that justice as well as care is needed in the household (Ruddick) and many assert that care as well as justice is needed in the public domain (Walker 1991; Tronto 1993; Held 1993; Ruddick). Dividing the moral labor so that justice and care regulate the public and private domains, respectively, makes justice primary over care because justice regulates the domain that not only has the higher status but also controls how the domains are demarcated. Care ethics, symbolically gendered feminine, then becomes analogous to housework: despite its indispensability, its contribution to the larger economy is disregarded or marginalized.

330 Although Seyla Benhabib retains a strong commitment to a universal ethics of justice, she seeks to rescue care thinking from what she calls Habermas's relegation of it "to the margins of ethical theory." Benhabib complains that, on Habermas's construal, the issues with which he takes care to be concerned become "'anomalies' or residual problems of an otherwise adequate scientific paradigm" (Benhabib 1992:183). She challenges Habermas's sharp distinction between the right and the good, noting, "The line between matters of justice and those of the good life is not given by some moral dictionary, but evolves as a result of historical and cultural struggles" (Benhabib 1992:75). In her view, questions of the good life are also susceptible to inter-

340 subjective debate and reflection, although she concedes that consensus here may not be possible, and she insists, in opposition to Habermas, that "questions of care are moral issues" (Benhabib 1992:186).

Most proponents of the ethics of care now dispute the possibility of any easy synthesis of care with justice. They note that in her later work, Gilligan presents care and justice as "two moral perspectives that organize thinking in different ways" (Gilligan 1987:20), dropping her early metaphor of a marriage in favor of explaining care and justice by reference to ambiguous figures that may be given alternative and incompatible interpretations. Rather than seeking to include care and justice in a unified account of moral reasoning, most contemporary advocates of an ethics of care are committed to exploring care's strengths as an independent style or practice of moral thinking. They present the ethics of care as a complete moral orientation or perspective or outlook, "a unified perspective on morality" (Walker 1989:123). In this view, care and justice both involve distinctive ontological, epistemological, and practical commitments, though this is not to deny that the concepts, themes, and priorities associated with both orientations are often loosely defined, permitting considerable disagreement between them. Sara Ruddick speaks for many in asserting that "justice" and "care" are "two non-assimilable moral orientations . . . which foster distinctive cognitive capacities, appeal to distinctive ideals of rationality, elicit distinctive moral emotions, presume distinctive conceptions of identity and relationships, recognize distinctive virtues and make distinctive requirements on institutions." On Ruddick's view, "justice" and "care" each offer

> "a point of view from which alone a certain sort of understanding of human life is possible." That is to say, each orientation is genuinely moral; neither can be replaced by or subsumed under the other; each covers the whole of the moral domain and therefore can check and inform the other; there is no third, "mature," single integrative moral perspective within which each orientation has its place. (Ruddick)

CARE THINKING'S SIGNIFICANCE FOR MORAL PHILOSOPHY

Even if the new interest in caring did no more than focus philosophical attention on previously disregarded aspects of moral thinking, it would have considerable significance for moral philosophy. Cheshire Calhoun has argued that the historical neglect of these aspects has produced a distorted and misleading representation of moral life (Calhoun 1988). For instance, focusing exclusively on people's shared humanity and equal membership in the moral community diverts attention from the ways in which people's basic interests and empirical desires may differ depending on their social location. Focusing exclusively on the adult capacity for consistent and universalizable moral reflection diverts attention from the indispensability of moral motivation and education and from the social availability of morally relevant information. Focusing exclusively on the dangers of egoism and partiality to one's own diverts attention from the dangers of self-sacrifice and devalues the moral significance of special relations. Calhoun argues that the traditional focus of Western moral philosophy has created a lopsided ideology of moral life and thought that reflects the moral preoccupations of propertied males and obscures the moral concerns of (among others) many women. The ethics of care, construed as a focus on hitherto neglected aspects of moral life and thought, can help to redress this gendered bias in moral theory.

390   If care thinking is construed in a stronger sense, as an independent style or practice of moral reasoning, then its advocates contend that it may generate actions morally superior to those that result from a concern for justice. Many examples purport to illustrate how people motivated primarily by justice frequently ignore the pressing needs of real people, often those closest to them, or subordinate individuals to abstract principle, with a "blind willingness to sacrifice people to truth" (Gilligan 1982:104; compare Baier 1987a and Noddings 1984). Care's ability to generate actions morally preferable to those produced by justice reasoning is credited in part to its reliance on the direct perception of particular situations. This direct perception is said to

400 facilitate action that is more context-sensitive than actions guided by moral rules that, because of their generality, are necessarily indeterminate.

Care is also asserted to be more reliable than justice thinking in motivating right action because justice often presents right action as requiring the sacrifice of one's own self-interest, whereas care thinking regards the interests of the self as inseparable from those of others. Unlike acting from a concern for justice, therefore, acting caringly does not require a prior act of moral will strong enough to overcome one's inclinations, and so caring action, unlike justice-motivated action, can hardly be inhibited by "weakness of the will." For instance, Noddings reports that of the non-Jews who risked their own

410 safety to save Jews during the Holocaust, only 11 percent acted on principle; the rest "responded either directly out of compassion or from a sense of themselves as decent, caring people" (Noddings 1990a:27).

Finally, the process of responding in a caring manner itself is said to have moral value, unlike the intellectual appeal to principle characteristic of the ethics of justice. As Blum observes, "Accurate moral perception is a good in its own right," expressing a praiseworthy moral sensitivity (Blum 1991:714).

Many of these claims seem to me persuasive, but rather than developing them here, I intend to discuss two features of care reasoning that I find especially problematic. Gilligan chose the analogy of the ambiguous figure to sug-

420 gest that the ethics of care draws attention to some things only at the expense of obscuring others. I am concerned about two of care thinking's apparent blind spots, which hamper and may even disable care from addressing certain questions crucial for feminist ethics.

JUSTIFYING "TRUE CARE"

In this section, I criticize the care tradition for failing to explain how care thinking may be properly critical of the moral validity of felt, perceived, or expressed needs, so that it can avoid permitting or even legitimating morally inadequate responses to them. I attribute this failure to the relative lack of attention to moral justification given so far by theorists of care ethics.

It would not be true to say that the tradition of care ethics fails to acknowledge any distinction between real necessities and objects of empirical desire, between felt or expressed needs, on the one hand, and genuine needs, on the other. On the contrary, such a distinction runs through the work of Gilligan, it is implicit in Ruddick's definition of caring in terms of what may usefully be given and received (Ruddick), and it is explicit in Tronto's observation that "a patient in the hospital who refuses to get up may be forced to do so. A child who wishes only to eat junk food may be disappointed by parents' reluctance to meet this wish" (Tronto 1989:177). But although most accounts of care reasoning assume such a distinction, they have provided only scanty explanations of how it should be drawn.

Accounts of care thinking that emphasize the directness of caring perception sometimes discourage even raising this epistemological question by treating care as a "success" concept. On this construal, caring perception of another's need is by definition veridical; if someone fails to assess another's situation accurately, she is not practicing care thinking. Tronto's assertion that hospital patients may be forced to get up and children prevented from eating junk food is followed immediately by the remark, "Genuine attentiveness would presumably allow the caretaker to see through these pseudo-needs and come to appreciate what the other really needs" (Tronto 1989:177). Such comments tend to obscure the question of how we distinguish "pseudo-needs" from "real needs" by suggesting that "genuine attentiveness," which Tronto takes as central to caring, is self-authenticating. From here, it is easy to slide into paternalism, authoritarianism, and dogmatism.

Many care theorists, including Tronto, are aware of these dangers and discuss such concerns as vicarious identification, projection, and carers' desires to control those for whom they care or to maintain them in a state of dependence. Frequently, care theorists maintain that these dangers may be avoided through improved practices of attentiveness, portraying attentiveness as a kind of discipline whose prerequisites include attitudes and capacities such as openness, receptivity, empathy, sensitivity, and imagination. Margaret Walker writes, "Acuity of moral perception, especially as regards the interests and perspectives of people, must result from the exercise of many complex, learned, and indefinitely improvable skills of attention, communication, and interpretation" (Walker 1991:771).

Among contemporary care theorists, Walker is probably the most insistent on the need that caring intentions be validated through communication with those cared-for. But Ruddick also mentions mothers attempting to figure out how to care for their children by talking with each other (Ruddick 1989), and Held emphasizes the need "to listen to each other in actual conversations in actual communities" (Held 1993:41). Noddings's argument that there must be fairly tight limits on the circle of those for whom we care depends partly on her insistence that the caring relation be completed by the recognition of those who are cared-for, and this insistence is in turn at least partially motivated by an epistemological concern. She says that if we do not

"check on the effects of our efforts" and attend to a "living other speaking to us directly—informing us, persuading us, getting us to change our minds," we can be led into "a dangerous inauthenticity" (Noddings 1991:98). In a similar vein, Walker writes, "A great deal of our best evidence about how it is with others requires talking with and listening to them . . . . Asking, telling, repeating, mutually clarifying, mulling over, and checking back are the most
480   dependable, accessible, and efficient devices for finding out how it is with others" (Walker 1991:769).

Theorists influenced by Simone Weil and Iris Murdoch sometimes speak as though care thinking requires forgetting the self; Noddings, for instance, asserts that "our attention, our mental engrossment is on the cared-for, not on ourselves" (Noddings 1984:24). But other theorists emphasize that care thinking also requires self-awareness and self-knowledge; Tronto says that attentiveness requires "a tremendous self-knowledge so that the caretaker does not simply transform the needs of the other into a projection of the self's own needs" (Tronto 1989:178).

490   The care perspective's attention to the subjects of moral consciousness contrasts with the justice perspective's efforts to disregard or bracket individual subjectivity through ingenious theoretical devices designed to approximate an impersonal "view from nowhere." Not only that strand of the justice tradition concerned primarily with rights but also the strand that concerns itself with welfare or utility typically focuses on relations "out there" in the world external to the self. This is not to say that the justice tradition dismisses all questions about the interests and obligations of the moral subject or about personal relationships but that, in both teleological and neo-Kantian deontological ethics, relationships between particular selves and particular others
500   are regarded as likely to be epistemologically subversive or morally corrupting. Theoretical postulates such as the ideal observer, the disinterested judge, the archangel, the original position, and the view from nowhere are designed to correct for the assumed bias of particular points of view.

Care reasoning is unlike justice reasoning in that it does not attempt to bracket or disregard the self, whose appropriate motivations, attitudes, sensibilities, and qualities of character are thought indispensable to morally acute perception. Furthermore, these qualities are regarded not simply as instrumental to producing a morally desirable outcome but as intrinsic to the quality of the caring relationship. Care thinking thus not only pays more atten-
510   tion than justice thinking to the subject or moral consciousness but also conceptualizes differently the relation between that subject and the objects of her moral concern. Justice thinking is impersonal and general because it regards both moral subjects and the objects of their moral concern in terms of their moral status as representatives of humanity or as beings capable of pleasure and pain rather than in terms of their concrete specificity; care thinking is personal and particularized in that both carers and those cared-for regard each other as unique, irreplaceable individuals.

The justice perspective's concern to depersonalize moral thinking reflects its interest in epistemological issues and its eagerness to identify a method for discovering which moral principles are most objectively just. Justice thinking often prides itself on being objective precisely insofar as it distances itself from the self and particular relationships and dismisses care thinking as subjective and therefore unreliable precisely because successful caring by definition involves particular relations between carers and those cared-for. However, it is mistaken to assume that bracketing subjectivity is the best way of achieving moral objectivity, in the sense of trustworthy moral responses.

Care's focus on the relation between the carer and the cared-for is valuable in raising questions often ignored by justice reasoning, questions that are important both morally and epistemologically. Turning our attention inward as well as outward encourages reflexive consideration of what the agent brings to the situation, her interests, her location, the context, her warrant for intervention. Conceiving moral reasoning as interactive encourages reflection not only on the moral implications for others of action or inaction but also on the implications for the self, how it expresses or develops her moral character. As Walker puts it, it encourages us to ask, What kind of person do I want to become? (Walker 1987). Acknowledging the moral dimension of perception and the epistemic dimension of emotion also encourages consideration of how people may develop the moral abilities for morally sensitive perception and loving attention. Finally, insisting on the importance of checking with the one cared-for, rather than assuming that we know her needs in advance, avoids the arrogance and presumptiveness of postulating hypothetical consent in what Walker calls "round robins of role-taking" in what she regards as the "alarming" "philosophical predilection for the game of imagination" (Walker 1991:769).

Although it is not true that moral objectivity is best achieved by bracketing subjectivity, it is equally mistaken to suppose that morally appropriate responses can be determined by focusing exclusively either on the attitude of the moral subject or even on the caring relationship. Yet care theorists often seem to assume that even if adequate caring cannot be guaranteed by the carer's intentions alone, the carer/cared-for dyad between them can be counted on to identify truly caring behavior.

On reflection, it is immediately evident that such an assumption is unwarranted. Overindulgence or "spoiling" are only the least of the moral mistakes that may be carried out in the name of care. Other, more clearly gendered, abuses include incest and even footbinding. Incestuous fathers often portray themselves as caring for their daughters, even as nurturing or initiating them, and the Chinese women who bound the feet of their daughters and granddaughters also equated the pain they caused with care (Blake 1994:682).[7] These examples show not only that appropriate caring is not guaranteed by the intentions of the one who claims to care but that such a guarantee is not supplied even by agreement on the part of the one who is cared-for. Children

characteristically retain a tenacious trust in the goodness of their "caretakers" intentions, finding it less psychologically devastating to interpret neglect or abuse as care than to believe that they are not cared for. Abused women also often regard violence as an expression of caring or love, and they may even identify empathically with their abusers. "Co-dependents" appeal to care to justify their facilitation of destructive or self-destructive behavior on the part of others. These examples demonstrate clearly that so long as care thinking focuses exclusively on the carer/cared-for dyad, it cannot reliably assess the
570   adequacy and appropriateness of responses that claim to be caring.

The care perspective is not necessarily without resources for addressing this issue, but so far few care theorists have given it more than perfunctory attention, perhaps because they have not yet clearly acknowledged it as a problem. The care literature contains relatively few direct discussions of how to identify care that is morally appropriate and has shown limited interest in moral justification. Noddings, here as often elsewhere the most radical of the care theorists, even explicitly rejects traditional concerns about justification. She writes,

580
> An ethic of caring does not emphasise justification. As one-caring, I am not seeking justification for my action; I am not standing alone before some tribunal. What I seek is completion in the other—the sense of being cared-for and, I hope, the renewed commitment of the cared-for to turn about and act as one-caring in the circles and chains within which he is defined. Thus, I am not justified but somehow fulfilled and completed in my own life and in the lives of those I have thus influenced. (Noddings 1984:95)

This passage may be read as expressing lack of concern for any perspectives external to the caring relation.

The recent work of Joan Tronto is one exception to care theorists' lack of
590   interest in justification. Because she recognizes that identifying and ranking needs is inherently contestable, Tronto asserts that care is a desirable political ideal only in the context of a just, pluralistic, democratic society in which open and equal discussion about needs and justice occurs (Tronto 1993:154–172). But in asserting the necessity of societywide dialogue about needs, which presumably involves assessing and ranking the needs of classes of people rather than specific individuals, Tronto seems to be concerned primarily with care as a political ideal and to depart from classic accounts of care thinking that describe it as distinguished by its focus on particular others.

These considerations suggest that care thinking, at least as it has been
600   described so far in the literature, is incomplete as a feminist account of moral rationality. The suggestion that dyadic relations of care are somehow self-justifying, a suggestion more often implied than explicit, is not only mystifying but evidently false. I suggest that claims to care, like other perceptual and moral claims, can be justified only by widening the circle of intersubjective validation.

Writer would perhaps say public + familial realms should be considered differently

CARE'S FOCUS ON THE PARTICULAR

Care reasoning is often described as responding directly to particular persons and situations, whereas justice reasoning is supposedly concerned with universal principles. Like several other alleged contrasts between care and justice, this contrast is often overstated, since justice and care reasoning each necessarily recognize both particular and universal aspects of situations. Justice reasoning, as we have seen already, requires perceiving and assessing the morally salient features of particular situations in order to know which general principles should be brought to bear. Similarly, care's recognition of particular situations necessarily utilizes general concepts; for instance, recognizing a particular individual's need for companionship presupposes an ability to deploy the concepts of person and loneliness in a range of relevantly similar situations. Since both care and justice reasoning logically involve reference to both particular and universal aspects of situations, this distinction between them may be regarded as one of degree rather than kind, a difference of emphasis or attention or focus.

Justice reasoning regards particular situations as tokens of more general types and so attends to what they have in common with other situations. Care reasoning, by contrast, focuses on the specificities of each situation, emphasizing the ways in which it is unique and responding to those involved as particular in the sense of nonsubstitutable or irreplaceable (Friedman 1993:136–137). Accounts of care reasoning emphasize its attentiveness to detail, its deep and rather narrow focus, whereas justice reasoning, which requires explicit comparisons, tends to have a wider but shallower focus. Although the state of the nation, the world, and the universe are all, in a logical sense, particular states of affairs, care reasoning, with its emphasis on detail, depth, and specificity, is typically practiced in small-scale or micro situations involving a very few people whom the carer knows or comes to know personally. Justice reasoning, by contrast, has often been thought inappropriate for small-scale situations involving personal relations (Sandel 1982) and is paradigmatically used to address large-scale or macro situations involving people not known by the agent in their concrete specificity. On those somewhat exceptional occasions when agents apply justice reasoning to situations in which they are personally acquainted with those involved, they are expected to bracket or discount their personal knowledge and feelings. Care thinking celebrates minute perception of detail, but justice is supposed to be blind to all aspects of situations other than the limited number of generalizable features taken to be morally salient.

Some critics of the ethics of care complain that care thinking is unable to address large-scale social or global problems, but that is not precisely my concern here. Instead, I want to discuss one limitation of care reasoning not in terms of its applicability or otherwise to large-scale situations or the so-called public realm but rather in terms of what care makes visible in any situation regardless of scale or publicity. Accepting that one strength of care reasoning lies in its ability to draw moral attention to aspects of situations often disregarded by justice reasoning, I shall argue that its weakness lies in its inability

650   to bring into focus other morally salient features of situations. When some
things are foregrounded, others recede into the background; in making some
things visible, care obscures others.

The distinctive feature of care reasoning that I address here is its focus on
the specificities of particular situations, especially the needs of particular
individuals. This focus is valuable in encouraging awareness of the moral
complexities of situations, which are always open to a variety of interpretations, and of individuals' responsibilities within situations. Its weakness is
that its attention to situations' specificity and particularity diverts attention
away from their general features such as the social institutions and groupings
660   that give them their structure and much of their meaning (Card 1990:205;
Hoagland 1991:253, 260). For instance, care's emphasis on responding to
immediate needs simultaneously takes those needs as givens, failing to question their source or why they are presently unfulfilled.

general social concern

My point is not that the care perspective excludes awareness of social
identities and structures; on the contrary, care presupposes such awareness,
since the identity of particular individuals is constituted partly by their group
membership and since particular actions or situations are made possible by
and gain their meaning from social structures. Thus, recognizing a situation
of racial privilege or sexual abuse inevitably presupposes an awareness of the
670   race or sex of the individuals involved and of the way that these aspects of
their identity influence particular situations. In an example of Lawrence
Blum's, for instance, when a taxi driver chooses a white male customer over
an African American woman, it would be impossible to perceive the affront
to the dignity of the African American woman unless one were aware of the
social meanings assigned to the skin colors of those involved; without this
awareness, one's perception would be aesthetic rather than moral. Conversely, social structures, such as race and sex, exist only in their specific manifestations, and understanding them requires recognizing their operation in
particular situations and experiences. The universal and particular aspects of
680   situations, what might be called their form and content, thus presuppose
each other in a way that the images of the duck and the rabbit in the ambiguous duck-rabbit figure do not presuppose each other. It is no more than a
contingent fact that the outline of the duck can also be seen as the shape of
a rabbit and vice versa, whereas it is not contingent that particular situations
gain their meaning from social structures and that social structures exist only
through their instantiation in particular situations. Despite this disanalogy,
reference to the ambiguous duck-rabbit figure helps illustrate one important
feature of the relationship between justice and care. This is that even when
one is aware of the presence of both images, one cannot focus on both at
690   once; when one is visible, the other becomes invisible. Similarly, when an
agent is focusing on the concrete specificities of a situation, she is not attending directly to the social institutions that structure it and vice versa. When
one is at the center of her consciousness, the other is at the margins. In care

thinking, social structure occupies a place comparable to the frame of a picture one is viewing; one must be aware of it in some sense but one pays it little direct attention.

From a feminist perspective, care's exclusive focus on particularity is sometimes a significant liability, since an important concern of feminist ethics must be the ways in which male-dominant social structures limit the life chances of women and men. Close attention to the specificities of small-scale situations may well obscure perception of the larger social context in which they are embedded. For instance, focusing on particular examples of oppression may facilitate perception of insensitive and bullying behavior on the part of individuals, but it can also divert moral attention away from the social structures of privilege that legitimate such behavior. Moral thinking that focuses on the specificities of particular situations is likely to see the source of problems as lying in the personal attitudes of individual men, whites or heterosexuals who benefit, sometimes unwittingly or unwillingly, from sexism, racism, and heterosexism, rather than in those larger institutions that give some individuals power and privilege over others. Similarly, attending to an individual's immediate needs for food, shelter, comfort, or companionship is likely to distract from moral scrutiny of the social structures that create those needs or leave them unfulfilled.

I do not wish to argue that individual attitudes and immediate needs are morally insignificant. On the contrary, social structures and institutions are human inventions that survive only because people conform their behavior to them; racism and sexism outlive legal prohibition because of individuals' insensitivity or callousness. Care reasoning encourages personal accountability and individual resistance to oppressive structures. But care's emphasis on individual responses to immediate needs also encourages what are sometimes called band-aid or social work approaches to moral problems rather than efforts to solve them institutionally or prevent their occurrence through social changes.

The characteristic strengths and limitations of the care perspective are revealed in Noddings's response to the criticism most commonly made of caring, namely, that it is partial or parochial because attention to intimates and proximate strangers can lead to neglecting those who are further away. Noddings readily acknowledges the legitimacy of moral concern for distant strangers or humanity at large but insists it is not properly addressed in ways such as giving money to famine-relief organizations, which she calls "caring about." "Caring about" is "a poor second-cousin to caring," in Noddings's view, (1984:112) because caring, as she defines it, is an interactive relation in which people recognize each other as particular individuals. When others are too distant or too numerous for personal caring relations to be established with them, Noddings suggests that we either press their neighbors to care for them or seek to empower them to help themselves (Noddings 1991:97–98). "Instead of presenting ourselves to the

what Jaggar is worried about [margin note, at line 720]

world as heroes, gangbusters, or saviors, we would act as friends and partners, carefully building and maintaining stable relations on which we as
740   well as others could depend in times of need" (Noddings 1991:97).

> From the perspective of caring, when we empower a group, we do not
> just give them things. Rather we help them to gain control over their
> own lives and, especially, to develop the resources and commitment to
> help others. The process of empowering is thus a part of caring. It nec-
> essarily requires a sort of "staying with" or "holding" as Sara Ruddick
> describes it, and this is a longterm program that involves the contin-
> uous construction and maintenance of caring relations. *It is still lim-
> ited in the individualist sense.* I have to trust others to do the direct
> work of caring when I cannot be present." (1991:98, emphasis added)

750   Care's insistence on personal engagement and individual responsibility is
a useful corrective to the impersonality, insensitivity, and frequent ineffec-
tiveness of social engineering. It reminds us not only that a new society needs
new people to make it work but that social change requires individual action
and challenges each of us to act now rather than wait for the authorities or
the revolution. Noddings's rejection of the masculine models of hero, gang-
buster, and savior is a characteristically feminist response to the "grandiose
universality" of the justice orientation (Friedman 1993:109) and the postur-
ing of leaders, paradigmatically male (Fisher 1980:12–13), who infantilize
and disempower their followers, positioning them as victims awaiting rescue
760   or salvation.

Despite the virtues of care thinking, its emphasis on the quality of individual relations seems to preclude its addressing the structural oppositions
between the interests of social groups that make caring difficult or unlikely
between members of those groups. Similarly, care's reliance on individual
efforts to meet individual needs disregards the social structures that make this
virtually impossible in many cases. Care thinking seems unable to focus on the
social causes of many individual problems, such as widespread homelessness
and hunger, both of which have disproportionately severe effects on women.

I am not aware that care theorists have addressed the question of home-
770   lessness in North America, but it seems compatible with the spirit of care
ethics to encourage moral responses such as personally helping homeless
individuals or families rehabilitate or build houses or even taking them into
one's own home, as opposed to challenging zoning and credit restrictions,
pressing for governmental provision of housing, or even questioning why so
many people, especially women, lack the money for housing. With respect to
the question of Third World hunger, we have seen that care thinking encourages local people to give food to individuals with whom they are acquainted
and even to help them grow their own food. But care thinking does not question why some "neighbors" have food while others do not, let alone identify

the larger social forces causing peasant dislocation and dispossession, the   780
assignment of land to cash crops for export rather than food for local people,
Third World deforestation and desertification, and the draining of Third
World resources to service its debt to international financial institutions.
Even if caring is capable eventually of producing a social transformation that
is evolutionary rather than revolutionary, the slowness and uncertainty of this
approach make it morally inadequate for tackling existing problems of home-
lessless or hunger, given the level and extent of dislocation, malnutrition, and
starvation as well as the interlinked and accelerating social and environmental crises.

Some care theorists have talked about making care applicable to large-   790
scale social or global issues by enlarging our moral imagination, learning to
care for distant others, including large populations with whom we have no
personal contact. But this is to treat care merely as a moral motive, not as a
distinctive mode of moral response, and it is incompatible with the characteristically interactive and personal relation that defines care thinking. At
best, it is what Noddings calls "caring about." At worst, it appropriates the
language of caring to refer to "caring that is *directed toward* inert and
unknown recipients" and is thus a form of colonization, "oblivious to the
possibility that [its] 'targets' might experience the proffered caring as insulting and invasive" (Code 1992:1–2).   800

Significantly improving the lives of the world's women certainly requires
the empathy, imagination, and responsiveness that distinguish care thinking;
but it also requires a kind of moral thinking that focuses not only on meeting immediate needs but on problematizing the structures that create those
needs or keep them unfulfilled. This is as true on the familial and local levels as it is on the national and international levels, and it presents a major
challenge for care theorists.

To note care thinking's difficulty in addressing some crucial questions of
feminist practical ethics is not necessarily to assume that justice thinking is
capable of dealing adequately with those questions. For instance, care rea-   810
soning addresses instances of rape and domestic violence by "strongly disapproving" of them (Noddings 1990b:125) and tries to protect victims and survivors by establishing moral authority over their assailants; justice reasoning,
as commonly construed, is likely to condemn these assaults as violations by
individuals of other individuals' rights. In order to fully comprehend sexual
violence, however, its meanings and functions as a systematic social practice
must be addressed, together with the ways in which many social institutions
implicitly condone and legitimate it. Neither care nor justice reasoning, as
ordinarily construed, constitutes the kind of hermeneutical moral thinking
capable of questioning conventional definitions of assault as well as of explor-   820
ing the complex assumptions about sexuality, aggression, and gender that
make rape not only thinkable but predictable and even normal. The feminists
of the late 1960s called this kind of thinking consciousness-raising.

CONCLUSION

At least as so far described by its theorists, care thinking has severe limitations. Its inability to focus on social structures restricts the scope of its moral critiques, and its lack of theoretical interest in justification renders its critical perspective unreliable even on those issues that it does address. Despite these shortcomings, the recent recognition of care thinking has made valuable contributions to philosophical understandings of moral rationality. Through 830 studying empirical examples of moral thinking, care theorists have raised questions hitherto largely neglected by moral philosophers and revealed that the conception of practical reason associated with the European Enlightenment has its own limitations. Among these are an inadequate portrayal of moral thinking that exaggerates the significance of principles and fails to recognize that affectively laden aspects of moral thinking have epistemic as well as motivational functions. In addition, and because care is generally associated with the personal realm, the ethics of care has contributed to rehabilitating personal life as an arena for moral scrutiny; it has thus expanded the domain of practical morality, exposing further limitations in traditional theory. Finally, 840 the ethics of care has revealed damaging biases, including gender biases, in Enlightenment moral theory, which has not only devalued the caring work assigned primarily to women, especially women of the lower classes, but also functioned as an ideology to rationalize selfishness as natural and normal.

ENDNOTES

1. Virginia Held and Sara Ruddick both read several earlier drafts of this essay and discussed them with me at length. I am deeply grateful for their help, although I must make the usual disclaimer that the views expressed here are still, in the end, not theirs but mine.

2. The Center for Human Caring was established in 1986 and its history and mission statement describes it as "the nation's first interdisciplinary center with an overall commitment to develop and use knowledge of human caring and healing as the foundation for transforming the health care system."

3. The contemporary ethics of care was pioneered by Milton Mayeroff's 1971 book, *On Caring,* (New York: Harper & Row) but this did not explore care's gendered dimensions and so was largely ignored by feminists. The name most widely associated with the contemporary feminist ethics of care is that of Nel Noddings (1984, 1989) but other philosophers who have endorsed some version of this approach to ethics include, but are not limited to Annette Baier (1987a, 1987b, 1994), Lawrence Blum (1988, 1991), Marilyn Friedman (1993), Virginia Held (1993), Rita Manning (1992), Sara Ruddick (1987, 1989, 1995), Joan Tronto (1993), and Margaret Urban Walker (1987, 1989, 1991, 1992).

4. There also appear to be convergences between the ethics of care and some non-Western moral thought. For instance, a recent article likens the ethics of care to the Confucian ethics of *Jen* (Chenyang Li 1994).

5. Contemporary feminist claims that women's morality is different from men's were foreshadowed in theories developing the neo-Marxist notion of a feminist standpoint (Smith 1974; Hartsock 1983), but the claims became best known in their psychological versions, through the work of Jean Baker Miller (1976), Nancy Chodorow (1978) and especially Carol Gilligan. In two influential articles published in the late 1970s in the *Harvard Educational Review*, followed by her landmark book, *In a Different Voice*, Gilligan argued that most accepted accounts of moral development were male biased not simply in focusing primarily on males but, more seriously, in measuring the development of both males and females by a standard derived exclusively from the study of men and boys (Gilligan 1982). Reflecting on the responses of girls and women interviewed initially about their abortion decisions, Gilligan claimed to hear "a different voice" expressing an understanding of morality that she called the ethics of care. She argued that this understanding contrasted in significant ways with what she called the ethics of justice assumed by her teacher and mentor Lawrence Kohlberg, whose own studies of moral development had drawn on the Kantian conception of morality embodied in the work of Jean Piaget and John Rawls.

6. Some suffragists argued for the vote on grounds that women's moral superiority would encourage cleaning up politics, and the "moral mothers" in Britain and the United States drew on cultural myths of women's innate peacefulness to oppose World War I. Contemporary feminist peace and environmental activists have sometimes portrayed their political work as a kind of global housekeeping.

7. The Chinese word *teng* may mean "pain," "care," or a conflation of both, as in the proverb that translates as "Beating is caring, scolding is loving" (Blake 1994).

REFERENCES

Baier, Annette C. 1987a. "The Need for More than Justice." *Science, Morality and Feminist Theory*, edited by Marsha Hanen and Kai Nielsen. Calgary, Canada: University of Calgary Press (*Canadian Journal of Philosophy*, Supplementary Volume 13).

————. 1987b. "Hume, the Women's Moral Theorist?" In *Women and Moral Theory*, edited by Eva Feder Kittay and Diana T. Meyers. Totowa, NJ: Rowman and Littlefield.

————. 1994. *Moral Prejudices: Essays on Ethics*. Cambridge, MA: Harvard University Press.

Baron, Marcia. 1984. "The Alleged Moral Repugnance of Acting from Duty." *Journal of Philosophy* 81:4 (April), 197–220.

Benhabib, Seyla. 1986. "The Generalized and the Concrete Other: The Kohlberg-Gilligan Controversy and Feminist Theory." *Praxis International* 5:4 (January), 402–424.

———. 1992. *Situating the Self: Gender, Community and Postmodernism in Contemporary Ethics.* New York: Routledge.

Blake, C. Fred. 1994. "Footbinding in Neo-Confucian China and the Appropriation of Female Labor." *Signs: Journal of Women in Culture and Society* 19:3 (Spring).

Blum, Lawrence. 1982. "Kant's and Hegel's Moral Rationalism: A Feminist Perspective." *Canadian Journal of Philosophy* 12:2 (June), 287–302.

———. 1987. "Particularity and Responsiveness." *The Emergence of Morality in Young Children*, edited by Jerome Kagan and Sharon Lamb. Chicago: University of Chicago Press.

———. 1988. "Gilligan and Kohlberg: Implications for Moral Theory." *Ethics* 98 (April), 472–491.

———. 1991. "Moral Perception and Particularity." *Ethics* 101:4 (July), 701–725.

———. 1992. "Care." In *Encyclopedia of Ethics*, edited by Lawrence C. Becker. New York: Garland.

Calhoun, Cheshire. 1988. "Justice, Care, Gender Bias." *Journal of Philosophy* 85:9 (September).

Card, Claudia. 1990. "Gender and Moral Luck." In *Identity, Character and Morality*, edited by Owen Flanagan and Amelie Oksenberg Rorty. Cambridge, MA: MIT Press.

Chodorow, Nancy. 1978. *The Reproduction of Mothering: Psychoanalysis and the Sociology of Gender.* Berkeley: University of California Press.

Code, Lorraine. 1992."Who Cares? The Poverty of Objectivism for a Moral Epistemology." *The Annals of Scholarship* 9:1–2, 1–17.

Coole, Diana. 1988. *Women in Political Theory: From Ancient Misogyny to Contemporary Feminism.* Brighton, UK, and Boulder, CO: Wheatsheaf and Lynne Rienner.

Dillon, Robin S. 1992. "Care and Respect." In *Explorations in Feminist Ethics: Theory and Practice*, edited by Eve Browning Cole and Susan Coultrap McQuin. Bloomington and Indianapolis: Indiana University Press.

Fisher, Berenice. 1980. "Who Needs Woman Heroes?" *Heresies* 3:1 (issue 9).

Flanagan, Owen, and Kathryn Jackson. 1987. "Justice, Care and Gender: The Kohlberg-Gilligan Debate Revisited." *Ethics* 97, 622–637.

Freud, Sigmund. 1933. "Femininity." In *New Introductory Lectures on Psychoanalysis*, translated from the German and edited by James Strachey. New York: W. W. Norton.

Friedman, Marilyn. 1993. *What Are Friends For? Feminist Perspectives on Personal Relationships and Moral Theory.* Ithaca: Cornell University Press.

Gilligan, Carol. 1982. *In a Different Voice: Psychological Theory and Women's Development*. Cambridge, MA: Harvard University Press.

———. 1987. "Moral Orientation and Moral Development." In *Women and Moral Theory*, edited by Eva Feder Kittay and Diana T. Meyers. Totowa, NJ: Rowman and Littlefield.

Habermas, Jürgen. 1990. "Moral Consciousness and Communicative Action." In *Moral Consciousness and Communicative Action*, translated by Christian Lenhardt and Shierry Weber Nicholsen. Boston: MIT Press, pp. 178–180.

Hacking, Ian. 1985. "Styles of Scientific Reasoning." In *Post-Analytic Philosophy*, edited by John Rajchman and Cornel West. New York: Columbia University Press.

Harding, Sandra. 1987. "The Curious Coincidence of Feminine and African Moralities: Challenges in Feminist Theory." In *Women and Moral Theory*, edited by Eva Feder Kittay and Diana T. Meyers. Totowa, NJ: Rowman and Littlefield.

Hartsock, Nancy. 1983. *Money, Sex and Power: Toward a Feminist Historical Materialism*. New York: Longman.

Held, Virginia. 1993. *Feminist Morality: Transforming Culture, Society and Politics*. Chicago: University of Chicago Press.

Herman, Barbara. 1983. "Integrity and Impartiality." *Monist* 66, 233–250.

Hoagland, Sarah Lucia. 1991. "Some Thoughts About 'Caring.'" In *Feminist Ethics*, edited by Claudia Card. Lawrence: University of Kansas Press.

Houston, Barbara. 1988. "Gilligan and the Politics of a Distinctive Women's Morality." In *Feminist Perspectives: Philosophical Essays on Method and Morals*, edited by Lorraine Code, Sheila Mullett, and Christine Overall. Toronto: University of Toronto Press.

Kant, Immanuel. 1965. *Critique of Pure Reason*, translated by L. W. Beck. New York: St. Martin's Press, p. 177:A133–A134.

Kohlberg, Lawrence. 1982. "A Reply to Owen Flanagan." *Ethics* 92, 513–528.

Kohlberg, Lawrence, Charles Levine, and Alexandra Hewer. 1983. *Moral Stages: A Current Reformulation and Response to Critics*. Basel: S. Karger.

Li, Chenyang. 1994. "The Confucian Concept of *Jen* and the Feminist Ethics of Care: A Comparative Study." *Hypatia* 9:1 (Winter), 70–89.

Mill, John Stuart. 1980. *The Subjection of Women*. Arlington Heights, IL: Harlan Davidson. Originally published in 1869.

Miller, Jean Baker. 1976. *Toward a New Psychology of Women*. Boston: Beacon Press.

Noddings, Nel. 1984. *Caring: A Feminine Approach to Ethics and Moral Education*. Berkeley: University of California Press.

———. 1989. *Women and Evil*. Berkeley: University of California Press.

———. 1990a. "Feminist Fears in Ethics." *Journal of Social Philosophy* 21:2–3 (Fall-Winter), 25–33.

———. 1990b. "A Response." *Hypatia* 5:1 (Spring).

————. 1991. "The Alleged Parochialism of Caring." *American Philosophical Association Newsletter on Feminism and Philosophy* 90:2 (Winter).

Okin, Susan. 1989. "Reason and Feeling in Thinking About Justice." *Ethics* 99:2 (January), 229–249.

O'Neill, Onora. 1984. "Kant After Virtue." *Inquiry* 26, 387–405.

Ruddick, Sara. 1987. "Remarks on the Sexual Politics of Reason." In *Women and Moral Theory*, edited by Eva Feder Kittay and Diana T. Meyers. Totowa, NJ: Rowman and Littlefield.

————. 1989. *Maternal Thinking: Towards a Politics of Peace.* Boston: Beacon Press.

Sandel, Michael. 1982. *Liberalism and the Limits of Justice.* Cambridge: Cambridge University Press.

Sher, George. 1987. "Other Voices, Other Rooms? Women's Psychology and Moral Theory." In *Women and Moral Theory*, edited by Eva Feder Kittay and Diana T. Meyers. Totowa, NJ: Rowman and Littlefield.

Smith, Dorothy. 1974. "Women's Perspective as a Radical Critique of Sociology." *Sociological Inquiry* 44.

Stack, Carol. 1986. "The Culture of Gender: Women and Men of Color." *Signs: Journal of Women in Culture and Society* 11:2 (Winter), 321–324.

Tronto, Joan. 1989. "Women and Caring: What Can Feminists Learn About Morality from Caring?" In *Gender/Body/Knowledge: Feminist Reconstructions of Being and Knowing*, edited by Alison M. Jaggar and Susan R. Bordo. New Brunswick, NJ: Rutgers University Press.

————. 1993. *Moral Boundaries: A Political Argument for the Ethics of Care.* New York: Routledge.

Walker, Lawrence J. 1984. "Sex Differences in the Development of Moral Reasoning." *Child Development* 55:3, 677–691.

Walker, Margaret Urban. 1987. "Moral Particularity." *Metaphilosophy* 18:3–4 (July-October).

————. 1989. "What Does the Different Voice Say? Gilligan's Women and Moral Philosophy." *Journal of Value Inquiry* 23, 123–134.

————. 1991. "Partial Consideration." *Ethics* 101:4 (July), 758–774.

————. 1992. "Moral Understandings: Alternative 'Epistemology' for a Feminist Ethics." In *Explorations in Feminist Ethics: Theory and Practice*, edited by Eve Browning Cole and Susan Coultrap McQuin. Bloomington and Indianapolis: Indiana University Press.

BULLYING AND THE PHOEBE PRINCE CASE
Wendy Kaminer

Two months ago, 15-year old Phoebe Prince hanged herself. Prince, a freshman at South Hadley High School in western Massachusetts, was widely acknowledged to have been a victim of bullying, and her suicide helped jolt the state legislature into passing stringent anti-bullying bills. Now, nine teenagers implicated in tormenting Prince are facing criminal charges, including criminal harassment, stalking, and statutory rape. District attorney Elizabeth Scheibel described Prince as the target of a "nearly three month campaign of verbally assaultive behavior and threats of physical violence . . . It appears that (her) death on January 14th followed a tortuous day for her, in which she was subjected to verbal harassment and threatened physical abuse."

Do these charges vindicate anti-bullying legislation? Not necessarily. If the prosecution of Prince's alleged tormenters is merited, it suggests that laws against bullying may be redundant, at best. At worst, (and often) anti-bullying regulation is overboard, exerting control over students outside of school and infringing unduly on speech, especially when it addresses cyber-bullying. The rash of recent cases targeting student online speech (especially speech critical of administrators), the use of child porn laws to prosecute teens for sexting, and the scandalous use of webcams to spy on students at home should make us skeptical of legislation aimed at curbing verbal "abuses." Unprecedented freedom to speak and opportunities to disseminate speech (for better and worse) have naturally resulted in some harsh crackdowns on speech.

This does not mean that school administrators should only respond to bullying that is so severe, willful, and prolonged that it constitutes criminal harassment or stalking; but it may mean that unless bullying does constitute a criminal offense, it is not the business of legislators. Or is it? Advocates of anti-bullying laws will argue that school officials may ignore abusive behavior by students if they are not required by law to address and even report it. Some teachers and administrators at South Hadley High School knew that Phoebe Prince was being harassed and did nothing to protect her, District Attorney Scheibel reported, calling official inaction "troublesome" (but not criminal).

But school officials who ignore obvious and extreme abuse of one student by small gang of teenage vipers are probably unfit to serve in schools; it's not clear that the problem of incompetent or grossly negligent officials can be solved with legislation. Focusing on cyber-bullying, in particular, may even distract administrators from addressing actual harassment and stalking of the sort allegedly suffered by Prince. It can also provide an excuse for inaction. South Hadley School Superintendent Gus A. Sayer initially tried blaming

40   Prince's suicide on cyber-bullying: "The real problem now is the texting stuff and the cyber-bullying," he told The Boston Globe, back in January. "Some kids can be very mean towards one another using that medium." Sayer has, so far, declined to comment on the criminal charges, but the Huffington Post seized on his previous statement in its report today (March 29th) on the Prince case: "Cyberbullies Charged with Harassing Phoebe Prince, Teen Who Killed Herself After Rape," its headline sensationally and inaccurately declares. As District Attorney Scheibel stressed (in a widely reported remark), the campaign against Phoebe Prince was "primarily conducted on school

50   grounds during school hours and while school was in session." Old-fashioned, in person harassment and stalking—not cyberbullying—allegedly drove Prince to suicide, and, if these allegations are true, then old-fashioned criminal laws can bring her abusers to justice.

LETTER FROM BIRMINGHAM JAIL
Martin Luther King, Jr.

April 16, 1963   1
MY DEAR FELLOW CLERGYMEN:

While confined here in the Birmingham city jail, I came across your recent statement calling my present activities "unwise and untimely." Seldom do I pause to answer criticism of my work and ideas. If I sought to answer all the criticisms that cross my desk, my secretaries would have little time for anything other than such correspondence in the course of the day, and I would have no time for constructive work. But since I feel that you are men of genuine good will and that your criticisms are sincerely set forth, I want to try to answer your statements in what I hope will be patient and rea-   10
sonable terms.

I think I should indicate why I am here In Birmingham, since you have been influenced by the view which argues against "outsiders coming in." I have the honor of serving as president of the Southern Christian Leadership Conference, an organization operating in every southern state, with headquarters in Atlanta, Georgia. We have some eighty-five affiliated organizations across the South, and one of them is the Alabama Christian Movement for Human Rights. Frequently we share staff, educational and financial resources with our affiliates. Several months ago the affiliate here in Birmingham asked us to be on call to engage in a nonviolent direct-action pro-   20
gram if such were deemed necessary. We readily consented, and when the hour came we lived up to our promise. So I, along with several members of my staff, am here because I was invited here. I am here because I have organizational ties here.

But more basically, I am in Birmingham because injustice is here. Just as the prophets of the eighth century B.C. left their villages and carried their "thus saith the Lord" far beyond the boundaries of their home towns, and just as the Apostle Paul left his village of Tarsus and carried the gospel of Jesus Christ to the far corners of the Greco-Roman world, so am I compelled to carry the gospel of freedom beyond my own home town. Like Paul, I must   30
constantly respond to the Macedonian call for aid.

Moreover, I am cognizant of the interrelatedness of all communities and states. I cannot sit idly by in Atlanta and not be concerned about what happens in Birmingham. Injustice anywhere is a threat to justice everywhere. We are caught in an inescapable network of mutuality, tied in a single garment of destiny. Whatever affects one directly, affects all indirectly. Never again can we afford to live with the narrow, provincial "outside agitator" idea. Anyone who lives inside the United States can never be considered an outsider anywhere within its bounds.

Reprinted by permission of Writers House, April 16, 1963.

① Collection of facts.
② Negotiation
③ Self-purification
④ Direct action

40   You deplore the demonstrations taking place in Birmingham. But your statement, I am sorry to say, fails to express a similar concern for the conditions that brought about the demonstrations. I am sure that none of you would want to rest content with the superficial kind of social analysis that deals merely with effects and does not grapple with underlying causes. It is unfortunate that demonstrations are taking place in Birmingham, but it is even more unfortunate that the city's white power structure left the Negro community with no alternative.

In any nonviolent campaign there are four basic steps: collection of the facts to determine whether injustices exist; negotiation; self-purification; and 50 direct action. We have gone through all these steps in Birmingham. There can be no gainsaying the fact that racial injustice engulfs this community. Birmingham is probably the most thoroughly segregated city in the United States. Its ugly record of brutality is widely known. Negroes have experienced grossly unjust treatment in the courts. There have been more unsolved bombings of Negro homes and churches in Birmingham than in any other city in the nation. These are the hard, brutal facts of the case. On the basis of these conditions, Negro leaders sought to negotiate with the city fathers. But the latter consistently refused to engage in good-faith negotiation.

Then, last September, came the opportunity to talk with leaders of Birm-60 ingham's economic community. In the course of the negotiations, certain promises were made by the merchants—for example, to remove the stores' humiliating racial signs. On the basis of these promises, the Reverend Fred Shuttlesworth and the leaders of the Alabama Christian Movement for Human Rights agreed to a moratorium on all demonstrations. As the weeks and months went by, we realized that we were the victims of a broken promise. A few signs, briefly removed, returned; the others remained.

As in so many past experiences, our hopes had been blasted, and the shadow of deep disappointment settled upon us. We had no alternative except to prepare for direct action, whereby we would present our very bod-70 ies as a means of laying our case before the conscience of the local and the national community. Mindful of the difficulties involved, we decided to undertake a process of self-purification. We began a series of workshops on nonviolence, and we repeatedly asked ourselves: "Are you able to accept blows without retaliating?" "Are you able to endure the ordeal of jail?" We decided to schedule our direct-action program for the Easter season, realizing that except for Christmas, this is the main shopping period of the year. Knowing that a strong economic withdrawal program would be the by-product of direct action, we felt that this would be the best time to bring pressure to bear on the merchants for the needed change.

80   Then it occurred to us that Birmingham's mayoralty election was coming up in March, and we speedily decided to postpone action until after election day. When we discovered that the Commissioner of Public Safety, Eugene "Bull" Connor, had piled up enough votes to be in the run-off we decided again to postpone action until the day after the run-off so that the demon-

strations could not be used to cloud the issues. Like many others, we waited to see Mr. Connor defeated, and to this end we endured postponement after postponement. Having aided in this community need, we felt that our direct-action program could be delayed no longer.

You may well ask: "Why direct action? Why sit-ins, marches and so forth? Isn't negotiation a better path?" You are quite right in calling for negotiation. Indeed, this is the very purpose of direct action. Nonviolent direct action seeks to create such a crisis and foster such a tension that a community which has constantly refused to negotiate is forced to confront the issue. It seeks so to dramatize the issue that it can no longer be ignored. My citing the creation of tension as part of the work of the nonviolent-resister may sound rather shocking. But I must confess that I am not afraid of the word "tension." I have earnestly opposed violent tension, but there is a type of constructive, nonviolent tension which is necessary for growth. Just as Socrates felt that it was necessary to create a tension in the mind so that individuals could rise from the bondage of myths and half-truths to the unfettered realm of creative analysis and objective appraisal, so must we see the need for nonviolent gad-flies to create the kind of tension in society that will help men rise from the dark depths of prejudice and racism to the majestic heights of understanding and brotherhood.

The purpose of our direct-action program is to create a situation so crisis-packed that it will inevitably open the door to negotiation. I therefore concur with you in your call for negotiation. Too long has our beloved Southland been bogged down in a tragic effort to live in monologue rather than dialogue.

One of the basic points in your statement is that the action that I and my associates have taken in Birmingham is untimely. Some have asked: "Why didn't you give the new city administration time to act?" The only answer that I can give to this query is that the new Birmingham administration must be prodded about as much as the outgoing one, before it will act. We are sadly mistaken if we feel that the election of Albert Boutwell as mayor will bring the millennium to Birmingham. While Mr. Boutwell is a much more gentle person than Mr. Connor, they are both segregationists, dedicated to maintenance of the status quo. I have hope that Mr. Boutwell will be reasonable enough to see the futility of massive resistance to desegregation. But he will not see this without pressure from devotees of civil rights. My friends, I must say to you that we have not made a single gain in civil rights without determined legal and nonviolent pressure. Lamentably, it is an historical fact that privileged groups seldom give up their privileges voluntarily. Individuals may see the moral light and voluntarily give up their unjust posture; but, as Reinhold Niebuhr has reminded us, groups tend to be more immoral than individuals.

We know through painful experience that freedom is never voluntarily given by the oppressor; it must be demanded by the oppressed. Frankly, I have yet to engage in a direct-action campaign that was "well timed" in the

130   view of those who have not suffered unduly from the disease of segregation. For years now I have heard the word "Wait!" It rings in the ear of every Negro with piercing familiarity. This "Wait" has almost always meant "Never." We must come to see, with one of our distinguished jurists, that "justice too long delayed is justice denied."

      We have waited for more than 340 years for our constitutional and God-given rights. The nations of Asia and Africa are moving with jetlike speed toward gaining political independence, but we still creep at horse-and-buggy pace toward gaining a cup of coffee at a lunch counter. Perhaps it is easy for those who have never felt the stinging dark of segregation to say, "Wait." But

140   when you have seen vicious mobs lynch your mothers and fathers at will and drown your sisters and brothers at whim; when you have seen hate-filled policemen curse, kick and even kill your black brothers and sisters; when you see the vast majority of your twenty million Negro brothers smothering in an airtight cage of poverty in the midst of an affluent society; when you suddenly find your tongue twisted and your speech stammering as you seek to explain to your six-year-old daughter why she can't go to the public amusement park that has just been advertised on television, and see tears welling up in her eyes when she is told that Funtown is closed to colored children, and see ominous clouds of inferiority beginning to form in her little mental

150   sky, and see her beginning to distort her personality by developing an unconscious bitterness toward white people; when you have to concoct an answer for a five-year-old son who is asking: "Daddy, why do white people treat colored people so mean?"; when you take a cross-county drive and find it necessary to sleep night after night in the uncomfortable corners of your automobile because no motel will accept you; when you are humiliated day in and day out by nagging signs reading "white" and "colored"; when your first name becomes "nigger," your middle name becomes "boy" (however old you are) and your last name becomes "John," and your wife and mother are never given the respected title "Mrs."; when you are harried by day and haunted by

160   night by the fact that you are a Negro, living constantly at tiptoe stance, never quite knowing what to expect next, and are plagued with inner fears and outer resentments; when you are forever fighting a degenerating sense of "nobodiness" then you will understand why we find it difficult to wait. There comes a time when the cup of endurance runs over, and men are no longer willing to be plunged into the abyss of despair. I hope, sirs, you can understand our legitimate and unavoidable impatience.

      You express a great deal of anxiety over our willingness to break laws. This is certainly a legitimate concern. Since we so diligently urge people to obey the Supreme Court's decision of 1954 outlawing segregation in the public

170   schools, at first glance it may seem rather paradoxical for us consciously to break laws. One may well ask: "How can you advocate breaking some laws and obeying others?" The answer lies in the fact that there are two types of laws: just and unjust. I would be the first to advocate obeying just laws. One has not only a legal but a moral responsibility to obey just laws. Conversely,

one has a moral responsibility to disobey unjust laws. I would agree with St. Augustine that "an unjust law is no law at all."

Now, what is the difference between the two? How does one determine whether a law is just or unjust? A just law is a man-made code that squares with the moral law or the law of God. An unjust law is a code that is out of harmony with the moral law. To put it in the terms of St. Thomas Aquinas: An unjust law is a human law that is not rooted in eternal law and natural law. Any law that uplifts human personality is just. Any law that degrades human personality is unjust. All segregation statutes are unjust because segregation distorts the soul and damages the personality. It gives the segregator a false sense of superiority and the segregated a false sense of inferiority. Segregation, to use the terminology of the Jewish philosopher Martin Buber, substitutes an "I-it" relationship for an "I-thou" relationship and ends up relegating persons to the status of things. Hence segregation is not only politically, economically and sociologically unsound, it is morally wrong and awful. Paul Tillich said that sin is separation. Is not segregation an existential expression of man's tragic separation, his awful estrangement, his terrible sinfulness? Thus it is that I can urge men to obey the 1954 decision of the Supreme Court, for it is morally right; and I can urge them to disobey segregation ordinances, for they are morally wrong.

Let us consider a more concrete example of just and unjust laws. An unjust law is a code that a numerical or power majority group compels a minority group to obey but does not make binding on itself. This is difference made legal. By the same token, a just law is a code that a majority compels a minority to follow and that it is willing to follow itself. This is sameness made legal.

Let me give another explanation. A law is unjust if it is inflicted on a minority that, as a result of being denied the right to vote, had no part in enacting or devising the law. Who can say that the legislature of Alabama which set up that state's segregation laws was democratically elected? Throughout Alabama all sorts of devious methods are used to prevent Negroes from becoming registered voters, and there are some counties in which, even though Negroes constitute a majority of the population, not a single Negro is registered. Can any law enacted under such circumstances be considered democratically structured?

Sometimes a law is just on its face and unjust in its application. For instance, I have been arrested on a charge of parading without a permit. Now, there is nothing wrong in having an ordinance which requires a permit for a parade. But such an ordinance becomes unjust when it is used to maintain segregation and to deny citizens the First Amendment privilege of peaceful assembly and protest.

I hope you are able to see the distinction I am trying to point out. In no sense do I advocate evading or defying the law, as would the rabid segregationist. That would lead to anarchy. One who breaks an unjust law must do so openly, lovingly, and with a willingness to accept the penalty. I submit that an individual who breaks a law that conscience tells him is unjust and who

220 willingly accepts the penalty of imprisonment in order to arouse the conscience of the community over its injustice, is in reality expressing the highest respect for law.

Of course, there is nothing new about this kind of civil disobedience. It was evidenced sublimely in the refusal of Shadrach, Meshach and Abednego to obey the laws of Nebuchadnezzar, on the ground that a higher moral law was at stake. It was practiced superbly by the early Christians, who were willing to face hungry lions and the excruciating pain of chopping blocks rather than submit to certain unjust laws of the Roman Empire. To a degree, academic freedom is a reality today because Socrates practiced civil disobedi-
230 ence. In our own nation, the Boston Tea Party represented a massive act of civil disobedience.

We should never forget that everything Adolf Hitler did in Germany was "legal" and everything the Hungarian freedom fighters did in Hungary was "illegal." It was "illegal" to aid and comfort a Jew in Hitler's Germany. Even so, I am sure that, had I lived in Germany at the time, I would have aided and comforted my Jewish brothers. If today I lived in a Communist country where certain principles dear to the Christian faith are suppressed, I would openly advocate disobeying that country's antireligious laws.

I must make two honest confessions to you, my Christian and Jewish
240 brothers. First, I must confess that over the past few years I have been gravely disappointed with the white moderate. I have almost reached the regrettable conclusion that the Negro's great stumbling block in his stride toward freedom is not the White Citizen's Councilor or the Ku Klux Klanner, but the white moderate, who is more devoted to "order" than to justice; who prefers a negative peace which is the absence of tension to a positive peace which is the presence of justice; who constantly says "I agree with you in the goal you seek, but I cannot agree with your methods of direct action"; who paternalistically believes he can set the timetable for another man's freedom; who lives by a mythical concept of time and who constantly advises the Negro to wait for a
250 "more convenient season." Shallow understanding from people of good will is more frustrating than absolute misunderstanding from people of ill will. Lukewarm acceptance is much more bewildering than outright rejection.

I had hoped that the white moderate would understand that law and order exist for the purpose of establishing justice and that when they fail in this purpose they become the dangerously structured dams that block the flow of social progress. I had hoped that the white moderate would understand that the present tension in the South is a necessary phase of the transition from an obnoxious negative peace, in which the Negro passively accepted his unjust plight, to a substantive and positive peace, in which all
260 men will respect the dignity and worth of human personality. Actually, we who engage in nonviolent direct action are not the creators of tension. We merely bring to the surface the hidden tension that is already alive. We bring it out in the open, where it can be seen and dealt with. Like a boil that can never be cured so long as it is covered up but must be opened with all its ugli-

ness to the natural medicines of air and light, injustice must be exposed, with all the tension its exposure creates, to the light of human conscience and the air of national opinion before it can be cured.

In your statement you assert that our actions, even though peaceful, must be condemned because they precipitate violence. But is this a logical assertion? Isn't this like condemning a robbed man because his possession of money precipitated the evil act of robbery? Isn't this like condemning Socrates because his unswerving commitment to truth and his philosophical inquiries precipitated the act by the misguided populace in which they made him drink hemlock? Isn't this like condemning Jesus because his unique God-consciousness and never-ceasing devotion to God's will precipitated the evil act of crucifixion? We must come to see that, as the federal courts have consistently affirmed, it is wrong to urge an individual to cease his efforts to gain his basic constitutional rights because the quest may precipitate violence. Society must protect the robbed and punish the robber.

I had also hoped that the white moderate would reject the myth concerning time in relation to the struggle for freedom. I have just received a letter from a white brother in Texas. He writes: "All Christians know that the colored people will receive equal rights eventually, but it is possible that you are in too great a religious hurry. It has taken Christianity almost two thousand years to accomplish what it has. The teachings of Christ take time to come to earth." Such an attitude stems from a tragic misconception of time, from the strangely rational notion that there is something in the very flow of time that will inevitably cure all ills. Actually, time itself is neutral; it can be used either destructively or constructively. More and more I feel that the people of ill will have used time much more effectively than have the people of good will. We will have to repent in this generation not merely for the hateful words and actions of the bad people but for the appalling silence of the good people. Human progress never rolls in on wheels of inevitability; it comes through the tireless efforts of men willing to be co-workers with God, and without this hard work, time itself becomes an ally of the forces of social stagnation. We must use time creatively, in the knowledge that the time is always ripe to do right. Now is the time to make real the promise of democracy and transform our pending national elegy into a creative psalm of brotherhood. Now is the time to lift our national policy from the quicksand of racial injustice to the solid rock of human dignity.

You speak of our activity in Birmingham as extreme. At first I was rather disappointed that fellow clergymen would see my nonviolent efforts as those of an extremist. I began thinking about the fact that I stand in the middle of two opposing forces in the Negro community. One is a force of complacency, made up in part of Negroes who, as a result of long years of oppression, are so drained of self-respect and a sense of "somebodiness" that they have adjusted to segregation; and in part of a few middle class Negroes who, because of a degree of academic and economic security and because in some ways they profit by segregation, have become insensitive to the problems of

[handwritten margin notes: "Bystanding", "time + stagnation"]

310   the masses. The other force is one of bitterness and hatred, and it comes perilously close to advocating violence. It is expressed in the various black nationalist groups that are springing up across the nation, the largest and best-known being Elijah Muhammad's Muslim movement. Nourished by the Negro's frustration over the continued existence of racial discrimination, this movement is made up of people who have lost faith in America, who have absolutely repudiated Christianity, and who have concluded that the white man is an incorrigible "devil."

I have tried to stand between these two forces, saying that we need emulate neither the "do-nothingism" of the complacent nor the hatred and

320   despair of the black nationalist. For there is the more excellent way of love and nonviolent protest. I am grateful to God that, through the influence of the Negro church, the way of nonviolence became an integral part of our struggle.

If this philosophy had not emerged, by now many streets of the South would, I am convinced, be flowing with blood. And I am further convinced that if our white brothers dismiss as "rabble-rousers" and "outside agitators" those of us who employ nonviolent direct action, and if they refuse to support our nonviolent efforts, millions of Negroes will, out of frustration and despair, seek solace and security in black-nationalist ideologies a development

330   that would inevitably lead to a frightening racial nightmare.

Oppressed people cannot remain oppressed forever. The yearning for freedom eventually manifests itself, and that is what has happened to the American Negro. Something within has reminded him of his birthright of freedom, and something without has reminded him that it can be gained. Consciously or unconsciously, he has been caught up by the Zeitgeist, and with his black brothers of Africa and his brown and yellow brothers of Asia, South America and the Caribbean, the United States Negro is moving with a sense of great urgency toward the promised land of racial justice. If one recognizes this vital urge that has engulfed the Negro community, one should

340   readily understand why public demonstrations are taking place. The Negro has many pent-up resentments and latent frustrations, and he must release them. So let him march; let him make prayer pilgrimages to the city hall; let him go on freedom rides—and try to understand why he must do so. If his repressed emotions are not released in nonviolent ways, they will seek expression through violence; this is not a threat but a fact of history. So I have not said to my people: "Get rid of your discontent." Rather, I have tried to say that this normal and healthy discontent can be channeled into the creative outlet of nonviolent direct action. And now this approach is being termed extremist.

350   But though I was initially disappointed at being categorized as an extremist, as I continued to think about the matter I gradually gained a measure of satisfaction from the label. Was not Jesus an extremist for love: "Love your enemies, bless them that curse you, do good to them that hate you, and pray for them which despitefully use you, and persecute you." Was not Amos an

extremist for justice: "Let justice roll down like waters and righteousness like an ever-flowing stream." Was not Paul an extremist for the Christian gospel: "I bear in my body the marks of the Lord Jesus." Was not Martin Luther an extremist: "Here I stand; I cannot do otherwise, so help me God." And John Bunyan: "I will stay in jail to the end of my days before I make a butchery of my conscience." And Abraham Lincoln: "This nation cannot survive half slave and half free." And Thomas Jefferson: "We hold these truths to be self-evident, that all men are created equal . . ." So the question is not whether we will be extremists, but what kind of extremists we will be. Will we be extremists for hate or for love? Will we be extremist for the preservation of injustice or for the extension of justice? In that dramatic scene on Calvary's hill three men were crucified. We must never forget that all three were crucified for the same crime—the crime of extremism. Two were extremists for immorality, and thus fell below their environment. The other, Jesus Christ, was an extremist for love, truth and goodness, and thereby rose above his environment. Perhaps the South, the nation and the world are in dire need of creative extremists. 370

I had hoped that the white moderate would see this need. Perhaps I was too optimistic; perhaps I expected too much. I suppose I should have realized that few members of the oppressor race can understand the deep groans and passionate yearnings of the oppressed race, and still fewer have the vision to see that injustice must be rooted out by strong, persistent and determined action. I am thankful, however, that some of our white brothers in the South have grasped the meaning of this social revolution and committed themselves to it. They are still too few in quantity, but they are big in quality. Some—such as Ralph McGill, Lillian Smith, Harry Golden, James McBride Dabbs, Ann Braden and Sarah Patton Boyle—have written about our struggle in elo- 380 quent and prophetic terms. Others have marched with us down nameless streets of the South. They have languished in filthy, roach-infested jails, suffering the abuse and brutality of policemen who view them as "dirty nigger lovers." Unlike so many of their moderate brothers and sisters, they have recognized the urgency of the moment and sensed the need for powerful "action" antidotes to combat the disease of segregation.

Let me take note of my other major disappointment. I have been so greatly disappointed with the white church and its leadership. Of course, there are some notable exceptions. I am not unmindful of the fact that each of you has taken some significant stands on this issue. I commend you, Reverend 390 Stallings, for your Christian stand on this past Sunday, in welcoming Negroes to your worship service on a non-segregated basis. I commend the Catholic leaders of this state for integrating Spring Hill College several years ago.

But despite these notable exceptions, I must honestly reiterate that I have been disappointed with the church. I do not say this as one of those negative critics who can always find something wrong with the church. I say this as a minister of the gospel, who loves the church; who was nurtured in its bosom; who has been sustained by its spiritual blessings and who will remain true to it as long as the cord of life shall lengthen.

400   When I was suddenly catapulted into the leadership of the bus protest in Montgomery, Alabama, a few years ago, I felt we would be supported by the white church. I felt that the white ministers, priests and rabbis of the South would be among our strongest allies. Instead, some have been outright opponents, refusing to understand the freedom movement and misrepresenting its leaders all too many others have been more cautious than courageous and have remained silent behind the anesthetizing security of stained-glass windows.

In spite of my shattered dreams, I came to Birmingham with the hope that the white religious leadership of this community would see the justice of our cause and, with deep moral concern, would serve as the channel through which our just grievances could reach the power structure. I had hoped that

410   each of you would understand. But again I have been disappointed.

I have heard numerous southern religious leaders admonish their worshipers to comply with a desegregation decision because it is the law, but I have longed to hear white ministers declare: "Follow this decree because integration is morally right and because the Negro is your brother." In the midst of blatant injustices inflicted upon the Negro, I have watched white churchmen stand on the sideline and mouth pious irrelevancies and sanctimonious trivialities. In the midst of a mighty struggle to rid our nation of racial and economic injustice, I have heard many ministers say: "Those are social issues,

420   with which the gospel has no real concern." And I have watched many churches commit themselves to a completely other worldly religion which makes a strange, un-Biblical distinction between body and soul, between the sacred and the secular.

I have traveled the length and breadth of Alabama, Mississippi and all the other southern states. On sweltering summer days and crisp autumn mornings I have looked at the South's beautiful churches with their lofty spires pointing heavenward. I have beheld the impressive outlines of her massive religious-education buildings. Over and over I have found myself asking: "What kind of people worship here? Who is their God? Where were their

430   voices when the lips of Governor Barnett dripped with words of interposition and nullification? Where were they when Governor Wallace gave a clarion call for defiance and hatred? Where were their voices of support when bruised and weary Negro men and women decided to rise from the dark dungeons of complacency to the bright hills of creative protest?"

Yes, these questions are still in my mind. In deep disappointment I have wept over the laxity of the church. But be assured that my tears have been tears of love. There can be no deep disappointment where there is not deep love. Yes, I love the church. How could I do otherwise? I am in the rather unique position of being the son, the grandson and the great-grandson of

440   preachers. Yes, I see the church as the body of Christ. But, oh! How we have blemished and scarred that body through social neglect and through fear of being nonconformists.

There was a time when the church was very powerful in the time when the early Christians rejoiced at being deemed worthy to suffer for what they believed. In those days the church was not merely a thermometer that recorded the ideas and principles of popular opinion; it was a thermostat that transformed the mores of society. Whenever the early Christians entered a town, the people in power became disturbed and immediately sought to convict the Christians for being "disturbers of the peace" and "outside agitators." But the Christians pressed on, in the conviction that they were "a colony of heaven," called to obey God rather than man. Small in number, they were big in commitment. They were too God intoxicated to be "astronomically intimidated." By their effort and example they brought an end to such ancient evils as infanticide, and gladiatorial contests.

Things are different now. So often the contemporary church is a weak, ineffectual voice with an uncertain sound. So often it is an archdefender of the status quo. Far from being disturbed by the presence of the church, the power structure of the average community is consoled by the church's silent and often even vocal sanction of things as they are.

But the judgment of God is upon the church as never before. If today's church does not recapture the sacrificial spirit of the early church, it will lose its authenticity, forfeit the loyalty of millions, and be dismissed as an irrelevant social club with no meaning for the twentieth century. Every day I meet young people whose disappointment with the church has turned into outright disgust.

Perhaps I have once again been too optimistic. Is organized religion too inextricably bound to the status quo to save our nation and the world? Perhaps I must turn my faith to the inner spiritual church, the church within the church, as the true ekklesia and the hope of the world. But again I am thankful to God that some noble souls from the ranks of organized religion have broken loose from the paralyzing chains of conformity and joined us as active partners in the struggle for freedom. They have left their secure congregations and walked the streets of Albany, Georgia, with us. They have gone down the highways of the South on tortuous rides for freedom. Yes, they have gone to jail with us. Some have been dismissed from their churches, have lost the support of their bishops and fellow ministers. But they have acted in the faith that right defeated is stronger than evil triumphant. Their witness has been the spiritual salt that has preserved the true meaning of the gospel in these troubled times. They have carved a tunnel of hope through the dark mountain of disappointment.

I hope the church as a whole will meet the challenge of this decisive hour. But even if the church does not come to the aid of justice, I have no despair about the future. I have no fear about the outcome of our struggle in Birmingham, even if our motives are at present misunderstood. We will reach the goal of freedom in Birmingham and all over the nation, because the goal of America is freedom. Abused and scorned though we may be, our destiny is tied up with America's destiny. Before the pilgrims landed at Plymouth, we were here. Before the pen of Jefferson etched the majestic words of the Declaration of Independence across the pages of history, we were here. For more

490 than two centuries our forebears labored in this country without wages; they made cotton king; they built the homes of their masters while suffering gross injustice and shameful humiliation—and yet out of a bottomless vitality they continued to thrive and develop. If the inexpressible cruelties of slavery could not stop us, the opposition we now face will surely fail. We will win our freedom because the sacred heritage of our nation and the eternal will of God are embodied in our echoing demands.

Before closing I feel impelled to mention one other point in your statement that has troubled me profoundly. You warmly commended the Birmingham police force for keeping "order" and "preventing violence." I doubt
500 that you would have so warmly commended the police force if you had seen its dogs sinking their teeth into unarmed, nonviolent Negroes. I doubt that you would so quickly commend the policemen if you were to observe their ugly and inhumane treatment of Negroes here in the city jail; if you were to watch them push and curse old Negro women and young Negro girls; if you were to see them slap and kick old Negro men and young boys; if you were to observe them, as they did on two occasions, refuse to give us food because we wanted to sing our grace together. I cannot join you in your praise of the Birmingham police department.

It is true that the police have exercised a degree of discipline in handling
510 the demonstrators. In this sense they have conducted themselves rather "nonviolently" in pubic. But for what purpose? To preserve the evil system of segregation. Over the past few years I have consistently preached that nonviolence demands that the means we use must be as pure as the ends we seek. I have tried to make clear that it is wrong to use immoral means to attain moral ends. But now I must affirm that it is just as wrong, or perhaps even more so, to use moral means to preserve immoral ends. Perhaps Mr. Connor and his policemen have been rather nonviolent in public, as was Chief Pritchett in Albany, Georgia but they have used the moral means of nonviolence to maintain the immoral end of racial injustice. As T. S. Eliot has said:
520 "The last temptation is the greatest treason: To do the right deed for the wrong reason."

I wish you had commended the Negro sit-inners and demonstrators of Birmingham for their sublime courage, their willingness to suffer and their amazing discipline in the midst of great provocation. One day the South will recognize its real heroes. They will be the James Merediths, with the noble sense of purpose that enables them to face jeering, and hostile mobs, and with the agonizing loneliness that characterizes the life of the pioneer. They will be old, oppressed, battered Negro women, symbolized in a seventy-two-year-old woman in Montgomery, Alabama, who rose up with a sense of dig-
530 nity and with her people decided not to ride segregated buses, and who responded with ungrammatical profundity to one who inquired about her weariness: "My feets is tired, but my soul is at rest." They will be the young high school and college students, the young ministers of the gospel and a host

of their elders, courageously and nonviolently sitting in at lunch counters and willingly going to jail for conscience' sake. One day the South will know that when these disinherited children of God sat down at lunch counters, they were in reality standing up for what is best in the American dream and for the most sacred values in our Judaeo-Christian heritage, thereby bringing our nation back to those great wells of democracy which were dug deep by the founding fathers in their formulation of the Constitution and the Declaration of Independence.   540

Never before have I written so long a letter. I'm afraid it is much too long to take your precious time. I can assure you that it would have been much shorter if I had been writing from a comfortable desk, but what else can one do when he is alone in a narrow jail cell, other than write long letters, think long thoughts and pray long prayers?

If I have said anything in this letter that overstates the truth and indicates an unreasonable impatience, I beg you to forgive me. If I have said anything that understates the truth and indicates my having a patience that allows me to settle for anything less than brotherhood, I beg God to forgive me.   550

I hope this letter finds you strong in the faith. I also hope that circumstances will soon make it possible for me to meet each of you, not as an integrationist or a civil rights leader but as a fellow clergyman and a Christian brother. Let us all hope that the dark clouds of racial prejudice will soon pass away and the deep fog of misunderstanding will be lifted from our fear-drenched communities, and in some not too distant tomorrow the radiant stars of love and brotherhood will shine over our great nation with all their scintillating beauty.

Yours for the cause of Peace and Brotherhood,

MARTIN LUTHER KING, JR.   560

1906-1995
Lithuanian-born
French Philosopher
and Talmudic commentator

THE FACE AND RESPONSIBILITY FOR THE OTHER
Emmanuel Levinas

[*Phillippe Nemo*]: In *Totality and Infinity* you speak at great length of the face. It is one of your frequent themes. What does this phenomenology of the face, that is, this analysis of what happens when I look at the Other face to face, consist in and what is its purpose?

[*Emmanuel Levinas*]: I do not know if one can speak of a "phenomenology" of the face, since phenomenology describes what appears. So, too, I wonder if one can speak of a look turned toward the face, for the look is knowledge, perception. I think rather that access to the face is straightaway ethical. You turn yourself toward the Other as toward an object when you see a nose, eyes, a forehead, a chin, and you can describe them. The best way of encountering the Other is not even to notice the color of his eyes! When one observes the color of the eyes one is not in social relationship with the Other. The relation with the face can surely be dominated by perception, but what is specifically the face is what cannot be reduced to that.

There is first the very uprightness of the face, its upright exposure, without defense. The skin of the face is that which stays most naked, most destitute. It is the most naked, though with a decent nudity. It is the most destitute also: there is an essential poverty in the face; the proof of this is that one tries to mask this poverty by putting on poses, by taking on a countenance. The face is exposed, menaced, as if inviting us to an act of violence. At the same time, the face is what forbids us to kill.

Ph.N.: War stories tell us in fact that it is difficult to kill someone who looks straight at you.

E.L.: The face is signification, and signification without a context. Other, in the rectitude of his face, is not a character within a context. Ordinarily one is a "character": a professor at the Sorbonne, a Supreme Court justice, son of so-and-so, everything that is in one's passport, the manner of dressing, of presenting oneself. And all signification in the usual sense of the term is relative to such a context: the meaning of something is in its relation to another thing. Here, to the contrary, the face is meaning all by itself. You are you. In this sense one can say that the face is not "seen". It is what cannot become a content, which your thought would embrace; it is uncontainable, it leads you beyond. It is in this that the signification of the face makes it escape from being, as a correlate of a knowing. Vision, to the contrary, is a search for adequation; it is what par excellence absorbs being. But the relation to the face is straightaway ethical. The face is what one cannot kill, or at least it is that whose *meaning* consists in saying: "thou shalt not kill." Murder, it is true, is a banal fact: one can kill the Other; the ethical exigency is not an ontological necessity. The prohibition against killing does not render murder impossible,

Reprinted from *Ethics and Infinity: Conversations with Phillipe Nemo* (1985), Duquesne University Press.

141

40 even if the authority of the prohibition is maintained in the bad conscience about the accomplished evil—malignancy of evil. It also appears in the Scriptures, to which the humanity of man is exposed inasmuch as it is engaged in the world. But to speak truly, the appearance in being of these "ethical peculiarities"—the humanity of man—is a rupture of being. It is significant, even if being resumes and recovers itself.

Ph.N.: The Other is face; but the Other, equally, speaks to me and I speak to him. Is not human discourse another way of breaking what you call "totality"?

50 *E.L.:* Certainly. Face and discourse are tied. The face speaks. It speaks, it is in this that it renders possible and begins all discourse. I have just refused the notion of vision to describe the authentic relationship with the Other; it is discourse and, more exactly, response or responsibility which is this authentic relationship.

Ph.N.: But since the ethical relationship is beyond knowledge, and, on the other hand, it is authentically assumed through discourse, it is thus that discourse itself is not something of the order of knowledge?

E.L.: In discourse I have always distinguished, in fact, between the *saying* and the *said.* That the *saying* must bear a *said* is a necessity of
60 the same order as that which imposes a society with laws, institutions and social relations. But the *saying* is the fact that before the face I do not simply remain there contemplating it, I respond to it. The saying is a way of greeting the Other, but to greet the Other is already to answer for him. It is difficult to be silent in someone's presence; this difficulty has its ultimate foundation in this signification proper to the saying, whatever is the said. It is necessary to speak of something, of the rain and fine weather, no matter what, but to speak, to respond to him and already to answer for him.

Ph.N.: In the face of the Other you say there is an "elevation," a "height."
70 The Other is higher than I am. What do you mean by that?

E.L.: The first word of the face is the "Thou shalt not kill." It is an order. There is a commandment in the appearance of the face, as if a master spoke to me. However, at the same time, the face of the Other is destitute; it is the poor for whom I can do all and to whom I owe all. And me, whoever I may be, but as a "first person," I am he who finds the resources to respond to the call.

Ph.N.: One is tempted to say to you: yes, in certain cases. But in other cases, to the contrary, the encounter with the Other occurs in the mode of violence, hate and disdain.

80 *E.L.:* To be sure. But I think that whatever the motivation which explains this inversion, the analysis of the face such as I have just made, with the mastery of the Other and his poverty, with my submission and my wealth, is primary. It is the presupposed in all human relationships. If it were not that, we

would not even say, before an open door, "After you, sir!" It is an original "After you, sir!" that I have tried to describe.

You have spoken of the passion of hate. I feared a much graver objection: How is it that one can punish and repress? How is it that there is justice? I answer that it is the fact of the multiplicity of men and the presence of someone else next to the Other, which condition the laws and establish justice. If I am alone with the Other, I owe him everything; but there is someone else. Do I know what my neighbor is in relation to someone else? Do I know if someone else has an understanding with him or his victim? Who is my neighbor? It is consequently necessary to weigh, to think, to judge, in comparing the incomparable. The interpersonal relation I establish with the Other, I must also establish with other men; there is thus a necessity to moderate this privilege of the Other; from whence comes justice. Justice, exercised through institutions, which are inevitable, must always be held in check by the initial interpersonal relation. . . .

Ph.N.: In your last great book published, *Otherwise than Being or Beyond Essence*, you speak of moral responsibility. Husserl had already spoken of responsibility, but of a responsibility for the truth; Heidegger had spoken of authenticity; as for yourself, what do you understand by responsibility?

E.L.: In this book I speak of responsibility as the essential, primary and fundamental structure of subjectivity. For I describe subjectivity in ethical terms. Ethics, here, does not supplement a preceding existential base; the very node of the subjective is knotted in ethics understood as responsibility.

I understand responsibility as responsibility for the Other, thus as responsibility for what is not my deed, or for what does not even matter to me; or which precisely does matter to me, is met by me as face.

Ph.N.: How, having discovered the Other in his face, does one discover him as he to whom one is responsible?

E.L.: In describing the face positively, and not merely negatively. You recall what we said: meeting the face is not of the order of pure and simple perception, of the intentionality which goes toward adequation. Positively, we will say that since the Other looks at me, I am responsible for him, without even having *taken* on responsibilities in his regard; his responsibility *is incumbent on me.* It is responsibility that goes beyond what I do. Usually, one is responsible for what one does oneself. I say, in *Otherwise than Being*, that responsibility is initially a *for the Other.* This means that I am responsible for his very responsibility.

Ph.N.: What in this responsibility for the Other defines the structure of subjectivity?

E.L.: Responsibility in fact is not a simple attribute of subjectivity, as if the latter already existed in itself, before the ethical relationship. Subjectivity is not for itself; it is, once again, initially for another. In the book, the proximity of the Other is presented as the fact that the Other is not simply close to me in space, or close like a parent, but he approaches me essentially insofar as I feel myself—insofar as I am—responsible for him. It is a structure

130 that in nowise resembles the intentional relation which in knowledge attaches us to the object—to no matter what object, be it a human object. Proximity does not revert to this intentionality; in particular it does not revert to the fact that the Other is known to me.

Ph.N.: I can know someone to perfection, but this knowledge will never by itself be a proximity?

E.L.: No. The tie with the Other is knotted only as responsibility, this moreover, whether accepted or refused, whether knowing or not knowing how to assume it, whether able or unable to do something concrete for the Other. To say: here I am [*me voici*].[1] To do something for the Other. To give. To be human spirit, that's it. The incarnation of human subjectivity guaran-
140 tees its spirituality (I do not see what angels could give one another or how they could help one another). Dia-chrony before all dialogue: I analyze the inter-human relationship as if, in proximity with the Other—beyond the image I myself make of the other man—his face, the expressive in the Other (and the whole human body is in this sense more or less face), were what *ordains* me to serve him. I employ this extreme formulation. The face orders and ordains me. Its signification is an order signified. To be precise, if the face signifies an order in my regard, this is not in the manner in which an ordinary sign signifies its signified; this order is the very signifyingness of the face.

Ph.N.: You say at once "it orders me" and "it ordains me." Is this not a
150 contradiction?

E.L.: It orders me as one orders someone one commands, as when one says: "Someone's asking for you."

Ph.N.: But is not the Other also responsible in my regard?

E.L.: Perhaps, but that is *his* affair. One of the fundamental themes of *Totality and Infinity* about which we have not yet spoken is that the intersubjective relation is a non-symmetrical relation. In this sense, I am responsible for the Other without waiting for reciprocity, were I to die for it. Reciprocity is *his* affair. It is precisely insofar as the relationship between the Other and me is not reciprocal that I am subjection to the Other; and I am
160 "subject" essentially in this sense. It is I who support all. You know that sentence in Dostoyevsky: *"We are all guilty of all and for all men before all, and I more than the others."*[2] This is not owing to such or such a guilt which is really mine, or to offenses that I would have committed; but because I am responsible for a total responsibility which answers for all the others and for all in the others, even for their responsibility. The I always has one responsibility *more* than all the others.

ENDNOTES

1. Cf., *Genesis* 22, lines 1, 7 and 11, and *Isaiah* 6, line 8, for *Hineni.* Also, cf., Emmanuel Levinas, "God and Philosophy," in *Philosophy Today*, Vol. XXII, no. 2, Summer 1978, pp. 127–145. [Tr. note]
2. Cf., Fyodor Dostoyevsky, *The Brothers Karamazou*, transl. by Constance Garnett (New York: New American Library, 1957), p. 264.

SELECTIONS FROM *IN THE NAME OF IDENTITY*
Amin Maalouf

Identity isn't given once and for all: it is built up and changes throughout a person's lifetime. This has been pointed out in numerous books and amply explained, but it is still worth emphasising again: not many of the elements that go to make up our identity are already in us at birth. A few physical characteristics of course—sex, colour and so on. And even at this point not everything is innate. Although, obviously, social environment doesn't determine sex, it does determine its significance. To be born a girl is not the same in Kabul as it is in Oslo: the condition of being a woman, like every other factor in a person's identity, is experienced differently in the two places. [1]

The same could be said of colour. To be born black is a different matter according to whether you come into the world in New York, Lagos, Pretoria or Luanda. One might almost say that, from the point of view of identity, we're not even talking about the same colour in the different places. For an infant who first sees the light of day in Nigeria, the operative factor as regards his identity is not whether he is black rather than white, but whether he is Yoruba, say, rather than Hausa. In South Africa, whether a person is black or white is still a significant element in his identity, but at least equally meaningful is his ethnic affiliation, whether Zulu, Xhosa or something else. In the United States it's of no consequence whether you have a Yoruba rather than a Hausa ancestor: it's chiefly among the whites—the Italians, the English, the Irish and the rest—that ethnic origin has a determining effect on identity. Moreover, someone with both whites and blacks among his ancestors would be regarded as "black" in the United States, whereas in South Africa or Angola he would be considered as "of mixed race." [10] [20]

Why is the idea of mixed race taken into account in some countries and not in others? Why is ethnic affiliation a determining factor in some societies but not in the rest? One could put forward various more or less convincing answers to both questions. But that is not what concerns me at this stage. I mention these examples only to underline the fact that even colour and sex are not "absolute" ingredients of identity. That being so, all the other ingredients are even more relative. [30]

To gauge what is really innate among the ingredients that go to make up identity, we may make use of a mental exercise which is extremely revealing. Imagine an infant removed immediately from its place of birth and set down in a different environment. Then compare the various "identities" the child might acquire in its new context, the battles it would now have to fight and those it would be spared. Needless to say, the child would have no recollection of his original religion, or of his country or language. And might he not one day find himself fighting to the death against those who ought to have been his nearest and dearest? [40]

Reprinted from *In the Name of Identity: Violence and the Need to Belong* (2000), Arcade Publishing, Inc.

What determines a person's affiliation to a given group is essentially the influence of others: the influence of those about him—relatives, fellow-countrymen, co-religionists—who try to make him one of them; together with the influence of those on the other side, who do their best to exclude him. Each one of us has to make his way while choosing between the paths that are urged upon him and those that are forbidden or strewn with obstacles. He is not himself from the outset; nor does he just "grow aware" of what he is; he *becomes* what he is. He doesn't merely grow aware of his identity; he acquires it step by step.

50   The apprenticeship starts very soon, in early childhood. Deliberately or otherwise, those around him mould him, shape him, instil into him family beliefs, rituals, attitudes and conventions, together of course with his native language and also certain fears, aspirations, prejudices and grudges, not forgetting various feelings of affiliation and non-affiliation, belonging and not belonging.

And soon, at home, at school and in the next street, he will suffer his first knocks. By their words and by their looks, other people will make him feel he is poor, or lame, short or lanky, swarthy or too fair, circumcised or uncircumcised, or an orphan; those innumerable differences, major and minor,

60   that define every personality and shape each individual's behaviour, opinions, fears and ambitions. Such factors may act as formative influences, but they can also cause permanent injuries.

It is these wounds that at every stage in life determine not only men's attitudes towards their affiliations but also the hierarchy that decides the relative importance of these ties. When someone has been bullied because of his religion, humiliated or mocked because of the colour of his skin, his accent or his shabby clothes, he will never forget it. Up till now I have stressed the fact that identity is made up of a number of allegiances. But it is just as necessary to emphasise that identity is also singular, something that we experience as a

70   complete whole. A person's identity is not an assemblage of separate affiliations, nor a kind of loose patchwork; it is like a pattern drawn on a tightly stretched parchment. Touch just one part of it, just one allegiance, and the whole person will react, the whole drum will sound.

People often see themselves in terms of whichever one of their allegiances is most under attack. And sometimes, when a person doesn't have the strength to defend that allegiance, he hides it. Then it remains buried deep down in the dark, awaiting its revenge. But whether he accepts or conceals it, proclaims it discreetly or flaunts it, it is with that allegiance that the person concerned identifies. And then, whether it relates to colour, religion, lan-

80   guage or class, it invades the person's whole identity. Other people who share the same allegiance sympathise; they all gather together, join forces, encourage one another, challenge "the other side." For them, "asserting their identity" inevitably becomes an act of courage, of liberation.

In the midst of any community that has been wounded, agitators naturally arise. Whether they are hot-heads or cool schemers, their intransigent speeches act as balm to their audience's wounds. They say one shouldn't beg others for respect: respect is a due and must be forced from those who would withhold it. They promise victory or vengeance, they inflame men's minds, sometimes they use extreme methods that some of their brothers may merely have dreamed of in secret. The scene is now set and the war can begin. Whatever happens "the others" will have deserved it. "We" can remember quite clearly "all they have made us suffer" since time immemorial: all the crimes, all the extortion, all the humiliations and fears, complete with names and dates and statistics.

I have lived in a country at war, in a neighbourhood being shelled from a nearby part of the same city. I have spent a night or two in a basement being used as an air-raid shelter, together with my young wife, who was pregnant, and my little son. From outside came the noise of explosions; inside, people exchanged rumours of imminent attack and stories about whole families being put to the sword. So I know very well that fear might make anyone take to crime. If, instead of mere rumours, there had been a real massacre in the neighbourhood where I lived, would I have remained calm and collected? If, instead of spending just a couple of days in that shelter, I had had to stay there for a month, would I have refused to take a gun if it had been put in my hand?

I prefer not to ask myself such questions too often. I had the good luck not to be put to the test; to emerge from the ordeal with my family unharmed, with my hands clean and with a clear conscience. But I speak of "good luck" because things could have turned out very differently if I'd been 16 instead of 26 when the war began in Lebanon. Or if I'd lost someone I loved. Or if I'd belonged to a different social class, or a different community.

After each new ethnic massacre we ask ourselves, quite rightly, how human beings can perpetrate such atrocities. Certain excesses seem incomprehensible; the logic behind them indecipherable. So we talk of murderous folly, of bloodthirsty ancestral or hereditary madness. In a way, we are right to talk of madness. When an otherwise normal man is transformed overnight into a killer, that is indeed insanity. But when there are thousands, millions of killers; when this phenomenon occurs in one country after another, in different cultures, among the faithful of all religions and among unbelievers alike, it's no longer enough to talk of madness. What we conveniently call "murderous folly" is the propensity of our fellow-creatures to turn into butchers when they suspect that their "tribe" is being threatened. The emotions of fear or insecurity don't always obey rational considerations. They may be exaggerated or even paranoid; but once a whole population is afraid, we are dealing with the reality of the fear rather than the reality of the threat.

I don't think any particular affiliation, be it ethnic, religious, national or anything else, predisposes anyone to murder. We have only to review the

events of the last few years to see that any human community that feels humiliated or fears for its existence will tend to produce killers. And these
130 killers will commit the most dreadful atrocities in the belief that they are right to do so and deserve the admiration of their fellows in this world and bliss in the next. There is a Mr. Hyde inside each one of us. What we have to do is prevent the conditions occurring that will bring the monster forth.

I shall not venture to propose a universal explanation of all the massacres, still less to suggest a miracle cure. I no more believe in simplistic solutions than I do in simplistic identities. The world is a complex machine that can't be dismantled with a screwdriver. But that shouldn't prevent us from observing, from trying to understand, from discussing, and sometimes suggesting a subject for reflection.
140   The theme that runs like a thread through the tapestry of this book might be formulated as follows: if the men of all countries, of all conditions and faiths can so easily be transformed into butchers, if fanatics of all kinds manage so easily to pass themselves off as defenders of identity, it's because the "tribal" concept of identity still prevalent all over the world facilitates such a distortion. It's a concept inherited from the conflicts of the past, and many of us would reject it if we examined it more closely. But we cling to it through habit, from lack of imagination or resignation, thus inadvertently contributing to the tragedies by which, tomorrow, we shall be genuinely shocked.

4

From the very beginning of this book I have been speaking of murderous or
150 mortal identities. Identities that kill. The expression doesn't strike me as inappropriate insofar as the idea I'm challenging—the notion that reduces identity to one single affiliation—encourages people to adopt an attitude that is partial, sectarian, intolerant, domineering, sometimes suicidal, and frequently even changes them into killers or supporters of killers. Their view of the world is biased and distorted. Those who belong to the same community as we do are "ours," we like to think ourselves concerned about what happens to them, but we also allow ourselves to tyrannise over them: if they are thought to be "lukewarm" we denounce them, intimidate them, punish them as "traitors" and "renegades." As for the others, those on the opposite side, we never try to
160 put ourselves in their place, we take good care not to ask ourselves whether on some point or other they might not be entirely in the wrong, and we won't let our hearts be softened by their complaints, their sufferings or the injustices that have been inflicted on them. The only thing that counts is the point of view of "our" side; a point of view that is often that of the most militant, the most demagogic and the most fanatical members of the community.

On the other hand, when one sees one's own identity as made up of a number of allegiances, some linked to an ethnic past and others not, some linked to a religious tradition and others not; when one observes in oneself, in

one's origins and in the course one's life has taken, a number of different con-
fluences and contributions, of different mixtures and influences, some of
them quite subtle or even incompatible with one another; then one enters into
a different relationship both with other people and with one's own "tribe." It's
no longer just a question of "them" and "us": two armies in battle order
preparing for the next confrontation, the next revenge match. From then on
there are people on "our" side with whom I ultimately have little in common,
while on "their" side there are some to whom I might feel very close.

But to return to the earlier state of mind, it's easy to imagine how it can
drive people to the worst kind of extremities: if they feel that "others" represent a threat to their own ethnic group or religion or nation, anything they
might do to ward off that danger seems to them entirely legitimate. Even
when they commit massacres they are convinced they are merely doing what
is necessary to save the lives of their nearest and dearest. And as this attitude
is shared by those around them, the butchers often have a clear conscience
and are amazed to hear themselves described as criminals. How can they be
criminals when all they are doing is protecting their aged mothers, their
brothers and sisters and children?

The feeling that they are fighting for the survival of their own loved ones
and are supported by their prayers; the belief that if not in the present
instance at least over the long term they can claim to be acting in legitimate
self-defence: these characteristics are common to all those who in recent
years, throughout the world, from Rwanda to former Yugoslavia, have committed the most abominable crimes.

We are not talking about isolated examples. The world is full of whole
communities that are wounded—either enduring present persecution or still
overshadowed by the memory of former sufferings—and who dream of
exacting revenge. We cannot remain unmoved by their martyrdom; we can
only sympathise with their desire to speak their own language freely, to prac-
tise their own religion without fear, and to preserve their own traditions. But
compassion sometimes tends towards complaisance: those who have suffered
from colonialist arrogance, racism and xenophobia are forgiven for excesses
they themselves have committed because of their own nationalistic arrogance, their own racism and xenophobia. This attitude means we turn a blind
eye to the fate of their victims, at least until rivers of blood have been shed.

The fact is, it's difficult to say where legitimate affirmation of identity
ends and encroachment on the rights of others begins. Did I not say that the
word identity was a "false friend"? It starts by reflecting a perfectly permissible aspiration, then before we know where we are it has become an instrument of war. The transition from one meaning to the other is imperceptible,
almost natural, and sometimes we all just go along with it. We are denouncing an injustice, we are defending the rights of a suffering people—then the
next day we find ourselves accomplices in a massacre.

All the massacres that have taken place in recent years, like most of
the bloody wars, have been linked to complex and long-standing "cases" of

identity. Sometimes the victims are forever desperately the same; sometimes the situation is reversed and the victimisers of yesterday become victims of today; or vice versa. Such words themselves, it must be said, are meaningful only to outside observers; for people directly involved in conflicts arising out of identity, for those who have suffered and been afraid, nothing else exists except "them" and "us," the insult and the atonement. "We" are necessarily
220 and by definition innocent victims; "they" are necessarily guilty and have long been so, regardless of what they may be enduring at present.

And when we, the outside observers, go in for this game and cast one community in the role of the sheep and another in that of the wolf, what we are unwittingly doing is granting the former community impunity in advance for its crimes. In recent conflicts some factions have even committed atrocities against their own people, knowing that international opinion would automatically lay the blame on their opponents.

This first type of complacency carries with it another, equally unfortunate form, whereby, at each new massacre arising out of identity, the eternal scep-
230 tics immediately declare that things have been the same since the dawn of history, and that it would be naive and self-deluding to hope they might change. Ethnic massacres are sometimes treated, consciously or otherwise, like collective crimes of passion, regrettable but comprehensible, and anyway inevitable because they are "inherent in human nature."

The *laisser-tuer* attitude has already done great harm, and the realism invoked to justify it is in my opinion a misnomer. Unfortunately the "tribal" notion of identity is still the one most commonly accepted everywhere, not only amongst fanatics. But many ideas that have been commonly accepted for centuries are no longer admissible today, among them the "natural"
240 ascendancy of men over women, the hierarchy between races, and even, closer to home, apartheid and the various other kinds of segregation. Torture, too, was for a long time regarded as a "normal" element in the execution of justice. For centuries, slavery seemed like a fact of life, and great minds of the past took care not to call it into question.

Then new ideas gradually managed to establish themselves: that every man had rights that must be defined and respected; that women should have the same rights as men; that nature too deserved to be protected; that the whole human race has interests in common in more and more areas—the environment, peace, international exchanges, the battle against the great
250 scourges of disease and natural disaster; that others might and even should interfere in the internal affairs of countries where fundamental human rights are abused. And so on.

In other words, ideas that have hitherto prevailed throughout history are not necessarily those that ought to prevail in times to come. When new facts emerge we need to reconsider our attitudes and habits. Sometimes, when such facts emerge too rapidly, our mental attitudes can't keep up with them and we find ourselves trying to fight fires by pouring oil on them.

But in the age of globalisation and of the ever-accelerating intermingling of elements in which we are all caught up, a new concept of identity is needed, and needed urgently. We cannot be satisfied with forcing billions of bewildered human beings to choose between excessive assertion of their identity and the loss of their identity altogether, between fundamentalism and disintegration. But that is the logical consequence of the prevailing attitude on the subject. If our contemporaries are not encouraged to accept their multiple affiliations and allegiances; if they cannot reconcile their need for identity with an open and unprejudiced tolerance of other cultures; if they feel they have to choose between denial of the self and denial of the other—then we shall be bringing into being legions of the lost and hordes of bloodthirsty madmen.

But let us return for a moment to some examples I quoted at the beginning of this book. A man with a Serbian mother and a Croatian father, and who manages to accept his dual affiliation, will never take part in any form of ethnic "cleansing." A man with a Hutu mother and a Tutsi father, if he can accept the two "tributaries" that brought him into the world, will never be a party to butchery or genocide. And neither the Franco-Algerian lad, nor the young man of mixed German and Turkish origin whom I mentioned earlier, will ever be on the side of the fanatics if they succeed in living peacefully in the context of their own complex identity.

Here again it would be a mistake to see such examples as extreme or unusual. Wherever there are groups of human beings living side by side who differ from one another in religion, colour, language, ethnic origin or nationality; wherever there are tensions, more or less longstanding, more or less violent, between immigrants and local populations, Blacks and Whites, Catholics and Protestants, Jews and Arabs, Hindus and Sikhs, Lithuanians and Russians, Serbs and Albanians, Greeks and Turks, English-speaking and French-speaking Canadians, Flemings and Walloons, Chinese and Malays— yes, wherever there is a divided society, there are men and women bearing within them contradictory allegiances, people who live on the frontier between opposed communities, and whose very being might be said to be traversed by ethnic or religious or other fault lines.

We are not dealing with a handful of marginal people. There are thousands, millions of such men and women, and there will be more and more of them. They are frontier-dwellers by birth, or through the changes and chances of life, or by deliberate choice, and they can influence events and affect their course one way or the other. Those who can accept their diversity fully will hand on the torch between communities and cultures, will be a kind of mortar joining together and strengthening the societies in which they live. On the other hand, those who cannot accept their own diversity may be among the most virulent of those prepared to kill for the sake of identity, attacking those who embody that part of themselves which they would like to see forgotten. History contains many examples of such self-hatred. . . .

And this not only as regards appearance, clothes, behaviour, way of life, work, habitat and the objects that surround us, but also as regards moral concepts and habits of thought.

The same applies to belief. We may call ourselves Christians—or Muslims, Jews, Buddhists or Hindus—but our vision of both this world and the next no longer bears much resemblance to that of our "co-religionists" who lived 500 years ago. For the great majority of them, Hell was as real a place as Asia Minor or Abyssinia, complete with cloven-hoofed devils thrusting sinners into eternal fire, as in apocalyptic paintings. Practically no one thinks like that now. The example I chose was extreme, but the observation itself applies equally well to all our ideas in every field. Many types of behaviour that are perfectly acceptable to a believer today would have struck his "co-religionists" in the past as inconceivable. I put the word in quotes because the religion practised by our ancestors was not the same as ours. If we had lived among them and behaved as we do nowadays we would have been stoned in the street, thrown into prison or burned at the stake for impiety, debauchery, heresy or witchcraft.

In short, each one of us has two heritages, a "vertical" one that comes to us from our ancestors, our religious community and our popular traditions, and a "horizontal" one transmitted to us by our contemporaries and by the age we live in. It seems to me that the latter is the more influential of the two, and that it becomes more so every day. Yet this fact is not reflected in our perception of ourselves, and the inheritance we invoke most frequently is the vertical one.

This is an essential point with regard to current concepts of identity. On the one hand there is what we are in reality and what we are becoming as a result of cultural globalisation: that is to say, beings woven out of many-coloured threads, who share most of their points of reference, their ways of behaving and their beliefs with the vast community of their contemporaries. And on the other hand there is what we think we are and what we claim to be: that is to say, members of one community rather than another, adherents of one faith rather than another. I do not deny the importance of our religious, national or other affiliations. I do not question the often decisive influence of our vertical heritage. But it is necessary at this point in time to draw attention to the gulf that exists between what we are and what we think we are.

To tell the truth, if we assert our differences so fiercely it is precisely because we are less and less different from one another. Because, in spite of our conflicts and our age-old enmities, each day that goes by reduces our differences and increases our likenesses a little bit more.

I seem to be glad of this. But should one rejoice to see people growing more and more like one another? Are we heading for an insipid world where we may soon speak only one language, where everyone shares the same bunch of minimal beliefs, and where everyone watches the same American TV soaps, munching the same sandwiches?

Caricature aside, the question needs to be seriously addressed. We are living in a very bewildering age, in which many of our fellow-creatures see globalisation not as a great and enriching amalgam with advantages for all, but as a standardisation and an impoverishment, a threat that the individual needs to fight against in order to preserve his own culture, identity and values.   350

These may be merely rear-guard actions, but in present circumstances we must have the humility to admit we don't really know. We may not always find what we expect in the dustbins of history. In any case, if so many people see globalisation as a threat it is only natural that we should examine it more closely.

Those who feel themselves to be in danger may of course be influenced in part by the fear of change that is as old as mankind itself. But there are other, more current anxieties which I'd hesitate to dismiss as irrelevant. For globalisation draws us simultaneously towards two contrasting results, one welcome and the other not: i.e., universality and uniformity. The two tracks   360
seem so alike and are so closely intermingled it's as if there were only one. You might almost wonder if one isn't just the presentable face of the other.

But for my part I'm sure there are two separate tracks, however much and however closely they intertwine. It would be over-optimistic to try to unravel the whole skein at once, but we might well attempt to tease out a thread or two.

Smuggled out of
Hungary

business ethics

"deploys a neo-Aristotelian
ethical stance whereby commercial
and business conduct gain their
moral standing by constituting
extensions of the virtues of productivity
and prudence."
— wikipedia

Hoover Inst. @ Stanford
Libertarian

SELECTIONS FROM *CLASSICAL INDIVIDUALISM*
INDIVIDUALISM AND CLASSICAL LIBERALISM
Tibor R. Machan

THE ROOTS OF RADICAL INDIVIDUALISM

What is this individualism that has disturbed so many people with different orientations on politics?

Radical individualism, as spelled out prominently first by the seventeenth-century English philosopher Thomas Hobbes, is derived from a type of materialist metaphysics and nominalist epistemology. All of reality, by the tenets of this view, is matter in motion, and our ideas do not reflect some objective reality but are constructed classifications produced so as to suit our interests. In turn, human nature does not exist independently of social invention and cannot be known objectively. Hobbes advanced a kind of raw, barren, radical—or "atomistic"—individualism: only pure, particular, moving material things—no general classes—exist in reality.

The individualism of Hobbes was meant to be the application of the laws of motion to human life. Motion would occur most effectively, with the greatest efficiency, if something were left unimpeded, as per classical physics. Applied to human social life, Hobbes believed, the laws of motion—manifest in human affairs as the universal drive toward self-preservation and self-advancement—would at first (in the state of nature) lead to conflict, whereupon human intelligence would be driven to introduce social rules. This would be an improvement on the efficiency of self-preservation that is possible in an increasingly crowded state of nature. Individuals would thereafter behave in a more orderly, peaceful fashion, provided the rules were upheld—via the instrumentality of an absolute monarch.

Hobbes's endorsement of absolute monarchy is a tactical detail that his philosophical sympathizers later dropped. They accepted from Hobbes that societies are made up of these unique individuals striving to aggrandize themselves—striving to seek their own advantage in every way possible. They also believed that the social contract would only produce rules of social conduct that would guarantee the enhancement of the members' subjective self-interest. But the political economists who went along with Hobbes that far rejected his belief that absolute monarchy served the ends of peace and prosperity; in fact, they believed quite the contrary. This was most clearly laid out by Adam Smith, who held that the attempt to organize society through feudal, monarchical, or mercantilist economics was inefficient. Smith, while otherwise embracing Hobbes, suggested the idea—later developed in ever more refined fashion by subsequent political economists—that if we just adopt rules to which everyone will agree and protect natural liberty (the right of all individuals to pursue their self-interest), overall social prosperity and success will result.

Reprinted from *Classical Individualism: The Supreme Importance of Each Human Being* (1998), Routledge.

157

INDIVIDUALISM: IS IT A LIABILITY?

Clearly, in light of these and related considerations, radical (subjectivist) individualism has become a target of not just criticism but even moral outrage.
40 Some have rejected such individualism—especially as advanced within the field of economics—on simple moral grounds. They say the view engenders selfishness, social isolation, and alienation. Others, following Karl Marx, claim that while it may have had some uses as an ideology during the seventeenth, eighteenth, and nineteenth centuries, it has lost its value in our "postmodern" era. They say we should no longer be concerned with amassing great material wealth, which radical individualism encouraged; instead, we should be concerned with the quality of our lives, its spiritual dimensions, the ecosystem, community values, and so forth, and in these areas radical individualism is not just useless but a disvalue.

50 Need we, then, dismiss individualism and the liberalism with which it is so closely aligned? Should we embrace a new version of collectivism, for example, communitarianism, in order to recover from the consequences of subjectivism?

I do not believe that is necessary. Individualism has not had a full hearing. There are forms of it distinct from the version the classical–liberal tradition inherited. The type of individualism I have in mind focuses on individual *human* beings. This humanist individualism, which I call classical individualism, recognizes that there is in nature a class of human individuals. And their human nature has a lot to teach us about social life and personal
60 ethics. It seems there are indeed good reasons to classify human beings as a distinct class of entities in nature. There is, however, also good reason to regard their individuality as one of their essential, central characteristics.

So, on one hand, we must abandon the radical individualism, but, on the other hand, we can firm up the foundation for individualism by noting that when we study human nature—when we carefully examine what it is to be a human being—we arrive at the conclusion that one of the crucial characteristics of human beings is that they are individuals. Instead of saying, with Hobbes, that there is no human essence, we can say, in opposition to both Marx and Hobbes, that the human essence is the true individuality of man.
70 This may appear paradoxical, especially to an existentialist, but it is not if the Aristotelian idea of potentiality is sound, since something could have as one of its distinctive attributes a potential to be unique.

CLASSICAL INDIVIDUALISM:
HUMANIZING THE RADICAL VERSION

A major criticism of the idea of an objective, or real, human nature has to do with the legacy of Platonism in both natural-law and natural-rights theories. There is a very serious problem with the Platonistic view of "the nature of something." In the Platonistic tradition, the nature of anything had to be a timeless, unchanging, perfect form. We may usefully think of the perfect circle this way, but that is because geometry is a purely formal field, concerned with measurement and precision, not with substance.

When we consider knowing the nature of human beings, justice, or governments, can we expect to know what is timeless, perfect, unchanging, eternal? Hardly. Human beings are actual, temporal. They are not unchanging, timeless. Nor are we in a position to demonstrate that a human or any other kind of being is timeless, perfect, and final. So Platonism in this area leads to skepticism. If we have to come up with a final truth to know the nature of man, we simply reach an impasse.

Such skepticism, of course, makes it impossible to rest any sort of stable social or political order or conception of a good society on human nature, natural law, or natural rights. This is what Hobbes concluded. We are now left with two extremes: radical skepticism, which issues in nominalism and radical individualism, à la Hobbes, and the Platonistic alternative of an unattainable, hopelessly Utopian and ideal conception of human nature. Both favor skepticism in the end.

RECONCEIVING NATURALISM

Might we, however, reconceive naturalism instead of abandoning it? Yes, and quite promisingly. When we talk about the nature of something, we should have in mind what is reasonably justifiable given what we know to be so beyond a reasonable doubt. The evidence we can gather will be limited to the context of our present knowledge, but if we are consistent and reasonably historically complete, the evidence will yield a conception of what the nature of something is. And that is firm enough to guide us in our political and even our personal lives, as firm as we can expect the world to be from our knowledge of history and from common sense.

Actual aspects of the world—its substance—should not be thought of as we think of its formal features, for example, in mathematics and geometry. The subject matter of these latter fields is capable of yielding final definitions—although some dispute even that—because these definitions concern measurement devices, not actual objects. But human beings, for example, are not mere measurements—they actually exist and undergo changes, which our theory of understanding them must also accommodate. Now, when we study *Homo sapiens* over the estimated 92,000 years that they have been in roughly their current form on Earth, we are justified in concluding that they do have a stable nature as thinking animals—biological entities that are distinctively facilitated to think and depend upon exercising this faculty in order to live and do well at that task.

Furthermore, human beings seem to be always confronted with the possibility of mishaps through their own agency, which accounts for the pervasive fact of criticism among them! They can be wrong as well as right in what they do, and unlike other animals, it is often up to them. And the way they can be wrong is by their failure to act in accordance with their distinctive

120 human nature—by not being in full focus, by failing to pay heed, by negligence, evasion, thoughtlessness, imprudence, dishonesty, and so forth.

These common features give rise to certain universal standards, but there is also an inescapable individuality to human nature. It is by their own particular initiative, circumscribed by their family backgrounds, traditions, habits, customs, environment, opportunities, climate, and so forth, that people must confront living their lives. So they must implement or establish their individuality every moment of their lives. This also points up the social nature of human life—being thinking animals implies that their flourishing is interwoven with their fellows. They will learn from them, find enjoyment

130 and love from them, trade and play with them, and carry on all the most exciting aspects of their humanity with them.

How does all this help us out of some of the problems and paradoxes of individualism that I described earlier? For one thing, with a viable conception of human nature, we can identify some general principles that we could count on to guide our lives. These principles, alluded to above, are general enough to apply over time, to succeeding generations, even if they are not guaranteed to hold for eternity.

As Aristotle recognized, the application of the general principles that rest on our knowledge of human nature will not be identical in different situa-

140 tions, at different times. Being honest in the twentieth century probably requires applying the principles to telephones, fax machines, and computers. Earlier people did not have the responsibility to be honest just as we do because, for one thing, their tools of communication differed from ours. So honesty, although a general human virtue along with all the other virtues, such as prudence, generosity, and courage, will have individual, regional, temporal, and cultural manifestations.

CLASSICAL INDIVIDUALISM AND THE FREE MARKET

So how would classical individualism approach the points that neoclassical economists provide in support of the free market?

Take the claim that in free-market exchanges both parties necessarily

150 benefit. Classical individualism rejects this understanding of market exchange. It is quite possible that a free exchange will not benefit both parties, or even either party. Both could be making a mistake. Sometimes people trade good money for bad goods or make exchanges that are harmful to one or both of the parties. Impulse buying and similarly thoughtless purchases also illustrate this clearly enough. (Nor will it do to try to refute this by claiming that "it seemed to them to be to their benefit," since such a claim is not falsifiable.)

Neoclassical economists tend to reject this because they think that if it is true, some central or collective planner might have second-guessed one or

160 both of the trading parties and ordered them to behave differently "for their own best interest." If it were possible to know (objectively) what would ben-

efit people in trade, even when they themselves deny this, it might be possible to admit to the legitimacy of paternalism and authoritarianism and to defeat free trade. In other words, the subjective theory of value stands for many of them as a bulwark against statism.

But does interventionism follow from classical individualism, simply because it rejects the theory of subjective value? No, not at all. A central feature of any objective ethical value judgment, as well as the ensuing conduct, is that a person must be able to choose. One must, that is, initiate one's ethically significant conduct. Bona fide moral theorists have all understood that one cannot force others to behave morally—ethical conduct must be of the agent's own choosing, meaning not that what is right is a matter of choice, but that doing it is morally right only if it has been chosen freely by the agent.

So a central feature of morally relevant conduct is that it is chosen; if imposed or regimented, its moral significance vanishes. Included in the range of choices every individual is confronted with is the entire array of issues concerned with the bulk of community life.

CLASSICAL INDIVIDUALISM AND MORALITY

Classical individualism, furthermore, places before us certain stable (enough) principles of community life that are necessary for us to even embark upon a morally independent, peaceful, and productive social existence. This aspect of the social moral nature of human life is a result of both one's humanity and one's inherent individuality as the author of one's moral character and conduct.

If one behaved as a good citizen or a charitable person simply because one was dreadfully scared of the state placing one in jail, one would not be a good citizen or person but barely more than a circus animal. So it is wrong to confuse conduct one should have engaged in of one's own free will with regimented behavior imposed by some planning authority, politburo, or regulatory agency. There is, in short, no such thing as coerced morally right conduct. Those aspects of the classical-liberal polity that concern individual rights, never mind whether they were founded on the right philosophical groundings, have validity here as well. Within the framework of individual rights, however, ample room for uncoerced communitarian values remains.

CLASSICAL INDIVIDUALISM AND PUBLIC AFFAIRS

This position also allows for moral criticism of commerce—including the behavior of commercial agents, from used-car sellers to corporate magnates—without sanctioning interference in it. Business ethics, for example, would be a branch of ethics. It would allow us to say, with full justice, that some individuals in the marketplace—some persons or entire firms—are behaving badly and should not do so. They might have chosen to do otherwise.

Of course, classical individualism and its resulting polity would not turn a blind eye toward corporate behavior with adverse impact in the form of violating individual rights. The entire sphere of corporate behavior *vis-à-vis* the environment, for example, as well as fraud, malpractice, and negligence in the production of goods and services, could still be seen, as it is by anti-individualists, as public wrongs that need to have legal sanctions applied. But these would be construed not, for example, in the murky fashion of the environmentalist ethics movement, as assaults upon nature or intrinsic values, but as dumping on and intruding upon individuals, as violations of their rights. The remedy would also shift from the more communitarian approach of social cost–benefit analysis to the individualist approach of giving full protection to those who might be dumped on or assaulted by means of toxic side effects of production or transportation processes. Furthermore, the conduct of merchants and corporations could be judged unethical, apart from any illegality, when such matters as tastelessness in advertising or mismanagement of employee relations are at issue.

CLASSICAL INDIVIDUALISM AND CLASSICAL LIBERALISM

Some of this is disturbing to various classical liberals because they realize that in terms of this form of individualism, sometimes what we do in the free market we *should not* do. Yet, as has been noted already, this does not at all imply that whatever I should not do may be prohibited or that what I should do may be commanded. Rather, it admits what common sense recognizes, namely, that free agents can do the wrong thing and that this may be pointed out to them in peaceful ways. Clearly, nothing about statist intervention follows.

What are the theoretical and political gains from classical individualism concerning how the classical liberal may analyze many aspects of contemporary society? For one thing, as noted before, this position allows for moral criticism of commerce without sanctioning the regulation of commerce. With perfect theoretical justification, we can write articles about unethical business practices and protest them by way of letters, boycotts, and ostracism. We might even attend a stockholders meeting and argue a company's management out of their current wrongheaded policy.

With radical—as distinct from classical—individualism, whatever people do in the marketplace has to be accepted as what they ought to do. That is because the only clue as to what they ought to do is their doing it. I have already indicated what kind of difficulties that produces. Classical individualism recognizes that individual market agents might behave either in a morally praiseworthy fashion or in a morally blameworthy fashion; yet for them to earn praise or blame, *it has to be their choice whether they do one or the other.* That is the only way in which a socioeconomic system avoids becoming demoralized. Within certain "rules of market conduct" that identify the borders around us—which is where natural-rights theory comes into the picture—individuals must be left free to misbehave, because that is the only way that their human dignity is preserved in a commercial setting.

All this makes sense because it could now be said that, objectively speaking, some of what these people do in the market they should not be doing. But since morally relevant conduct must be chosen, it follows that market agents may not be regimented unless their morally wrong conduct infringes on the rights of others—that is, unless their conduct obstructs other people's liberty to make moral choices, the only avenue toward influencing them is to persuade them to do otherwise.   250

what dignity in Poverty or poisoning?

CLASSICAL INDIVIDUALISM AND NEOCLASSICAL ECONOMICS

Embracing classical individualism involves no loss at all to classical liberalism and neoclassical economics. Diversity of values still holds—not, however, because of ethical subjectivity, but because of enormous individual variations among people. The price system remains the best means by which to communicate human choices, although at times this means that wrong choices will also be communicated and responded to by market agents (for example, choices that may lead to the production of harmful drugs or trivial pursuits or pornography). Still, the point made by public-choice theorists still holds: any attempt to remedy market failures by means of political intervention involves the far greater risk of enshrining the errors of politicians in an aspect   260 of a culture that is much less flexible than its market, namely, in its legal system. In addition, the point about trying to make people good by means of coercion must also be recalled. Both of these points count against any interventionist policies, so the free market remains intact, despite its somewhat altered philosophical foundations.

natural rights

SELECTIONS FROM *CLASSICAL INDIVIDUALISM*
INDIVIDUAL RIGHTS AND THE COMMON GOOD
The Case of the Environment

A TEST CASE FOR INDIVIDUALISM

1   It may be one of the most frequently cited general problems of political life in modern times, with traces of it found in every age: The supposed conflict between the rights of individuals and the welfare or good of the community as a whole. Examples of such alleged conflicts abound: Environmentalists stress that the power conferred upon individuals by the principles of the right to private property is extremely hazardous to the common welfare; some criminologists stress that upholding the individual rights of the accused is threatening the good of the community by helping to leave criminals go unpunished; those who are concerned about the general moral climate of our
10   society claim that upholding the individual's right to use harmful drugs will surely undermine public morals, while others, who are concerned about the ethics of the marketplace, often express impatience with the right to freedom of commerce, claiming that such freedom unleashes the forces of avarice and greed at the expense of decency and harmony. No doubt, other examples can be cited. The curtailment of *individual* rights rarely occurs without claiming some *public* benefit from it. And the dominant political forces tend to claim for their agenda of such curtailment just that kind of public benefit.

But does it have to be thus? Must individual rights conflict with the common welfare? Certainly those who proposed the doctrine of individual natu-
20   ral rights didn't think so. It was precisely to show the congruence of the protection of individuals and the enhancement of the community that many advocated the protection of individual rights. John Locke would never have admitted that there has to be conflict in this area. Rather, the conflict, if there is any, stems from a basic misunderstanding. This involves thinking that the community is anything but *a community of human individuals who share certain community concerns which will best be served if each individual has his or her rights fully protected.*

The idea is that human nature unites us into one species and gives us standards by which community life may be fully harmonized, at least poten-
30   tially. And the natural rights tradition held that such harmony is best secured by granting every individual a sphere of personal jurisdiction. Within this jurisdiction each person is most likely to accomplish the best he or she can, giving rise to the least degree of mischief in the process, since by not granting persons the authority to intrude on others, the evil or harm they do is most likely to hurt only them. This will certainly serve as a discouragement to wrong doing, which, in turn, confers overall benefit to the community.

Even many thinkers who believed that ideally the best course of conduct for everyone is to serve the community believed, also, along with Bernard

Mandeville and Adam Smith, that public benefit could be procured *via* private vice, provided certain principles of liberty are upheld. And, even earlier, Aristotle believed that the right to private property would enhance public welfare, when he wrote:

> That all persons call the same thing mine in the sense in which each does so may be a fine thing, but it is impracticable; or if the words are taken in the other sense, such a unity in no way conduces to harmony. And there is another objection to the proposal. For that which is common to the greatest number has the least care bestowed upon it. Every one thinks chiefly of his own, hardly at all of the common interest; and only when he is himself concerned as an individual. For besides other considerations, everybody is more inclined to neglect the duty which he expects another to fulfill; as in families many attendants are often less useful than a few.

One way to support the idea of the harmony of individual rights and the common good is to demonstrate the compossibility of individual goods and rights—i.e., that no one's objective good need obstruct another's objective good, which, in turn, suggests that the pursuit of individual goods within the framework of individual rights will bring about the maximum well-being of the community. But are the objective goods or values of individuals really compossible, that is, fully capable of being realized for all? Some argue that this isn't even conceivable, let alone possible. They believe that no common human nature exists so as to be able to identify some common standards of good or value. Or they argue that human nature is a myth, so any idea of compatible values is hopelessly futile. Then there are the more empirically minded critics who point to how history is replete with major and minor conflicts among human beings, so any belief in some kind of harmony is utopian, even if theoretically not entirely absurd.

Yet, of course, there is plenty that's problematic even with the idea of a common good, over and above individual goods. How are we to identify some transcendent specific common good in the first place? Will any candidate not always be the candidate of some special group of human beings and thus by definition not the common good? Is there even such a being as humanity or society apart from the individuals who comprise it? So what else is there but the good of individuals?

But perhaps the more immediate issue that springs to mind under the heading "individual rights vs. the community" has to do with environmentalism. There are very few people involved in the international discussion of the environment who do not believe that some inherent conflict between the individual and the common welfare faces us here. Consider the alleged problem of the ozone layer. It seems that in the long run the right of individuals to secure for themselves, for example, refrigeration and air conditioning simply cannot help but conflict with the prospects of a healthy (current and future) human race. Free trade, the freedom to pursue one's happiness, even the freedom to express oneself freely seem to some not to be rights but occasional, highly circumscribed privileges that can and ought to be revoked by government whenever the environment or some other value is being threatened by them.

So there are a few who would protest and argue that, in fact, environmental well-being and other values not only are compatible with but entirely depend on the respect for individual rights.

ECOLOGY: A NEW EXCUSE FOR STATISM?

90 As we noted in the previous chapter, in the early part of the twentieth century Ludwig von Mises observed the same principle identified by Aristotle. Mises, as Heilbroner has reminded us, argued that collectivist management of resource allocation can simply never work. Effective information dissemination and communication of what something is worth to whom and how much they want requires that individuals enjoy the freedom to buy and sell, which, in turn, requires the protection of their right to private property.

More recently, Professor Garrett Hardin, in his famous essay "The Tragedy of the Commons," argued that the difficulties first noticed by Aristotle plague us in the context of our concerns with the quintessentially pub-
100 lic realm, namely, the ecological environment. Here over-usage is most likely because the realm seems to be inherently resistant to privatization. Hardin did not draw optimistic conclusions from this. Nevertheless we can conclude that the collectivist system, which rejects individual rights, does not appear to solve problems very well.

These various indictments of collectivism, coupled with the few moral arguments against it, didn't manage to dissuade many intellectuals from, the task of attempting to implement various forms of the idea. Our own century is filled with enthusiastic, stubborn, visionary, opportunistic but almost always bloody efforts to implement the collectivist dream. Not until the crum-
110 pling of the Soviet attempt, in the form of its Marxist–Leninist internationalist socialist revolution, did it dawn on most people that collectivism is not going to do the job of enabling people to live a decent human social life. Although most admit that in small units—convents, kibbutzes, the family—a limited, temporary collectivist arrangement is feasible, they no longer look with much hope toward the transformation of entire societies into collectivist human organizations.

Heilbroner, who was for a long time sympathetic to socialism, admitted, finally, that ". . . Ludwig von Mises . . . was right . . ." But, unlike previous thinkers who have seen various examples of the failure of idealist nor-
120 mative moral or political schemes, Heilbroner does not abandon the hope for government regulation of some essentially peaceful areas of human life. He notes that there are two ways central regulation may remain something of a handy concept. First, it may leave us piecemeal social objectives to strive for. Second, it may reemerge as the adjunct of the ecological movement. And just

as we noted earlier that the planned economy is misguided, we need now to examine in that light Heilbroner's suggestion, that coping with the challenges of environmental problems must involve considerable government interference. Heilbroner tells us that:

> The ecological crisis toward which we are moving at a quickening pace has occasioned much scientific comment but surprisingly little economic attention. [Professor Heilbroner does not follow the burgeoning literature of free market environmentalist; e.g., the works of John Baden and Richard Stroup.] Yet if there is any single problem that will have to be faced by any socioeconomic order over the coming decades it is the problem of making our economic peace with the demands of the environment. Making that peace means insuring that the vital processes of material provisioning do not contaminate the green-blue film on which life itself depends. This imperative need not affect all social formations, but none so profoundly as capitalism. 130

To this idea, that a new problem faces us that is too complicated for free men and women to handle, we may respond by recalling that since this is not in principle different from other problems, Heilbroner's call for more meddling from government is unjustified. As we have already seen Heilbroner issues the "new" warning that capitalism needs to be restrained, now so as to secure environmental objectives. As Heilbroner put it, the system needs to be "monitored, regulated, and contained to such a degree that it would be difficult to call the final social order capitalism." Despite already having attended to such objections to the free market economic, this recast skepticism about individualism needs to be addressed, if only because it is time that the technique it exhibits of undermining confidence in human freedom needs to be exposed. 140 150

THE PROBLEM OF INDIVIDUALISM *VIS-A-VIS* ENVIRONMENTAL PROBLEMS

Clearly, the ecological realms mostly affected adversely by human agency are public realms—the air mass, lakes, oceans, many parks and beaches, and, of course, the treasuries of democratic states (for what is deficit spending but a tragedy of the commons?), etc. The ultimate harm, of course, befalls individual human beings—now or in the future—and other living things upon which human life often depends or from which it gains a great deal of benefit and satisfaction. Yet the injury occurs not in a way that is judicially manageable—namely, where victim and culprit can be linked and the crime may be dealt with. 160

Let us for the sake of argument understand Heilbroner not to be advocating out and out collectivism but rather something of a compromise between an individualist-capitalist and a collectivist system, namely, what we have come to call the welfare state. After all, he admits that he envisions an eco-logically prudent socioeconomic system to be substantially individualist—i.e., the institution of private property has not been entirely abolished in such a system—but one that is also "monitored, regulated, and contained to such a degree that it would be difficult to call the final social order capitalism."

Do we really need once again to abandon the individualist alternative for 170 some such regimented order? Let us take the environmental problem as a test case and ever so briefly present the case for why an individual rights approach will more likely solve it and, thus, be more conducive to the common good—as understood within a framework that acknowledges the ontological priority of human individuals to their various groupings—than alternatives that proposed to violate individual rights. While this may appear to be ques-tion begging—by denying at the outset any meaningful non-individualist sense of the common good—it will turn out not to be, once the individual-ist environmentalism that emerges comes to full light.

First of all, we need to stress the individual rights position on pollution: 180 Wherever activities issuing in pollution cannot be carried out without injury to third (non-consenting) parties, such activities have to be prohibited as inherently in violation of the rights of members of the community. (This would not include trade in pesticide-treated fruits, for example, where the risk of harm from eating such fruit is lower than or equal to normal risks encountered in everyday life.)

When pollution occurs along lines of thresholds, such that only once so much emission has occurred could the emission be actually polluting (i.e., harmful to persons) rather than simply defiling, a system of first come, first served might be instituted, so that those who start the production first would 190 be permitted to continue, while others, who would raise the threshold to a harmful level, would not. This may appear arbitrary, but in fact numerous areas of human life, including especially commerce, make good use of this system, and human ingenuity could well be expended toward making sure that one's firm is not a latecomer.

A word about thresholds. The earth—as well as any part of the universe where life support is reasonably imaginable—can often absorb some measure of potentially injurious waste. (This can be expected, since life itself produces waste!) Most toxic substances can dissipate up to a point. Arguably this is no different from the simple observation that within a given territory only so 200 much life can be supported, after which the quantity and quality of life must be lowered. Barring the privatization of such spheres, where they can be kept apart and separated from others, a judicially efficient management of toxic substance disposal must take into consideration how far disposal can con-tinue before the vital point—whereby the waste is harmlessly absorbed and dissipated—is reached. Technical measurements would need to be employed and correlated with information about the levels of human tolerance for the toxic substance in question. Risk analysis would need to be performed so as to learn whether the risk of falling victim to toxic substance disposal corresponds with or exceeds expected risks not produced by human pollution.

It is important to state that the natural rights individualist standard of tolerance might very well be far lower than even those who support it would imagine. Many free market advocates favor a social cost–benefit approach here, based on the utilitarian idea that what ultimately matters is the achievement of some state of collective satisfaction. This is not the approach that flows from the idea that individuals have natural negative rights to life, liberty and property.

Assuming the soundness of the natural rights stance, it may be necessary to prepare for some drastic life style changes, so that some past abuses can be rectified. For example, whereas automobile wastes have been poured into the atmosphere with an understanding that from a utilitarian perspective it is worth doing so (based on social cost–benefit analysis), from the natural rights individualist-Capitalist viewpoint it would be necessary to insist on the full initial cost being borne by automobile drivers/owners, thereby at least temporarily prompting a considerable rise in the prices of vehicles. (That the overall cost may be borne wider, since more expensive manufacturing and transportation processes will prompt more expensive goods and services, is not relevant here. The issue is what persons can choose to do or avoid doing in light of their understanding of what may harm them.)

Certainly, the government of an individualist political economy would not have the authority to rely on the utilitarian notion, used by many courts today in their refusal to enforce "public nuisance laws," that those harmed by pollution have to "pay" since the benefits of industrial growth outweigh such costs in health and property damage as are caused by pollution. Instead the principle of strict liability would apply: The polluter or others who are bound by contract with the polluter, such as nuclear utilities which may have a pact to share insurance premiums and liability resulting from accident at one member's plant, would be held liable. Benefits not solicited cannot be charged for if one respects the individual's right to choose, as the individualist system is committed to do.

SELECTIONS FROM *CLASSICAL INDIVIDUALISM* INDIVIDUALISM VERSUS ITS CRITICS

WHY ANTI-INDIVIDUALISM NEEDS SCRUTINY

1   In the bulk of this work I have been spelling out various elements of a form of individualism I have called "classical." I have made the point in various places that this individualism may be traced to a view of human nature that emerges out of Aristotelian metaphysics and epistemology, one that respects the idea of "the nature of X" in a fashion that avoids the difficulties associated with the Platonic essentialism of the theory of forms or ideas.

What I wish to do here is address directly some of the criticisms of individualism that have been aired over the years, some ancient, others modern and most quite contemporary. This may involve some repetition of argu-
10   ments and points but it will be useful to have before us these responses all under one roof, as it were. One reason is that anti-individualism is still very popular and despite the setbacks suffered by collectivism in the wake of the demise of the most prominent standard bearers, namely, centrally planned socialist political economy, there are renewed efforts to suggest that the individualist system of capitalism, of the regime of natural individual rights, is ill conceived and neglects what is supposed to be the essentially communitarian nature of human life.

Even by those who reject Marxism in all of its varieties, many versions of socialism, in particular democratic–socialist and market–socialist visions, are
20   still widely championed. And all non-Marxian socialist views share this feature of the Marxian version, namely, that human beings are primarily if not exclusively social parts, with society, the class, or some other large collective as the significant entity to be considered as we organize our lives. Not that every communitarian champions the abolition of individualist type constitutional rights and liberties. Rather, many favor diluting those rights with measures that stress the solidarity or cohesive nature of various communities that we ought to consider of prior importance, of value over and above the individual's rights and liberties.

Communitarianism has been gaining prominence, particularly because
30   its endorsement of the group is not linked explicitly to the term "socialism." The communities that stand above individuals in importance can be families, tribes, nations, races, or all of humanity. The main point here is only to note that in rejecting individualism of any kind, one is usually going to opt for one or another of these collective beings. (The term "collective" is, of course, problematic because it must refer back to the individuals who comprise it. At that point it becomes interesting just what the status of these individuals turns out to be.)

ESSENTIALS OF INDIVIDUALISM

Mary Midgley makes the point that "our own culture, in particular, has grossly exaggerated the degree of independence that individuals have, their separateness from other organisms, and also their degree of inner harmony." However, she goes on to add:

> But these exaggerations do not affect the more modest facts that underlie them. Whenever people have to make decisions, the language of agency has to be used, and the reasons why it had to be invented constantly become obvious. The language of impersonal process, by contrast, can scarcely be used at all for many important aspects of human behavior and, when it is used there, it often serves only for fatalistic evasions.

What are those modest facts that underlie an exaggerated individualism? They are few but vital for human existence. These facts may be distinguished, though not separated.

One such fact is a certain indispensable level of separateness of every person. A human being is an individual in part insofar as he or she experiences a measure of separateness—for example, that his or her death does not require the death of another human being. One dies by oneself. Insofar as that involves the extinction of one's identity in some important respect, one is an individual with some sort of separate identity.

Another component is an element of self-directedness. This lies in the social-psychological dimension of human life. Self-determination and free will are a part of individualism insofar as an individual is someone whose initiative—choices, decisions, and actions—is instrumental in who he or she is and will become. Individualism regards everyone as something of a self-made person, even if only in a minimal respect, culminating in no more than acquiescence. Individuals, according to the individualist tradition, do have a determining, decisive influence on their own lives, on who and what they will become over their lifetime of development. The idea is that how human beings develop is not reducible to the influence of other people, of history, or even of their parents.

Furthermore, the capacity for self-generated rationality is a part of the individualist conception of the human being. Every human being is capable of engaging—and, within different individual conceptions, more or less responsible to engage—in creative reasoning, figuring things out, learning of the world, understanding the world to some perhaps minimal but essential extent. Cognition, at least at the conceptual, idea-forming level, has to be generated by the person—it cannot be imposed. A person is not a container into which ideas are funneled or poured, or something that responds to various stimuli passively. There is an element of self-generated understanding, however minimal, on the part of the individual, according to the individual-ist social–philosophical tradition.

80 Individualism also upholds moral autonomy for human beings, in the sense that it identifies the individual as the source of moral choice. The point is not, as Steven Lukes argues, that individualism involves the sort of subjec-tive autonomy that "will eventuate in ethical individualism, the doctrine that the final authority of ethical behavior, values, and principles is the individual alone." What individualism requires is that the initiative to do what is right or wrong must come from persons and cannot be wholly explained by refer-ence to external or structural causal forces (for example, cultural or genetic forces). It is neither others nor one's DNA or environment that is held responsible for what the individual does.

90 Thus, quite independently of whatever moral stance is applicable to guid-ing individual conduct—whether utilitarian, altruist, egoist, hedonist, Bud-dhist, Christian, or whatever—it is an essential point of individualism that it is the individual free agent who makes the moral choice, whose input is the most vital for whether that person takes the morally right or wrong action. Indeed, all bona fide moral blaming and praising are implicitly individualist. Those, for example, who are very concerned with recent legal developments whereby people are able to plead as an exonerating condition that they could not help themselves—where the defense of mental incapacitation comes in—are understandably associating this with the demise of individualism and the

100 rise of "group thinking," where the notion reigns that "I" do not do any-thing; rather, "we" do things or things happen to us.

Also associated with individualism is the idea of the political sovereignty of the human being, the idea that in a polity, ultimately it is the individual members of that polity who are sovereign—not the polity itself, not the lead-ers of the polity, not some representative crook of the polity. It is you and I, as citizens, who are sovereign, who are not subjects of some other sovereign whose natural position or superiority or divine selection has come to entitle him or her to power over us. The political individualism that this sovereignty notion is associated with is, I think, very much a part of the American polit-

110 ical tradition. Indeed, those of us who come to the United States from out-side, from the very beginnings of our stirrings as Americaphiles, have kind of associated America with this individualism precisely for that reason; we always thought that when you come within the borders of the United States, you are not anyone else's master and neither is anyone else your master; you are sovereign. This is a form of individualism for which America is well known and also often criticized.

Finally, there is the idea that individual rights, negative rights to life, lib-erty, and property, are by nature to be ascribed to every adult human being.

I think individualism can be pretty much characterized by these six con-

120 ditions (a certain level of separateness of every person, an element of self-directedness, the capacity for self-generated rationality, moral autonomy, individual political sovereignty, and individual rights to life, liberty, and

property). I might have mentioned a seventh, but it takes us into the realm of metaphysics and is probably beyond the debate that I am participating in here. There was a hint of it in the first one—separateness. There is a metaphysical form of individualism that maintains that every being is a particular in an essential respect. There are no general or concrete universal beings. There is no such thing as society. There is no such thing as family as a concrete thing. There is no such thing as the team, or America, or blacks or whites, or women or men; there are beings and there are all beings; they can   130 be of a specific kind, but in their actuality, they are individuals. This form of individualism is slightly distinct from the one with which I am concerned here, although the two forms are often mixed up.

THE PLATONISTIC CRITICISM

We have seen a sketch of the nature of individualism. Let us now examine a few of the more severe criticisms of individualism. To begin with, here is another brief look at the most traditional, anti-individualist thesis, namely, a certain understanding of Platonism.

If one takes Plato's dialogues to actually spell out a philosophical viewpoint (which many authors and teachers do, although there is dispute about whether one should), then I think one comes to the conclusion that Plato   140 favors the reality of *concrete universals* over concrete particulars or individual beings.

According to Plato, particular beings, you and I as we manifest ourselves in this actual, visible world, are in some sense inferior, imperfect versions of the perfect rendition of this being in a concrete universal. This can be taken on analogy to the way a perfect circle, as defined in geometry, is superior to any actual circular being. Thus it is human nature—the form of humanity—that has the elevated or noble status. We who imperfectly participate in this form are always inferior, and lamentably so. It is, accordingly, no accident that Western civilization has always had something of a disdain toward the   150 body, whether it be in connection with work, sex, business, or material possessions. There is this legacy of the pure idea as superior to the actual approximation of it here in this world.

This is anti-individualist in that the individual is always an inferior part of reality. The truly elevated part of reality is the universal, the ideal. The criticism of individualism derivative of this Platonistic outlook is obviously embodied in a very comprehensive, philosophical point of view. In response, one would have to deal with at least some aspects of that point of view, which I will do below.

ARISTOTLE AS ANTI-INDIVIDUALIST

There is a more moderate view of ancient anti-individualism: the Aristotelian   160 notion that the human being can be realized only as a part of the whole. We considered it briefly at the outset of this work and even indicated reasons why taking Aristotle to have embraced it might be seriously misguided.

The whole, as Aristotle's communitarianism is usually conveyed, does not have to be all of humanity, as is implicit in a certain reading of Plato, but something like the family, the *polis*, or some other group. Because Aristotle identifies human beings as essentially social, it is said to follow from his view that no individual can flourish apart from the realization of this communitarian good.

170   Aristotle himself seems to have been ambivalent on this matter, for the self-sufficiency he associates with living in the *polis* need not deny an essential individuality to every human being. One can be essentially both individual and social, given a certain understanding of these notions. But in histories of political theory, it is often claimed that Aristotle's much revered and highly influential position implies the rejection of individualism, mainly because everyone does best in life when belonging to a community.

There are many echoes of this view in our own time, what with the reemergence of communitarianism in the writings of MacIntyre, Rorty, Robert Bellah and colleagues, and Amitai Etzioni. There are certain elements
180   in Aristotle's position, as we have already seen, that stress individualism. He gives a prominent place to self-directedness, for one, something that does not square fully with an exclusively communitarian conception of human flourishing. The idea in Aristotle is that it is, in fact, the individual agent of conduct who is virtuous or vicious. It is in part, not wholly, through the individual's own effort that his or her character is achieved and thus the ethical (or unethical) life is lived. Still, certainly a lot of scholars who are critical of individualism draw on Aristotle in their criticism.

CHRISTIANITY *VIS-A-VIS* INDIVIDUALISM

Then there are some elements of Christianity that do not completely square with the individualist requirements that I have laid out, despite some that do.
190   Crucial elements of individualism are suggested clearly enough by the idea that each human being is a distinct, unique child of God and that the saving of each individual's everlasting soul is the task of the ethical life. But there are also anti-individualist directions that one can find in Christian theology.

For example, Saint Augustine said that every part of the community belongs to the whole. Thus holism also seems to be present in Christianity, although there are aspects of Christianity that are individualist—such as that each individual has a separate soul and ought to seek salvation. Still, there appear to be certain ways in Christianity that the individual may be sacrificed to the whole, or at least the purposes of the whole. When Jesus
200   said, "Compel them to come in," he was taken by some—for example, the more zealous missionaries—to suggest *coercing* people to join the faith; this is anti-individualist.

Debate as to whether Christianity is more individualist or more collectivist is certainly widespread in theological circles. Michael Novak and Robert Sirico seem to stress the individualist element in the American debate, while the Catholic bishops tend to stress the collectivist element, whereby compelling people to help the poor, thus denying their free choice in the matter of practicing the virtues of charity and generosity, seems to be favored.

Furthermore, the idea that knowledge *begins* with community runs aground when we consider just how this could happen. No community has a brain. It is the members who have brains. So even if after centuries of human history, the bulk of what any of us knows does come by way of what others teach us, *it could not have been like that from the start.* Nor is it always like that now—there are plenty of cases in which children stand their ground against their teachers, citizens against their leaders, ones who often try to indoctrinate or brainwash them and whose efforts often enough need to be and do get thwarted by individual resistance. (For Rorty and other communitarians, the heroic stance of the dissident is impossible—such folks are either deluded in thinking they are lone rebels or actually amount to lunatics.)

INDIVIDUALISM HUMANIZED

Now, how does all this help us out of some of the problems and paradoxes that critics of individualism tend to focus upon? For one thing, since we now have a viable, sound, feasible conception of human nature—one that need not be timeless and yet has the stability one expects of what the nature of something is—we can identify some general principles that we could count on to guide our lives. These principles are going to be general enough to apply over time to succeeding generations, even if they will not be guaranteed to hold for eternity, as earlier naturalists had hoped.

Of course, as Aristotle already recognized, the precise application of the general principles that rest on our knowledge of human nature may not be exactly identical in different situations, at different times. Being honest in the twentieth century probably requires applying the principles to telephones, fax machines, and computers. Two hundred years ago, people did not have the responsibility to be honest in just this way. So honesty, although it may well be a very general human virtue that we all ought to practice, will have individual, regional, temporal, and cultural manifestations, as will other virtues, such as courage, prudence, and justice.

There can be very many general human traits of character that we ought to practice because they make for human excellence. That these must be applied in particular circumstances does not imply at all that they have to be subjective, mere preferences or choices that we invent at a given moment. These could well be human virtues, so that, for example, if we discover that a person four hundred years ago was a liar, we could say objectively that he did something morally wrong.

What is most unfortunate in the critiques of individualism is that no attempt is made by any of the critics to discover a more generous rendition of this social philosophy, one that sees the high regard individualism has for the human individual as somewhat meritorious, somewhat sensible, somewhat morally palatable. Instead, we find the critics stressing elements of individualism that seem obviously morally repugnant and often wholly unrealis-

250 tic. Individualists are presented as isolated, atomistic creatures whose "independence" is not the virtuous motivation of someone who is set on ascertaining truth and justice objectively, without prejudice and free of group pressure, but the vice of fantasizing some kind of solitary existence, of denying moral connection and responsibilities to family, friends, and others. The fact that the individualist is mainly concerned with avoiding oppression and denying a natural subservience of the human being to some supposedly higher group—which is most often translated as subservience to some select other persons—does not appear to phase the critics very much (although some, such as Mary Midgley, make mention of this motivation).

260 In any case, the individualist stance is not by any means so unpalatable from the viewpoints of philosophy, ethics, science and common sense as some of its critics suggest. The main alternative placed before us in our time is a rather ambiguous kind of *we-ism*, a communitarianism in which the community is quite undefined. No answers are given to crucial questions: Which is the community to which we belong? Where is it? How long does it last? How do we come to belong to it? How do we leave one of them and go to the other? By what standard of assessment do we judge some communities to be barbaric or corrupt and make our way, if we can, to some others?

Despite what individualism's critics keep telling us, the story could indeed
270 be exactly the opposite, at the end of the day. What the world needs most is a serious, thoughtful individualism, not a continued emphasis on groups.

THE VIRTUES, THE UNITY OF A HUMAN LIFE AND THE CONCEPT OF A TRADITION
Alasdair MacIntyre

Any contemporary attempt to envisage each human life as a whole, as a unity, whose character provides the virtues with an adequate *telos* encounters two different kinds of obstacle, one social and one philosophical. The social obstacles derive from the way in which modernity partitions each human life into a variety of segments, each with its own norms and modes of behavior. So work is divided from leisure, private life from public, the corporate from the personal. So both childhood and old age have been wrenched away from the rest of human life and made over into distinct realms. And all these separations have been achieved so that it is the distinctiveness of each and not the unity of the life of the individual who passes through those parts in terms of which we are taught to think and to feel. . . .

That particular actions derive their character as parts of larger wholes is a point of view alien to our dominant ways of thinking and yet one which it is necessary at least to consider if we are to begin to understand how a life may be more than a sequence of individual actions and episodes.

Equally the unity of a human life becomes invisible to us when a sharp separation is made either between the individual and the roles that he or she plays.

At the same time the liquidation of the self into a set of demarcated areas of role-playing allows no scope for the exercise of dispositions which could genuinely be accounted virtues in any sense remotely Aristotelian. For a virtue is not a disposition that makes for success only in some one particular type of situation. What are spoken of as the virtues of a good committee man or of a good administrator or of a gambler or a pool hustler are professional skills professionally deployed in those situations where they can be effective, not virtues. Someone who genuinely possesses a virtue can be expected to manifest it in very different types of situation, many of them situations where the practice of a virtue cannot be expected to be effective in the way that we expect a professional skill to be. . . .

A central thesis then begins to emerge: man is in his actions and practice, as well as in his fictions, essentially a story-telling animal. He is not essentially, but becomes through his history, a teller of stories that aspire to truth. But the key question for men is not about their own authorship; I can only answer the question 'What am I to do?' if I can answer the prior question 'Of what story or stories do I find myself a part?' We enter human society, that is, with one or more imputed characters—roles into which we have been drafted—and we have to learn what they are in order to be able to understand how others respond to us and how our responses to them are apt to be construed. It is through hearing stories about wicked stepmothers, lost children, good but

Reprinted from *After Virtue: A Study of Moral Theory* (2007), by permission of University of Notre Dame Press.

40 misguided kings, wolves that suckle twin boys, youngest sons who receive no inheritance but must make their own way in the world and eldest sons who waste their inheritance on riotous living and go into exile to live with the swine, that children learn or mislearn both what a child and what a parent is, what the cast of characters may be in the drama into which they have been born and what the ways of the world are. Deprive children of stories and you leave them unscripted, anxious stutterers in their actions as in their words. Hence there is no way to give us an understanding of any society, including our own, except through the stock of stories which constitute its initial dramatic resources. Mythology, in its original sense, is at the heart of things. Vico

50 was right and so was Joyce. And so too of course is that moral tradition from heroic society to its medieval heirs according to which the telling of stories has a key part in educating us into the virtues.

What the narrative concept of selfhood requires is thus twofold. On the one hand, I am what I may justifiably be taken by others to be in the course of living out a story that runs from my birth to my death; I am the *subject* of a history that is my own and no one else's, that has its own peculiar meaning. When someone complains—as do some of those who attempt or commit suicide—that his or her life is meaningless, he or she is often and perhaps characteristically complaining that the narrative of their life has become

60 unintelligible to them, that it lacks any point, any movement towards a climax or a *telos*. Hence the point of doing any one thing rather than another at crucial junctures in their lives seems to such person to have been lost.

To be the subject of a narrative that runs from one's birth to one's death is, I remarked earlier, to be accountable for the actions and experiences which compose a narratable life. It is, that is, to be open to being asked to give a certain kind of account of what one did or what happened to one or what one witnessed at any earlier point in one's life than the time at which the question is posed. . . .

The other aspect of narrative selfhood is correlative: I am not only

70 accountable, I am one who can always ask others for an account, who can put others to the question. I am part of their story, as they are part of mine. The narrative of any one life is part of an interlocking set of narratives. Moreover this asking for and giving of accounts itself plays an important part in constituting narratives. Asking you what you did and why, saying what I did and why, pondering the differences between your account of what I did and my account of what I did, and *vice versa*, these are essential constituents of all but the very simplest and barest of narratives. Thus without the accountability of the self those trains of events that constitute all but the simplest and barest of narratives could not occur; and without that same accountability narra-

80 tives would lack that continuity required to make both them and the actions that constitute them intelligible. . . .

It is now possible to return to the question from which this enquiry into the nature of human action and identity started: In what does the unity of an individual life consist? The answer is that its unity is the unity of narrative embodied in a single life. To ask 'What is the good for me to ask how best I might live out that unity and bring it to completion.' To ask 'What is the good for man?' is to ask what all answers to the former question must have in common. But now it is important to emphasize that it is the systematic asking of these two questions and the attempt to answer them in deed as well as in word which provide the moral life with its unity. The unity of a human life is the unity of a narrative quest. Quests sometimes fail, are frustrated, abandoned or dissipated into distractions; and human lives may in all these ways also fail. But the only criteria for success or failure in a human life as a whole are the criteria of success or failure in a narrated or to-be-narrated quest. A quest for what?

Two key features of the medieval conception of a quest need to be recalled. The first is that without some at least partly determinate conception of the final *telos* there could not be any beginning to a quest. Some conception of the good for man is required. Whence is such a conception to be drawn? Precisely from those questions which led us to attempt to transcend that limited conception of the virtues which is available in and through practices. It is in looking for a conception of *the* good which will enable us to order other goods, for a conception of *the* good which will enable us to extend our understanding of the purpose and content of the virtues, for a conception of *the* good which will enable us to understand the place of integrity and constancy in life, that we initially define the kind of life which is a quest for the good. But secondly it is clear the medieval conception of a quest is not at all that of a search for something already adequately characterized, as miners search for gold or geologists for oil. It is in the course of the quest and only through encountering and coping with the various particular harms, dangers, temptations and distractions which provide any quest with its episodes and incidents that the goal of the quest is finally to be understood. A quest is always an education both as to the character of that which is sought and in self-knowledge.

The virtues therefore are to be understood as those dispositions which enable us to overcome the harms, dangers, temptations and distractions which we encounter, and which will furnish us with increasing self-knowledge and increasing knowledge of the good. The catalogue of the virtues will therefore include the virtues required to sustain the kind of households and the kind of political communities in which men and women can seek for the good together and the virtues necessary for philosophical enquiry about the character of the good. We have then arrived at a provisional conclusion about the good life for man: the good life for man is the life spent in seeking for the good life for man, and the virtues necessary for the seeking are those which will enable us to understand what more and what else the good life for man is. . . .

I am never able to seek for the good or exercise the virtues only *qua* individual. This is partly because what it is to live the good life concretely varies

130   from circumstance to circumstance even when it is one and the same conception of the good life and one and the same set of virtues which are being
embodied in a human life. What the good life is for a fifth-century Athenian
general will not be the same as what it was for a medieval nun or a
seventeenth-century farmer. But it is not just that different individuals live in
different social circumstances; it is also that we all approach our own circumstances as bearers of a particular social identity. I am someone's son or
daughter, someone else's cousin or uncle; I am a citizen of this or that city, a
member of this or that guild or profession; I belong to this clan, that tribe,
this nation. Hence what is good for me has to be the good for one who
140   inhabits these roles. As such, I inherit from the past of my family, my city,
my tribe, my nation, a variety of debts, inheritances, rightful expectations
and obligations. These constitute the given of my life, my moral starting
point. This is in part what gives my life its own moral particularity.

    This thought is likely to appear alien and even surprising from the stand-
point of modern individualism. From the standpoint of individualism, I wish
to put in question, what are taken to be the merely contingent social features
of my existence. I may biologically be my father's son; but I cannot be held
responsible for what he did unless I choose implicitly or explicitly to assume
such responsibility. I may legally be a citizen of a certain country; but I can-
150   not be held responsible for what my country does or has done unless I choose
implicitly or explicitly to assume such responsibility. . . .

    The contrast with the narrative view of the self is clear. For the story of
my life is always embedded in the story of those communities from which I
derive my identity. I am born with a past; and to try to cut myself off from
that past, in the individualist mode, is to deform my present relationships.
The possession of an historical identity and the possession of a social identity
coincide. Notice that rebellion against my identity is always one possible
mode of expressing it. . . .

    What I am, therefore, is in key part what I inherit, a specific past that is
160   present to some degree in my present. I find myself part of a history and that
is generally to say, whether I like it or not, whether I recognize it or not, one
of the bearers of a tradition. . . .

    A living tradition then is an historically extended, socially embodied argu-
ment, and an argument precisely in part about the goods which constitute
that tradition. Within a tradition the pursuit of goods extends through generations, sometimes through many generations. Hence the individual's search
for his or her good is generally and characteristically conducted within a context defined by those traditions of which the individual's life is a part, and this
is true both of those goods which are internal to practices and of the goods of
170   a single life. Once again the narrative phenomenon of embedding is crucial:
the history of a practice in our time is generally and characteristically embedded in and made intelligible in terms of the larger and longer history of the
tradition through which the practice in its present form was conveyed to us;

the history of each of our own lives is generally and characteristically embedded in and made intelligible in terms of the larger and longer histories of a number of traditions. I have to say 'generally and characteristically' rather than 'always,' for traditions decay, disintegrate and disappear. What then sustains and strengthens traditions? What weakens and destroys them?

The answer in key part is: the exercise or the lack of exercise of the relevant virtues. The virtues find their point and purpose not only in sustaining those relationships necessary if the variety of goods internal to practices are to be achieved and not only in sustaining the form of an individual life in which that individual may seek out his or her good as the good of his or her whole life, but also in sustaining those traditions which provide both practices and individual lives with their necessary historical context. Lack of justice, lack of truthfulness, lack of courage, lack of the relevant intellectual virtues—these corrupt traditions, just as they do those institutions and practices which derive their life from the traditions of which they are the contemporary embodiments. To recognize this is of course also to recognize the existence of an additional virtue, one whose importance is perhaps most obvious when it is least present, the virtue of having an adequate sense of the traditions to which one belongs or which confront one. This virtue is not to be confused with any form of conservative antiquarianism; I am not praising those who choose the conventional conservative role of *laudator temporis acti.* It is rather the case that an adequate sense of tradition manifests itself in a grasp of those future possibilities which the past has made available to the present. Living traditions, just because they continue a not-yet-completed narrative, confront a future whose determinate and determinable character, so far as it possesses any, derives from the past.

INDIVIDUALISM: A NEW VIEW OF FEMINISM
Wendy McElroy

From a talk presented for the Institute for Humane Studies, at Marymount University, Arlington, Virginia, on June 22, 2001.

Women are the equals of men and should be treated as such. 1

For most people, the foregoing statement is the core of what feminism means. But what is equal? How is equality defined?

For example, does it mean equality under existing laws and equal representation in existing institutions? Or does it involve a socio-economic equality—a redistribution of wealth and power—that, in turn, requires new laws and an overturning of existing institutions. It could involve cultural equality by which women are accorded the same level of respect as men with sexual harassment laws, for example, enforcing that respect. 5/6

The manner in which the word "equality" is defined is a litmus test by 10
which different schools of feminism can be distinguished from each other.

Throughout the 19th century, the mainstream of American feminism defined "equality" as equal treatment with men under existing laws and equal representation within existing institutions. More revolutionary feminists protested that the existing laws and institutions were the source of injustice and, as such, could not be reformed. The system had to be swept away before women's rights could be secured. *what kind of laws*

In simplistic terms, the two more revolutionary traditions were socialist feminism, from which contemporary radical feminism draws heavily, and individualist feminism, which is sometimes called libertarian feminism. These 20
two traditions differed dramatically in their approaches to equality.

To socialist feminism, equality was a socioeconomic term. Women could be equal only after private property and the economic relationships it encouraged—that is, capitalism—were eliminated. Equality was also a cultural goal. The 19th century parallel to the 20th century rebellion against 'white male culture'—against pornography, for example—is to be found in the 19th century social purity crusades over such issues as temperance. The social purity campaigns attempted to impose 'virtue'—that is, to impose a morally proper behavior upon society through the force of law—in much the same way that modern feminism attempts to impose political correctness. 30 *not a very good comparison*

To individualist feminism, equality was achieved when the individual rights of women were fully acknowledged under laws that identically protected the person and property of men and women. It made no reference to being economically or socially equal, only to equal treatment under the laws that governed society in such a manner as to protect person and property.

In an ideal society, the legal system would make no distinction based upon secondary characteristics, such as sex, but would protect the rights each

individual equally. Women would neither be oppressed by nor receive any privileges under the law. This society does not exist. As long as the law dis-
40   tinguishes between the sexes, women need to stand up and demand their full and equal rights. No more, no less. This demand forms the political crux of individualist feminism.

This article focuses on the two revolutionary forms of feminism, which are diametrically opposite to each other ideologically and define the two extremes of feminism: radical feminism and individualist feminism.

Speaking in 20th century terms, how do they define equality? For radical feminism, equality is socio-economic and cultural. That is, the class distinc-tions between the genders must be eliminated so that men and women can enjoy social, economic, political and sexual parity. To achieve this, it is nec-
50   essary to sweep away patriarchy, which is a combination of white male cul-ture and capitalism.

For individualist feminism, equality still means equal treatment of men and women under laws that protect person and property. Individualist femi-nism says nothing about whether the resulting wealth should be spread equally between the sexes. That kind of division could only be achieved through the imposition of law, through State intervention over people's lives and property. This is precisely what individualist feminism opposes—the use of force in society.

Let me provide an example of why this last statement is as revolutionary.
60   Consider the issue of marriage. Mainstream feminism says, "Reform divorce laws to make them just." Individualist feminism says, "the very existence of marriage/divorce laws is an injustice because the State has no proper author-ity over what should be a private contract between individuals."

The word "just" has appeared. Briefly, I want to consider how the two forms of feminism approach the concept of justice.

Radical feminism approaches justice as an end state; by which I mean, it provides a specific picture of what constitutes a just society. A just society would be one without patriarchy or capitalism in which the socio-economic and cultural equality of women was fully expressed. In other words, justice is
70   a specific end state in which society embodies specific economic, political and cultural arrangements. It says employers shall pay men and women equally, no one should publish pornography, sexual comments in the work-place must be outlawed.

By contrast, the individualist feminist approach to justice is means-oriented: that is it refers primarily to methodology. The methodology is "any-thing that is peaceful." The only end-state individualist feminism envisions is the protection of person and property—that is, the removal of force and fraud from society.

Otherwise stated, justice is not embodied in a specifically defined end-
80   state: whatever society results from the free and peaceful choices of individu-als are, *politically-speaking*, a just society. Aspects of the society may not be moral and individualist feminists may use education, protest, boycott, and

moral suasion—the whole slate of persuasive strategies—to affect change. What they will not do is use force in the form of government law to restrict peaceful choices.

The conflicting concepts of justice between radical and individualist feminism highlight one of the key differences in their approach to social problems: namely, the willingness of socialist or radical feminists to use the State. This difference is not surprising when you realize that the radical feminist ideal of justice *can* by established by the use of force, by the State. You can, for example, impose a specific economic arrangement on society. You can arrest people for overcharging or for bad hiring practices. But you cannot use force to impose a purely voluntary society: it is a contradiction in terms.

Leaving theory, I want to provide a sense of the unique history of individualist feminism within America.

As an organized force, feminism can be dated from the abolitionist movement that arose in the early 1830s. And the two dominant ideological influences on the feminism that arose were Quakerism and individualism. Many courageous women advanced the status of women prior to that date. For example, in the 17th century, Anne Hutchinson led the first organized attack on the Puritan orthodoxy of the Massachusetts Bay Colony. But these women spoke out as individuals rather than as part of a self-conscious movement dedicated to women's rights.

Abolitionism was the radical anti-slavery movement that demanded the immediate cessation of slavery on the grounds that every human being was a self-owner: every human being had a moral jurisdiction over his or her own body.

Gradually, abolitionist women began to apply the principle of self-ownership to themselves. The abolitionist feminist Abbie Kelley observed: "We have good cause to be grateful to the slave, for the benefit we have received to ourselves, in working for him. In striving to strike his irons off, we found most surely that we were manacled ourselves."

Within abolitionism, women's rights stirred hot debate. Perhaps the strongest advocate of women's rights was the libertarian William Lloyd Garrison, editor of the Liberator, who insisted that anti-slavery was a battle for human rights, not male rights.

Then, a watershed event occurred: the 1840 World Anti-Slavery Conference in London, England. The abolitionist feminism Elizabeth Cady Stanton, who attended the 1840 World Anti-Slavery Conference in London, was embittered by the dismissive treatment women received from the less-enlightened Englishmen. Garrison, who also attended, had been so outraged that he withdrew from the floor to the curtained off section to which the women were relegated.

Later, with the Quaker Lucretia Mott, Stanton planned the 1848 Seneca Falls Convention to discuss women's rights. There, women's suffrage resolution was introduced: "Resolved, that it is the duty of the women of this country to secure to themselves their sacred right to the elective franchise." The

What does it matter that one person is acting in force over another - none for her.

resolution met strong resistance from Mott and other members of the old guard of abolitionist feminists who were <u>deeply opposed to using govern-</u>

130 <u>ment to solve social problems.</u> But it passed.

Unfortunately for the American individualist tradition—in all its manifestations—the Civil War erupted. If 'War is the <u>health of state</u>', as Randolph Bourne claimed, then it is the <u>death of individualism.</u> There are many reasons for this; one of them being that individualism is, at its roots, an anti-Statist ideology, and war involves an increase in State power that never seems to roll back to its prewar level when peace is declared.

After the war, the key issue for feminism became the Constitution; women wished to be included in the wording of the Fourteenth and Fifteenth Amendments that aimed at securing freedom for blacks. The Four-

140 teenth Amendment introduced the word "male" into the United States Constitution. The Fifteenth Amendment assured that the right to vote could not be abridged because of "race, color, or previous condition of servitude." It made no reference to sex. The abolitionist women felt betrayed. Susan B. Anthony wrote, "We repudiated man's counsels forever." This became a pivotal point at which mainstream feminism became alienated from men.

At this juncture, the feminist movement diversified, with the mainstream focusing its efforts into a drive for woman's suffrage. Other feminists were suspicious of political solutions to social problems.

Individualist feminism found expression within a variety of social move-

150 ments, especially free love, free thought, and individualist anarchism. There, these feminists functioned as a radical segment, where they represented and pursued the interests of women.

The most important vehicle was the free love movement that sought to separate the State from sexual matters such as marriage, adultery, divorce, and birth control. Free love demanded that such matters be left to the conscience and contracts of those involved. Consider free love, very briefly. . .

In 1889, a woman who had just risked her life in a self-induced abortion wrote to the libertarian periodical, *Lucifer the Light Bearer*, pleading:

"I know I am dreadful wicked, but I am sure to be in the condition from

160 which I risked my life to be free, and I cannot stand it. . . Would you know of any appliance that will prevent conception? If there is anything reliable, you will save my life by telling me of it."

The woman wrote to Lucifer—published and edited by Moses Harman— because, in the late 1800s, it was one of the few forums openly promoting birth control. Moses Harman insisted that woman's self-ownership be fully acknowledged in all sexual arrangements.

Unfortunately, Harman ran counter to the Comstock Act (1873), which prohibited the mailing of obscene matter but did not define what constituted obscenity. Whatever it was, it specifically included contraceptives and birth

170 control information. A witchhunt ensued.

Against this backdrop, Harman began his "<u>free word</u>" policy by which he refused to edit correspondence to Lucifer that contained explicit language. Harman maintained, "Words are not deeds, and it is not the province of civil law to take preventative measures against remote or possible consequences of words, no matter how violent or incendiary." He openly discussed birth control.

In 1887, the staff of Lucifer was arrested for the publication of three letters and indicted on 270 counts of obscenity. One letter had described the plight of a woman whose husband forced sex upon her even though it tore the stitches from a recent operation. It is a very early analysis of forced sex within marriage constituting rape.

Harman's legal battles against the Comstock laws continued from 1887 through to 1906, his last imprisonment during which he spent a year at hard labor, often breaking rocks for eight hours a day in the Illinois snow. Harman was 75 at the time."

Interestingly, when the authorities came to arrest Harman in 1887, his 16-year old daughter Lillian was not present. She was in jail herself, having been arrested for engaging in a private marriage—that is, a marriage that consisted of a private contract, without Church or State involvement. At that ceremony, Moses had refused to give his daughter away, stating that she was the owner of her person.

The Harman episode is not a tale of individualist feminism because he championed birth control. A number of traditions did that. Harman was an individualist feminist because of the ideology and methodology he used. He based his arguments on women's self-ownership and extended this principle to all arrangements, sexual and economic. He refused to use the State in personal relationships because he considered it to be the institutionalization of force in society. He actively opposed laws that restricted peaceful behavior.

Moses Harman—along with Voltairine de Cleyre—are the most prominent figures from the 19th century. In their own time, such figures as Harman were well recognized by contemporary radicals. Emma Goldman in her autobiography "Living My Life" credited him with being a pioneer who made her birth control work possible. In 1907, when George Bernard Shaw was asked why he did not tour America, he replied if the "brigands" could imprison Moses Harman for expressing basically the same views set forth, in his play *Man and Superman* he did not care to come to America and test his luck. It is a travesty that he is forgotten today.

So with a small taste of history, let's move back to theory.

Arguably, the most important concept in feminism today is "class." There are men, there are women, they are separate classes. . . or so the theory goes.

The foregoing statement is different than the tradition "war between the sexes." That war refers to the fact that, in the same circumstances, men and women often want different things and, so, come into conflict. For example, on a date men are typically said to want sex whereas women are said to seek a relationship. This is not the conflict to which I am referring. I am talking about a war of the gender.

A class is nothing more than an arbitrary grouping of entities that share common characteristics as determined from a certain epistemological point of view. In short, what constitutes a class is defined by the purposes of the definer. For example, a researcher studying drug addiction may break society into classes of drug using and non-drug using people. Classes can be defined by almost any factor salient to the definer.

For radical feminists, gender is the salient factor. Many fields of endeavor use biology as a dividing line. For example, medicine often separates the sexes in order to apply different medical treatment and techniques. Women are examined for breast cancer and men for prostate problems. But medicine does not claim that the basic interests of men and women as human beings conflict or even diverge. The sexes share a basic biology that requires the same approach of nutrition, exercise and common sense lifestyle choices. In short, although the biology of the sexes differs, they share the same goal of good health, which can be defined and pursued in roughly the same manner.

By contrast, radical feminism advocates a theory of fundamental class conflict based on gender. It claims that males not only share a biological identity but also a political and social one. The political interests of men are in necessary conflict with those of women.

The concept of class conflict is widely associated with Karl Marx, who popularized it as a tool to predict the political interests and social behavior of individuals. Once the class affiliation of an individual was known, his or her behavior became predictable. To Marx, the salient feature defining a person's class was his relationship to the means of production: was he a capitalist or a worker? This is a form of relational class analysis that describes a class in terms of its relationship to an institution.

Radical feminism has adapted this theory. Catherine MacKinnon refers to the analysis as "post-Marxist." By this, she means that radical feminism embraces many aspects of Marxism but rejects its insistence that economic status, not gender, is the salient political factor that determines a class. Thus, radical feminism incorporates such Marxist/socialist ideas as "surplus labor" through which one class is said to use the free market in order to commit economic theft upon another class. (An example of surplus labor in radical feminism is unsalaried housework.) The classification 'male' becomes so significant that it predicts and determines how the individuals within that class will behave. Thus, radical feminists can level accusations of "rapist" at non-violent men because they are beneficiaries of 'the rape culture' established by patriarchy.

To prevent the oppression of women, it is necessary to deconstruct the institutions through which men control women—institutions such as the free market.

This class analysis makes no sense within the framework of individualist feminism that declares all human beings to have the same political interests.

Individualism has a long and differing tradition of class analysis. The salient factor by which people are categorized is whether he or she uses force in society. Do they acquire wealth or power through merit and productivity or do they use aggression, often in the form of law, to appropriate wealth and power from others? Expressed in the most basic form, individualist feminism asks, "are you a member of the political or productive class?" This, too, is a form of relational class analysis because it asks, "What is your relationship to the State?"

Individualist feminism class analysis does not predict the behavior of individuals. Both men and women can use the political means. An individual can change his or her class affiliation at will, abandoning the use of force and adopting the economic means instead. In short, classes within individualist feminist analysis are fluid. This is not true of radical feminist analysis that is based on biology. Within radical feminism, classes are static.

This difference has many implications. One is that individualist feminist class analysis offers no predictive value. Just because an individual has been a member of the political class in the past says nothing about whether he or she will continue to be so in the future.

This fluidity has a further implication. Namely, there is no necessary conflict between the genders. The fact that men have oppressed women in the past says nothing about whether they will oppress women in the future. Whether an individual man is an oppressor or a friend depends on whether he uses the political means and this is a matter of his conscious choice. Men are not the enemy.

CONCLUSION

Radical and individualist feminism constitute the two extremes of the feminist movement. One advocates state-control; the other, self-control. One considers men to be the enemy; the other embraces men as valued partners. But the most important feature of the ideological divide is individualist feminism's insistence on applying the radically personal principle "A woman's body, a woman's right" across the board to all issues.

WHITE PRIVILEGE AND MALE PRIVILEGE: A PERSONAL ACCOUNT OF COMING TO SEE CORRESPONDENCES THROUGH WORK IN WOMEN'S STUDIES
Peggy McIntosh

Through work to bring materials and perspectives from Women's Studies into the rest of the curriculum, I have often noticed men's unwillingness to grant that they are overprivileged in the curriculum, even though they may grant that women are disadvantaged. Denials that amount to taboos surround the subject of advantages that men gain from women's disadvantages. These denials protect male privilege from being fully recognized, acknowledged, lessened, or ended.

Thinking through unacknowledged male privilege as a phenomenon with a life of its won, I realized that since hierarchies in our society are interlocking, there was most likely a phenomenon of white privilege that was similarly denied and protected, but alive and real in its effects. As a white person, I realized I had been taught about racism as something that puts others at a disadvantage, but had been taught not to see one of its corollary aspects, white privilege, which puts me at an advantage.

I think whites are carefully taught not to recognize white privilege, as males are taught not to recognize male privilege. So I have begun in an untutored way to ask what it is like to have white privilege. This paper is a partial record of my personal observations and not a scholarly analysis. It is based on my daily experiences within my particular circumstances.

I have come to see white privilege as an invisible package of unearned assets that I can count on cashing in each day, but about which I was "meant" to remain oblivious. White privilege is like an invisible weightless knapsack of special provisions, assurances, tools, maps, guides, codebooks, passports, visas, clothes, compass, emergency gear, and blank checks.

Since I have had trouble facing white privilege, and describing its results in my life, I saw parallels here with men's reluctance to acknowledge male privilege. Only rarely will a man go beyond acknowledging that women are disadvantaged to acknowledging that men have unearned advantage, or that unearned privilege has not been good for men's development as human beings, or for society's development, or that privilege systems might ever be challenged and *changed*.

I will review here several types or layers of denial that I see at work protecting, and preventing awareness about, entrenched male privilege. Then I will draw parallels, from my own experience, with the denials that veil the facts of white privilege. Finally, I will list forty-six ordinary and daily ways in which I

experience having white privilege, by contrast with my African American colleagues in the same building. This list is not intended to be generalizable. Others can make their own lists from within their own life circumstances.

40   Writing this paper has been difficult, despite warm receptions for the
talks on which it is based.[1] For describing white privilege makes one newly
accountable. As we in Women's Studies work reveal male privilege and ask
men to give up some of their power, so one who writes about having white
privilege must ask, "Having described it, what will I do to lessen or end it?"

The denial of men's overprivileged state takes many forms in discussions
of curriculum change work. Some claim that men must be central in the curriculum because they have done most of what is important or distinctive in
life or in civilization. Some recognize sexism in the curriculum but deny that
it makes male students seem unduly important in life. Others agree that certain *individual* thinkers are male oriented but deny that there is any systemic
50   tendency in disciplinary frameworks or epistemology to overempower men as
a group. Those men who do grant that male privilege takes institutionalized
and embedded forms are still likely to deny that male hegemony has opened
doors for them personally. Virtually all men deny that male overreward alone
can explain men's centrality in all the inner sanctums of our most powerful
institutions. Moreover, those few who will acknowledge that male privilege
systems have overempowered them usually end up doubting that we could
dismantle these privilege systems. They may say they will work to improve
women's status, in the society or in the university, but they can't or won't support the idea of lessening men's. In curricular terms, this is the point at which
60   they say that they regret they cannot use any of the interesting new scholarship on women because the syllabus is full. When the talk turns to giving
men less cultural room, even the most thoughtful and fair-minded of the
men I know will tend to reflect, or fall back on, conservative assumptions
about the inevitability of present gender relations and distributions of power,
calling on precedent or sociobiology and psychobiology to demonstrate that
male domination is natural and follows inevitably from evolutionary pressures. Others resort to arguments from "experience" or religion or social
responsibility or wishing and dreaming.

After I realized, through faculty development work in Women's Studies,
70   the extent to which men work from a base of unacknowledged privilege, I
understood that much of their oppressiveness was unconscious. Then I
remembered the frequent charges from women of color that white women
whom they encounter are oppressive. I began to understand why we are justly
seen as oppressive, even when we don't see ourselves that way. At the very
least, obliviousness of one's privileged state can make a person or group irri-
tating to be with. I began to count the ways in which I enjoy unearned skin
privilege and have been conditioned into oblivion about its existence, unable
to see that it put me "ahead" in any way, or put in my people ahead, overre-
warding us and yet also paradoxically damaging us, or that it could or should
80   be changed.

My schooling gave me no training in seeing myself as an oppressor, as an unfairly advantaged person, or as a participant in a damaged culture. I was taught to see myself as an individual whose moral state depended on her individual moral will. At school, we were not taught about slavery in any depth; we were not taught to see slaveholders as damaged people. Slaves were seen as the only group at risk of being dehumanized. My schooling followed the pattern which Elizabeth Minnich has pointed out: whites are taught to think of their fives as morally neutral, normative, and average, and also ideal, so that when we work to benefit others, this is seen as work that will allow "them" to be more like "us." I think many of us know how obnoxious this   90
attitude can be in men.

After frustration with men who would not recognize male privilege, I decided to try to work on myself at least by identifying some of the daily effects of white privilege in my life. It is crude work, at this stage, but I will give here a list of special circumstances and conditions I experience that I did not earn but that I have been made to feel are mine by birth, by citizenship, and by virtue of being a conscientious law-abiding "normal" person of good-will. I have chosen those conditions that I think in my case *attach somewhat more to skin-color privilege* than to class, religion, ethnic status, or geographi-cal location, though these other privileging factors are intricately intertwined.   100
As far as I can see, my Afro-American co-workers, friends, and acquaintances with whom I come into daily or frequent contact in this particular time, place, and line of work cannot count on most of these conditions.

1. I can, if I wish, arrange to be in the company of people of my race most of the time.
2. I can avoid spending time with people whom I was trained to mis-trust and who have learned to mistrust my kind or me.
3. If I should need to move, I can be pretty sure of renting or purchas-ing housing in an area which I can afford and in which I would want to live.   110
4. I can be reasonably sure that my neighbors in such a location will be neutral or pleasant to me.
5. I can go shopping alone most of the time, fairly well assured that I will not be followed or harassed by store detectives.
6. I can turn on the television or open to the front page of the paper and see people of my race widely and positively represented.
7. When I am told about our national heritage or about "civilization," I am shown that people of my color made it what it is.
8. I can be sure that my children will be given curricular materials that testify to the existence of their race.   120
9. If I want to, I can be pretty sure of finding a publisher for this piece on white privilege.
10. I can be fairly sure of having my voice heard in a group in which I am the only member of my race.

11. I can be casual about whether or not to listen to another woman's voice in a group in which she is the only member of her race.

12. I can go into a book shop and count on finding the writing of my race represented, into a supermarket and find the staple foods that fit with my cultural traditions, into a hairdresser's shop and find someone who can deal with my hair.

13. Whether I use checks, credit cards, or cash, I can count on my skin color not to work against the appearance that I am financially reliable.

14. I could arrange to protect our young children most of the time from people who might not like them.

15. I did not have to educate our children to be aware of systemic racism for their own daily physical protection.

16. I can be pretty sure that my children's teachers and employers will tolerate them if they fit school and workplace norms; my chief worries about them do not concern others' attitudes toward their race.

17. I can talk with my mouth full and not have people put this down to my color.

18. I can swear, or dress in secondhand clothes, or not answer letters, without having people attribute these choices to the bad morals, the poverty, or the illiteracy of my race.

19. I can speak in public to a powerful male group without putting my race on trial.

20. I can do well in a challenging situation without being called a credit to my race.

21. I am never asked to speak for all the people of my racial group.

22. I can remain oblivious to the language and customs of persons of color who constitute the world's majority without feeling in my culture any penalty for such oblivion.

23. I can criticize our government and talk about how much I fear its policies and behavior without being seen as a cultural outsider.

24. I can be reasonably sure that if I ask to talk to "the person in charge," I will be facing a person of my race.

25. If a traffic cop pulls me over or if the IRS audits my tax return, I can be sure I haven't been singled out because of my race.

26. I can easily buy posters, postcards, picture books, greeting cards, dolls, toys, and children's magazines featuring people of my race.

27. I can go home from most meetings of organizations I belong to feeling somewhat tied in, rather than isolated, out of place, outnumbered, unheard, held at a distance, or feared.

28. I can be pretty sure that an argument with a colleague of another race is more likely to jeopardize her chances for advancement than to jeopardize mine.

29. I can be fairly sure that if I argue for the promotion of a person of another race, or a program centering on race, this is not likely to cost me heavily within my present setting, even if my colleagues disagree with me.

30. If I declare there is a racial issue at hand, or there isn't a racial issue at hand, my race will lend me more credibility for either position than a person of color will have.

31. I can choose to ignore developments in minority writing and minority activist programs, or disparage them, or learn from them, but in any case, I can find ways to be more or less protected from negative consequences of any of these choices.

32. My culture gives me little fear about ignoring the perspectives and powers of people of other races.

33. I am not made acutely aware that my shape, bearing, or body odor   180
will be taken as a reflection on my race.

34. I can worry about racism without being seen as self-interested or self-seeking.

35. I can take a job with an affirmative action employer without having my co-workers on the job suspect that I got it because of my race.

36. If my day, week, or year is going badly, I need not ask of each negative episode or situation whether it has racial overtones.

37. I can be pretty sure of finding people who would be willing to talk with me and advise me about my next steps, professionally.

38. I can think over many options, social, political, imaginative, or pro-   190
fessional, without asking whether a person of my race would be accepted or allowed to do what I want to do.

39. I can be late to a meeting without having the lateness reflect on my race.

40. I can choose public accommodation without fearing that people of my race cannot get in or will be mistreated in the places I have chosen.

41. I can be sure that if I need legal or medical help, my race will not work against me.

42. I can arrange my activities so that I will never have to experience feel-   200
ings of rejection owing to my race.

43. If I have low credibility as a leader, I can be sure that my race is not the problem.

44. I can easily find academic courses and institutions that give attention only to people of my race.

45. I can expect figurative language and imagery in all of the arts to testify to experiences of my race.

46. I can choose blemish cover or bandages in "flesh" color and have them more or less match my skin.

I repeatedly forgot each of the realizations on this list until I wrote it   210
down. For me, white privilege has turned out to be an elusive and fugitive subject. The pressure to avoid it is great, for in facing it I must give up the myth of meritocracy. If these things are true, this is not such a free country; one's life is not what one makes it; many doors open for certain people through no virtues of their own. These perceptions mean also that my moral

condition is not what I had been led to believe. The appearance of being a good citizen rather than a troublemaker comes in large part from having all sorts of doors open automatically because of my color.

220   A further paralysis of nerve comes from literary silence protecting privilege. My clearest memories of finding such analysis are in Lillian Smith's unparalleled *Killers of the Dream* and Margaret Andersen's review of Karen and Mamie Fields' *Lemon Swamp*. Smith, for example, wrote about walking toward black children on the street and knowing they would step into the gutter; Andersen contrasted the pleasure that she, as a white child, took on summer driving trips to the south with Karen Fields' memories of driving in a closed car stocked with all necessities lest, in stopping, her black family should suffer "insult, or worse." Adrienne Rich also recognizes and writes about daily experiences of privilege, but in my observation, white women's writing in this area is far more often on systemic racism than on our daily

230   lives as light-skinned women.[2]

In unpacking this invisible knapsack of white privilege, I have listed conditions of daily experience that I once took for granted, as neutral, normal, and universally available to everybody, just as I once thought of a male-focused curriculum as the neutral or accurate account that can speak for all. Nor did I think of any of these perquisites as bad for the holder. I now think that we need a more finely differentiated taxonomy of privilege, for some of these varieties are only what one would want for everyone in a just society, and others give license to be ignorant, oblivious, arrogant, and destructive. Before proposing some more finely tuned categorization, I will make some

240   observations about the general effects of these conditions on my life and expectations.

In this potpourri of examples, some privileges make me feel at home in the world. Others allow me to escape penalties or dangers that others suffer. Through some, I escape fear, anxiety, insult, injury, or a sense of not being welcome, not being real. Some keep me from having to hide, to be in disguise, to feel sick or crazy, to negotiate each transaction from the position of being an outsider or, within my group, a person who is suspected of having too close links with a dominant culture. Most keep me from having to be angry.

I see a pattern running through the matrix of white privilege, a pattern of

250   assumptions that were passed on to me as a white person. There was one main piece of cultural turf; it was my own turf, and I was among those who could control the turf. I could measure up to the cultural standards and take advantage of the many options I saw around me to make what the culture would call a success of my life. *My skin color was an asset for any move I was educated to want to make.* I could think of myself as "belonging" in major ways and of making social systems work for me. I could freely disparage, fear, neglect, or be oblivious to anything outside of the dominant cultural forms. Being of the main culture, I could also criticize it fairly freely. My life was reflected back to me frequently enough so that I felt, with regard to my race,

260   if not to my sex, like one of the real people.

Whether through the curriculum or in the newspaper, the television, the economic system, or the general look of people in the streets, I received daily signals and indications that my people counted and that others *either didn't exist or must be trying, not very successfully, to be like people of my race.* I was given cultural permission not to hear voices of people of other races or a tepid cultural tolerance for hearing or acting on such voices. I was also raised not to suffer seriously from anything that darker-skinned people might say about my group, "protected," though perhaps I should more accurately say *prohibited*, through the habits of my economic class and social group, from living in racially mixed groups or being reflective about interactions between people of differing races.

In proportion as my racial group was being made confident, comfortable, and oblivious, other groups were likely being made unconfident, uncomfortable, and alienated. Whiteness protected me from many kinds of hostility, distress, and violence, which I was being subtly trained to visit in turn upon people of color.

For this reason, the word "privilege" now seems to me misleading. Its connotations are too positive to fit the conditions and behaviors which "privilege systems" produce. We usually think of privilege as being a favored state, whether earned, or conferred by birth or luck. School graduates are reminded they are privileged and urged to use their (enviable) assets well. The word "privilege" carries the connotation of being something everyone must want. Yet some of the conditions I have described here work to systemically overempower certain groups. Such privilege simply *confers dominance*, gives permission to control, because of one's race or sex. The kind of privilege that gives license to some people to be, at best, thoughtless and, at worst, murderous should not continue to be referred to as a desirable attribute. Such "privilege" may be widely desired without being in any way beneficial to the whole society.

Moreover, though "privilege" may confer power, it does not confer moral strength. Those who do not depend on conferred dominance have straits and qualities that may never develop in those who do. Just as Women's Studies courses indicate that women survive their political circumstances to lead lives that hold the human race together, so "underprivileged" people of color who are the world's majority have survived their oppression and lived survivors' lives from which the white global minority can and must learn. In some groups, those dominated have actually become strong through *not* having all of these unearned advantages, and this gives them a great deal to teach the others. Members of so-called privileged groups can seem foolish, ridiculous, infantile, or dangerous by contrast.

I want, then, to distinguish between earned strength and unearned power conferred systematically. Power from unearned privilege can look like strength when it is, in fact, permission to escape or to dominate. But not all of the privileges on my list are inevitably damaging. Some, like the expectation that neighbors will be decent to you, or that your race will not count

against you in court, should be the norm in a just society and should be considered as the entitlement of everyone. Others, like the privilege not to listen to less powerful people, distort the humanity of the holders as well as the ignored groups. Still others, like finding one's staple foods everywhere, may
310   be a function of being a member of a numerical majority in the population. Others have to do with not having to labor under pervasive negative stereotyping and mythology.

We might at least start by distinguishing between positive advantages that we can work to spread, to the point where they are not advantages at all but simply part of the normal civic and social fabric, and negative types of advantage that unless rejected will always reinforce our present hierarchies. For example, the positive "privilege" of belonging, the feeling that one belongs within the human circle, as Native Americans say, fosters development and should not be seen as privilege for a few. It is, let us say, an entitlement that
320   none of us should have to earn; ideally it is an *unearned entitlement*. At present, since only a few have it, it is an *unearned advantage* for them. The negative "privilege" that gave me cultural permission not to take darker-skinned others seriously can be seen as arbitrarily conferred dominance and should not be desirable for anyone. This paper results from a process of coming to see that some of the power that I originally saw as attendant on being a human being in the United States consisted in *unearned advantage* and *conferred dominance*, as well as other kinds of special circumstances not universally taken for granted.

In writing this paper I have also realized that white identity and status (as
330   well as class identity and status) give me considerable power to choose whether to broach this subject and its trouble. I can pretty well decide whether to disappear and avoid and not listen and escape the dislike I may engender in other people through this essay, or interrupt, answer, interpret, preach, correct, criticize, and control to some extent what goes on in reaction to it. Being white, I am given considerable power to escape many kinds of danger or penalty as well as to choose which risks I want to take.

There is an analogy here, once again, with Women's Studies. Our male colleagues do not have a great deal to lose in supporting Women's Studies, but they do not have a great deal to lose if they oppose it either. They simply
340   have the power to decide whether to commit themselves to more equitable distributions of power. They will probably feel few penalties whatever choice they make; they do not seem, in any obvious short-term sense, the ones at risk, though they and we are all at risk because of the behaviors that have been rewarded in them.

Through Women's Studies work I have met very few men who are truly distressed about systemic, unearned male advantage and conferred dominance. And so one question for me and others like me is whether we will be like them, or whether we will get truly distressed, even outraged, about unearned race advantage and conferred dominance and if so, what we will do
350   to lessen them. In any case, we need to do more work in identifying how they

actually affect our daily lives. We need more down-to-earth writing by people about these taboo subjects. We need more understanding of the ways in which white "privilege" damages white people, for these are not the same ways in which it damages the victimized. Skewed white psyches are an inseparable part of the picture, though I do not want to confuse the kinds of damage done to the holders of special assets and to those who suffer the deficits. Many, perhaps most, of our white students in the United States think that racism doesn't affect them because they are not people of color; they do not see "whiteness" as a racial identity. Many men likewise think that Women's Studies does not bear on their own existences because they are not female; they do not see themselves as having gendered identities. Insisting on the universal "effects" of "privilege" systems, then, becomes one of our chief tasks, and being more explicit about the *particular* effects in particular contexts is another. Men need to join us in this work.

In addition, since race and sex are not the only advantaging systems at work, we need to similarly examine the daily experience of having age advantage, or ethnic advantage, or physical ability, or advantage related to nationality, religion, or sexual orientation. Professor Marine Evans suggested to me that in many ways the list I made also applies directly to heterosexual privilege. This is a still more taboo subject than race privilege: the daily ways in which heterosexual privilege makes some persons comfortable or powerful, providing supports, assets, approvals, and rewards to those who live or expect to live in heterosexual pairs. Unpacking that content is still more difficult, owing to the deeper imbeddedness of heterosexual advantage and dominance and stricter taboos surrounding these.

But to start such an analysis I would put this observation from my own experience: The fact that I live under the same roof with a man triggers all kinds of societal assumptions about my worth, politics, life, and values and triggers a host of unearned advantages and powers. After recasting many elements from the original list I would add further observations like these:

1. My children do not have to answer questions about why I live with my partner (my husband).
2. I have no difficulty finding neighborhoods where people approve of our household.
3. Our children are given texts and classes that implicitly support our kind of family unit and do not turn them against my choice of domestic partnership.
4. I can travel alone or with my husband without expecting embarrassment or hostility in those who deal with us.
5. Most people I meet will see my marital arrangements as an asset to my life or as a favorable comment on my likeability, my competence, or my mental health.
6. I can talk about the social events of a weekend without fearing most listeners' reactions.

7. I will feel welcomed and "normal" in the usual walks of public life, institutional and social.
8. In many contexts, I am seen as "all right" in daily work on women because I do not live chiefly with women.

Difficulties and dangers surrounding the task of finding parallels are
400 many. Since racism, sexism, and heterosexism are not the same, the advantages associated with them should not be seen as the same. In addition, it is hard to isolate aspects of unearned advantage that derive chiefly from social class, economic class, race, religion, region, sex, or ethnic identity. The oppressions are both distinct and interlocking, as the Combahee River Collective statement of 1977 continues to remind us eloquently.[3]

One factor seems clear about all of the interlocking oppressions. They take both active forms that we can see and embedded forms that members of the dominant group are taught not to see. In my class and place, I did not see myself as racist because I was taught to recognize racism only in individ-
410 ual acts of meanness by members of my group, never in invisible systems conferring racial dominance on my group from birth. Likewise, we are taught to think that sexism or heterosexism is carried on only through intentional, individual acts of discrimination, meanness, or cruelty, rather than in invisible systems conferring unsought dominance on certain groups. Disapproving of the systems won't be enough to change them. I was taught to think that racism could end if white individuals changed their attitudes; many men think sexism can be ended by individual changes in daily behavior toward women. But a man's sex provides advantage for him whether or not he approves of the way in which dominance has been conferred on his group. A
420 "white" skin in the United States opens many doors for whites whether or not we approve of the way dominance has been conferred on us. Individual acts can palliate, but cannot end, these problems. To redesign social systems, we need first to acknowledge their colossal unseen dimensions. The silences and denials surrounding privilege are the key political tool here. They keep the thinking about equality or equity incomplete, protecting unearned advantage and conferred dominance by making these taboo subjects. Most talk by whites about equal opportunity seems to me now to be about equal opportunity to try to get into a position of dominance while denying that systems of dominance exist.

430 Obliviousness about white advantage, like obliviousness about male advantage, is kept strongly inculturated in the United States so as to maintain the myth of meritocracy, the myth that democratic choice is equally available to all. Keeping most people unaware that freedom of confident action is there for just a small number of people props up those in power and serves to keep power in the hands of the same groups that have most of it already. Though systemic change takes many decades, there are pressing questions for me and I imagine for some others like me if we raise our daily

consciousness on the perquisites of being light-skinned. What will we do with such knowledge? As we know from watching men, it is an open question whether we will choose to use unearned advantage to weaken invisible privilege systems and whether we will use any of our arbitrarily awarded power to try to reconstruct power systems on a broader base.   440

ENDNOTES

1. This paper was presented at the Virginia Women's Studies Association conference in Richmond in April, 1986, and the American Educational Research Association conference in Boston in October, 1986, and discussed with two groups of participants in the Dodge seminars for Secondary School Teachers in New York and Boston in the spring of 1987.

2. Andersen, Margaret, "Race and the Social Science Curriculum: A Teaching and Learning Discussion." *Radical Teacher*, November, 1984, pp. 17–20. Smith, Lillian, *Killers of the Dream*, New York: W. W. Norton, 1949.

3. "A Black Feminist Statement," The Combahee River Collective, pp. 13–22 in G. Hull, P. Scott, B. Smith, Eds., *All the Women Are White, All the Blacks Are Men, But Some of Us Are Brave: Black Women's Studies*, Old Westbury, NY: The Feminist Press, 1982.

WHAT'S SO GOOD ABOUT A COLLEGE EDUCATION?
Andrew P. Mills[1]

W hy is it good to go to college? What is so valuable about a college education? College is expensive, and you wouldn't spend all that money
on something that wasn't valuable. Moreover, college requires a great deal of
work, and it requires that you spend time reading and writing and studying
and going to class and taking tests—time that you could spend doing other
things—and you wouldn't spend your time on all those college-related tasks
unless you thought you were getting something valuable for all your effort.
You are in college, and so you think that getting a college education is a good
thing—that it is valuable in some way or other—but what sort of value does
it have? It's worthwhile to spend some time thinking about the answer to this
question, for it will affect the way you spend your time at college, and it will
affect the sort of education that you get there. If you don't know why college
is valuable, you're very likely wasting your time and money and effort during
your college years.

   Most people give what I will call the simple "Can Opener Answer" to this
question. I think there are two serious problems with that answer, and that is
what I want to convince you of. Once we see what is wrong with the simple
Can Opener Answer, we can talk about some of the differences between high
school and college, and the right way to approach your college education.

THE CAN OPENER ANSWER

Why is it good to have a can opener? People pay money for can openers, and
people spend time with can openers, so they must think that can openers are
valuable in some way or other, but how are they valuable? The answer here is
easy: can openers are valuable because they allow you to open cans. There's
tasty stuff inside of cans, and you can't get at the tasty stuff unless the can is
open, and you can't open the can unless you've got a can opener. If you could
open cans by snapping your fingers, then you wouldn't need a can opener.
Can openers are *tools:* they are valuable, but only as tools or instruments are
valuable. That is, they are valuable because of what you can get with them.
Once we acquire the ability to open cans by snapping our fingers, or once
they stop hiding the tasty stuff inside of cans, then can openers will be useless. They will cease to have the sort of value they now have.[2]

   So what's the Can Opener Answer to the question about the value of college? It's this: a college education is valuable because of what you can do with
it. In particular, it's valuable because you can trade it for a job. Crudely put,
you can take your diploma, show it to an employer, and then you'll get a job.
Of course the job interview process is not that easy, but in rough outline
that's how many people (maybe even you!) think about the value of a college

Reprinted by permission of the author.

education. I hope you can see the analogy with the can opener case. The job is the analogue of the tasty stuff in the can. If you could get a job without a

40 college education, then, it would seem, it's silly and wasteful and foolish to spend all that time and money and effort at college. Just as it would be silly to spend money on a can opener if you could open the can by snapping your fingers.

People who ask the question, "So, what are you going to do with an English major?", or "How much money do Sociology majors make?" are thinking in can opener terms. They think that the only thing valuable about a college education is what sort of job (and how high-paying a job) you can get with that college education. And they also think that people who major in Classics or Philosophy or Women's Studies won't get very good jobs. So, they think, since

50 you're spending all that time and money and effort on college, you should get yourself the sort of education that is *useful* for getting a good job. So, they might say, you should major in Nursing or Education or Business or Journalism or Computer Science because those are the sort of majors that you can trade for good jobs.

Now I think there is something right about the Can Opener Answer, but there are two serious problems with it. Let me now turn to those.

THE FIRST PROBLEM WITH THE CAN OPENER ANSWER

What the Can Opener Answer has right is that a college education is useful for getting a job. After all, college graduates, in general, have better, higher paying, more interesting, potentially more fulfilling jobs than those without

60 college degrees. But that is not the only thing a college education is useful for. A college education—in particular, a broad-based, multi-disciplinary, liberal arts education—is useful for so much more. The problem with the simple Can Opener Answer is that it misses this "so much more" when it focuses merely on the job-getting features of a college degree. Here are just some of the other things that college educated people are able to do.

- College can equip us for our leisure time just as much, if not more so, than it can equip us for our working lives. College educated people are able to appreciate and enjoy literature, art, music, essays, movies, and other products of the culture. Or, to put it better, the sort of apprecia-

70 tion and enjoyment that they have is deeper because of their education: those with a liberal arts education see things in movies and music and literature that those without the education don't. And, as a consequence, their experience is richer.

- We live in a democracy, the success of which requires that each of us participates actively and intelligently in the democratic institutions. Such participation includes not simply voting, but critically examining the candidates' positions, speaking out as an advocate for policy change, perhaps even serving in a leadership role on a governmental body. Moreover, it requires being critical of the institutions themselves, and seeing what needs changing and why. The appreciation of history, the ability to formulate a persuasive argument, an analytic skill with budgets and statistics and polling data—these are all skills you get as a college educated person and they are skills necessary for successful participation as a citizen in a democracy.

• The developments in technology and the advances in science (especially medical science) are an ever-present, and ever-more-important part of our lives. The growing presence of medications in the treatment of psychological maladies, the possibilities opened up by study and manipulation of DNA, and the prospects for artificial intelligence (just to name a few) are developments that require an intelligent response. Which of the many possibilities opened up to us by science should be pursued? How reliable is DNA testing? Should we treat depression with a drug or with traditional therapy? College graduates are well-positioned to answer these questions because they know some science, and can distinguish quackery from good scientific practice. Moreover, they are accustomed to asking questions about *value*[3] and these are the sorts of questions which very much need to be asked about technological developments.

• This last point applies not simply to the advances in science and technology, but to the information that comes to us via the media. We need to be able to distinguish the foolish fad from the important trend; we need to be able to determine which news outlets are reliable and which are overly biased; we need to be able to figure out where to turn for information and how to navigate between the twin vices of gullibility (believing everything you read in the newspaper, or see on the internet, or hear from a TV anchor) and skepticism (believing nothing that anybody else tells you). Because during your college education you will spend a significant amount of time doing research and evaluating sources, you will be, once you finish college, perfectly situated to be intelligent consumers of information.

• Finally, a college education equips people with the tools for self-examination that renders them able to make informed and intelligent choices about the direction of their own lives. College may equip you for a career, but you have to decide which career to pursue, and how to balance the competing demands of work and family. At what point do you leave the safety of an old but boring job for the insecurity of a new but exciting job? How important a role should your religious or political beliefs play in the life you lead? Should you work for (or buy the products of) a company that exploits child laborers? Should you buy your groceries from a large national chain or from the local, but perhaps more expensive, market? At what point should you put a moral principle ahead of economic interest? These are decisions that we all must make; if we don't, someone else will make them for us.

And by providing the experience and guidance at thinking through these sorts of questions (and other, much more difficult ones) a college education will turn you into a reflective, morally mature person.

The point I'm making can be put this way. A college education isn't valuable like a can opener is valuable. It's valuable like a Swiss army knife is valuable. Or like a computer is valuable. People who focus simply on the job-getting

140   feature of a college education are like people who think that the belt-punch is the only useful feature of a Swiss army knife.

I would argue that the benefits of a college education that I just listed are actually *more valuable* than the fact that you can get a good job with a college diploma. First, it is becoming increasingly unlikely you will spend the 40 years following college in one career, let alone in one job. To devote your college years to preparing for life as a lab assistant will turn out to be a waste when you leave the biomedical industry for a job in book publishing. But the features I listed above will be of use no matter what job you have. Secondly, and I think more importantly, the job you have is but one element in

150   what I would hope is a complex and multi-layered life. Living your life involves so much more than working at a job. It involves being a citizen, a spouse, a friend, a parent, a decision-maker, and someone who has leisure time to fill, and a college education contributes toward improving these aspects of your life.

THE SECOND PROBLEM WITH THE CAN OPENER ANSWER

That's the first problem with the simple Can Opener Answer: it mistakes something that has many uses for something that performs merely one task. But even when we do focus on the way in which a college education translates into a job, I think many people fail fully to grasp precisely why employers value employees who are college educated. And this failure is the second

160   problem with the simple Can Opener Answer.

The reason that college degrees translate into high-end salaries and good jobs has, I would argue, more to do with the *skills* one acquires in college than with the discipline-specific *knowledge* of the individual courses. No one is going to give you a better job because of your knowledge of Shakespeare or Plato or the Napoleonic Wars. But students who are successful in their English, philosophy, and history classes are independent and creative thinkers who can write and speak clearly, who can juggle many responsibilities, who can research a project, and who can take steps to educate themselves. And employers will be falling all over themselves to hire people with

170   these skills. Consequently, it doesn't matter so much what your major is as much as it does that you acquire these more general skills. So select a major that you find interesting, which will challenge you, which will make you smarter, and don't worry exclusively about "what you can do" with a degree in, say, religious studies.

Even when it comes to the more vocationally-related majors like nursing or business or education or biology, it is sure to be the case that the knowledge you will need in your job will far outstrip what you will learn in your college classes. This is not a failing of the college classes, it is just a fact that specific industries and jobs require highly specific knowledge. It is also a fact that what you need to know to be an accountant or a teacher or a nurse or a biologist will change in response to advances in those fields. (Think, for example, about how much more today's middle school teachers need to know about computers compared to their predecessors 30 years ago.) One of the goals of a college education is to give you the general knowledge into which you can fit the more specific knowledge required by your particular job. And, more importantly, a college education will give you the ability to teach yourself, so that when you need a new job skill, you'll be prepared.

When you get a job, the employer very likely will train you to do whatever it is that needs to be done. Large corporations have entire human resources departments and internal "universities" the sole purpose of which is to train the new employees to perform the necessary tasks. The Widget Corporation will understand if you can't come in on the first day of the job and start making the widgets; their trainers will show you how to do that. But what they won't show you is how to write clearly, how to organize your time, how to give a presentation to the Board of Directors, how to ask questions, and how to make decisions. What an employer wants above all is an employee who can *think,* and that is what they expect from people with a college education. Once you understand that it is these more generally intellectual skills which employers desire, you'll realize that they can be acquired in just about any major.

The second problem, then, with the simple Can Opener Answer is that it fails to recognize that it is the general skills and not simply the domain-specific content knowledge which turns college graduates into desirable employees. I think I can put the point this way. A college education does not, as most people believe, prepare you to do *something.* Rather, it prepares you to do *anything.*[4]

HOW TO GET THE MOST OUT OF COLLEGE

Now that we understand the value of a college education, we can think about what you should do in college, and how you can make the most of your college years. Given that college is valuable not simply because it gets you a job, but because it prepares you to be a complete person, *and* given that what you want from college in the way of job-related skills are general intellectual abilities more than particular, task-specific knowledge, what should you do? I don't have all the answers, but here are some about which I'm fairly confident.

1. Write as much as you can. Then write some more. The written word is the medium of academic communication. Academics talk to one

another through books and published articles. Students talk to their professors through exams and termpapers. If you cannot write well, you will not succeed in college, it's as simple as that. I once spoke to a group of college juniors, and I asked them what they wish they knew about college when they were entering freshmen. One of them[5] said that he wished he had known how much writing he would have to do, and to how high a standard his writing would be held. So now you know: writing is crucially important.

And since writing is a skill like juggling or playing the guitar, the only way to get better at it is to practice. Write at every opportunity. Keep a class journal. Take notes when you read (and don't simply underline or highlight your books. This is next to worthless.). Write drafts of your assigned papers. Demand feedback on your writing from your professors. The more you write, the better a writer you will become. And, you will find, the better a *thinker* you will become, because more than anything else, writing is a form of thinking out loud. Write for yourself, to clarify your own thinking, not simply because you have a paper due at the end of the term. Because writing is the medium of academic communication, you need to treat it that way—as a form of communication. Don't think of your papers as something that you turn in for a grade, but as an opportunity to talk to your professors—to tell them what you have been thinking about. I hardly need say that if you are a talented writer, you will succeed in the workplace. You won't have to write essays on Jane Austen or the Protestant Reformation once you leave college, but you will have to write memos and reports and presentations and speeches, and honing this skill in college will serve you well once you leave.

2. Talk. And not just about your weekend plans or about the details of your friends' love lives. Talk about ideas that fascinate you. Talk about politics and religion and racism and abortion and all the other issues that are important but which are not usually talked about in "polite society". It is through talking about these issues that you may very well come to turn confusion into clarity. Many of these questions can only be solved when a number of minds come together at once, and gathering in a group and talking is the best way to bring minds together. How will you know if there is a flaw in your position if you don't show it to someone else? Moreover, you can use your talking about these issues as practice for the talking that you will have to do with your spouse, your children, your coworkers, your boss, and the members of your town council. Speaking to others in private and to groups in public is one of those life and job skills that I was talking about above, and if you can treat college as an opportunity for honing that skill, you will be ready to talk in these other sorts of situations. Finally, as you will soon learn, talking about ideas is valuable for its own sake. The late-night conversations at coffee houses or

in dorm rooms about the meaning of life and the way to fix the world are just plain fun. Do it as often as you can.

3. Take responsibility for your education. Here's the part where college distinguishes itself from high school. High school students are there because they have to be. College students are in college because they want to be. (And make sure you really *want* to be in college before you go. It is a sizeable investment of time and money, and if there's something else you'd rather be doing, you should take some time and re-assess your situation. Taking a year off to figure out what you want, and entering college with a clear plan in mind can make all the difference in the world.) You are paying dearly for your college education, so you should go out and *get* it. Don't wait for someone else to hand it to you; it won't come. Taking responsibility for your own education manifests itself in small ways, and in larger ways. On the small side it means going to the dictionary when you run across a word you don't know. It also means asking your professor to read a draft of your essay, or raising your hand in class to ask for a difficult point to be repeated. But taking responsibility for your education means more than this. It means seeking out challenging courses and inspiring professors, for only if you push yourself by taking hard courses will you improve your academic and intellectual skills. It means having the courage to change your major if you find your current one uninteresting. It means engaging your friends in the dormitories and coffee shops about what you are learning in the classroom. It means speaking up and agitating for change if things aren't going the way you want. If you sit passively through your classes, skipping the readings, and taking only the easy courses, you will fail to gain the very education to which you are committing so much time and money.

It might help to think of college as a sort of health club—a health club for the mind.[6] There are all sorts of machines in the health club: these are your professors, your classes, and the many extra-curricular activity opportunities. The machines at this intellectual health club can improve your mind in the way that the weights and stair-climbers at your gym can improve your body. But, just as at the gym, the machines are useless if you don't use them. Merely buying a health club membership won't turn flab into muscle; you have to lift weights and do sit-ups. And merely enrolling in college won't turn an uneducated person into an educated one. Doing the reading, talking in class, visiting your professors in office hours, pursuing research topics outside of class—this is the sort of "machine using" behavior that will turn the gray matter inside your head into a well-toned mental muscle.

4. Do something completely different. I see so many students who take the same menu of courses they took in high school: history, English,

270

280

290

*Health
Club
analogy*

300

math, science, and a foreign language. All of those are important classes, but a quick glance at any college's course catalog will show that there are dozens if not hundreds of comparatively exotic courses. Religious studies, communication, anthropology, economics, psychology, film theory—the list goes on. Take a course that is completely different from anything you have taken before. Explore the unknown. Not only might the strange and exotic be something you like (and have a talent for!), but the challenge of these new courses will push you to develop the intellectual skills I have been talking about. This injunction to do something completely different shouldn't stop at the course catalog, however. Find the person on campus most different from you and take them out to coffee. Try out for a play, join the debate team, write for the newspaper, join a campus service organization. Try your hand at some of those activities that you would never have done in high school. Of course you will meet new people, but the primary reason for engaging in these pursuits is to discover something about yourself. Maybe you would enjoy the theatre or find that you have a talent for organizing fund-drives (and can translate that into a career!). It is foolish to commit yourself to a life-plan before you have discovered what you like and what talents you have. And after you get a "real job" and "settle down" you will find precious little time for these extra-curricular pursuits.

5. Become curious. The late Canadian novelist Robertson Davies has hit upon the essence of college. "Energy and curiosity are the lifeblood of universities," Davies had one of his characters say. "The desire to find out, to uncover, to dig deeper, to puzzle out obscurities, is the spirit of the university and it is a channeling of that unresting curiosity that holds mankind together."[7] Since this 'unresting curiosity' is the essence of any college, succeeding during the next four years requires that you tap into this energy, and that you become an unrestingly curious person yourself. Feed your curiosity by taking courses that interest you, rather than the courses which might look good on a law school application. Find those issues and problems that interest you and pursue them doggedly. Become curious about everything—about medieval history, about the structure of the cell, about what your roommates are learning in their classes, about the research interests of your professors—and you will find not only that you are getting better grades, but that you are becoming a smarter, more intellectually independent person. And that is, at the end, the goal of a college education.[8]

ENDNOTES

1. Andrew P. Mills is an assistant professor of philosophy at Otterbein College, where he teaches a wide array of philosophy courses. He received his B.A. from the University of Michigan, and his M.A. and Ph.D. in philosophy from The University of North Carolina at Chapel Hill. He is the author of scholarly articles in the philosophy of language and in philosophical logic.

2. Of course in such a situation can openers may have value as antiques, or as objects of art. And that is a real sort of value, but it is not (at least not standardly) why we think can openers are valuable now.

3. Like this very essay: it's an examination of the value of a college education.

4. I learned of this way of putting the point from Ami Berger, though I don't think she was the originator of this thought.

5. His name is Caleb Bell.

6. For this health club analogy I am indebted to Craig Froehle.

7. This is from Davies' novel, *The Rebel Angels.*

8. An earlier, abbreviated, version of this essay was published under the title "College is more than job training" in *The Blade* (Toledo, Ohio) on September 30, 2000. For helpful conversation on this essay, I would like to thank Lori Aronson, Ami Berger, Brad Cohen, Craig Froehle, Glenna Jackson, Brian Lindeman, Kristine LaLonde, Mary MacLeod, Lisa Pollak, Charles Salter, and the audiences at Otterbein College to whom I have presented the main ideas contained above. I would like to dedicate this essay to Jack Meiland, who ignited my thinking on the question of why a college education is valuable. His little book, *College Thinking* is as valuable a guide to college as I can think of.

CURBING SPEECH AT QUINNIPIAC

People who follow politics know Quinnipiac University as the home of the polling institute that bears its name. But lately it has been making a name for itself—a bad name—for a different reason.

The university has gone to unusual lengths this semester to try to curb the activities of student journalists who are running an independent, online newspaper that is affiliated with the school and called Quad News. Students began the upstart newspaper over frustration with the administration's attempts to control the official student newspaper, a common enough conflict between students and university officials.

But Quinnipiac's reaction was anything but ordinary. First, the university tried to stonewall student attempts to report stories by imposing a gag order on administrators, coaches and athletes. Then last month, the institution, in writing, threatened to ban from campus the student chapter of the Society of Professional Journalists, a nationwide media advocacy group of working journalists that includes about 200 student chapters.

Apparently the university became irate when an information booth for the professional journalists' group on campus included a sign-up sheet inviting students to become involved with Quad News. The university sent a letter to Jaclyn Hirsch, the student president of Quinnipiac's chapter of the Society of Professional Journalists, threatening to kick the group off campus if it continued any "interactions or endorsements" with Quad News. That's a difficult task, considering that many student reporters, including Ms. Hirsch, are members of the group.

Such intimidation does not speak well of Quinnipiac's commitment to freedom of speech, open-mindedness or academic inquiry. Instead of encouraging the students for their remarkable initiative, the school tried to retaliate against them for resisting its control and not toeing the line.

Students say that the university lifted the gag order last week, making it easier for them to interview administrators and athletes. That's a good start. But Quinnipiac should take the next necessary step and withdraw its threat against the school's chapter of the professional journalists' organization—and put it in writing.

Reprinted from the *New York Times*, October 28, 2008, by permission of the New York Times Company.

THE ARTIFICIAL NIGGER
Flannery O'Connor

Mr. Head awakened to discover that the room was full of moonlight. He sat up and stared at the floor boards—the color of silver—and then at the ticking on his pillow, which might have been brocade, and after a second, he saw half of the moon five feet away in his shaving mirror, paused as if it were waiting for his permission to enter. It rolled forward and cast a dignifying light on everything. The straight chair against the wall looked stiff and attentive as if it were awaiting an order and Mr. Head's trousers, hanging to the back of it, had an almost noble air, like the garment some great man had just flung to his servant; but the face on the moon was a grave one. It gazed across the room and out the window where it floated over the horse stall and appeared to contemplate itself with the look of a young man who sees his old age before him.

Mr. Head could have said to it that age was a choice blessing and that only with years does a man enter into that calm understanding of life that makes him a suitable guide for the young. This, at least, had been his own experience.

He sat up and grasped the iron posts at the foot of his bed and raised himself until he could see the face on the alarm clock which sat on an overturned bucket beside the chair. The hour was two in the morning. The alarm on the clock did not work but he was not dependent on any mechanical means to awaken him. Sixty years had not dulled his responses; his physical reactions, like his moral ones, were guided by his will and strong character, and these could be seen plainly in his features. He had a long tube-like face with a long rounded open jaw and a long depressed nose. His eyes were alert but quiet, and in the miraculous moonlight they had a look of composure and of ancient wisdom as if they belonged to one of the great guides of men. He might have been Vergil summoned in the middle of the night to go to Dante, or better, Raphael, awakened by a blast of God's light to fly to the side of Tobias. The only dark spot in the room was Nelson's pallet, underneath the shadow of the window.

Nelson was hunched over on his side, his knees under his chin and his heels under his bottom. His new suit and hat were in the boxes that they had been sent in and these were on the floor at the foot of the pallet where he could get his hands on them as soon as he woke up. The slop jar, out of the shadow and made snow-white in the moonlight, appeared to stand guard over him like a small personal angel. Mr. Head lay back down, feeling entirely confident that he could carry out the moral mission of the coming day. He meant to be up before Nelson and to have the breakfast cooking by the time he awakened. The boy was always irked when Mr. Head was the first

Reprinted from *A Good Man Is Hard to Find* (1955), Harcourt Brace Co., Inc.

40   up. They would have to leave the house at four to get to the railroad junction by five-thirty. The train was to stop for them at five forty-five and they had to be there on time for this train was stopping merely to accommodate them.

This would be the boy's first trip to the city though he claimed it would be his second because he had been born there. Mr. Head had tried to point out to him that when he was born he didn't have the intelligence to determine his whereabouts but this had made no impression on the child at all and he continued to insist that this was to be his second trip. It would be Mr. Head's third trip. Nelson had said, "I will've already been there twict and
50   I ain't but ten."

Mr. Head had contradicted him.

"If you ain't been there in fifteen years, how you know you'll be able to find your way about?" Nelson had asked. "How you know it hasn't changed some?"

"Have you ever," Mr. Head had asked, "seen me lost?"

Nelson certainly had not but he was a child who was never satisfied until he had given an impudent answer and he replied, "It's nowhere around here to get lost at."

"The day is going to come," Mr. Head prophesied, "when you'll find you
60   ain't as smart as you think you are." He had been thinking about this trip for several months but it was for the most part in moral terms that he conceived it. It was to be a lesson that the boy would never forget. He was to find out from it that he had no cause for pride merely because he had been born in a city. He was to find out that the city is not a great place. Mr. Head meant him to see everything there is to see in a city so that he would be content to stay at home for the rest of his life. He fell asleep thinking how the boy would at last find out that he was not as smart as he thought he was.

He was awakened at three-thirty by the smell of fatback frying and he leaped off his cot. The pallet was empty and the clothes boxes had been
70   thrown open. He put on his trousers and ran into the other room. The boy had a corn pone on cooking and had fried the meat. He was sitting in the half-dark at the table, drinking cold coffee out of a can. He had on his new suit and his new gray hat pulled low over his eyes. It was too big for him but they had ordered it a size large because they expected his head to grow. He didn't say anything but his entire figure suggested satisfaction at having arisen before Mr. Head.

Mr. Head went to the stove and brought the meat to the table in the skillet. "It's no hurry," he said. "You'll get there soon enough and it's no guarantee you'll like it when you do neither," and he sat down across from the boy whose
80   hat teetered back slowly to reveal a fiercely expressionless face, very much the same shape as the old man's. They were grandfather and grandson but they looked enough alike to be brothers and brothers not too far apart in age, for Mr. Head had a youthful expression by daylight, while the boy's look was ancient, as if he knew everything already and would be pleased to forget it.

Mr. Head had once had a wife and daughter and when the wife died, the daughter ran away and returned after an interval with Nelson. Then one morning, without getting out of bed, she died and left Mr. Head with sole care of the year-old child. He had made the mistake of telling Nelson that he had been born in Atlanta. If he hadn't told him that, Nelson couldn't have insisted that this was going to be his second trip.

"You may not like it a bit," Mr. Head continued. "It'll be full of niggers."

The boy made a face as if he could handle a nigger.

"All right," Mr. Head said. "You ain't ever seen a nigger."

"You wasn't up very early," Nelson said.

"You ain't ever seen a nigger," Mr. Head repeated. "There hasn't been a nigger in this county since we run that one out twelve years ago and that was before you were born." He looked at the boy as if he were daring him to say he had ever seen a Negro.

"How you know I never saw a nigger when I lived there before?" Nelson asked. "I probably saw a lot of niggers."

"If you seen one you didn't know what he was," Mr. Head said, completely exasperated. "A six-month-old child don't know a nigger from anybody else."

"I reckon I'll know a nigger if I see one," the boy said and got up and straightened his slick sharply creased gray hat and went outside to the privy.

They reached the junction some time before the train was due to arrive and stood about two feet from the first set of tracks. Mr. Head carried a paper sack with some biscuits and a can of sardines in it for their lunch. A coarse-looking orange-colored sun coming up behind the east range of mountains was making the sky a dull red behind them, but in front of them it was still gray and they faced a gray transparent moon, hardly stronger than a thumbprint and completely without light. A small tin switch box and a black fuel tank were all there was to mark the place as a junction; the tracks were double and did not converge again until they were hidden behind the bends at either end of the clearing. Trains passing appeared to emerge from a tunnel of trees and, hit for a second by the cold sky, vanish terrified into the woods again. Mr. Head had had to make special arrangements with the ticket agent to have this train stop and he was secretly afraid it would not, in which case, he knew Nelson would say, "I never thought no train was going to stop for you." Under the useless morning moon the tracks looked white and fragile. Both the old man and the child stared ahead as if they were awaiting an apparition.

Then suddenly, before Mr. Head could make up his mind to turn back, there was a deep warning bleat and the train appeared, gliding very slowly, almost silently around the bend of trees about two hundred yards down the track, with one yellow front light shining. Mr. Head was still not certain it would stop and he felt it would make an even bigger idiot of him if it went by slowly. Both he and Nelson, however, were prepared to ignore the train if it passed them.

130 The engine charged by, filling their noses with the smell of hot metal and then the second coach came to a stop exactly where they were standing. A conductor with the face of an ancient bloated bulldog was on the step as if he expected them, though he did not look as if it mattered one way or the other to him if they got on or not. "To the right," he said.

Their entry took only a fraction of a second and the train was already speeding on as they entered the quiet car. Most of the travelers were still sleeping, some with their heads hanging off the chair arms, some stretched across two seats, and some sprawled out with their feet in the aisle. Mr. Head saw two unoccupied seats and pushed Nelson toward them. "Get in there by

140 the winder," he said in his normal voice which was very loud at this hour of the morning. "Nobody cares if you sit there because it's nobody in it. Sit right there."

"I heard you," the boy muttered. "It's no use in you yelling," and he sat down and turned his head to the glass. There he saw a pale ghost-like face scowling at him beneath the brim of a pale ghost-like hat. His grandfather, looking quickly too, saw a different ghost, pale but grinning, under a black hat.

Mr. Head sat down and settled himself and took out his ticket and started reading aloud everything that was printed on it. People began to stir. Several woke up and stared at him. "Take off your hat," he said to Nelson and took

150 off his own and put it on his knee. He had a small amount of white hair that had turned tobacco-colored over the years and this lay flat across the back of his head. The front of his head was bald and creased. Nelson took off his hat and put it on his knee and they waited for the conductor to come ask for their tickets.

The man across the aisle from them was spread out over two seats, his feet propped on the window and his head jutting into the aisle. He had on a light blue suit and a yellow shirt unbuttoned at the neck. His eyes had just opened and Mr. Head was ready to introduce himself when the conductor came up from behind and growled, "Tickets."

160 When the conductor had gone, Mr. Head gave Nelson the return half of his ticket and said, "Now put that in your pocket and don't lose it or you'll have to stay in the city."

"Maybe I will," Nelson said as if this were a reasonable suggestion.

Mr. Head ignored him. "First time this boy has ever been on a train," he explained to the man across the aisle, who was sitting up now on the edge of his seat with both feet on the floor.

Nelson jerked his hat on again and turned angrily to the window.

"He's never seen anything before," Mr. Head continued. "Ignorant as the day he was born, but I mean for him to get his fill once and for all."

170 The boy leaned forward, across his grandfather and toward the stranger. "I was born in the city," he said. "I was born there. This is my second trip." He said it in a high positive voice but the man across the aisle didn't look as if he understood. There were heavy purple circles under his eyes.

Mr. Head reached across the aisle and tapped him on the arm. "The thing to do with a boy," he said sagely, "is to show him all it is to show. Don't hold nothing back."

"Yeah," the man said. He gazed down at his swollen feet and lifted the left one about ten inches from the floor. After a minute he put it down and lifted the other. All through the car people began to get up and move about and yawn and stretch. Separate voices could be heard here and there and then a general hum. Suddenly Mr. Head's serene expression changed. His mouth almost closed and a light, fierce and cautious both, came into his eyes. He was looking down the length of the car. Without turning, he caught Nelson by the arm and pulled him forward. "Look," he said.

A huge coffee-colored man was coming slowly forward. He had on a light suit and a yellow satin tie with a ruby pin in it. One of his hands rested on his stomach which rode majestically under his buttoned coat, and in the other he held the head of a black walking stick that he picked up and set down with a deliberate outward motion each time he took a step. He was proceeding very slowly, his large brown eyes gazing over the heads of the passengers. He had a small white mustache and white crinkly hair. Behind him there were two young women, both coffee-colored, one in a yellow dress and one in a green. Their progress was kept at the rate of his and they chatted in low throaty voices as they followed him.

Mr. Head's grip was tightening insistently on Nelson's arm. As the procession passed them, the light from a sapphire ring on the brown hand that picked up the cane reflected in Mr. Head's eye, but he did not look up nor did the tremendous man look at him. The group proceeded up the rest of the aisle and out of the car. Mr. Head's grip on Nelson's arm loosened. "What was that?" he asked.

"A man," the boy said and gave him an indignant look as if he were tired of having his intelligence insulted.

"What kind of a man?" Mr. Head persisted, his voice expressionless.

"A fat man," Nelson said. He was beginning to feel that he had better be cautious.

"You don't know what kind?" Mr. Head said in a final tone.

"An old man," the boy said and had a sudden foreboding that he was not going to enjoy the day.

"That was a nigger," Mr. Head said and sat back.

Nelson jumped up on the seat and stood looking backward to the end of the car but the Negro had gone.

"I'd of thought you'd know a nigger since you seen so many when you was in the city on your first visit," Mr. Head continued. "That's his first nigger," he said to the man across the aisle.

The boy slid down into the seat. "You said they were black," he said in an angry voice. "You never said they were tan. How do you expect me to know anything when you don't tell me right?"

"You're just ignorant is all," Mr. Head said and he got up and moved over in the vacant seat by the man across the aisle.

220   Nelson turned backward again and looked where the Negro had disappeared. He felt that the Negro had deliberately walked down the aisle in order to make a fool of him and he hated him with a fierce raw fresh hate; and also, he understood now why his grandfather disliked them. He looked toward the window and the face there seemed to suggest that he might be inadequate to the day's exactions. He wondered if he would even recognize the city when they came to it.

After he had told several stories, Mr. Head realized that the man he was talking to was asleep and he got up and suggested to Nelson that they walk over the train and see the parts of it. He particularly wanted the boy to see

230   the toilet so they went first to the men's room and examined the plumbing. Mr. Head demonstrated the ice-water cooler as if he had invented it and showed Nelson the bowl with the single spigot where the travelers brushed their teeth. They went through several cars and came to the diner.

This was the most elegant car in the train. It was painted a rich egg-yellow and had a wine-colored carpet on the floor. There were wide windows over the tables and great spaces of the rolling view were caught in miniature in the sides of the coffee pots and in the glasses. Three very black Negroes in white suits and aprons were running up and down the aisle, swinging trays and bowing and bending over the travelers eating breakfast. One of them

240   rushed up to Mr. Head and Nelson and said, holding up two fingers, "Space for two!" but Mr. Head replied in a loud voice, "We eaten before we left!"

The waiter wore large brown spectacles that increased the size of his eye whites. "Stan' aside then please," he said with an airy wave of the arm as if he were brushing aside flies.

Neither Nelson nor Mr. Head moved a fraction of an inch. "Look," Mr. Head said.

The near corner of the diner, containing two tables, was set off from the rest by a saffron-colored curtain. One table was set but empty but at the other, facing them, his back to the drape, sat the tremendous Negro. He was

250   speaking in a soft voice to the two women while he buttered a muffin. He had a heavy sad face and his neck bulged over his white collar on either side. "They rope them off," Mr. Head explained. Then he said, "Let's go see the kitchen," and they walked the length of the diner but the black waiter was coming fast behind them.

"Passengers are not allowed in the kitchen!" he said in a haughty voice. "Passengers are NOT allowed in the kitchen!"

Mr. Head stopped where he was and turned. "And there's good reason for that," he shouted into the Negro's chest, "because the cockroaches would run the passengers out!"

260   All the travelers laughed and Mr. Head and Nelson walked out, grinning. Mr. Head was known at home for his quick wit and Nelson felt a sudden keen pride in him. He realized the old man would be his only support in the

strange place they were approaching. He would be entirely alone in the world if he were ever lost from his grandfather. A terrible excitement shook him and he wanted to take hold of Mr. Head's coat and hold on like a child.

As they went back to their seats they could see through the passing windows that the countryside was becoming speckled with small houses and shacks and that a highway ran alongside the train. Cars sped by on it, very small and fast. Nelson felt that there was less breath in the air than there had been thirty minutes ago. The man across the aisle had left and there was no one near for Mr. Head to hold a conversation with so he looked out the window, through his own reflection, and read aloud the names of the buildings they were passing. "The Dixie Chemical Corp!" he announced. "Southern Maid Flour! Dixie Doors! Southern Belle Cotton Products! Patty's Peanut Butter! Southern Mammy Cane Syrup!"

"Hush up!" Nelson hissed.

All over the car people were beginning to get up and take their luggage off the overhead racks. Women were putting on their coats and hats. The conductor stuck his head in the car and snarled, "Firstopppppmry," and Nelson lunged out of his sitting position, trembling. Mr. Head pushed him down by the shoulder.

"Keep your seat," he said in dignified tones. "The first stop is on the edge of town. The second stop is at the main railroad station." He had come by this knowledge on his first trip when he had got off at the first stop and had had to pay a man fifteen cents to take him into the heart of town. Nelson sat back down, very pale. For the first time in his life, he understood that his grandfather was indispensable to him.

The train stopped and let off a few passengers and glided on as if it had never ceased moving. Outside, behind rows of brown rickety houses, a line of blue buildings stood up, and beyond them a pale rose-gray sky faded away to nothing. The train moved into the railroad yard. Looking down, Nelson saw lines and lines of silver tracks multiplying and criss-crossing. Then before he could start counting them, the face in the window started out at him, gray but distinct, and he looked the other way. The train was in the station. Both he and Mr. Head jumped up and ran to the door. Neither noticed that they had left the paper sack with the lunch in it on the seat.

They walked stiffly through the small station and came out of a heavy door into the squall of traffic. Crowds were hurrying to work. Nelson didn't know where to look. Mr. Head leaned against the side of the building and glared in front of him.

Finally Nelson said, "Well, how do you see what all it is to see?"

Mr. Head didn't answer. Then as if the sight of people passing had given him the clue, he said, "You walk," and started off down the street. Nelson followed, steadying his hat. So many sights and sounds were flooding in on him that for the first block he hardly knew what he was seeing. At the second corner, Mr. Head turned and looked behind him at the station they had left, a putty-colored terminal with a concrete dome on top. He thought that if he could keep the dome always in sight, he would be able to get back in the afternoon to catch the train again.

310   As they walked along, Nelson began to distinguish details and take note of the store windows, jammed with every kind of equipment—hardware, drygoods, chicken feed, liquor. They passed one that Mr. Head called his particular attention to where you walked in and sat on a chair with your feet upon two rests and let a Negro polish your shoes. They walked slowly and stopped and stood at the entrances so he could see what went on in each place but they did not go into any of them. Mr. Head was determined not to go into any city store because on his first trip here, he had got lost in a large one and had found his way out only after many people had insulted him.

They came in the middle of the next block to a store that had a weighing
320   machine in front of it and they both in turn stepped up on it and put in a penny and received a ticket. Mr. Head's ticket said, "You weigh 120 pounds. You are upright and brave and all your friends admire you." He put the ticket in his pocket, surprised that the machine should have got his character correct but his weight wrong, for he had weighed on a grain scale not long before and knew he weighed 110. Nelson's ticket said, "You weigh 98 pounds. You have a great destiny ahead of you but beware of dark women." Nelson did not know any women and he weighed only 68 pounds but Mr. Head pointed out that the machine had probably printed the number upside down, meaning the 9 for a 6.

330   They walked on and at the end of five blocks the dome of the terminal sank out of sight and Mr. Head turned to the left. Nelson could have stood in front of every store window for an hour if there had not been another more interesting one next to it. Suddenly he said, "I was born here!" Mr. Head turned and looked at him with horror. There was a sweaty brightness about his face. "This is where I come from!" he said.

Mr. Head was appalled. He saw the moment had come for drastic action. "Lemme show you one thing you ain't seen yet," he said and took him to the corner where there was a sewer entrance. "Squat down," he said, "and stick you head in there," and he held the back of the boy's coat while he got down
340   and put his head in the sewer. He drew it back quickly, hearing a gurgling in the depths under the sidewalk. Then Mr. Head explained the sewer system, how the entire city was underlined with it, how it contained all the drainage and was full of rats and how a man could slide into it and be sucked along down endless pitchblack tunnels. At any minute any man in the city might be sucked into the sewer and never heard from again. He described it so well that Nelson was for some seconds shaken. He connected the sewer passages with the entrance to hell and understood for the first time how the world was put together in its lower parts. He drew away from the curb.

Then he said, "Yes, but you can stay away from the holes," and his face
350   took on that stubborn look that was so exasperating to his grandfather. "This is where I come from!" he said.

Mr. Head was dismayed but he only muttered, "You'll get your fill," and they walked on. At the end of two more blocks he turned to the left, feeling that he was circling the dome; and he was correct for in a half-hour they passed in front of the railroad station again. At first Nelson did not notice that he was seeing the same stores twice but when they passed the one where you put your feet on the rests while the Negro polished your shoes, he perceived that they were walking in a circle.

"We done been here!" he shouted. "I don't believe you know where you're at!"   360

"The direction just slipped my mind for a minute," Mr. Head said and they turned down a different street. He still did not intend to let the dome get too far away and after two blocks in their new direction, he turned to the left. This street contained two- and three-story wooden dwellings. Anyone passing on the sidewalk could see into the rooms and Mr. Head, glancing through one window, saw a woman lying on an iron bed, looking out, with a sheet pulled over her. Her knowing expression shook him. A fierce-looking boy on a bicycle came driving down out of nowhere and he had to jump to the side to keep from being hit. "It's nothing to them if they knock you down," he said. "You better keep closer to me."   370

They walked on for some time on streets like this before he remembered to turn again. The houses they were passing now were all unpainted and the wood in them looked rotten; the street between was narrower. Nelson saw a colored man. Then another. Then another. "Niggers live in these houses," he observed.

"Well come on and we'll go somewheres else," Mr. Head said. "We didn't come to look at niggers," and they turned down another street but they continued to see Negroes everywhere. Nelson's skin began to prickle and they stepped along at a faster pace in order to leave the neighborhood as soon as possible. There were colored men in their undershirts standing in the doors   380 and colored women rocking on the sagging porches. Colored children played in the gutters and stopped what they were doing to look at them. Before long they began to pass rows of stores with colored customers in them but they didn't pause at the entrances of these. Black eyes in black faces were watching them from every direction. "Yes," Mr. Head said, "this is where you were born—right here with all these niggers."

Nelson scowled. "I think you done got us lost," he said.

Mr. Head swung around sharply and looked for the dome. It was nowhere in sight. "I ain't got us lost either," he said. "You're just tired of walking."

"I ain't tired, I'm hungry," Nelson said. "Give me a biscuit."   390

They discovered then that they had lost the lunch.

"You were the one holding the sack," Nelson said. "I would have kepa-holt of it."

"If you want to direct this trip, I'll go on by myself and leave you right here," Mr. Head said and was pleased to see the boy turn white. However, he

realized they were lost and drifting farther every minute from the station. He was hungry himself and beginning to be thirsty and since they had been in the colored neighborhood, they had both begun to sweat. Nelson had on his shoes and he was unaccustomed to them. The concrete sidewalks were very
400   hard. They both wanted to find a place to sit down but this was impossible and they kept on walking, the boy muttering under his breath, "First you lost the sack and then you lost the way," and Mr. Head growling from time to time, "Anybody wants to be from this nigger heaven can be from it!"

By now the sun was well forward in the sky. The odor of dinners cooking drifted out to them. The Negroes were all at their doors to see them pass. "Whyn't you ast one of these niggers the way?" Nelson said. "You got us lost."

"This is where you were born," Mr. Head said. "You can ast one yourself if you want to."

Nelson was afraid of the colored men and he didn't want to be laughed at
410   by the colored children. Up ahead he saw a large colored woman leaning in a doorway that opened onto the sidewalk. Her hair stood straight out from her head for about four inches all around and she was resting on bare brown feet that turned pink at the sides. She had on a pink dress that showed her exact shape. As they came abreast of her, she lazily lifted one hand to her head and her fingers disappeared into her hair.

Nelson stopped. He felt his breath drawn up by the woman's dark eyes. "How do you get back to town?" he said in a voice that did not sound like his own.

After a minute she said, "You in town now," in a rich low tone that made
420   Nelson feel as if a cool spray had been turned on him.

"How do you get back to the train?" he said in the same reed-like voice.

"You can catch you a car," she said.

He understood she was making fun of him but he was too paralyzed even to scowl. He stood drinking in every detail of her. His eyes traveled up from her great knees to her forehead and then made a triangular path from the glistening sweat on her neck down and across her tremendous bosom and over her bare arm back to where her fingers lay hidden in her hair. He suddenly wanted her to reach down and pick him up and draw him against her and then he wanted to feel her breath on his face. He wanted to look down and
430   down into her eyes while she held him tighter and tighter. He had never had such a feeling before. He felt as if he were reeling down through a pitchblack tunnel.

"You can go a block down yonder and catch you a car take you to the railroad station, Sugarpie," she said.

Nelson would have collapsed at her feet if Mr. Head had not pulled him roughly away. "You act like you don't have any sense!" the old man growled.

They hurried down the street and Nelson did not look back at the woman. He pushed his hat sharply forward over his face which was already burning with shame. The sneering ghost he had seen in the train window and
440   all the foreboding feelings he had on the way returned to him and he remem-

bered that his ticket from the scale had said to beware of dark women and that his grandfather's had said he was upright and brave. He took hold of the old man's hand, a sign of dependence that he seldom showed.

They headed down the street toward the car tracks where a long yellow rattling trolley was coming. Mr. Head had never boarded a streetcar and he let that one pass. Nelson was silent. From time to time his mouth trembled slightly but his grandfather, occupied with his own problems, paid him no attention. They stood on the corner and neither looked at the Negroes who were passing, going about their business just as if they had been white, except that most of them stopped and eyed Mr. Head and Nelson. It occurred to 450 Mr. Head that since the streetcar ran on tracks, they could simply follow the tracks. He gave Nelson a slight push and explained that they would follow the tracks on into the railroad station, walking, and they set off.

Presently to their great relief they began to see white people again and Nelson sat down on the sidewalk against the wall of a building. "I got to rest myself some," he said. "You lost the sack and the direction. You can just wait on me to rest myself."

"There's the tracks in front of us," Mr. Head said. "All we got to do is keep them in sight and you could have remembered the sack as good as me. This is where you were born. This is your old home town. This is your sec- 460 ond trip. You ought to know how to do," and he squatted down and continued in this vein but the boy, easing his burning feet out of his shoes, did not answer.

"And standing there grinning like a chim-pan-zee while a nigger woman gives you direction. Great Gawd!" Mr. Head said.

"I never said I was nothing but born here," the boy said in a shaky voice. "I never said I would or wouldn't like it. I never said I wanted to come. I only said I was born here and I never had nothing to do with that. I want to go home. I never wanted to come in the first place. It was all your big idea. How you know you ain't following the tracks in the wrong direction?" 470

This last had occurred to Mr. Head too. "All these people are white," he said.

"We ain't passed here before," Nelson said. This was a neighborhood of brick buildings that might have been lived in or might not. A few empty automobiles were parked along the curb and there was an occasional passerby. The heat of the pavement came up through Nelson's thin suit. His eyelids began to droop, and after a few minutes his head tilted forward. His shoulders twitched once or twice and then he fell over on his side and lay sprawled in an exhausted fit of sleep.

Mr. Head watched him silently. He was very tired himself but they could 480 not both sleep at the same time and he could not have slept anyway because he did not know where he was. In a few minutes Nelson would wake up, refreshed by his sleep and very cocky, and would begin complaining that he had lost the sack and the way. You'd have a mighty sorry time if I wasn't here, Mr. Head thought; and then another idea occurred to him. He looked at the

sprawled figure for several minutes; presently he stood up. He justified what he was going to do on the grounds that it is sometimes necessary to teach a child a lesson he won't forget, particularly when the child is always reasserting his position with some new impudence. He walked without a sound to
490 the corner about twenty feet away and sat down on a covered garbage can in the alley where he could look out and watch Nelson wake up alone.

The boy was dozing fitfully, half conscious of vague noises and black forms moving up from some dark part of him into the light. His face worked in his sleep and he had pulled his knees up under his chin. The sun shed a dull dry light on the narrow street; everything looked like exactly what it was. After a while Mr. Head, hunched like an old monkey on the garbage can lid, decided that if Nelson didn't wake up soon, he would make a loud noise by bamming his foot against the can. He looked at his watch and discovered that it was two o'clock. Their train left at six and the possibility of missing it was
500 too awful for him to think of. He kicked his foot backwards on the can and a hollow boom reverberated in the alley.

Nelson shot up onto his feet with a shout. He looked where his grandfather should have been and stared. He seemed to whirl several times and then, picking up his feet and throwing his head back, he dashed down the street like a wild maddened pony. Mr. Head jumped off the can and galloped after but the child was almost out of sight. He saw a streak of gray disappearing diagonally a block ahead. He ran as fast as he could, looking both ways down every intersection, but without sight of him again. Then as he passed the third intersection, completely winded, he saw about half a block down the
510 street a scene that stopped him altogether. He crouched behind a trash box to watch and get his bearings.

Nelson was sitting with both legs spread out and by his side lay an elderly woman, screaming. Groceries were scattered about the sidewalk. A crowd of women had already gathered to see justice done and Mr. Head distinctly heard the old woman on the pavement shout, "You've broken my ankle and your daddy'll pay for it! Every nickel! Police! Police!" Several of the women were plucking at Nelson's shoulder but the boy seemed too dazed to get up.

Something forced Mr. Head from behind the trash box and forward, but
520 only at a creeping pace. He had never in his life been accosted by a policeman. The women were milling around Nelson as if they might suddenly all dive on him at once and tear him to pieces, and the old woman continued to scream that her ankle was broken and to call for an officer. Mr. Head came on so slowly that he could have been taking a backward step after each forward one, but when he was about ten feet away, Nelson saw him and sprang. The child caught him around the hips and clung panting against him.

The women all turned on Mr. Head. The injured one sat up and shouted, "You sir! You'll pay every penny of my doctor's bill that your boy has caused. He's a juve-nile deliquent! Where is an officer? Somebody take this man's
530 name and address!"

Mr. Head was trying to detach Nelson's fingers from the flesh in the back of his legs. The old man's head had lowered itself into his collar like a turtle's; his eyes were glazed with fear and caution.

"Your boy has broken my ankle!" the old woman shouted. "Police!"

Mr. Head sensed the approach of the policeman from behind. He stared straight ahead at the women who were massed in their fury like a solid wall to block his escape, "This is not my boy," he said. "I never seen him before."

He felt Nelson's fingers fall out of his flesh.

The women dropped back, staring at him with horror, as if they were so repulsed by a man who would deny his own image and likeness that they could not bear to lay hands on him. Mr. Head walked on, through a space they silently cleared, and left Nelson behind. Ahead of him he saw nothing but a hollow tunnel that had once been the street. 540

The boy remained standing where he was, his neck craned forward and his hands hanging by his sides. His hat was jammed on his head so that there were no longer any creases in it. The injured woman got up and shook her fist at him and the others gave him pitying looks, but he didn't notice any of them. There was no policeman in sight.

In a minute he began to move mechanically, making no effort to catch up with his grandfather but merely following at about twenty paces. They walked on for five blocks in this way. Mr. Head's shoulders were sagging and his neck hung forward at such an angle that it was not visible from behind. He was afraid to turn his head. Finally he cut a short hopeful glance over his shoulder. Twenty feet behind him, he saw two small eyes piercing into his back like pitchfork prongs. 550

The boy was not of a forgiving nature but this was the first time he had ever had anything to forgive. Mr. Head had never disgraced himself before. After two more blocks, he turned and called over his shoulder in a high desperately gay voice, "Let's us go get us a Co' Cola somewheres!"

Nelson, with a dignity he had never shown before, turned and stood with his back to his grandfather. 560

Mr. Head began to feel the depth of his denial. His face as they walked on became all hollows and bare ridges. He saw nothing they were passing but he perceived that they had lost the car tracks. There was no dome to be seen anywhere and the afternoon was advancing. He knew that if dark overtook them in the city, they would be beaten and robbed. The speed of God's justice was only what he expected for himself, but he could not stand to think that his sins would be visited upon Nelson and that even now, he was leading the boy to his doom.

They continued to walk on block after block through an endless section 570 of small brick houses until Mr. Head almost fell over a water spigot sticking up about six inches off the edge of a grass plot. He had not had a drink of water since early morning but he felt he did not deserve it now. Then he thought that Nelson would be thirsty and they would both drink and be brought together. He squatted down and put his mouth to the nozzle and turned a cold stream of water into his throat. Then he called out in the high desperate voice, "Come on and getcher some water!"

This time the child stared through him for nearly sixty seconds. Mr. Head got up and walked on as if he had drunk poison. Nelson, though he had not
580 had water since some he had drunk out of a paper cup on the train, passed by the spigot, disdaining to drink where his grandfather had. When Mr. Head realized this, he lost all hope. His face in the waning afternoon light looked ravaged and abandoned. He could feel the boy's steady hate, traveling at an even pace behind him and he knew that (if by some miracle they escaped being murdered in the city) it would continue just that way for the rest of his life. He knew that now he was wandering into a black strange place where nothing was like it had ever been before, a long old age without respect and an end that would be welcome because it would be the end.

As for Nelson, his mind had frozen around his grandfather's treachery as
590 if he were trying to preserve it intact to present at the final judgment. He walked without looking to one side or the other, but every now and then his mouth would twitch and this was when he felt, from some remote place inside himself, a black mysterious form reach up as if it would melt his frozen vision in one hot grasp.

The sun dropped down behind a row of houses and hardly noticing, they passed into an elegant suburban section where mansions were set back from the road by lawns with birdbaths on them. Here everything was entirely deserted. For blocks they didn't pass even a dog. The big white houses were like partially submerged icebergs in the distance. There were no sidewalks,
600 only drives, and these wound around and around in endless ridiculous circles. Nelson made no move to come nearer to Mr. Head. The old man felt that if he saw a sewer entrance he would drop down into it and let himself be carried away; and he could imagine the boy standing by, watching with only a slight interest, while he disappeared.

A loud bark jarred him to attention and he looked up to see a fat man approaching with two bulldogs. He waved both arms like someone shipwrecked on a desert island. "I'm lost!" he called. "I'm lost and can't find my way and me and this boy have got to catch this train and I can't find the station. Oh Gawd I'm lost! Oh hep me Gawd I'm lost!"
610 The man, who was bald-headed and had on golf knickers, asked him what train he was trying to catch and Mr. Head began to get out his tickets, trembling so violently he could hardly hold them. Nelson had come up to within fifteen feet and stood watching.

"Well," the fat man said, giving him back the tickets, "you won't have time to get back to town to make this but you can catch it at the suburb stop. That's three blocks from here," and he began explaining how to get there.

Mr. Head stared as if he were slowly returning from the dead and when the man had finished and gone off with the dogs jumping at his heels, he turned to Nelson and said breathlessly, "We're going to get home!"

The child was standing about ten feet away, his face bloodless under the   620
gray hat. His eyes were triumphantly cold. There was no light in them, no
feeling, no interest. He was merely there, a small figure, waiting. Home was
nothing to him.

Mr. Head turned slowly. He felt he knew now what time would be like
without seasons and what heat would be like without light and what man
would be like without salvation. He didn't care if he never made the train and
if it had not been for what suddenly caught his attention, like a cry out of
the gathering dusk, he might have forgotten there was a station to go to.

He had not walked five hundred yards down the road when he saw,
within reach of him, the plaster figure of a Negro sitting bent over on a low   630
yellow brick fence that curved around a wide lawn. The Negro was about
Nelson's size and he was pitched forward at an unsteady angle because the
putty that held him to the wall had cracked. One of his eyes was entirely
white and he held a piece of brown watermelon.

Mr. Head stood looking at him silently until Nelson stopped at a little
distance. Then as the two of them stood there, Mr. Head breathed, "An artificial nigger!"

It was not possible to tell if the artificial Negro were meant to be young
or old; he looked too miserable to be either. He was meant to look happy
because his mouth was stretched up at the corners but the chipped eye and   640
the angle he was cocked at gave him a wild look of misery instead.

"An artificial nigger!" Nelson repeated in Mr. Head's exact tone.

The two of them stood there with their necks forward at almost the same
angle and their shoulders curved in almost exactly the same way and their
hands trembling identically in their pockets. Mr. Head looked like an ancient
child and Nelson like a miniature old man. They stood gazing at the artificial Negro as if they were faced with some great mystery, some monument to
another's victory that brought them together in their common defeat. They
could both feel it dissolving their differences like an action of mercy.
Mr. Head had never known before what mercy felt like because he had been   650
too good to deserve any, but he felt he knew now. He looked at Nelson and
understood that he must say something to the child to show that he was still
wise and in the look the boy returned he saw a hungry need for that assur-
ance. Nelson's eyes seemed to implore him to explain once and for all the
mystery of existence.

Mr. Head opened his lips to make a lofty statement and heard himself say,
"They ain't got enough real ones here. They got to have an artificial one."

After a second, the boy nodded with a strange shivering about his mouth,
and said, "Let's go home before we get ourselves lost again."

Their train glided into the suburb stop just as they reached the station   660
and they boarded it together, and ten minutes before it was due to arrive at
the junction, they went to the door and stood ready to jump off if it did not
stop; but it did, just as the moon, restored to its full splendor, sprang from a

cloud and flooded the clearing with light. As they stepped off, the sage grass was shivering gently in shades of silver and the clinkers under their feet glittered with a fresh black light. The treetops, fencing the junction like the protecting walls of a garden, were darker than the sky which was hung with gigantic white clouds illuminated like lanterns.

Mr. Head stood very still and felt the action of mercy touch him again but this time he knew that there were no words in the world that could name it. He understood that it grew out of agony, which is not denied to any man and which is given in strange ways to children. He understood it was all a man could carry into death to give his Maker and he suddenly burned with shame that he had so little of it to take with him. He stood appalled, judging himself with the thoroughness of God, while the action of mercy covered his pride like a flame and consumed it. He had never thought himself a great sinner before but he saw now that his true depravity had been hidden from him lest it cause him despair. He realized that he was forgiven for sins from the beginning of time, when he had conceived in his own heart the sin of Adam, until the present, when he had denied poor Nelson. He saw that no sin was too monstrous for him to claim as his own, and since God loved in proportion as He forgave, he felt ready at that instant to enter Paradise.

Nelson, composing his expression under the shadow of his hat brim, watched him with a mixture of fatigue and suspicion, but as the train glided past them and disappeared like a frightened serpent into the woods, even his face lightened and he muttered, "I'm glad I've went once, but I'll never go back again!"

THE MORAL INSTINCT
Steven Pinker

Steven Pinker is the Johnstone Family Professor of Psychology at Harvard University and the author of "The Language Instinct" and "The Stuff of Thought: Language as a Window Into Human Nature."

Which of the following people would you say is the most admirable: Mother Teresa, Bill Gates or Norman Borlaug? And which do you think is the least admirable? For most people, it's an easy question. Mother Teresa, famous for ministering to the poor in Calcutta, has been beatified by the Vatican, awarded the Nobel Peace Prize and ranked in an American poll as the most admired person of the 20th century. Bill Gates, infamous for giving us the Microsoft dancing paper clip and the blue screen of death, has been decapitated in effigy in "I Hate Gates" Web sites and hit with a pie in the face. As for Norman Borlaug . . . who the heck is Norman Borlaug?

Yet a deeper look might lead you to rethink your answers. Borlaug, father of the "Green Revolution" that used agricultural science to reduce world hunger, has been credited with saving a billion lives, more than anyone else in history. Gates, in deciding what to do with his fortune, crunched the numbers and determined that he could alleviate the most misery by fighting everyday scourges in the developing world like malaria, diarrhea and parasites. Mother Teresa, for her part, extolled the virtue of suffering and ran her well-financed missions accordingly: their sick patrons were offered plenty of prayer but harsh conditions, few analgesics and dangerously primitive medical care.

It's not hard to see why the moral reputations of this trio should be so out of line with the good they have done. Mother Teresa was the very embodiment of saintliness: white-clad, sad-eyed, ascetic and often photographed with the wretched of the earth. Gates is a nerd's nerd and the world's richest man, as likely to enter heaven as the proverbial camel squeezing through the needle's eye. And Borlaug, now 93, is an agronomist who has spent his life in labs and nonprofits, seldom walking onto the media stage, and hence into our consciousness, at all.

I doubt these examples will persuade anyone to favor Bill Gates over Mother Teresa for sainthood. But they show that our heads can be turned by an aura of sanctity, distracting us from a more objective reckoning of the actions that make people suffer or flourish. It seems we may all be vulnerable to moral illusions the ethical equivalent of the bending lines that trick the eye on cereal boxes and in psychology textbooks. Illusions are a favorite tool

Reprinted from *The New York Times Magazine*, January 13, 2008, by permission of The New York Times Company.

of perception scientists for exposing the workings of the five senses, and of philosophers for shaking people out of the naive belief that our minds give us a transparent window onto the world (since if our eyes can be fooled by an illusion, why should we trust them at other times?). Today, a new field is using illusions to unmask a sixth sense, the moral sense. Moral intuitions are being drawn out of people in the lab, on Web sites and in brain scanners, and
40   are being explained with tools from game theory, neuroscience and evolutionary biology.

"Two things fill the mind with ever new and increasing admiration and awe, the oftener and more steadily we reflect on them," wrote Immanuel Kant, "the starry heavens above and the moral law within." These days, the moral law within is being viewed with increasing awe, if not always admiration. The human moral sense turns out to be an organ of considerable complexity, with quirks that reflect its evolutionary history and its neurobiological foundations.

These quirks are bound to have implications for the human predicament.
50   Morality is not just any old topic in psychology but close to our conception of the meaning of life. Moral goodness is what gives each of us the sense that we are worthy human beings. We seek it in our friends and mates, nurture it in our children, advance it in our politics and justify it with our religions. A disrespect for morality is blamed for everyday sins and history's worst atrocities. To carry this weight, the concept of morality would have to be bigger than any of us and outside all of us.

So dissecting moral intuitions is no small matter. If morality is a mere trick of the brain, some may fear, our very grounds for being moral could be eroded. Yet as we shall see, the science of the moral sense can instead be seen
60   as a way to strengthen those grounds, by clarifying what morality is and how it should steer our actions.

THE MORALIZATION SWITCH

The starting point for appreciating that there is a distinctive part of our psychology for morality is seeing how moral judgments differ from other kinds of opinions we have on how people ought to behave. Moralization is a psychological state that can be turned on and off like a switch, and when it is on, a distinctive mind-set commandeers our thinking. This is the mind-set that makes us deem actions immoral ("killing is wrong"), rather than merely disagreeable ("I hate brussels sprouts"), unfashionable ("bell-bottoms are out") or imprudent ("don't scratch mosquito bites").
70   The first hallmark of moralization is that the rules it invokes are felt to be universal. Prohibitions of rape and murder, for example, are felt not to be matters of local custom but to be universally and objectively warranted. One can easily say, "I don't like brussels sprouts, but I don't care if you eat them," but no one would say, "I don't like killing, but I don't care if you murder someone."

The other hallmark is that people feel that those who commit immoral acts deserve to be punished. Not only is it allowable to inflict pain on a person who has broken a moral rule; it is wrong not to, to "let them get away with it." People are thus untroubled in inviting divine retribution or the power of the state to harm other people they deem immoral. Bertrand Russell wrote, "The infliction of cruelty with a good conscience is a delight to moralists—that is why they invented hell."

We all know what it feels like when the moralization switch flips inside us—the righteous glow, the burning dudgeon, the drive to recruit others to the cause. The psychologist Paul Rozin has studied the toggle switch by comparing two kinds of people who engage in the same behavior but with different switch settings. Health vegetarians avoid meat for practical reasons, like lowering cholesterol and avoiding toxins. Moral vegetarians avoid meat for ethical reasons: to avoid complicity in the suffering of animals. By investigating their feelings about meat-eating, Rozin showed that the moral motive sets off a cascade of opinions. Moral vegetarians are more likely to treat meat as a contaminant—they refuse, for example, to eat a bowl of soup into which a drop of beef broth has fallen. They are more likely to think that other people ought to be vegetarians, and are more likely to imbue their dietary habits with other virtues, like believing that meat avoidance makes people less aggressive and bestial.

Much of our recent social history, including the culture wars between liberals and conservatives, consists of the moralization or amoralization of particular kinds of behavior. Even when people agree that an outcome is desirable, they may disagree on whether it should be treated as a matter of preference and prudence or as a matter of sin and virtue. Rozin notes, for example, that smoking has lately been moralized. Until recently, it was understood that some people didn't enjoy smoking or avoided it because it was hazardous to their health. But with the discovery of the harmful effects of secondhand smoke, smoking is now treated as immoral. Smokers are ostracized; images of people smoking are censored; and entities touched by smoke are felt to be contaminated (so hotels have not only nonsmoking rooms but nonsmoking floors). The desire for retribution has been visited on tobacco companies, who have been slapped with staggering "punitive damages."

At the same time, many behaviors have been amoralized, switched from moral failings to lifestyle choices. They include divorce, illegitimacy, being a working mother, marijuana use and homosexuality. Many afflictions have been reassigned from payback for bad choices to unlucky misfortunes. There used to be people called "bums" and "tramps"; today they are "homeless." Drug addiction is a "disease"; syphilis was rebranded from the price of wanton behavior to a "sexually transmitted disease" and more recently a "sexually transmitted infection."

This wave of amoralization has led the cultural right to lament that morality itself is under assault, as we see in the group that anointed itself the Moral Majority. In fact there seems to be a Law of Conservation of Moralization, so that as old behaviors are taken out of the moralized column, new ones are added to it. Dozens of things that past generations treated as practical matters are now ethical battlegrounds, including disposable diapers, I.Q. tests, poultry farms, Barbie dolls and research on breast cancer. Food alone has become a minefield, with critics sermonizing about the size of sodas, the chemistry of fat, the freedom of chickens, the price of coffee beans, the species of fish and now the distance the food has traveled from farm to plate.

Many of these moralizations, like the assault on smoking, may be understood as practical tactics to reduce some recently identified harm. But whether an activity flips our mental switches to the "moral" setting isn't just a matter of how much harm it does. We don't show contempt to the man who fails to change the batteries in his smoke alarms or takes his family on a driving vacation, both of which multiply the risk they will die in an accident. Driving a gas-guzzling Hummer is reprehensible, but driving a gas-guzzling old Volvo is not; eating a Big Mac is unconscionable, but not imported cheese or creme brulee. The reason for these double standards is obvious: people tend to align their moralization with their own lifestyles.

REASONING AND RATIONALIZING

It's not just the content of our moral judgments that is often questionable, but the way we arrive at them. We like to think that when we have a conviction, there are good reasons that drove us to adopt it. That is why an older approach to moral psychology, led by Jean Piaget and Lawrence Kohlberg, tried to document the lines of reasoning that guided people to moral conclusions. But consider these situations, originally devised by the psychologist Jonathan Haidt:

Julie is traveling in France on summer vacation from college with her brother Mark. One night they decide that it would be interesting and fun if they tried making love. Julie was already taking birth-control pills, but Mark uses a condom, too, just to be safe. They both enjoy the sex but decide not to do it again. They keep the night as a special secret, which makes them feel closer to each other. What do you think about that—was it O.K. for them to make love?

A woman is cleaning out her closet and she finds her old American flag. She doesn't want the flag anymore, so she cuts it up into pieces and uses the rags to clean her bathroom.

A family's dog is killed by a car in front of their house. They heard that dog meat was delicious, so they cut up the dog's body and cook it and eat it for dinner.

Most people immediately declare that these acts are wrong and then grope to justify why they are wrong. It's not so easy. In the case of Julie and Mark, people raise the possibility of children with birth defects, but they are reminded that the couple were diligent about contraception. They suggest that the siblings will be emotionally hurt, but the story makes it clear that they weren't. They submit that the act would offend the community, but then recall that it was kept a secret. Eventually many people admit, "I don't know, I can't explain it, I just know it's wrong." People don't generally engage in moral reasoning, Haidt argues, but moral rationalization: they begin with the conclusion, coughed up by an unconscious emotion, and then work backward to a plausible justification.

The gap between people's convictions and their justifications is also on display in the favorite new sandbox for moral psychologists, a thought experiment devised by the philosophers Philippa Foot and Judith Jarvis Thomson called the Trolley Problem. On your morning walk, you see a trolley car hurtling down the track, the conductor slumped over the controls. In the path of the trolley are five men working on the track, oblivious to the danger. You are standing at a fork in the track and can pull a lever that will divert the trolley onto a spur, saving the five men. Unfortunately, the trolley would then run over a single worker who is laboring on the spur. Is it permissible to throw the switch, killing one man to save five? Almost everyone says "yes."

Consider now a different scene. You are on a bridge overlooking the tracks and have spotted the runaway trolley bearing down on the five workers. Now the only way to stop the trolley is to throw a heavy object in its path. And the only heavy object within reach is a fat man standing next to you. Should you throw the man off the bridge? Both dilemmas present you with the option of sacrificing one life to save five, and so, by the utilitarian standard of what would result in the greatest good for the greatest number, the two dilemmas are morally equivalent. But most people don't see it that way: though they would pull the switch in the first dilemma, they would not heave the fat man in the second. When pressed for a reason, they can't come up with anything coherent, though moral philosophers haven't had an easy time coming up with a relevant difference, either.

When psychologists say "most people" they usually mean "most of the two dozen sophomores who filled out a questionnaire for beer money." But in this case it means most of the 200,000 people from a hundred countries who shared their intuitions on a Web-based experiment conducted by the psychologists Fiery Cushman and Liane Young and the biologist Marc Hauser. A difference between the acceptability of switch-pulling and man-heaving, and an inability to justify the choice, was found in respondents from Europe, Asia and North and South America; among men and women, blacks and whites, teenagers and octogenarians, Hindus, Muslims, Buddhists, Christians, Jews and atheists; people with elementary-school educations and people with Ph.D.'s.

Joshua Greene, a philosopher and cognitive neuroscientist, suggests that evolution equipped people with a revulsion to manhandling an innocent person. This instinct, he suggests, tends to overwhelm any utilitarian calculus that would tote up the lives saved and lost. The impulse against roughing up a fellow human would explain other examples in which people abjure killing one to save many, like euthanizing a hospital patient to harvest his organs and save five dying patients in need of transplants, or throwing someone out of a crowded lifeboat to keep it afloat.

210   By itself this would be no more than a plausible story, but Greene teamed up with the cognitive neuroscientist Jonathan Cohen and several Princeton colleagues to peer into people's brains using functional M.R.I. They sought to find signs of a conflict between brain areas associated with emotion (the ones that recoil from harming someone) and areas dedicated to rational analysis (the ones that calculate lives lost and saved).

When people pondered the dilemmas that required killing someone with their bare hands, several networks in their brains lighted up. One, which included the medial (inward-facing) parts of the frontal lobes, has been implicated in emotions about other people. A second, the dorsolateral (upper and 220 outer-facing) surface of the frontal lobes, has been implicated in ongoing mental computation (including nonmoral reasoning, like deciding whether to get somewhere by plane or train). And a third region, the anterior cingulate cortex (an evolutionarily ancient strip lying at the base of the inner surface of each cerebral hemisphere), registers a conflict between an urge coming from one part of the brain and an advisory coming from another.

But when the people were pondering a hands-off dilemma, like switching the trolley onto the spur with the single worker, the brain reacted differently: only the area involved in rational calculation stood out. Other studies have shown that neurological patients who have blunted emotions because of 230 damage to the frontal lobes become utilitarians: they think it makes perfect sense to throw the fat man off the bridge. Together, the findings corroborate Greene's theory that our nonutilitarian intuitions come from the victory of an emotional impulse over a cost-benefit analysis.

A UNIVERSAL MORALITY?

The findings of trolleyology—complex, instinctive and worldwide moral intuitions—led Hauser and John Mikhail (a legal scholar) to revive an analogy from the philosopher John Rawls between the moral sense and language. According to Noam Chomsky, we are born with a "universal grammar" that forces us to analyze speech in terms of its grammatical structure, with no conscious awareness of the rules in play. By analogy, we are born with a univer-240 sal moral grammar that forces us to analyze human action in terms of its moral structure, with just as little awareness.

The idea that the moral sense is an innate part of human nature is not far-fetched. A list of human universals collected by the anthropologist Donald E. Brown includes many moral concepts and emotions, including a distinction between right and wrong; empathy; fairness; admiration of generosity; rights and obligations; proscription of murder, rape and other forms of violence; redress of wrongs; sanctions for wrongs against the community; shame; and taboos.

The stirrings of morality emerge early in childhood. Toddlers spontaneously offer toys and help to others and try to comfort people they see in distress. And according to the psychologists Elliot Turiel and Judith Smetana, preschoolers have an inkling of the difference between societal conventions and moral principles. Four-year-olds say that it is not O.K. to wear pajamas to school (a convention) and also not O.K. to hit a little girl for no reason (a moral principle). But when asked whether these actions would be O.K. if the teacher allowed them, most of the children said that wearing pajamas would now be fine but that hitting a little girl would still not be.

Though no one has identified genes for morality, there is circumstantial evidence they exist. The character traits called "conscientiousness" and "agreeableness" are far more correlated in identical twins separated at birth (who share their genes but not their environment) than in adoptive siblings raised together (who share their environment but not their genes). People given diagnoses of "antisocial personality disorder" or "psychopathy" show signs of morality blindness from the time they are children. They bully younger children, torture animals, habitually lie and seem incapable of empathy or remorse, often despite normal family backgrounds. Some of these children grow up into the monsters who bilk elderly people out of their savings, rape a succession of women or shoot convenience-store clerks lying on the floor during a robbery.

Though psychopathy probably comes from a genetic predisposition, a milder version can be caused by damage to frontal regions of the brain (including the areas that inhibit intact people from throwing the hypothetical fat man off the bridge). The neuroscientists Hanna and Antonio Damasio and their colleagues found that some children who sustain severe injuries to their frontal lobes can grow up into callous and irresponsible adults, despite normal intelligence. They lie, steal, ignore punishment, endanger their own children and can't think through even the simplest moral dilemmas, like what two people should do if they disagreed on which TV channel to watch or whether a man ought to steal a drug to save his dying wife.

The moral sense, then, may be rooted in the design of the normal human brain. Yet for all the awe that may fill our minds when we reflect on an innate moral law within, the idea is at best incomplete. Consider this moral dilemma: A runaway trolley is about to kill a schoolteacher. You can divert the trolley onto a sidetrack, but the trolley would trip a switch sending a signal to a class of 6-year-olds, giving them permission to name a teddy bear Muhammad. Is it permissible to pull the lever?

This is no joke. Last month a British woman teaching in a private school in Sudan allowed her class to name a teddy bear after the most popular boy in the class, who bore the name of the founder of Islam. She was jailed for blasphemy and threatened with a public flogging, while a mob outside the prison demanded her death. To the protesters, the woman's life clearly had less value than maximizing the dignity of their religion, and their judgment on whether it is right to divert the hypothetical trolley would have differed from ours. Whatever grammar guides people's moral judgments can't be all that universal. Anyone who stayed awake through Anthropology 101 can offer many other examples.

Of course, languages vary, too. In Chomsky's theory, languages conform to an abstract blueprint, like having phrases built out of verbs and objects, while the details vary, like whether the verb or the object comes first. Could 300 we be wired with an abstract spec sheet that embraces all the strange ideas that people in different cultures moralize?

THE VARIETIES OF MORAL EXPERIENCE

When anthropologists like Richard Shweder and Alan Fiske survey moral concerns across the globe, they find that a few themes keep popping up from amid the diversity. People everywhere, at least in some circumstances and with certain other folks in mind, think it's bad to harm others and good to help them. They have a sense of fairness: that one should reciprocate favors, reward benefactors and punish cheaters. They value loyalty to a group, sharing and solidarity among its members and conformity to its norms. They believe that it is right to defer to legitimate authorities and to respect people with high sta-310 tus. And they exalt purity, cleanliness and sanctity while loathing defilement, contamination and carnality.

The exact number of themes depends on whether you're a lumper or a splitter, but Haidt counts five—harm, fairness, community (or group loyalty), authority and purity—and suggests that they are the primary colors of our moral sense. Not only do they keep reappearing in cross-cultural surveys, but each one tugs on the moral intuitions of people in our own culture. Haidt asks us to consider how much money someone would have to pay us to do hypothetical acts like the following:

Stick a pin into your palm.
320 Stick a pin into the palm of a child you don't know. (Harm.)
Accept a wide-screen TV from a friend who received it at no charge
    because of a computer error.
Accept a wide-screen TV from a friend who received it from a thief who
    had stolen it from a wealthy family. (Fairness.)
Say something bad about your nation (which you don't believe) on a
    talk-radio show in your nation.
Say something bad about your nation (which you don't believe) on a
    talk-radio show in a foreign nation. (Community.)
Slap a friend in the face, with his permission, as part of a comedy skit.
330 Slap your minister in the face, with his permission, as part of a comedy
    skit. (Authority.)
Attend a performance-art piece in which the actors act like idiots for
    30 minutes, including flubbing simple problems and falling down
    on stage.

Attend a performance-art piece in which the actors act like animals for
30 minutes, including crawling around naked and urinating on stage.
(Purity.)

In each pair, the second action feels far more repugnant. Most of the moral
illusions we have visited come from an unwarranted intrusion of one of the
moral spheres into our judgments. A violation of community led people to   340
frown on using an old flag to clean a bathroom. Violations of purity repelled
the people who judged the morality of consensual incest and prevented the
moral vegetarians and nonsmokers from tolerating the slightest trace of a vile
contaminant. At the other end of the scale, displays of extreme purity lead
people to venerate religious leaders who dress in white and affect an aura of
chastity and asceticism.

THE GENEALOGY OF MORALS

The five spheres are good candidates for a periodic table of the moral sense
not only because they are ubiquitous but also because they appear to have
deep evolutionary roots. The impulse to avoid harm, which gives trolley pon-
derers the willies when they consider throwing a man off a bridge, can also   350
be found in rhesus monkey, who go hungry rather than pull a chain that
delivers food to them and a shock to another monkey. Respect for authority
is clearly related to the pecking orders of dominance and appeasement that
are widespread in the animal kingdom. The purity-defilement contrast taps
the emotion of disgust that is triggered by potential disease vectors like bodily effluvia, decaying flesh and unconventional forms of meat, and by risky
sexual practices like incest.

The other two moralized spheres match up with the classic examples of
how altruism can evolve that were worked out by sociobiologists in the 1960s
and 1970s and made famous by Richard Dawkins in his book *The Selfish Gene*.   360
Fairness is very close to what scientists call reciprocal altruism, where a willingness to be nice to others can evolve as long as the favor helps the recipient
more than it costs the giver and the recipient returns the favor when fortunes
reverse. The analysis makes it sound as if reciprocal altruism comes out of a
robotlike calculation, but in fact Robert Trivers, the biologist who devised the
theory, argued that it is implemented in the brain as a suite of moral emotions.
Sympathy prompts a person to offer the first favor, particularly to someone in
need for whom it would go the furthest. Anger protects a person against
cheaters who accept a favor without reciprocating, by impelling him to punish
the ingrate or sever the relationship. Gratitude impels a beneficiary to reward   370
those who helped him in the past. Guilt prompts a cheater in danger of being
found out to repair the relationship by redressing the misdeed and advertising
that he will behave better in the future (consistent with Mencken's definition
of conscience as "the inner voice which warns us that someone might be looking"). Many experiments on who helps whom, who likes whom, who punishes
whom and who feels guilty about what have confirmed these predictions.

Community, the very different emotion that prompts people to share and sacrifice without an expectation of payback, may be rooted in nepotistic altruism, the empathy and solidarity we feel toward our relatives (and which evolved because any gene that pushed an organism to aid a relative would have helped copies of itself sitting inside that relative). In humans, of course, communal feelings can be lavished on nonrelatives as well. Sometimes it pays people (in an evolutionary sense) to love their companions because their interests are yoked, like spouses with common children, in-laws with common relatives, friends with common tastes or allies with common enemies. And sometimes it doesn't pay them at all, but their kinship-detectors have been tricked into treating their groupmates as if they were relatives by tactics like kinship metaphors (blood brothers, fraternities, the fatherland), origin myths, communal meals and other bonding rituals.

JUGGLING THE SPHERES

All this brings us to a theory of how the moral sense can be universal and variable at the same time. The five moral spheres are universal, a legacy of evolution. But how they are ranked in importance, and which is brought in to moralize which area of social life—sex, government, commerce, religion, diet and so on—depends on the culture. Many of the flabbergasting practices in faraway places become more intelligible when you recognize that the same moralizing impulse that Western elites channel toward violations of harm and fairness (our moral obsessions) is channeled elsewhere to violations in the other spheres. Think of the Japanese fear of nonconformity (community), the holy ablutions and dietary restrictions of Hindus and Orthodox Jews (purity), the outrage at insulting the Prophet among Muslims (authority). In the West, we believe that in business and government, fairness should trump community and try to root out nepotism and cronyism. In other parts of the world this is incomprehensible—what heartless creep would favor a perfect stranger over his own brother?

The ranking and placement of moral spheres also divides the cultures of liberals and conservatives in the United States. Many bones of contention, like homosexuality, atheism and one-parent families from the right, or racial imbalances, sweatshops and executive pay from the left, reflect different weightings of the spheres. In a large Web survey, Haidt found that liberals put a lopsided moral weight on harm and fairness while playing down group loyalty, authority and purity. Conservatives instead place a moderately high weight on all five. It's not surprising that each side thinks it is driven by lofty ethical values and that the other side is base and unprincipled.

Reassigning an activity to a different sphere, or taking it out of the moral spheres altogether, isn't easy. People think that a behavior belongs in its sphere as a matter of sacred necessity and that the very act of questioning an assignment is a moral outrage. The psychologist Philip Tetlock has shown that the mentality of taboo—a conviction that some thoughts are sinful to think—is not just a superstition of Polynesians but a mind-set that can easily be triggered in college-educated Americans. Just ask them to think about applying the sphere of reciprocity to relationships customarily governed by community or authority. When Tetlock asked subjects for their opinions on whether adoption agencies should place children with the couples willing to pay the most, whether people should have the right to sell their organs and whether they should be able to buy their way out of jury duty, the subjects not only disagreed but felt personally insulted and were outraged that anyone would raise the question.

The institutions of modernity often question and experiment with the way activities are assigned to moral spheres. Market economies tend to put everything up for sale. Science amoralizes the world by seeking to understand phenomena rather than pass judgment on them. Secular philosophy is in the business of scrutinizing all beliefs, including those entrenched by authority and tradition. It's not surprising that these institutions are often seen to be morally corrosive.

IS NOTHING SACRED?

And "morally corrosive" is exactly the term that some critics would apply to the new science of the moral sense. The attempt to dissect our moral intuitions can look like an attempt to debunk them. Evolutionary psychologists seem to want to unmask our noblest motives as ultimately self-interested—to show that our love for children, compassion for the unfortunate and sense of justice are just tactics in a Darwinian struggle to perpetuate our genes. The explanation of how different cultures appeal to different spheres could lead to a spineless relativism, in which we would never have grounds to criticize the practice of another culture, no matter how barbaric, because "we have our kind of morality and they have theirs." And the whole enterprise seems to be dragging us to an amoral nihilism, in which morality itself would be demoted from a transcendent principle to a figment of our neural circuitry.

In reality, none of these fears are warranted, and it's important to see why not. The first misunderstanding involves the logic of evolutionary explanations. Evolutionary biologists sometimes anthropomorphize DNA for the same reason that science teachers find it useful to have their students imagine the world from the viewpoint of a molecule or a beam of light. One shortcut to understanding the theory of selection without working through the math is to imagine that the genes are little agents that try to make copies of themselves.

Unfortunately, the meme of the selfish gene escaped from popular biology books and mutated into the idea that organisms (including people) are ruthlessly self-serving. And this doesn't follow. Genes are not a reservoir of our dark unconscious wishes. "Selfish" genes are perfectly compatible with

selfless organisms, because a gene's metaphorical goal of selfishly replicating
460 itself can be implemented by wiring up the brain of the organism to do
unselfish things, like being nice to relatives or doing good deeds for needy
strangers. When a mother stays up all night comforting a sick child, the genes
that endowed her with that tenderness were "selfish" in a metaphorical sense,
but by no stretch of the imagination is she being selfish.

Nor does reciprocal altruism—the evolutionary rationale behind fairness—
imply that people do good deeds in the cynical expectation of repayment down
the line. We all know of unrequited good deeds, like tipping a waitress in a city
you will never visit again and falling on a grenade to save platoonmates. These
bursts of goodness are not as anomalous to a biologist as they might appear.

470 In his classic 1971 article, Trivers, the biologist, showed how natural
selection could push in the direction of true selflessness. The emergence of
tit-for-tat reciprocity, which lets organisms trade favors without being
cheated, is just a first step. A favor-giver not only has to avoid blatant cheaters
(those who would accept a favor but not return it) but also prefer generous
reciprocators (those who return the biggest favor they can afford) over stingy
ones (those who return the smallest favor they can get away with). Since
it's good to be chosen as a recipient of favors, a competition arises to be the
most generous partner around. More accurately, a competition arises to
appear to be the most generous partner around, since the favor-giver can't lit-
480 erally read minds or see into the future. A reputation for fairness and generosity becomes an asset.

Now this just sets up a competition for potential beneficiaries to inflate
their reputations without making the sacrifices to back them up. But it also
pressures the favor-giver to develop ever-more-sensitive radar to distinguish
the genuinely generous partners from the hypocrites. This arms race will
eventually reach a logical conclusion. The most effective way to seem generous and fair, under harsh scrutiny, is to be generous and fair. In the long
run, then, reputation can be secured only by commitment. At least some
agents evolve to be genuinely high-minded and self-sacrificing—they are
490 moral not because of what it brings them but because that's the kind of people they are.

Of course, a theory that predicted that everyone always sacrificed themselves for another's good would be as preposterous as a theory that predicted
that no one ever did. Alongside the niches for saints there are niches for more
grudging reciprocators, who attract fewer and poorer partners but don't make
the sacrifices necessary for a sterling reputation. And both may coexist with
outright cheaters, who exploit the unwary in one-shot encounters. An ecosystem of niches, each with a distinct strategy, can evolve when the payoff of
each strategy depends on how many players are playing the other strategies.
500 The human social environment does have its share of generous, grudging and
crooked characters, and the genetic variation in personality seems to bear the
fingerprints of this evolutionary process.

IS MORALITY A FIGMENT?

So a biological understanding of the moral sense does not entail that people are calculating maximizers of their genes or self-interest. But where does it leave the concept of morality itself?

Here is the worry. The scientific outlook has taught us that some parts of our subjective experience are products of our biological makeup and have no objective counterpart in the world. The qualitative difference between red and green, the tastiness of fruit and foulness of carrion, the scariness of heights and prettiness of flowers are design features of our common nervous system, and if our species had evolved in a different ecosystem or if we were missing a few genes, our reactions could go the other way. Now, if the distinction between right and wrong is also a product of brain wiring, why should we believe it is any more real than the distinction between red and green? And if it is just a collective hallucination, how could we argue that evils like genocide and slavery are wrong for everyone, rather than just distasteful to us?

Putting God in charge of morality is one way to solve the problem, of course, but Plato made short work of it 2,400 years ago. Does God have a good reason for designating certain acts as moral and others as immoral? If not—if his dictates are divine whims—why should we take them seriously? Suppose that God commanded us to torture a child. Would that make it all right, or would some other standard give us reasons to resist? And if, on the other hand, God was forced by moral reasons to issue some dictates and not others—if a command to torture a child was never an option—then why not appeal to those reasons directly?

This throws us back to wondering where those reasons could come from, if they are more than just figments of our brains. They certainly aren't in the physical world like wavelength or mass. The only other option is that moral truths exist in some abstract Platonic realm, there for us to discover, perhaps in the same way that mathematical truths (according to most mathematicians) are there for us to discover. On this analogy, we are born with a rudimentary concept of number, but as soon as we build on it with formal mathematical reasoning, the nature of mathematical reality forces us to discover some truths and not others. (No one who understands the concept of two, the concept of four and the concept of addition can come to any conclusion but that 2 + 2 = 4.) Perhaps we are born with a rudimentary moral sense, and as soon as we build on it with moral reasoning, the nature of moral reality forces us to some conclusions but not others.

Moral realism, as this idea is called, is too rich for many philosophers' blood. Yet a diluted version of the idea—if not a list of cosmically inscribed Thou-Shalts, then at least a few If-Thens—is not crazy. Two features of reality point any rational, self-preserving social agent in a moral direction. And they could provide a benchmark for determining when the judgments of our moral sense are aligned with morality itself.

One is the prevalence of nonzero-sum games. In many arenas of life, two parties are objectively better off if they both act in a nonselfish way than if each of them acts selfishly. You and I are both better off if we share our surpluses, rescue each other's children in danger and refrain from shooting at each other, compared with hoarding our surpluses while they rot, letting the other's child drown while we file our nails or feuding like the Hatfields and McCoys. Granted, I might be a bit better off if I acted selfishly at your expense and you played the sucker, but the same is true for you with me, so if each of us tried for these advantages, we'd both end up worse off. Any neutral observer, and you and I if we could talk it over rationally, would have to conclude that the state we should aim for is the one in which we both are unselfish. These spreadsheet projections are not quirks of brain wiring, nor are they dictated by a supernatural power; they are in the nature of things.

The other external support for morality is a feature of rationality itself: that it cannot depend on the egocentric vantage point of the reasoner. If I appeal to you to do anything that affects me—to get off my foot, or tell me the time or not run me over with your car—then I can't do it in a way that privileges my interests over yours (say, retaining my right to run you over with my car) if I want you to take me seriously. Unless I am Galactic Overlord, I have to state my case in a way that would force me to treat you in kind. I can't act as if my interests are special just because I'm me and you're not, any more than I can persuade you that the spot I am standing on is a special place in the universe just because I happen to be standing on it.

Not coincidentally, the core of this idea—the interchangeability of perspectives—keeps reappearing in history's best-thought-through moral philosophies, including the Golden Rule (itself discovered many times); Spinoza's Viewpoint of Eternity; the Social Contract of Hobbes, Rousseau and Locke; Kant's Categorical Imperative; and Rawls's Veil of Ignorance. It also underlies Peter Singer's theory of the Expanding Circle—the optimistic proposal that our moral sense, though shaped by evolution to overvalue self, kin and clan, can propel us on a path of moral progress, as our reasoning forces us to generalize it to larger and larger circles of sentient beings.

DOING BETTER BY KNOWING OURSELVES

Morality, then, is still something larger than our inherited moral sense, and the new science of the moral sense does not make moral reasoning and conviction obsolete. At the same time, its implications for our moral universe are profound.

At the very least, the science tells us that even when our adversaries' agenda is most baffling, they may not be amoral psychopaths but in the throes of a moral mind-set that appears to them to be every bit as mandatory and universal as ours does to us. Of course, some adversaries really are psychopaths, and others are so poisoned by a punitive moralization that they are beyond the pale of reason. (The actor Will Smith had many historians on his side when he recently speculated to the press that Hitler thought he was acting morally.) But in any conflict in which a meeting of the minds is not completely hopeless, a recognition that the other guy is acting from moral rather than venal reasons can be a first patch of common ground. One side can acknowledge the other's concern for community or stability or fairness or dignity, even while arguing that some other value should trump it in that instance. With affirmative action, for example, the opponents can be seen as arguing from a sense of fairness, not racism, and the defenders can be seen as acting from a concern with community, not bureaucratic power. Liberals can ratify conservatives' concern with families while noting that gay marriage is perfectly consistent with that concern.

The science of the moral sense also alerts us to ways in which our psychological makeup can get in the way of our arriving at the most defensible moral conclusions. The moral sense, we are learning, is as vulnerable to illusions as the other senses. It is apt to confuse morality per se with purity, status and conformity. It tends to reframe practical problems as moral crusades and thus see their solution in punitive aggression. It imposes taboos that make certain ideas indiscussible. And it has the nasty habit of always putting the self on the side of the angels.

Though wise people have long reflected on how we can be blinded by our own sanctimony, our public discourse still fails to discount it appropriately. In the worst cases, the thoughtlessness of our brute intuitions can be celebrated as a virtue. In his influential essay "The Wisdom of Repugnance," Leon Kass, former chair of the President's Council on Bioethics, argued that we should disregard reason when it comes to cloning and other biomedical technologies and go with our gut: "We are repelled by the prospect of cloning human beings . . . because we intuit and feel, immediately and without argument, the violation of things that we rightfully hold dear. . . . In this age in which everything is held to be permissible so long as it is freely done . . . repugnance may be the only voice left that speaks up to defend the central core of our humanity. Shallow are the souls that have forgotten how to shudder."

There are, of course, good reasons to regulate human cloning, but the shudder test is not one of them. People have shuddered at all kinds of morally irrelevant violations of purity in their culture: touching an untouchable, drinking from the same water fountain as a Negro, allowing Jewish blood to mix with Aryan blood, tolerating sodomy between consenting men. And if our ancestors' repugnance had carried the day, we never would have had autopsies, vaccinations, blood transfusions, artificial insemination, organ transplants and in vitro fertilization, all of which were denounced as immoral when they were new.

There are many other issues for which we are too quick to hit the moralization button and look for villains rather than bug fixes. What should we do when a hospital patient is killed by a nurse who administers the wrong drug in a patient's intravenous line? Should we make it easier to sue the hospital for damages? Or should we redesign the IV fittings so that it's physically impossible to connect the wrong bottle to the line?

And nowhere is moralization more of a hazard than in our greatest global challenge. The threat of human-induced climate change has become the occasion for a moralistic revival meeting. In many discussions, the cause of climate change is overindulgence (too many S.U.V.'s) and defilement (sullying the atmosphere), and the solution is temperance (conservation) and expiation (buying carbon offset coupons). Yet the experts agree that these numbers don't add up: even if every last American became conscientious about his or her carbon emissions, the effects on climate change would be trifling, if for no other reason than that two billion Indians and Chinese are unlikely to copy our born-again abstemiousness. Though voluntary conservation may be one wedge in an effective carbon-reduction pie, the other wedges will have to be morally boring, like a carbon tax and new energy technologies, or even taboo, like nuclear power and deliberate manipulation of the ocean and atmosphere. Our habit of moralizing problems, merging them with intuitions of purity and contamination, and resting content when we feel the right feelings, can get in the way of doing the right thing.

Far from debunking morality, then, the science of the moral sense can advance it, by allowing us to see through the illusions that evolution and culture have saddled us with and to focus on goals we can share and defend. As Anton Chekhov wrote, "Man will become better when you show him what he is like."

SELECTIONS FROM *THE REPUBLIC*
Plato

BOOK II

JUSTICE WRIT LARGE IN THE STATE (367E–369B)

Socrates: The inquiry we are undertaking is not trivial, but requires sharp   1
sight, as it appears to me. So since we are not clever, I said, I think we should
make this sort of inquiry as though we were not very sharp-sighted and someone ordered us to read small letters at a distance. If one next realized that the
same letters exist elsewhere, larger and on a larger surface, it would appear to
be a stroke of luck, I think, to be able to read those first and in this way examine the smaller, to see if they happen to be the same.

Of course, said Adeimantus. But what do you see of this sort in the
inquiry about justice, Socrates?

I will tell you, I said. Justice, we say, belongs to one man, but surely also   10
to a whole city?

Of course, he replied.

Now, a city is greater than one man?

Yes, he said.

Perhaps then justice would be larger and easier to understand in what is
greater. If you will, then, let us first seek to discover what it is in cities; afterward, we will thus also examine it in the individual, looking for the likeness
of the greater in the character of the less.

Why, I think that is an excellent suggestion, he said.

Then if we should watch a city come to be in discourse, I replied, we   20
would also see the justice and the injustice of it come to be?

Perhaps, he replied.

So if that happened, there is hope that what we seek would be easier
to see?

Yes, much easier.

Do you think we should try to go through with it? For I suspect it is no
small task. Think about it.

I have Adeimantus replied. Please continue.

THE GUARDIANS' NATIVE DISPOSITION (374E–376E)

Then in as much as the work of the Guardians is of greatest importance, I
replied, it would by so much require utmost leisure from other activities, and   30
again, the greatest amount of art and training.

Yes, I think so, he replied.

Does it also require a nature suited to the occupation itself?

Of course.

Reprinted from *The Republic*, translated by R.E. Allen (2006), Yale University Press.

So it would be our task, it seems, to pick out, if we can, which and what sorts of nature are suitable for guardianship of a city.

Indeed.

Really then, I replied, we have perhaps taken on ourselves no mean task. Nevertheless, it is not to be shirked, so far as ability permits.

40 No, he said.

Do you suppose then, I replied, in respect to guardianship, that there is any difference in nature between a well-bred young pup and a well-born young lad?

How do you mean?

For example, each of the two must be sharp of perception and quick in pursuit of what he perceives, and strong too, if he must subdue what he has caught.

Why, they require all this, he said.

Yes, and courage too, if they are to fight well.

50 Of course.

Will a horse or dog or any other animal be courageous if it is not spirited? Or have you not realized how irresistible and invincible spirit is? Its presence makes every soul fearless and indomitable in everything.

Yes.

It is clear then what bodily characteristics the Guardian must have.

Yes.

And further, those of his soul—at least that it be spirited.

That too.

Then if their natures are of this sort, Glaucon, I replied, how will they not 60 be savage with one another and the other citizens?

Really, it is not easy to see, he replied.

Nevertheless, they must be hard on their enemies but gentle with their friends. Otherwise, they will not need to wait around for others to destroy them; they will be beforehand in doing it themselves.

True, he said.

What shall we do, then? I replied. Where shall we find a character at once gentle and high spirited? For gentle nature is surely opposite to spirited.

It appears so.

A nature deprived of either would never become a good guardian. Yet 70 they seem incompatible, and thus then it follows that a good guardian is impossible.

Very likely, he said.

I was at a loss, and reflected on what had gone before. We are rightly perplexed, my friend, I said, for we have departed from the image we set before ourselves.

How do you mean?

We did not realize that there are, after all, natures which have these opposites, of a sort we did not consider.

Where?

One might see it even in other animals, but especially in the animal we   80
compared to the guardian. For you surely know that it is the natural character of well-bred dogs to be as gentle as possible to those they know and are
accustomed to, but the opposite to those they do not know.

Yes, certainly.

So it is possible, I replied, and the sort of guardian we are seeking is not
contrary to nature.

It seems not.

Now, in addition to being spirited, do you think our future guardian will
in nature still further need to be a philosopher?

How so? he said. I don't understand.   90

You see it even in dogs, I replied. Indeed, it is worth admiring in the
beast.

What's that?

The dog is roused to anger at seeing someone he does not know, without
ever having suffered any evil; but he welcomes someone he knows even if he
has never experienced anything good at the other's hands. Have you never yet
wondered at that?

I had not paid much attention to it before this, he said. But clearly, they
do act that way.

But surely this shows a fine trait of his nature, and that it is truly   100
philosophical.

How so?

Because, I replied, he distinguishes a friendly from an unfriendly face on
no other basis than having learned to know the one but not the other. And
yet, if he can distinguish what is his own and what is alien on the basis of
knowledge and ignorance, how would he not be a lover of learning?

He must be, he replied.

Again, I said, love of learning and love of wisdom are the same?

Yes, he said.

Then we may confidently assume also in man, that if he is to be gentle   110
toward his own and those he knows, he must by nature be a philosopher and
lover of learning?

Let's assume it, he said.

Then anyone who is to be a good and noble Guardian of our city will be
a lover of wisdom, and spirited and quick and strong in nature.

Most assuredly, he said.

So that is their natural disposition. But how will they be raised and educated? Is it helpful to examine the question relative to discerning the object
of our whole inquiry: how justice and injustice come to be present in a city?
We must not curtail argument, nor yet draw it out at length.   120

And Glaucon's brother said, I certainly think this inquiry is helpful in
respect to that.

Then we surely must not give it up, dear Adeimantus, I replied, even if it happens to be rather lengthy.

No.

Come then. As though telling a story at our leisure, we will educate these men in discourse.

Why, so we must.

BOOK V

PHILOSOPHERS AND LOVERS OF SIGHTS AND SOUNDS: THE THEORY OF FORMS (475D–476B)

And Glaucon said, Then many strange folk will be philosophers. For all
130 lovers of sights and spectacles, it seems to me, are like this, because they delight in learning. And lovers of sounds are among the strangest to rank as philosophers, because they will not willingly engage in arguments and such pursuits as that, but run around to Dionysiac festivals as though they had rented out their ears to every chorus, omitting no performance either in city or country village. Shall we then say that all these are philosophers too? And others who learn other things of this same sort, or practice the minor arts?

No, I said, but they are like philosophers.

Who do you say are the genuine philosophers? he said.

Those who love the sight and spectacle of truth, I replied.

140 No doubt, he said. But what do you mean?

It's not easily explained to another, I replied, but I think you will agree with me in this.

What?

Since beautiful is opposite to ugly,[12] they are two.

Of course.

Then since two, each is also one?

Yes.

And the same account for just and unjust, good and evil, and all the forms: each in itself is one, but by communion with actions and bodies and
150 each other, they make their appearance everywhere, and each appears many.

You are right, he said.

In this way, then, I replied, I distinguish separately on one side those whom you just now described as lovers of sights and spectacles and lovers of arts and practical men, and separately again on the other side those with whom the argument is concerned, and whom one alone would rightly call philosophers or lovers of wisdom.

How do you mean? he said.

Lovers of sights and sounds, I replied, surely delight in beautiful tones and colors and figures and all that is fashioned from such things, but their
160 understanding is incapable of seeing and delighting in the nature of the beautiful itself.

Yes, that is certainly so, he said.

KNOWLEDGE AND OPINION (476D–477B)

Then we would rightly say that the understanding of the one is knowledge, since he knows, but that of the other is opinion, since he judges by appearances.

Of course.

What if this person whom we say judges by appearances but does not know became angry at us, and contended that we do not speak truly? Can we soothe and gently persuade him, while disguising the fact that he is unsound?[13]

We must at least try, he said.

Come then, consider what we will say to him. Or would you have us inquire of him in this way, suggesting that if he knows something no one begrudges him; on the contrary, we would be delighted to see that he knows something. But he must please tell us this: does someone who knows, know something or nothing? You answer me in his behalf.

I will answer that he knows something, he said.

Something that is, or is not?

Something that is. For how could something be known if it is not?

Then we are sufficiently assured, from whatever point of view we may examine it, that the perfectly real is perfectly knowable, but what in no way is, is in every way utterly unknowable?

Yes.

Very well. But if there is something such that it both exists and does not exist, would it not lie intermediate between what purely is, and again, what in no way is?

Yes.

Then since knowledge is directed to what is, but ignorance of necessity to what is not, something intermediate between knowledge and ignorance must also be sought, if there happens to be such a thing, directed to this intermediate.

Of course.

Now, we say that opinion or judgment of appearances is something?

Certainly.

Is it a power other than knowledge, or the same?

Other.

So judgment of appearances is ordered to one object, knowledge to another, each according to its own respective power.[14]

That is so.

BOOK VI

PHILOSOPHERS AND GUARDIANS (484A–487A)

Then following out a somewhat lengthy way, Glaucon, I replied, those who are philosophers and those who are not have, with some difficulty, revealed who they each are.

Perhaps the way could not easily have been shortened, he said.

It appears not, I said. At any rate, I think it might have been still better revealed if this were the only thing we had to talk about, and so many other things did not also require explanation in order to discern how a just life differs from an unjust life.

What is next, then? he said.

What else but what's next in order? I replied. Since philosophers are able to grasp what is always the same with respect to the same things, while those who cannot do this are not philosophers and wander amid manifold and diverse multiplicity, which of them then should be leaders of a city?

How might we fairly respond? he said.

Whichever of the two appear capable of guarding the laws and practices of cities should be established as Guardians, I replied.

Rightly, he said.

But it is clear, I replied, that a Guardian must not be blind but sharp of sight if he is to guard anything at all.

Of course it is clear, he said.

Then do you think that those really deprived of knowledge of the reality of each thing which is, and who have no clear paradigm or standard in their souls, differ at all from the blind? They cannot, like painters, look to what is most true and ever refer to it yonder and contemplate it as exactly as possible, and thus then, if there is need, establish conventional notions here about things beautiful and just and good, and guard and preserve what has been established.

No, he replied, it's not much different from being blind.

Shall we then rather establish them as Guardians, or those who know what each reality is, and do not fall short of the others in experience, nor are inferior in any other part of virtue?

If the latter do not fall short in other respects, he said, it would be absurd to choose the others; for it is in this very knowledge that their superiority would mainly consist.

Shall we then tell how it will be possible for the same people to have both the former and the latter?

Of course.

Well as we said to begin with, it is first necessary to understand their nature. I think if we once sufficiently agree on that, we'll also agree that it is possible for the same people to have both, and that no others should lead cities.

How so?

Let us first agree that philosophical natures are always in love with a study which makes clear to them the nature and reality of what always is, and is not caused to wander by coming to be and passing away.

Agreed.

And further, I replied, that they desire all of it, and will not voluntarily give up any part, small or larger, more valuable or less, even as we formerly described lovers and those ambitious for honor.

You're right, he said.

Then next consider whether people who are to be such as we described necessarily have this additional element in their nature:

What?

Lack of falseness and refusal willingly to accept falsehood in any way, but   250
to hate it and desire the truth.

Likely enough, he said.

Not only likely, my friend, but there is every necessity that someone in love by nature delights in everything akin and closely related to what he loves.

Right, he said.

Now, would you find anything more closely related to wisdom than truth?

No, he replied.

Then is it possible for the same nature to love wisdom and love falsehood?

Surely not.

So the real lover of learning must, from childhood up, strive as much as   260
possible after all truth.

Certainly.

Again, when the desires set strongly in one direction, we know they flow more weakly by the same amount in others, like a stream diverted into another bed.

Of course.

So when they flow toward learning and everything of that sort, I suppose they would be concerned for the pleasure of the soul alone by itself, and forsake the pleasures obtained through the body, if one is not a pretender but truly a lover of wisdom.   270

Quite necessary.

Such a person would surely be temperate and in no way a lover of money; for he is the last person to take seriously the things for which money is eagerly sought and lavishly spent.

That is so.

Again, if you intend to distinguish a philosophical from an unphilosophical nature, you must also consider this:

What is that?

That you not overlook any share of slavishness. For surely, pettiness of   *baseness*
mind is utterly opposite to a soul whose desire is always set on the Whole and   280
the All, human and divine.

Very true, he said.

Do you then think that an understanding lofty enough to contemplate all time and all existence can suppose this our human life a thing of great importance?

Impossible, he replied.

Then indeed, such a person will not believe death something terrible?

Hardly.

There is no share of genuine philosophy for a cowardly and slavish nature, it seems.

I think not.   290

Well then, is it possible that a well-ordered person, neither money-loving nor slavish, neither braggart nor coward, would ever become hard to deal with or unjust?

It is impossible.

So too then, in considering whether or not a person is philosophical in soul, you will observe from youth up whether he is just and kind, or unsociable and wild.

Of course.

300   Again, you will not omit this, I suppose:

What is that?

Ease and difficulty in learning. Or do you expect anyone ever to sufficiently love something if he does what he does in pain and with difficulty accomplishes little?

No.

What if he were able to retain nothing of what he learned and was full of forgetfulness? Could he possibly fail to be empty of knowledge?

Of course not.

So he will labor in vain, you think, compelled in the end to hate both himself and this kind of activity?

310

Of course.

Let us not then enroll a forgetful soul among those adequate to pursue philosophy. Let us require a good memory.

Of course.

But surely, we would also deny that graceless awkwardness of nature tends anywhere except to excess and disproportion.

Yes.

Do you believe that truth is akin to excess and disproportion, or to due measure?

320   To due measure.

Then in addition to the rest, let us seek an understanding naturally measured and graceful, which will easily lead of its own growth to the Idea of each thing which is.

Of course.

Now, we think that all we have described is in some way necessary, and follows each upon the other in a soul which intends sufficiently and perfectly to come to have a share of what is?

Most necessarily, he said.

Is there then any way to find fault with a pursuit which one could not

330   sufficiently practice unless he were not by nature of good memory, quick to learn, high-minded, graceful, friendly and akin to truth, and to justice and courage and temperance?

Why, Momus himself[1] could not find fault with it, he said.

But when such people are perfected by education and age, I replied, you would turn the city over only to them?

ADEIMANTUS OBJECTS: PEOPLE THINK PHILOSOPHERS USELESS (487B–E)

And Adeimantus said, No one can gainsay you in this, Socrates. Still, when you talk this way, your hearers are often affected somewhat like this: they believe that through inexperience in question and answer, they are little by little led astray by the argument at every question, and when the little mistakes are collected at the end, they turn out to be a big slip and opposite to what was said at first. Just as less skillful players at backgammon are finally shut out by clever ones and can't make a move, so also they themselves are finally shut out in this other kind of game where the counters are not pebbles but words, and don't have a thing to say—though it's not at all the more true for being that way. I speak with a view to the present argument. For as it is, someone might say that he cannot oppose you on any given question in word, but he sees in deed, among those who turn to philosophy and continue in it too long instead of taking it up to complete their education while young and then dropping it, that the greater part become very strange, not to say rotten, and even those who seem best nevertheless become useless to their cities as an effect of the study you praise.

And I listened and said, Well, do you think those who say this are mistaken?

I don't know, he replied. I'd gladly hear what you think.

You would hear that they appear to me to tell the truth.

THE SHIP OF STATE (487E–489D)

Then how can it be proper, he said, to claim that cities will find no surcease from evils until philosophers—whom we agree are useless to them—rule in them?

You ask a question, I replied, which needs an answer stated through an image.

I think you are not unaccustomed to speak through images, he said.

Well, well, I replied. You poke fun at me, after throwing me into an argument so hard to prove? Then hear the image, so that you may still better see how hard I strain to draw it. The experience of the best sort of men in relation to their cities is so difficult that nothing else is like it; to defend them by offering an image, one must collect it from many sources, as painters mix things up to draw goat-stags and such. Conceive this then as happening on many ships or one. A shipmaster is big and strong beyond everyone else on board, but also a bit deaf and somewhat near-sighted; and his knowledge of navigation is like that too. The sailors quarrel with each other over the helm; each thinks he ought to steer though he has never learned the art and cannot point to a teacher or a time in which he learned. They claim in addition that navigation cannot be taught, and they are ready to cut to pieces anyone who claims it can. They crowd around the shipmaster, begging him, prepared to do anything if only he will turn the rudder over to them. Sometimes, if they do not persuade him, but others do, they kill them or throw them overboard and banish them. Using drugs[2] or drink or something else, they bind the noble shipmaster hand and foot, seize the ship, plunder its stores, and sail on as one might expect, drinking and feasting. In addition, they praise and call a man a navigator, a pilot, and a master of seamanship if only he is clever at persuading or compelling the shipmaster to let them govern; anyone not like

380   that they condemn as useless. They do not realize that a genuine pilot must be concerned with the year and its seasons, with sky and stars and winds and all that belongs to his art, if he really intends to be governor of a ship. Neither do they suppose that there is an art or study of steering, whether one wishes it so or not, nor that it is possible to grasp it and therewith the art of the pilot. When things like this occur, don't you believe that sailors on ships managed this way will call the true pilot really a stargazer and an idle babbler, and useless to them?

Indeed, said Adeimantus.

Then you understand what I mean, I replied. I doubt you need examine

390   the image further to see that it is like the disposition of cities toward genuine philosophers.

Yes, he said.

Then first teach this image to anyone who is surprised that philosophers are not honored in their cities, and try to persuade him that it would be much more surprising if they were.

Why, I will teach it, he said.

And further, that he is right to claim that the best among those in philosophy are useless to the multitude. However, he is not to blame good men for their uselessness, but rather those who make no use of them. For it is not

400   natural that a pilot should beg sailors to be governed by himself, or for the wise to go to the doors of the rich; whoever invented that bit of cleverness was wrong. The actual truth is that, rich or poor, a sick man must go to the doors of doctors, and all who need to be ruled to the doors of someone capable of ruling; it is not for the ruler to beg those who need ruling to submit to being ruled, if he in truth confers a benefit. But you will not be mistaken in comparing present-day political rulers to the sailors we just described, and those whom they call useless babbling stargazers to true pilots.

Quite right, he said.

In consequence then, and under these conditions, the most noble pursuit

410   is not easily held in high esteem by those who practice occupations opposed to it. But by far the greatest and strongest prejudice against philosophy arises through those who claim to practice it. The accuser of philosophy, you say, claims that most of those who go to her are thoroughly bad, and the best sort useless. And I conceded that is true, did I not?

Yes.

Then we have explained the cause of uselessness of the better sort?

Indeed.

THAT A PHILOSOPHICAL RULER IS POSSIBLE (497A–502C)

I think it has fairly been told why there is prejudice against philosophy, and why the prejudice is unjust—unless you have something more to add.

No, I have nothing more to say about it, he replied. But among present-day constitutions, which do you claim is suitable?   420

Not a one of them, I said. On the contrary, that is exactly what I am complaining about: not a single city as now constituted is worthy of a philosophical nature. That is why that nature is twisted and altered. As foreign seed sown in alien soil is like to be overmastered and vanish into the native growth, so also this kind does not now receive its own power, but is cast out into an alien character. But if ever it gets the best constitution, then even as it is itself best, it will at that point make clear that it really is divine, and the others in nature and practice merely human. Clearly then, you are next going to ask what this constitution is.   430

No, he replied. I wasn't going to ask that, but whether it is this constitution we have described in founding the city or another.

In other respects, I replied, it is this. But there is also the exact thing we mentioned before: that there must always be some element present in the city which holds the same account of the constitution that you as lawgiver held in giving its laws.

Yes, that was said, he replied.

But not sufficiently made clear, I said, for fear of topics[9] which require, as your objections show, a long and difficult proof. Indeed, the hardest part still remains.   440

What is that?

How a city can deal with philosophy and not be destroyed. For all great things are dangerous, and, as the proverb has it, excellent things really are hard.

That is evident, he said. Nevertheless, please carry the demonstration through to the end.

If I do not, I replied, it will not be for want of trying, but for lack of ability. "You're here, and you'll witness my effort." Consider how eagerly and even rashly I mean to claim that a city must deal with this pursuit, the opposite of now.

How so?

As things stand now, I replied, those who touch philosophy at all are   450
young men just past childhood, in the interval before setting up a household and beginning to earn their own living. Just when they approach the hardest part of it, they quit—and yet, they are made out to be most accomplished in philosophy. By the hardest part I mean what has to do with reasoning. Later on, if invited by others who engage in philosophical conversation, they think it a great thing if they consent even to become hearers, because they suppose philosophy should be engaged in only as a hobby. With few exceptions, as they approach old age, their light is quenched more thoroughly than the Sun of Heraclitus, inasmuch as it is not again rekindled.

460 How should it be, then? he said.

Exactly the opposite. As boys and young men they should deal with education and philosophy in a way suited to their youth, and while growing into manhood take very good care of their bodies as a support to philosophy. As age advances and the soul begins to reach maturity, they should intensify exercise of the body; when strength abates and they are beyond political and military service, they should at that point be allowed to graze unfettered and do nothing but philosophy except as a hobby, if they are to live happily and, in dying, add a fitting apportionment in the other world to the life they have lived here.

470 Truly, you seem much in earnest, Socrates. Though I suppose most of your hearers are even more earnest in their opposition. They do not at all intend to be persuaded . . . .

THE GOOD IS NOT KNOWLEDGE OR PLEASURE (504D–506D)

Is it not ridiculous to strain every nerve to get the most pure and accurate knowledge of other things of little worth, but not to demand greatest accuracy in matters of greatest importance?

Yes, he said. But do you think anyone will let you off without asking what the greatest and most important study is, what you say it is about?

Of course, I replied. Go ahead and ask. You've certainly heard it often enough. Either you do not now realize that, or you intend to make trouble
480 by raising objections. I think it is the latter. For you have often heard that the greatest and most important study is the Idea of the Good, by which just things and the rest become useful and beneficial. And you pretty well now know that I intend to mention it, and to say in addition that we do not sufficiently know it. But if we do not know it, then however well we may know other things without it, you know we gain no benefit, even as we gain no benefit if we possess anything without the Good. Or do you think there is profit in any possession, if it is not Good? Or in understanding all other things without the Good, but understanding nothing beautiful and good?

I certainly do not, he said.

490 Furthermore, you also know that most people think the Good is pleasure, though the cleverer sort think it is knowledge.

Of course.

Yes, and those who believe the latter, my friend, cannot show what kind of knowledge, but are compelled in the end to say knowledge of the Good.

And quite ridiculously, he said.

Of course, I replied. How should it not be so, if they blame us because we do not know the Good, and again, speak as if they thought we knew it. For they say it is knowledge of good, supposing that we do after all understand what they mean when they utter the word "good."

500 Very true, he said.

What about those who define the Good as pleasure? Are they any less filled with wandering than the others? Are they not compelled also to agree that there are bad pleasures?

Yes, certainly.

It follows then, I suppose, that they agree that the same things are good and bad. Not so?

Certainly.

Then evidently there are many great disputes about it?

Of course.

But then, is it not evident that though many people would choose what   510
seems just and beautiful, even if it is not really so, they nevertheless do and possess and judge these things? But it is not enough to possess things which merely seem good; instead, they seek what really is good. Here, at this point, all disdain the seeming.

Yes, he said.

This then is what every soul pursues and for the sake of which it acts in everything, dimly divining that it is something but perplexed and unable sufficiently to grasp what it is, or to attain to the sort of steadfast belief she has about other things—thereby also missing any benefit those other things might have. Shall the best men in the city, in whose hands we are placing   520
everything, be left in the dark about such and so great a matter?

Surely not, he said.

At any rate, I said, I suppose that if it is not known in what way just and beautiful things are good, someone ignorant of this would be far from possessing a worthy guardian of themselves. My guess is that no one will sufficiently know anything before he sufficiently knows this.

An excellent guess, he said.

Now, our constitution will have been perfectly ordered, if the sort of guardian who knows these things oversees it?

Necessarily, he said. But what about you, Socrates? Do you claim the   530
Good is knowledge, or pleasure? Or something else besides?

What a man! I replied. You have shown all along that what seemed so to the others would not suffice for you.

No, Socrates, he said, because it does not appear just in me to try to state the judgments of others but not my own, after spending so much time worrying about it.

Well, but do you think it just to speak of what one does not know as if he thought he knew? I replied.

Certainly not as if he thought he knew, he said, but nevertheless as one who is willing to say what he thinks, given that he thinks it.   540

Are you not aware, I said, that all opinions without knowledge are flawed? The best of them are blind. Or do you think those who judge something truly without thought differ at all from blind men traveling the right road?

No, he said.

Would you then contemplate flawed things, halt and blind, when it is possible to hear bright and beautiful things from others?

For heavens sake, Socrates, Glaucon replied, don't stop as if you were at an end. Oblige us. As you explained about justice and temperance and the rest, please also explain about the Good.

THE SUN AND THE IDEA OF THE GOOD (506D–509C)

550   In fact, I will be very glad to oblige, my friend, I replied. But I fear I will not be able to, that in my eagerness I will only invite ridicule for my clumsiness. For the present, my friends, let us dismiss what the Good is in itself—for that appears to me a larger task than to arrive, according to the present line of attack, at what now seems true to me. What appears to be both offspring of the Good and most like it, I am willing to tell, if it pleases you.[16] If not, let it go.

Please speak, he said. You will pay your debt another time for the explanation you owe of the father.

I might wish, I said, that I were able to pay the debt and allow you to receive the principal, rather than, as now, only the interest.[17] But at any rate
560   accept the interest and offspring of the Good itself. Take care, however, that I do not in some way mislead you against my will, and render a false account of the offspring.

We will take care as best we can, he said. Only speak.

Yes, I said, once we've come to agreement. Recollect what was said before and at this point has often been said elsewhere.

What is that? he replied.

We say there are many beautiful things and many good things, and so on, I replied, and we distinguish them in discourse.

Yes, we do.

570   And again, there is beautiful itself, and good itself, and so for everything which we formerly assumed to be many. But now we turn and assume one single Idea of each, supposing that it is one, and in each case we call it what is.

That's so.

And some things are visible but not intelligible, we say, but the Ideas again are intelligible but not visible.

Certainly.

Then by what of ourselves do we see things seen?

By sight, he said.

Then also we hear things heard by hearing, I replied, and everything sen-
580   sible by the other senses?

Of course.

Then have you ever realized, I replied, with what extraordinary lavishness the craftsman of the senses has wrought the power to see and to be seen?[18]

Why, no, he said.

Consider this: do hearing and sound need in addition another kind in respect to hearing and being heard, such that if a third thing is not present, the one will not hear, the other not be heard?

No, he said, they need nothing in addition.

Nor I suppose are there many other senses—in order not to say none—that need in addition anything of this sort.[19] Can you mention any?   590

I cannot, he replied.

But don't you realize that sight and the visible need something in addition?

How so?

Sight may be in eyes, surely, and he who has it may try to use it; and color may be present in objects; but if a third kind of thing proper and peculiar to this very thing is not present in addition, you know that sight will see nothing and the colors will be invisible.

What is it you mean? he said.

Why, what you call light, I replied.[20]   600

True, he said.

So it is by no small idea that the sensation of seeing and the power of being seen are yoked together by a yoke more valuable than that yoking the rest, if indeed light is not itself without value.

But surely, it is far from being without value, he said.

Now, which among the gods in heaven[21] do you hold responsible as master of this—whose light causes vision to see what is most beautiful, and things seen to be seen?

Just what you and other people say, he replied: it is clear you are asking about the Sun.   610

Now, vision is dependent upon this god in the following way:

How?

Vision is not the Sun—neither itself nor that in which it comes to be present, which we call the eye.

No.

Yes, but I suppose the eye is the most sunlike of the organs of sensation?[22]

By far.

Then too, the power which it has is dispensed by the Sun, and possessed as a kind of overflow?

Of course.   620

Then again, the Sun is not vision, but, as cause of vision, is seen by vision itself?

That's so, he said.

This then, I replied, you may say is what I meant as the offspring of the Good, which the Good generated in analogy to itself: that as the Good stands to thought and things known in the intelligible place, so the Sun stands to vision and things seen in the visible place.

How do you mean? he said. Please explain further.

You know that eyes, I replied, when one no longer turns them toward those things whose colors are overspread by the light of day, but by moon-   630
light or starlight, become dull and appear nearly blind, as if pure vision were not present.

Indeed, he said.

Yes, but I suppose when the Sun illuminates their object, they see clearly, and vision proves to be present in these same eyes.

Of course.

So also then conceive what belongs to the soul: when it is fixed upon what truth and reality illuminate, it conceives and knows it, and proves to possess thought. But when it is fixed upon what is mixed with darkness, upon what

640   comes to be and passes away, it judges and becomes dull and changes opinions back and forth, and seems not to possess thought.

Yes.

This then, which provides truth to things known and gives to the knower the power of knowing, you must say is the Idea of the Good. As cause of knowledge and of truth, you must understand it as being known. But beautiful as knowledge and truth both are, you will rightly believe it is other and still more beautiful than they. Even as there it is right to regard light and vision as Sun-like, but wrong to believe them the Sun, so also here it is right to regard knowledge and truth as Good-like, but wrong to believe either of them the

650   Good. Instead, the possession of the Good is still more to be valued.[23]

You mean a matchless beauty, he said, if it provides knowledge and truth, but is itself beyond them in beauty. For you surely don't mean it is pleasure.

Don't blaspheme, I replied. But examine the image of it still further in this way:

How?

I suppose you will say that the Sun provides not only the power of being seen to things seen, but also of becoming and growth and nurture, though it is not itself becoming.

Of course.

660   And say also for things known, then, not only that intelligibility is present by agency of the Good, but reality and being is also present to them by it, though the Good is not being, but even beyond being, surpassing it in respect to dignity and power.

And Glaucon was quite amused: By Apollo![24] he said, Divine superiority!

It is your own fault, I replied, for making me say what I think about it.

BOOK VII

THE CAVE (514A–517A)

Next then, I said, concerning education and the lack of it, compare our own nature to a situation like this: Picture people as dwelling in a cavernous underground chamber, with an entrance opening upward to the light, and a long passageway running down the whole length of the cave. They have been

670   there since childhood, legs and necks fettered so they cannot move: they see only what is in front of them, unable to turn their heads because of the bonds. But light reaches them from a fire burning some distance behind and above them. Between the fire and the prisoners, picture a track a bit higher up, and a little wall built along it like the screens in front of the performers at puppet shows, above which they show the puppets.

I see it, he said.

See also then people carrying all sorts of artificial objects alongside this little wall, statues of men and other animals, made of wood and stone and all sorts of things. Some of the carriers are talking, it is likely, others silent.

A strange image, he said, and strange prisoners. 680

Like ourselves, I replied. For first, do you think such prisoners see anything of themselves or one another except the shadows cast by the fire on the wall of the cave in front of them?

Why, how could they, he said, if they had been compelled to hold their heads motionless throughout life?

What about the objects being carried along. Isn't it the same?

Of course.

Then if they were able to converse with one another, don't you think they would acknowledge as things which are, the things that they saw?[1]

Necessarily. 690

What if the prison also had an echo from the wall opposite. Whenever some one of those passing gave utterance, do you think they would believe anything except the passing shadow spoke?

Emphatically not, he said.

Such prisoners, then, I replied, would not acknowledge as true anything except shadows of artificial objects.

Quite necessarily, he said.

Consider then, I replied, what release and healing from the bonds of unwisdom would consist in, if it by nature occurred to them in this way: whenever one of them was released, and suddenly compelled to stand upright and turn 700 his head and walk and look upward to the light, he would feel pain in doing all this, and because his eyes were dazzled, he would be unable to discern those things yonder whose shadows he had seen before. What do you suppose he would say, if someone told him that what he had seen before was foolishness, but that now, being somewhat nearer to what is and turned toward more real objects, he would see more correctly? Especially if, after being shown each of the things which are passing, he was compelled by questioning to answer what it is? Don't you suppose he would be perplexed and at a loss, and believe the things he saw before more true than those pointed out to him now?

Yes, he said. 710

Then suppose he were also compelled to look toward the light itself. It would hurt his eyes, and he would turn away in order to escape to the things he was able to see, and acknowledge them as really more clear than what was being shown him.

That's so, he said.

But if someone forcibly dragged him from there up the rugged steep ascent, I replied, and did not let go until he had hauled him into the light of the sun, wouldn't he suffer and be distressed as he was dragged along? And when he came to the light, his eyes would be so filled with its brightness that he would be unable to see even one among the things now claimed to be true? 720

No, he said, at least not immediately.

Then I suppose he would have to become accustomed to it, if he is going to see the things above. It would be easiest first to look at shadows, next, at images in water of men and other things, and afterward at the things themselves; after this, it would be easier to contemplate things in the heaven and the heaven itself by night, and gaze at the light of the stars and the moon, than at the sun and its light by day.

Of course.

Finally then, I suppose, the sun. Not appearances of it in water or in alien
730   seats: he would be able to look at it alone by itself in its own place, and contemplate it as it is.

Necessarily, he said.

After this, he would at that point infer of it that it is this which produces the seasons and the years and governs everything in the visible place, and is in some manner cause of all the things they used to see.

It is clear, he said, that he would arrive next at this conclusion along with that.

Suppose he were to recall his first dwelling place, and the wisdom there, and his fellow prisoners then. Wouldn't he think himself happy in the
740   change, and pity them?

Indeed.

Suppose they had honors and prizes for those who most acutely discern and best remember the shadows that pass—which of them usually comes before, and after, and at the same time—and from this was then best able to guess what was coming next. Do you think he would want what they have, and envy them their honors and positions of power? Or would he feel, as Homer has it, that he would much prefer to be the slave of a landless man and suffer anything at all, rather than believe those things and live that life?[2]

Yes, he said, I think he would suffer anything rather than accept that life.
750   Consider this too, I replied. If such a man went down again and sat upon the same seat,[3] would not his eyes be filled with darkness, coming suddenly from the sun?

Yes, indeed, he said.

Suppose then he had to compete again in judging those shadows with people who had always been prisoners, while his vision was dim, before his eyes settled down—and it would take some little time to get used to the darkness. Wouldn't he be laughed at? Wouldn't it be said of him that he had journeyed upward only to return with his eyes ruined, that it wasn't worth it even to try to go up? And if they were able somehow to lay hands on the man try-
760   ing to release them and lead them up, and kill him, they would kill him.[4]

Certainly, he said.

THE CAVE APPLIED TO THE SUN AND THE LINE (517A–518B)

This image, my dear Glaucon, I replied, must be applied as a whole to what was said before, likening the seat which appears through sight to the prison dwelling, and the light of the fire in it to the power of the sun. If you assume that the ascent upward and the vision of things above is the upward journey of the soul to the intelligible place, you will not mistake my surmise, since you desire to hear it. God alone knows whether it happens to be true, but these appearances appear thus to me. In the intelligible place, the Idea of the Good is seen finally and with difficulty, but once seen, it must be inferred that it is the cause of all things right and beautiful. In the visible place it gives birth to Light and to the Sun, the Lord of Light; in the intelligible place it is itself Lord, and provides intelligence and truth. It must also be inferred that whoever intends to act wisely in public or private must see it.   770

So far as I am able, he said, I concur.

Come then, I replied, and concur also in this: do not be surprised that those who arrive here refuse to take part in the affairs of men; rather, their souls ever press on to spend their time above. For it is surely likely to be so, if the foregoing image once again applies.

Yes, he said.

Then do you think it at all surprising, I replied, if someone who has come   780 from contemplation of divine things to the evils of human life is awkward, and appears quite ridiculous when, with vision still dim and before becoming sufficiently accustomed to the present darkness, he is compelled, in law courts or elsewhere, to contend about the shadows of what is just, or about images of the things of which they are shadows, and to dispute about how they are understood by those who have never seen justice itself?

It would not at all be surprising, he said.

But a reasonable man might remember, I replied, that eyes become disturbed in two ways and for two reasons: by shifting from light to darkness, and from darkness to light. He would acknowledge that this same thing also   790 happens with soul, and whenever he saw it disturbed and unable to see something, he would not thoughtlessly laugh, but inquire whether it had been blinded by unaccustomed darkness after coming from a brighter life, or whether in passing from greater ignorance to a brighter life it had been dazzled by yet more light; and thus he would count one soul happy in its experience and its life, but pity the other, and if he wished to laugh at it, his laughter would be less ridiculous than laughter at a soul come down from the light above.

A very fair statement, he said.

EDUCATION AND VIRTUE (518B–519D)

If this is true, I said, we must acknowledge that education is not what it is   800 said to be by some, who profess to be able to put knowledge into a soul where it is not present, as though putting sight into blind eyes.

They do claim that, he said.

The present account signifies, I replied, that this power is present in the soul of each person, along with the instrument by which each person understands. It is as if an eye could not turn from darkness to what is bright except in company with the whole body. Just so, this instrument must be converted from what becomes by turning in company with the whole soul until it has become capable of being lifted up to contemplate what is, and the brightest of what is. But this, we say, is the Good. Not so?

Yes.

Then there would be an art whose object is to effect this very thing, this conversion, I replied, to turn the soul around in the easiest and most effective way. Not to put sight into it, for we may suppose it already has it, but to contrive that it not be turned to look in the wrong direction, but where it should.

It seems so, he said.

The other virtues commonly said to belong to the soul are not far removed from things of the body—for they are afterward produced by habits and practices where they were not really present before—but the virtue of intelligence assuredly happens to be something more divine, it seems: it never loses its power, but becomes useful and beneficial or useless and harmful because of the way it is turned. Or have you never noticed, among those said to be bad but wise, how shrewd is the vision of their petty souls and how keenly it sees the things toward which it is turned? There's nothing the matter with their vision, but it is compelled to the service of evil, so that the more keenly it sees, the more evils it works.

Of course, he replied.

And yet, I replied, if such a nature were pruned from childhood up—cleared, as it were, of those leaden weights, akin to becoming, which are attached to it by gluttony and greedy pleasures of that kind and bend the vision of the soul downward—if, freed from these, it were turned round at last to things which are true, then this same thing belonging to these same people would see things yonder most keenly, even as the objects toward which it is now turned.

Yes, likely enough, he said.

But isn't it also likely, I replied, and even necessary from what has been said, that a city cannot ever sufficiently be governed by those who are uneducated and without experience of truth, nor again by those allowed to pass their whole time in education? Not the one, because they have no single target in life at which to aim in every action, public and private; not the other, because they'll be unwilling to act, believing they've been transported to the Isles of the Blessed while still alive.

True, he said.

Then it is our own task as founders, I replied, to compel the best natures to attain to the knowledge which we formerly described as most important: to see the Good and rise upward in that ascent. And when they have ascended and sufficiently seen, not to allow to them what is now allowed.

What is that?

To abide there, I replied, and refuse to go back down again among the prisoners and share their labors and honors, whether of lesser or more serious worth.

Marginalia: 810 · (3) · 820 · Nurture after nature 830 · 840 · Must be compelled to return and teach others · 850

THE DUTY TO GOVERN (519D–521B)

Then we'll do them an injustice? he said. "We'll cause them to live a worse life when they're capable of better?

You again forget, my friend, I replied, that it is not a concern of law that some one class in a city should do and fare surpassingly well, but to contrive that this should come to be present in the city as a whole, harmoniously uniting citizens by persuasion and necessity, causing them to share with each other the benefit each is capable of providing to the community at large. Law produces such men in a city not in order to allow them to turn in any direction they each may wish, but in order that it may use them to bind the city together.

True, he said. I did forget.

Consider further, Glaucon, I said, that we will not do an injustice to the philosophers who arise among us; we will speak justly to them in requiring them to care for and guard the rest. For we shall say that people of their sort born in other cities reasonably do not share their labors; for they grew up on their own in spite of the constitution in each city, and it is right that as self-sustaining and indebted for nurture to no one, they should not be quick to make payment for being nurtured. But as for you, we will say, we bred you for yourselves and for the rest of the city, as kings and leaders in the hive. You are better and more perfectly educated than the rest, and more able to have a share of both ways of life. You must go down then, each in his turn, to dwell with the others and become accustomed to see in the darkness. For once used to it, you will see immeasurably better than those there, and you will know each of the images for what it is, and of what it is an image,[5] through having seen the truth of things beautiful and just and good. And in this way you will govern our city wide awake instead of in a dream, as most cities are now governed, where people fight over shadows and quarrel about office, supposing it a great good. The truth is surely this: that city is necessarily best and most free of faction in which those least eager to rule shall rule, and the city governed oppositely gains the opposite.

Of course, he said.

Then do you suppose those we have nurtured, when they hear this, will disobey and refuse to take their turn in sharing the labors of the city, but dwell most of the time with one another in what is pure?

Impossible, he said. For we require just things of just men. Still, each of them will assuredly enter upon office as a necessity, the opposite of those who rule in each city now.

That's so, my friend, I replied. It is possible to have a well-governed city only if you find a life better than ruling for those who are to rule. For in it only will the really rich rule—rich not in gold but in the wealth required for happiness, namely, a good and reasonable life. But if beggars starved of good things in their private lives enter on the public business, thinking there to seize the Good, it is impossible. When office comes to be fought over, this inner war destroys them and the rest of the city.

Margin notes:
"greater good" nature of community

True others live in self-interest, but we "bred you" as leaders

③

What would Plato think of our campaigns?

Very true, he said.

Can you suggest any life which scorns political office, I replied, except that of genuine philosophy?

I most certainly cannot, he replied.

900   But it is those who are not in love with office who must go to it; otherwise, rivals will fight.

Of course.

Then who will you compel to guardianship of the city, except those who are wisest about the things through which a city is best governed, and have other honors and a better life than the political life?

No one else at all, he said.

HOW GUARDIANS ARE LED UPWARD TO THE LIGHT
(521C–522D)

Would you then have us at this point consider how such people as this will come to be present and how to lead them upward to the light, as some are said to have ascended from the Underworld to the gods?

910   How could I not wish it? he said.

This then, it seems, is no mere flip of an oystershell,[6] but a conversion of soul from a day which is like night to genuine day, an ascent to what is real which we say is true philosophy.

Of course.

Then we must examine which studies have this power?

Certainly.

What study, Glaucon, would draw a soul from what becomes to what is? It occurs to me even as I speak: didn't we say that while young they must become athletes of war?

920   Yes.

So the study we seek must have this in addition:

What?

It must not be useless to soldiers.

Certainly, he said, if that's possible.

In what went before we educated them in gymnastic and in music and literature.

Yes, he said.

And gymnastic, I take it, is wholly devoted to what comes to be and perishes: for it presides over bodily growth and decay.

930   It appears so.

So this is not the study we seek.

No.

But perhaps instead music, as we've previously explained it?

Hardly, he said. That was the counterpart of gymnastic, if you recall. It educated the Guardians by habit, not knowledge, imparting a kind of tunefulness by mode and gracefulness by rhythm, and certain other dispositions akin to these in the content of the verse, whether fictional or true. But there was no study in it leading to a good of the sort you are now seeking.

You remind me most exactly, I replied: for really, it contained nothing of this sort. And yet, dear Glaucon, what does? For the arts all doubtless seem   940
base and vulgar.

Of course. But what other study is still left, apart from music and gymnastic and the arts?

Come, I replied. If we cannot grasp anything outside them, let us grasp something that stretches through them all.

Such as?

Such as that common thing which every art and branch of understanding and knowledge makes use of—indeed, among the first things everyone has to learn.

What's that? he said.   950

DIALECTIC (531C–535A)

Yes, I replied, and I suppose that if the investigation of everything we have discussed has arrived at their communion and kinship with one another, and they are reckoned together by their near relation to one another, then our concern for them is relevant to what we wish, and not work done in vain. Otherwise, it is in vain.

I guess so, he said. But it is an immense task you describe, Socrates.

You mean it is merely a prelude, I replied. Don't we know that all this is a preamble to the law itself, a prelude to the song we must learn? For you surely don't think people skilled in this are dialecticians?

Most certainly not, he said, unless perhaps a very few of those I've met.   960

But further, I said; do you think that anyone who cannot render and receive an account will ever know anything of what we claim must be known?

No again, he said.

Well, Glaucon, I said, is this at last the very law which dialectic fulfills, the song which it performs? Being intelligible, the power of vision, which we said undertakes to look at the animals by themselves, and at the stars by themselves and finally at the Sun itself, would imitate it. So also, when one undertakes by dialectical conversation, without any of the senses, to begin to make his way through reason to what each thing is by itself, and does not give over until he grasps by thought itself what the Good is by itself, he reaches   970
the end of the intelligible, even as, before, the power of vision reached the end of the visible.

Certainly, he said.

Well then, don't you call this journey dialectic?

Of course.

Yes, I replied. It is release from bondage and conversion from shadows to images and the light, and ascent out of the cave into the sunlight—and there, even still, inability to look at animals and plants and the light of the sun, but

only at divine[17] appearances in water and shadows of things which are, though
980 not shadows of images cast by that different sort of light which is itself a
shadow compared to the Sun. This whole business of the arts we have described
has this power to lead what is noblest in soul upward to the vision of what is
best among things which are, even as before what was clearest in body led
upward to the vision of what is brightest in the bodily and visible place.

I accept this, he said. And yet, I think it is very hard to accept, though in
another way hard to reject. Nevertheless—because it must not only be heard
now but often repeated hereafter—let us assume that these things are as now
told and proceed to the melody itself, and explain it as we explained the prelude. State then what character the power of dialectic has and according to
990 what forms it is divided, and again, what its methods are. For at this point
they would lead, it seems, to where upon arrival there would be, as it were, a
stopping place on the way and an end of the journey.

You will no longer be able to follow, my dear Glaucon, I replied—
though not for any unwillingness on my part—you would not then see an
image of what I mean, but the very truth itself, at least as it appears to me,
though whether it really is that way or not, I cannot yet worthily affirm. But
it must be strongly maintained that something of this sort is there for the
seeing. Not so?

Of course.

1000 And also that the power of dialectic would alone reveal it to someone
experienced in what we have just now described. It is possible in no other
way.

This too, he said, is worth affirming.

At any rate, I replied, no one will dispute us and claim that any other
method of inquiry undertakes to grasp in every case what each thing by itself
is. On the contrary: the other arts are all directed either to the beliefs and
desires of men, or to generation and combination, or to the service of things
which grow and are put together. And we see that the remaining arts—
geometry and the studies which follow on it, which we said grasp something
1010 of what is—merely dream about reality. They cannot see with waking vision
so long as they make use of hypotheses and leave them undisturbed, unable
to render an account of them. For with a starting point which one does not
know, and a conclusion and intermediate premises woven together from
what one does not know—by what device can this sort of agreement and
implication ever become knowledge?

None, he replied.

Dialectic, I rejoined, is the only method of inquiry which proceeds in this
way: it does away with hypotheses[18] and proceeds to the starting point and
the first principle itself in order to make its results secure. Finding that the
1020 eye of the soul is really sunk in a slough of barbarous mud, dialectic gently
draws and leads it upward, using as assistants and helpers the arts we have
described—which we often through force of habit call branches of knowl-

Dialectic

edge, though they need another name, in that they are more clear than opinion but more obscure than knowledge. In what went before we marked this off as understanding; but when an inquiry of such great magnitude lies before us, the dispute, I think, is not about a name.

Of course not, he said.[19]

Then as before, I replied, it suffices to call the first portion knowledge, the second understanding, the third belief, and the fourth imagination. The latter two together are opinion, the former two, thought. And opinion is concerned with becoming, thought with being. And being is to becoming as thought is to opinion, and thought is to opinion as knowledge is to belief, and understanding to imagination. But let us dismiss the proportionality of that to which they are directed, Glaucon, and the twofold division of each of the two, opinable and intelligible, so that we do not get involved in discussions many times as long as those we've had.

Why, I agree with you about the others, he said, in so far as I am able to follow.

And do you also call a dialectician one who accepts a reasoned account of the nature and reality of each thing? Will you deny that insofar as one cannot render a reasoned account to himself and to another, he in that degree cannot be said to have intelligence about it?

How could I deny it, he replied?

Then so in like manner about the Good. Whoever cannot distinguish the Idea of the Good by reason and set it apart from all other things, and, as though in battle, fight his way through all refutations in his eagerness to argue not according to opinion but according to reality, and proceed in all this without tripping up in argument—you will claim that someone like that knows neither the Good itself nor any other good. Rather, if in some way he grasps a deficient image of it, he does so by opinion, not knowledge, and sleeps and dreams away his present life. Before ever he awakens here, he will go to the place of the dead and fall asleep completely.

Yes, he replied. I shall emphatically assert all of this.

Moreover, these children of yours whom you are raising and educating in discourse—if ever you should raise them in fact, you would not, I think, allow them to be rulers in the city and to control matters of utmost importance, while being, as it were, irrational quantities?

Of course not, he said.

Then you will provide by law that they should instead receive this education, from which they will be able to ask and answer questions with utmost knowledge?

I will so provide, he said, in company with you.

Do you think then, I said, that dialectic is set like a copingstone over the subjects of study, and that no other study higher than it would rightly be put above it, but at this point the subjects of study have an end?

Yes, he said.

1030

[margin note:] Knowledge / understanding } thought / being
belief / imagination } opinion / becoming

1040

1050

1060

ENDNOTES

Book V

12. Or "since beauty is opposite to ugliness . . . " The neuter adjective, with or without article, may be used to the corresponding abstract noun.

13. Or unhealthy. "He who has opinion is, in comparison with the man who knows, not in a healthy state as far as truth is concerned." *Meta.* IV 1008b 30–31, trans. Ross.

14. It is here claimed that opinion involves knowledge minus something; it is not infallible, and does not have the real for its object. Compare *Timeaus* 51e–52c. The more popular alternative is that knowledge involves opinion plus something: this is examined in the *Theaetetus*, where knowledge is successively considered as sensation or perception, as true or right opinion, and as true or right opinion with an account. That all of these proposed definitions fail does not imply, since they are not exhaustive, that opinion is not prior to knowledge, or that knowledge is prior to opinion. The *Theaetetus* is not demonstrative but aporetic.

Book VI

1. The spirit of faultfinding.

2. Mandrake, a plant with a large forked root, used as a drug with analgesic and narcotic properties—in effect an opiate. The association of mandrake with fertility—cf. John Donne's "Go and catch a falling star / Get with child a mandrake root"—traced to Genesis 30, is perhaps based on a doctrine of signatures; *mandragoritis* is an epithet of Aphrodite. Adam remarks: "False rulers dull the senses of the Demos by the opiate of Pleasure, and so escape detection."

9. The reference is to the discussion of the status of women and children (V 449b ff.) and to the possibility of realizing the perfect city. (471c ff.)

16. Plural. Socrates is addressing the group.

17. *tokos.* An untranslatable pun: the Greek word means both interest and offspring.

18. Lavish because sight is unique in requiring an additional valuable element, namely light.

19. It may be objected that sound requires a third thing, namely, air, as Plato himself acknowledged (*Timaeus* 67b–c). But unlike sight and the light of the eyes, hearing is passive, a stroke (πληγή) through the ears by air on brain and blood, reaching the soul; if sound is a stroke of air, air is not "a third thing."

20. If sound is produced by particles striking the ear, it may be treated as an extension of touch, and therefore not analogous to light. The disanalogy becomes more evident if we correct for anachronism. We conceive light as rays impinging on the eye, a passive receptor, as sound waves impinge upon the ears. Plato thought of the eye as active, the visual image being the product of rays issuing from things

seen and meeting with rays issuing from the eye which sees them. Cf. *Timaeus* 45b–d, 58c, 67b, 80a.

21. The stars are gods—that is, immortal living animals. *Laws* 821b, 899b, 950d; *Epinomis* 985b, 988d; *Apology* 26d. Cf. *Cratylus* 397d.

22. Because the eye emits rays—the light in the eyes.

23. The passage offers a series of ratios, explicable in terms of proportionality: the Good is to the Sun as truth is to light, as Ideas are to objects of sight, as knowledge is to vision, as thought is to sight, as mind is to eye.

24. Apollo, god of music and poetry, is also god of the Sun.

Book VII

1. Shorey comments: "As we use the word tree of the trees we see, though the reality is the idea of a tree, so they would speak of the shadows as the world, though the real reference unknown to them would be to the objects that cause the shadows, and back of the objects to the things of the 'real' world of which they are copies. The general meaning, which is quite certain, is that they would suppose the shadows to be the realities. . . . They suppose that the names refer to the passing shadows, but (as we know) they really apply to the objects. Ideas and particulars are homonymous."

2. *Odyssey* XI 489–490. Achilles visits the place of the dead and declares that he would rather be the servant of a landless man on earth than king of the flickering shades of the dead. By implication, the prisoners chained in the cave suffer a living death.

3. *thakon*: seat, but also privy seat. Plato is sometimes careless of the neo-Victorian sensibilities of his translators.

4. An allusion to the trial and death of Socrates.

5. These images evidently include both the shadows on the wall of the cave and the objects, imitations of things outside, which cast those shadows.

6. The reference is to a children's game: the shell was black on one side, white on the other, indicating randomness of result, the flip of a coin.

17. The appearances of things outside the cave are divine because they are images of divine agency, as opposed to the shadows within the cave, cast by images which are products of human craftsmanship and a fire which is an image of the Sun.

18. There is a standing dispute as to whether doing away with hypotheses means merely doing away with their hypothetical character or altering their content. Both, surely: for example, the mathematician will define number as a plurality of units, a definition the dialectician will not accept.

19. The translation omits a sentence (533e) which is certainly corrupt, athetized by Adam and Shorey as an interpolation, and not printed either by Aldus or Stephanus, who had access to many older manuscripts now lost. Davies and Vaughn give: "You are quite right, said he: we only want a name which when applied to a mental state shall indicate clearly what phenomena it describes."

THINKING ABOUT SOCIAL CHANGE IN AMERICA
Robert D. Putnam

What happened next to civic and social life in American communities is the subject of this book. In recent years social scientists have framed concerns about the changing character of American society in terms of the concept of "social capital." By analogy with notions of physical capital and human capital—tools and training that enhance individual productivity—the core idea of social capital theory is that social networks have value. Just as a screwdriver (physical capital) or a college education (human capital) can increase productivity (both individual and collective), so too social contacts affect the productivity of individuals and groups.

Whereas physical capital refers to physical objects and human capital refers to properties of individuals, social capital refers to connections among individuals—social networks and the norms of reciprocity and trustworthiness that arise from them. In that sense social capital is closely related to what some have called "civic virtue." The difference is that "social capital" calls attention to the fact that civic virtue is most powerful when embedded in a dense network of reciprocal social relations. A society of many virtuous but isolated individuals is not necessarily rich in social capital.

The term *social capital* itself turns out to have been independently invented at least six times over the twentieth century, each time to call attention to the ways in which our lives are made more productive by social ties. The first known use of the concept was not by some cloistered theoretician, but by a practical reformer of the Progressive Era—L. J. Hanifan, state supervisor of rural schools in West Virginia. Writing in 1916 to urge the importance of community involvement for successful schools, Hanifan invoked the idea of "social capital" to explain why. For Hanifan, social capital referred to

those tangible substances [that] count for most in the daily lives of people: namely good will, fellowship, sympathy, and social intercourse among the individuals and families who make up a social unit. . . . The individual is helpless socially, if left to himself. . . . If he comes into contact with his neighbor, and they with other neighbors, there will be an accumulation of social capital, which may immediately satisfy his social needs and which may bear a social potentiality sufficient to the substantial improvement of living conditions in the whole community. The community as a whole will benefit by the cooperation of all its parts, while the individual will find in his associations the advantages of the help, the sympathy, and the fellowship of his neighbors.[1]

Reprinted from *Bowling Alone: The Collapse and Revival of American Community* (2000), by permission of Simon & Schuster, Inc.

Hanifan's account of social capital anticipated virtually all the crucial elements in later interpretations, but his conceptual invention apparently attracted no notice from other social commentators and disappeared without a trace. But like sunken treasure recurrently revealed by shifting sands and tides, the same idea was independently rediscovered in the 1950s by Canadian sociologists to characterize the club memberships of arriviste suburbanites, in the 1960s by urbanist Jane Jacobs to laud neighborliness in the modern metropolis, in the 1970s by economist Glenn Loury to analyze the social legacy of slavery, and in the 1980s by French social theorist Pierre Bourdieu and by German economist Ekkehart Schlicht to underline the social and economic resources embodied in social networks. Sociologist James S. Coleman put the term firmly and finally on the intellectual agenda in the late 1980s, using it (as Hanifan had originally done) to highlight the social context of education.[2]

As this array of independent coinages indicates, social capital has both an individual and a collective aspect—a private face and a public face. First, individuals form connections that benefit our own interests. One pervasive strategem of ambitious job seekers is "networking," for most of us get our jobs because of whom we know, not what we know—that is, our social capital, not our human capital. Economic sociologist Ronald Burt has shown that executives with bounteous Rolodex files enjoy faster career advancement. Nor is the private return to social capital limited to economic rewards. As Claude S. Fischer, a sociologist of friendship, has noted, "Social networks are important in all our lives, often for finding jobs, more often for finding a helping hand, companionship, or a shoulder to cry on.[3]

If individual clout and companionship were all there were to social capital, we'd expect foresighted, self-interested individuals to invest the right amount of time and energy in creating or acquiring it. However, social capital also can have "externalities" that affect the wider community, so that not all the costs and benefits of social connections accrue to the person making the contact.[4] As we shall see later in this book, a well-connected individual in a poorly connected society is not as productive as a well-connected individual in a well-connected society. And even a poorly connected individual may derive some of the spillover benefits from living in a well-connected community. If the crime rate in my neighborhood is lowered by neighbors keeping an eye on one another's homes, I benefit even if I personally spend most of my time on the road and never even nod to another resident on the street.

Social capital can thus be simultaneously a "private good" and a "public good." Some of the benefit from an investment in social capital goes to bystanders, while some of the benefit redounds to the immediate interest of the person making the investment. For example, service clubs, like Rotary or Lions, mobilize local energies to raise scholarships or fight disease at the same time that they provide members with friendships and business connections that pay off personally.

Social connections are also important for the rules of conduct that they sustain. Networks involve (almost by definition) mutual obligations; they are not interesting as mere "contacts." Networks of community engagement foster sturdy norms of reciprocity: I'll do this for you now, in the expectation that you (or perhaps someone else) will return the favor. "Social capital is akin to what Tom Wolfe called 'the favor bank' in his novel *The Bonfire of the Vanities*," notes economist Robert Frank.[5] It was, however, neither a novelist nor an economist, but Yogi Berra who offered the most succinct definition of reciprocity: "If you don't go to somebody's funeral, they won't come to yours."   90

Sometimes, as in these cases, reciprocity is *specific:* I'll do this for you if you do that for me. Even more valuable, however, is a norm of *generalized* reciprocity: I'll do this for you without expecting anything specific back from you, in the confident expectation that someone else will do something for me down the road. The Golden Rule is one formulation of generalized reciprocity. Equally instructive is the T-shirt slogan used by the Gold Beach, Oregon, Volunteer Fire Department to publicize their annual fund-raising effort: "Come to our breakfast, we'll come to your fire." "We act on a norm of specific reciprocity," the firefighters seem to be saying, but onlookers smile because they recognize the underlying norm of generalized reciprocity—the   100 firefighters will come even if *you* don't. When Blanche DuBois depended on the kindness of strangers, she too was relying on generalized reciprocity.

A society characterized by generalized reciprocity is more efficient than a distrustful society, for the same reason that money is more efficient than barter. If we don't have to balance every exchange instantly, we can get a lot more accomplished. Trustworthiness lubricates social life. Frequent interaction among a diverse set of people tends to produce a norm of generalized reciprocity. Civic engagement and social capital entail mutual obligation and responsibility for action. As L. J. Hanifan and his successors recognized, social networks and norms of reciprocity can facilitate cooperation for   110 mutual benefit. When economic and political dealing is embedded in dense networks of social interaction, incentives for opportunism and malfeasance are reduced. This is why the diamond trade, with its extreme possibilities for fraud, is concentrated within close-knit ethnic enclaves. Dense social ties facilitate gossip and other valuable ways of cultivating reputation—an essential foundation for trust in a complex society.

Physical capital is not a single "thing," and different forms of physical capital are not interchangeable. An eggbeater and an aircraft carrier both appear as physical capital in our national accounts, but the eggbeater is not much use for national defense, and the carrier would not be much help with   120 your morning omelet. Similarly, social capital—that is, social networks and the associated norms of reciprocity—comes in many different shapes and sizes with many different uses. Your extended family represents a form of social capital, as do your Sunday school class, the regulars who play poker on your commuter train, your college roommates, the civic organizations to which you belong, the Internet chat group in which you participate, and the network of professional acquaintances recorded in your address book.

Sometimes "social capital," like its conceptual cousin "community," sounds warm and cuddly. Urban sociologist Xavier de Souza Briggs, however,
130 properly warns us to beware of a treacly sweet, "kumbaya" interpretation of social capital.[6] Networks and the associated norms of reciprocity are generally good for those inside the network, but the external effects of social capital are by no means always positive. It was social capital, for example, that enabled Timothy McVeigh to bomb the Alfred P. Murrah Federal Building in Oklahoma City. McVeigh's network of friends, bound together by a norm of reciprocity, enabled him to do what he could not have done alone. Similarly, urban gangs, NIMBY ("not in my backyard") movements, and power elites often exploit social capital to achieve ends that are antisocial from a wider perspective. Indeed, it is rhetorically useful for such groups to obscure the
140 difference between the pro-social and antisocial consequences of community organizations. When Floridians objected to plans by the Ku Klux Klan to "adopt a highway," Jeff Coleman, grand wizard of the Royal Knights of the KKK, protested, "Really, we're just like the Lions or the Elks. We want to be involved in the community."[7]

Social capital, in short, can be directed toward malevolent, antisocial purposes, just like any other form of capital.[8] (McVeigh also relied on physical capital, like the explosive-laden truck, and human capital, like bomb-making expertise, to achieve his purposes.) Therefore it is important to ask how the positive consequences of social capital—mutual support, cooperation, trust, insti-
150 tutional effectiveness—can be maximized and the negative manifestations—sectarianism, ethnocentrism, corruption—minimized. Toward this end, scholars have begun to distinguish many different forms of social capital.

Some forms involve repeated, intensive, multistranded networks—like a group of steelworkers who meet for drinks every Friday after work and see each other at mass on Sunday—and some are episodic, single stranded, and anonymous, like the faintly familiar face you see several times a month in the supermarket checkout line. Some types of social capital, like a Parent-Teacher Association, are formally organized, with incorporation papers, regular meetings, a written constitution, and connection to a national federation, whereas
160 others, like a pickup basketball game, are more informal. Some forms of social capital, like a volunteer ambulance squad, have explicit public-regarding purposes; some, like a bridge club, exist for the private enjoyment of the members; and some, like the Rotary club mentioned earlier, serve both public and private ends.

Of all the dimensions along which forms of social capital vary, perhaps the most important is the distinction between *bridging* (or inclusive) and *bonding* (or exclusive).[9] Some forms of social capital are, by choice or necessity, inward looking and tend to reinforce exclusive identities and homogeneous groups. Examples of bonding social capital include ethnic fraternal organizations,
170 church-based women's reading groups, and fashionable country clubs. Other

networks are outward looking and encompass people across diverse social cleavages. Examples of bridging social capital include the civil rights movement, many youth service groups, and ecumenical religious organizations.

Bonding social capital is good for undergirding specific reciprocity and mobilizing solidarity. Dense networks in ethnic enclaves, for example, provide crucial social and psychological support for less fortunate members of the community, while furnishing start-up financing, markets, and reliable labor for local entrepreneurs. Bridging networks, by contrast, are better for linkage to external assets and for information diffusion. Economic sociologist Mark Granovetter has pointed out that when seeking jobs—or political allies—the "weak" ties that link me to distant acquaintances who move in different circles from mine are actually more valuable than the "strong" ties that link me to relatives and intimate friends whose sociological niche is very like my own. Bonding social capital is, as Xavier de Souza Briggs puts it, good for "getting by," but bridging social capital is crucial for "getting ahead."[10]

Moreover, bridging social capital can generate broader identities and reciprocity, whereas bonding social capital bolsters our narrower selves. In 1829 at the founding of a community lyceum in the bustling whaling port of New Bedford, Massachusetts, Thomas Greene eloquently expressed this crucial insight:

> We come from all the divisions, ranks and classes of society . . . to teach and to be taught in our turn. While we mingle together in these pursuits, we shall learn to know each other more intimately; we shall remove many of the prejudices which ignorance or partial acquaintance with each other had fostered. . . . In the parties and sects into which we are divided, we sometimes learn to love our brother at the expense of him whom we do not in so many respects regard as a brother. . . . We may return to our homes and firesides [from the lyceum] with kindlier feelings toward one another, because we have learned to know one another better.[11]

Bonding social capital constitutes a kind of sociological superglue, whereas bridging social capital provides a sociological WD-40. Bonding social capital, by creating strong in-group loyalty, may also create strong out-group antagonism; as Thomas Greene and his neighbors in New Bedford knew, and for that reason we might expect negative external effects to be more common with this form of social capital. Nevertheless, under many circumstances both bridging and bonding social capital can have powerfully positive social effects.

Many groups simultaneously bond along some social dimensions and bridge across others. The black church, for example, brings together people of the same race and religion across class lines. The Knights of Columbus was created to bridge cleavages among different ethnic communities while bonding along religious and gender lines. Internet chat groups may bridge across geography, gender, age, and religion, while being tightly homogeneous in education and ideology. In short, bonding and bridging are not "either-or" categories into which social networks can be neatly divided, but "more or less" dimensions along which we can compare different forms of social capital.

220 It would obviously be valuable to have distinct measures of the evolution of these various forms of social capital over time. However, like researchers on global warming, we must make do with the imperfect evidence that we can find, not merely lament its deficiencies. Exhaustive descriptions of social networks in America—even at a single point in time—do not exist. I have found no reliable, comprehensive, nationwide measures of social capital that neatly distinguish "bridgingness" and "bondingness." In our empirical account of recent social trends in this book, therefore, this distinction will be less prominent than I would prefer. On the other hand, we must keep this conceptual differentiation at the back of our minds as we proceed, recognizing that bridging and bonding social capital are not interchangeable.

230 "Social Capital" is to some extent merely new language for a very old debate in American intellectual circles. Community has warred incessantly with individualism for preeminence in our political hagiology. Liberation from ossified community bonds is a recurrent and honored theme in our culture, from the Pilgrims' storied escape from religious convention in the seventeenth century to the lyric nineteenth-century paeans to individualism by Emerson ("Self-Reliance"), Thoreau ("Civil Disobedience"), and Whitman ("Song of Myself") to Sherwood Anderson's twentieth-century celebration of the struggle against conformism by ordinary citizens in *Winesburg, Ohio* to the latest Clint Eastwood film. Even Alexis de Tocqueville, patron saint of American communitarians, acknowledged the uniquely democratic claim of 240 individualism, "a calm and considered feeling which disposes each citizen to isolate himself from the mass of his fellows and withdraw into the circle of family and friends; with this little society formed to his taste, he gladly leaves the greater society to look after itself."[12]

Our national myths often exaggerate the role of individual heroes and understate the importance of collective effort. Historian David Hackett Fischer's gripping account of opening night in the American Revolution, for example, reminds us that Paul Revere's alarum was successful only because of networks of civic engagement in the Middlesex villages. Towns without well-organized local militia, no matter how patriotic their inhabitants, were 250 AWOL from Lexington and Concord.[13] Nevertheless, the myth of rugged individualism continues to strike a powerful inner chord in the American psyche.

Debates about the waxing and waning of "community" have been endemic for at least two centuries. "Declensionist narrative"—postmodernist jargon for tales of decline and fall—have a long pedigree in our letters. We seem perennially tempted to contrast our tawdry todays with past golden ages. We apparently share this nostalgic predilection with the rest of humanity. As sociologist Barry Wellman observes,

It is likely that pundits have worried about the impact of social change on communities ever since human beings ventured beyond their caves. . . . In the [past] two centuries many leading social commentators have been gainfully employed suggesting various ways in which large-scale social changes associated with the Industrial Revolution may have affected the structure and operation of communities. . . . This ambivalence about the consequences of large-scale changes continued well into the twentieth century. Analysts have kept asking if things have, in fact, fallen apart.[14]

At the conclusion of the twentieth century, ordinary Americans shared this sense of civic malaise. We were reasonably content about our economic prospects, hardly a surprise after an expansion of unprecedented length, but we were not equally convinced that we were on the right track morally or culturally. Of baby boomers interviewed in 1987, 53 percent thought their parents' generation was better in terms of "being a concerned citizen, involved in helping others in the community," as compared with only 21 percent who thought their own generation was better. Fully 77 percent said the nation was worse off because of "less involvement in community activities." In 1992 three-quarters of the U.S. workforce said that "the breakdown of community" and "selfishness" were "serious" or "extremely serious" problems in America. In 1996 only 8 percent of all Americans said that "the honesty and integrity of the average American" were improving, as compared with 50 percent of us who thought we were becoming less trustworthy. Those of us who said that people had become less civil over the preceding ten years outnumbered those who thought people had become more civil, 80 percent to 12 percent. In several surveys in 1999 two-thirds of Americans said that America's civic life had weakened in recent years, that social and moral values were higher when they were growing up, and that our society was focused more on the individual than the community. More than 80 percent said there should be more emphasis on community, even if that put more demands on individuals.[15] Americans' concern about weakening community bonds may be misplaced or exaggerated, but a decent respect for the opinion of our fellow citizens suggests that we should explore the issue more thoroughly.

It is emphatically not my view that community bonds in America have weakened steadily throughout our history—or even throughout the last hundred years. On the contrary, American history carefully examined is a story of ups and downs in civic engagement, *not just downs*—a story of collapse *and* of renewal. As I have already hinted in the opening pages of this book, within living memory the bonds of community in America were becoming stronger, not weaker, and as I shall argue in the concluding pages, it is within our power to reverse the decline of the last several decades.

Nevertheless, my argument is, at least in appearance, in the declensionist tradition, so it is important to avoid simple nostalgia. Precisely because the theme of this book might lend itself to gauzy self-deception, our methods must be transparent. Is life in communities as we enter the twenty-first century really so different after all from the reality of American communities in the 1950s and 1960s? One way of curbing nostalgia is to count things. Are club meetings really less crowded today than yesterday, or does it just seem so? Do we really know our neighbors less well than our parents did, or is our childhood recollection of neighborhood barbecues suffused with a golden glow of wishful reminiscence? Are friendly poker games less common now, or

310 is it merely that we ourselves have outgrown poker? League bowling may be passé, but how about softball and soccer? Are strangers less trustworthy now? Are boomers and X'ers really less engaged in community life? After all, it was the preceding generation that was once scorned as "silent." Perhaps the younger generation today is no less engaged than their predecessors, but engaged in new ways. In the chapters that follow we explore these questions with the best available evidence.

The challenge of studying the evolving social climate is analogous in some respects to the challenge facing meteorologists who measure global warming: We know what kind of evidence we would ideally want from the

320 past, but time's arrow means that we can't go back to conduct those well-designed studies. Thus if we are to explore how our society is like or unlike our parents', we must make imperfect inferences from all the evidence that we can find.

The most powerful strategy for paleometeorologists seeking to assess global climate change is to triangulate among diverse sources of evidence. If pollen counts in polar ice, and the width of southwestern tree rings, and temperature records of the British Admiralty all point in a similar direction, the inference of global warming is stronger than if the cord of evidence has only a single strand. For much the same reason, prudent journalists follow a "two

330 source" rule: Never report anything unless at least two independent sources confirm it.

In this book I follow that same maxim. Nearly every major generalization here rests on more than one body of independent evidence, and where I have discovered divergent results from credible sources, I note that disparity as well. I have a case to make, but like any officer of the court, I have a professional obligation to present all relevant evidence I have found, exculpatory as well as incriminating. To avoid cluttering the text with masses of redundant evidence, I have typically put confirmatory evidence from multiple studies in

340 the notes, so skeptical "show me" readers should examine those notes as well as the text.[16]

I have sought as diverse a range of evidence as possible on continuities and change in American social life. If the transformation that I discern is as broad and deep as I believe it to be, it ought to show up in many different places, so I have cast a broad net. Of course, social change, like climatic change, is inevitably uneven. Life is not lived in a single dimension. We should not expect to find everything changing in the same direction and at the same speed, but those very anomalies may contain important clues to what is happening.

American society, like the continent on which we live, is massive and   350
polymorphous, and our civic engagement historically has come in many sizes
and shapes. A few of us still share plowing chores with neighbors, while many
more pitch in to wire classrooms to the Internet. Some of us run for Congress, and others join self-help groups. Some of us hang out at the local bar
association and others at the local bar. Some of us attend mass once a day,
while others struggle to remember to send holiday greetings once a year. The
forms of our social capital—the ways in which we connect with friends and
neighbors and strangers—are varied.

So our review of trends in social capital and civic engagement ranges
widely across various sectors of this complex society. In the chapters that fol-   360
low we begin by charting Americans' participation in the most public
forum—politics and public affairs. We next turn to the institutions of our
communities—clubs and community associations, religious bodies, and
work-related organizations, such as unions and professional societies. Then
we explore the almost infinite variety of informal ties that link Americans—
card parties and bowling leagues, bar cliques and ball games, picnics and
parties. Next we examine the changing patterns of trust and altruism in
America—philanthropy, volunteering, honesty, reciprocity. Finally we turn
to three apparent counterexamples to the decline of connectedness—small
groups, social movements, and the Internet.   370

In each domain we shall encounter currents and crosscurrents and eddies,
but in each we shall also discover common, powerful tidal movements that
have swept across American society in the twentieth century. The dominant
theme is simple: For the first two-thirds of the twentieth century a powerful
tide bore Americans into ever deeper engagement in the life of their communities, but a few decades ago—silently, without warning—that tide
reversed and we were overtaken by a treacherous rip current. Without at first
noticing, we have been pulled apart from one another and from our communities over the last third of the century.

ENDNOTES

1. Lyda Judson Hanifan, "The Rural School Community Center,"
   Annals of the American Academy of Political and Social Science 67
   (1916): 130–138, quotation at 130. Ever the practical reformer,
   Hanifan was self-conscious about using the term *capital* to encourage hard-nosed businessmen and economists to recognize the productive importance of social assets. Having introduced the idea of
   social capital, he observes, "That there is a great lack of such social
   capital in some rural districts need not be retold in this chapter. The
   important question at this time is: How can these conditions be
   improved? The story which follows is an account of the way a West
   Virginia rural community in a single year actually developed social
   capital and then used this capital in the improvement of its recre-
   ational, intellectual, moral, and economic conditions." His essay,

which included a list of practical exercises for community-based activists, was originally prepared in 1913 for West Virginia schoolteachers as "a handbook for community meetings at rural schoolhouses," and it was subsequently incorporated in L. J. Hanifan, *The Community Center* (Boston: Silver, Burdett, 1920). I am grateful to Brad Clarke for first spotting this usage of the term *social capital*.

2. John R. Seeley, Alexander R. Sim, and Elizabeth W. Loosley, *Crestwood Heights: A Study of the Culture of Suburban Life* (New York: Basic Books, 1956); Jane Jacobs, *The Death and Life of Great American Cities* (New York: Random House, 1961); Glenn Loury, "A Dynamic Theory of Racial Income Differences; in *Women, Minorities, and Employment Discrimination,* ed. P. A. Wallace and A. LeMund (Lexington, Mass.: Lexington Books, 1977), 153–188; Pierre Bourdieu, "Forms of Capital," in *Handbook of Theory and Research for the Sociology of Education,* ed. John G. Richardson (New York: Greenwood Press, 1983), 241–258; Ekkehart Schlicht, "Cognitive Dissonance in Economics," in *Normengeleitetes Verhalten in den Sozialwissenschaften* (Berlin: Duncker and Humblot, 1984), 61–81; James S. Coleman, "Social Capital in the Creation of Human Capital," *American Journal of Sociology* 94 (1988): S95–SI20; and James S. Coleman, *Foundations of Social Theory* (Cambridge, Mass.: Harvard University Press, 1990). See also George C. Homans, *Social Behavior: Its Elementary Forms* (New York: Harcourt, Brace & World, 1961), 378–98. Except for a brief acknowledgment by Coleman of Loury's work, I can find no evidence that any of these theorists were aware of any of the preceding usages. For a comprehensive overview of the conceptual history of "social capital," see Michael Woolcock, "Social Capital and Economic Development: Toward a Theoretical Synthesis and Policy Framework," *Theory and Society* 27 (1998): 151–208.

3. Ronald S. Burt, *Structural Holes: The Social Structure of Competition* (Cambridge, Mass.: Harvard University Press, 1992); Ronald S. Burt, "The Contingent Value of Social Capital," *Administrative Science Quarterly* 42 (1997): 339–365; and Ronald S. Burt, "The Gender of Social Capital," *Rationality & Society* 10 (1998): 5–46; Claude S. Fischer, "Network Analysis and Urban Studies," in *Networks and Places: Social Relations in the Urban Setting,* ed. Claude S. Fischer (New York: Free Press, 1977), 19; James D. Montgomery, "Social Networks and Labor-Market Outcomes: Toward an Economic Analysis," *American Economic Review* 81 (1991): 1408–1418, esp. table 1.

4. In earlier work I emphasized this public dimension of social capital almost to the exclusion of the private returns to social capital. See Robert D. Putnam, "The Prosperous Community: Social Capital and Public Affairs," *The American Prospect* 13 (1993): 35–42, on which the present text draws. For a literature review that highlights the private returns almost to the exclusion of the collective dimension, see

Alejandro Portes, "Social Capital: Its Origins and Applications in Modern Sociology," *Annual Review of Sociology* 22 (1998): 1–24.

5. Robert Frank in private conversation.

6. Xavier de Souza Briggs, "Social Capital and the Cities: Advice to Change Agents," *National Civic Review* 86 (summer 1997): 111–117.

7. *U.S. News & World Report* (August 4, 1997): 18. Fareed Zakaria, "Bigger Than the Family, Smaller Than the State," *New York Times Book Review,* August 13, 1995: 1, pointed out that McVeigh and his co-conspirators spent evenings together in a bowling alley and concluded that "we would all have been better off if Mr. McVeigh had gone bowling alone." Sometimes, as in certain cults or clans, even the *internal* effects of social capital can be negative, but these are less common than negative *external* effects.

8. In *Making Democracy Work: Civic Traditions in Modern Italy* (Princeton, N.J.: Princeton University Press, 1993), I ignored the possibility that social capital might have antisocial effects, but I recognized this possibility explicitly in "The Prosperous Community," published that same year.

9. So far as I can tell, credit for coining these labels belongs to Ross Gittell and Avis Vidal, *Community Organizing Building Social Capital as a Development Strategy* (Thousand Oaks, Calif.: Sage, 1998), 8.

10. Mark S. Granovetter, "The Strength of Weak Ties," *American Journal of Sociology* 78 (1973): 1360–1380; Xavier de Souza Briggs, "Doing Democracy Up Close: Culture, Power, and Communication in Community Building," *Journal of Planning Education and Research* 18 (1998): 1–13.

11. As quoted in Richard D. Brown, "The Emergence of Voluntary Associations in Massachusetts," *Journal of Voluntary Action Research* 2 (April 1973): 64–73, at 69. See also Ashutosh Varshney, *Ethnic Conflict and Civic Life: Hindus and Muslims in India* (New Haven, Conn.: Yale University Press, 2000).

12. Alexis de Tocqueville, *Democracy in America,* ed. J. P. Mayer, trans. George Lawrence (Garden City, N.Y.: Doubleday, 1969), 506. See also Wilson Carey McWilliams, *The Idea of Fraternity in America,* (Berkeley: University of California Press, 1973), and Thomas Bender, *Community and Social Change in America* (Baltimore, Md.: Johns Hopkins University Press, 1978).

13. David Hackett Fischer, *Paul Revere's Ride* (New York: Oxford University Press, 1994).

14. Barry Wellman, "The Community Question Re-Evaluated," in *Power, Community, and the City,* Michael Peter Smith, ed. (New Brunswick, N.J.: Transaction 1988), 81–107, quotation at 82–83. Pamela Paxton, "Is Social Capital Declining in the United States? A Multiple Indicator Assessment," *American Journal of Sociology* 105 (1999): 88–127.

15. *The Public Perspective* 8 (December/January 1997): 64; Robert Wuthnow, "Changing Character of Social Capital in the United States," in *The Dynamics of Social Capital in Comparative Perspective,* Robert D. Putnam, ed. (2000, forthcoming); *The Public Perspective* 10 (April/May 1999): 15; *Wall Street Journal,* June 24, 1999, A12; Mark J. Penn, "The Community Consensus," *Blueprint: Ideas for a New Century* (spring 1999). Respondents with no opinion are excluded.

16. For example, figures 31–33 present data from six independent sources on trends in philanthropy, but I have also discovered four additional sources that confirm the basic pattern, and those sources are mentioned briefly in the notes. For additional discussion of methodology, see the appendixes.

THE SOCIAL CONTRACT
Jean-Jacques Rousseau

Translated by George Douglas and Howard Cole

BOOK I

1. Subject of the First Book

Man is born free; and everywhere he is in chains. One thinks himself the   1
master of others, and still remains a greater slave than they. How did this
change come about? I do not know. What can make it legitimate? That question I think I can answer.

If I took into account only force, and the effects derived from it, I should
say: "As long as a people is compelled to obey, and obeys, it does well; as soon
as it can shake off the yoke, and shakes it off, it does still better; for, regain-
ing its liberty by the same right as took it away, either it is justified in resum-
ing it, or there was no justification for those who took it away." But the social
order is a sacred right which is the basis of all other rights. Nevertheless, this   10
right does not come from nature, and must therefore be founded on conventions. Before coming to that, I have to prove what I have just asserted.

2. The First Societies

The most ancient of all societies, and the only one that is natural, is the family: and even so the children remain attached to the father only so long as they
need him for their preservation. As soon as this need ceases, the natural bond
is dissolved. The children, released from the obedience they owed to the father,
and the father, released from the care he owed his children, return equally to
independence. If they remain united, they continue so no longer naturally, but
voluntarily; and the family itself is then maintained only by convention.

This common liberty results from the nature of man. His first law is to   20
provide for his own preservation, his first cares are those which he owes to
himself; and, as soon as he reaches years of discretion, he is the sole judge of
the proper means of preserving himself, and consequently becomes his own
master.

The family then may be called the first model of political societies: the
ruler corresponds to the father, and the people to the children; and all, being
born free and equal, alienate their liberty only for their own advantage. The
whole difference is that, in the family, the love of the father for his children
repays him for the care he takes of them, while, in the State, the pleasure of
commanding takes the place of the love which the chief cannot have for the   30
peoples under him.

nature of man = independent

What is the pleasure of commanding?

Reprinted from *The Social Contract* (1762).

Grotius denies that all human power is established in favour of the governed, and quotes slavery as an example. His usual method of reasoning is constantly to establish right by fact. It would be possible to employ a more logical method, but none could be more favourable to tyrants.

It is then, according to Grotius, doubtful whether the human race belongs to a hundred men, or that hundred men to the human race: and, throughout his book, he seems to incline to the former alternative, which is also the view of Hobbes. On this showing, the human species is divided into so many herds of cattle, each with its ruler, who keeps guard over them for the purpose of devouring them.

As a shepherd is of a nature superior to that of his flock, the shepherds of men, i.e., their rulers, are of a nature superior to that of the peoples under them. Thus, Philo tells us, the Emperor Caligula reasoned, concluding equally well either that kings were gods, or that men were beasts.

The reasoning of Caligula agrees with that of Hobbes and Grotius. Aristotle, before any of them, had said that men are by no means equal naturally, but that some are born for slavery, and others for dominion.

Aristotle was right; but he took the effect for the cause. Nothing can be more certain than that every man born in slavery is born for slavery. Slaves lose everything in their chains, even the desire of escaping from them: they love their servitude, as the comrades of Ulysses loved their brutish condition. If then there are slaves by nature, it is because there have been slaves against nature. Force made the first slaves, and their cowardice perpetuated the condition.

I have said nothing of King Adam, or Emperor Noah, father of the three great monarchs who shared out the universe, like the children of Saturn, whom some scholars have recognised in them. I trust to getting due thanks for my moderation; for, being a direct descendant of one of these princes, perhaps of the eldest branch, how do I know that a verification of titles might not leave me the legitimate king of the human race? In any case, there can be no doubt that Adam was sovereign of the world, as Robinson Crusoe was of his island, as long as he was its only inhabitant; and this empire had the advantage that the monarch, safe on his throne, had no rebellions, wars, or conspirators to fear.

3. The Right of the Strongest

The strongest is never strong enough to be always the master, unless he transforms strength into right, and obedience into duty. Hence the right of the strongest, which, though to all seeming meant ironically, is really laid down as a fundamental principle. But are we never to have an explanation of this phrase? Force is a physical power, and I fail to see what moral effect it can have. To yield to force is an act of necessity, not of will—at the most, an act of prudence. In what sense can it be a duty?

Suppose for a moment that this so-called "right" exists. I maintain that the sole result is a mass of inexplicable nonsense. For, if force creates right, the effect changes with the cause: every force that is greater than the first succeeds to its right. As soon as it is possible to disobey with impunity, disobedience is legitimate; and, the strongest being always in the right, the only thing that matters is to act so as to become the strongest. But what kind of right is that which perishes when force fails? If we must obey perforce, there is no need to obey because we ought; and if we are not forced to obey, we are under no obligation to do so. Clearly, the word "right" adds nothing to force: in this connection, it means absolutely nothing.

Obey the powers that be. If this means yield to force, it is a good precept, but superfluous: I can answer for its never being violated. All power comes from God, I admit; but so does all sickness: does that mean that we are forbidden to call in the doctor? A brigand surprises me at the edge of a wood: must I not merely surrender my purse on compulsion; but, even if I could withhold it, am I in conscience bound to give it up? For certainly the pistol he holds is also a power.

Let us then admit that force does not create right, and that we are obliged to obey only legitimate powers. In that case, my original question recurs.

4. Slavery

Since no man has a natural authority over his fellow, and force creates no right, we must conclude that conventions form the basis of all legitimate authority among men.

If an individual, says Grotius, can alienate his liberty and make himself the slave of a master, why could not a whole people do the same and make itself subject to a king? There are in this passage plenty of ambiguous words which would need explaining; but let us confine ourselves to the word *alienate*. To alienate is to give or to sell. Now, a man who becomes the slave of another does not give himself; he sells himself, at the least for his subsistence: but for what does a people sell itself? A king is so far from furnishing his subjects with their subsistence that he gets his own only from them; and, according to Rabelais, kings do not live on nothing. Do subjects then give their persons on condition that the king takes their goods also? I fail to see what they have left to preserve.

It will be said that the despot assures his subjects civil tranquillity. Granted; but what do they gain, if the wars his ambition brings down upon them, his insatiable avidity, and the vexatious conduct of his ministers press harder on them than their own dissensions would have done? What do they gain, if the very tranquillity they enjoy is one of their miseries? Tranquillity is found also in dungeons; but is that enough to make them desirable places to live in? The Greeks imprisoned in the cave of the Cyclops lived there very tranquilly, while they were awaiting their turn to be devoured.

To say that a man gives himself gratuitously, is to say what is absurd and inconceivable; such an act is null and illegitimate, from the mere fact that he who does it is out of his mind. To say the same of a whole people is to suppose a people of madmen; and madness creates no right.

Even if each man could alienate himself, he could not alienate his children: they are born men and free; their liberty belongs to them, and no one but they has the right to dispose of it. Before they come to years of discretion, the father can, in their name, lay down conditions for their preservation and well-being, but he cannot give them irrevocably and without conditions: such a gift is contrary to the ends of nature, and exceeds the rights of paternity. It would therefore be necessary, in order to legitimise an arbitrary government, that in every generation the people should be in a position to accept or reject it; but, were this so, the government would be no longer arbitrary.

To renounce liberty is to renounce being a man, to surrender the rights of humanity and even its duties. For him who renounces everything no indemnity is possible. Such a renunciation is incompatible with man's nature; to remove all liberty from his will is to remove all morality from his acts. Finally, it is an empty and contradictory convention that sets up, on the one side, absolute authority, and, on the other, unlimited obedience. Is it not clear that we can be under no obligation to a person from whom we have the right to exact everything? Does not this condition alone, in the absence of equivalence or exchange, in itself involve the nullity of the act? For what right can my slave have against me, when all that he has belongs to me, and, his right being mine, this right of mine against myself is a phrase devoid of meaning?

Grotius and the rest find in war another origin for the so-called right of slavery. The victor having, as they hold, the right of killing the vanquished, the latter can buy back his life at the price of his liberty; and this convention is the more legitimate because it is to the advantage of both parties.

But it is clear that this supposed right to kill the conquered is by no means deducible from the state of war. Men, from the mere fact that, while they are living in their primitive independence, they have no mutual relations stable enough to constitute either the state of peace or the state of war, cannot be naturally enemies. War is constituted by a relation between things, and not between persons; and, as the state of war cannot arise out of simple personal relations, but only out of real relations, private war, or war of man with man, can exist neither in the state of nature, where there is no constant property, nor in the social state, where everything is under the authority of the laws.

Individual combats, duels and encounters, are acts which cannot constitute a state; while the private wars, authorised by the Establishments of Louis IX, King of France, and suspended by the Peace of God, are abuses of feudalism, in itself an absurd system if ever there was one, and contrary to the principles of natural right and to all good polity.

War then is a relation, not between man and man, but between State and State, and individuals are enemies only accidentally, not as men, nor even as citizens, but as soldiers; not as members of their country, but as its defenders. Finally, each State can have for enemies only other States, and not men; for between things disparate in nature there can be no real relation.

Furthermore, this principle is in conformity with the established rules of all times and the constant practice of all civilised peoples. Declarations of war are intimations less to powers than to their subjects. The foreigner, whether king, individual, or people, who robs, kills or detains the subjects, without declaring war on the prince, is not an enemy, but a brigand. Even in real war, a just prince, while laying hands, in the enemy's country, on all that belongs to the public, respects the lives and goods of individuals: he respects rights on which his own are founded. The object of the war being the destruction of the hostile State, the other side has a right to kill its defenders, while they are bearing arms; but as soon as they lay them down and surrender, they cease to be enemies or instruments of the enemy, and become once more merely men, whose life no one has any right to take. Sometimes it is possible to kill the State without killing a single one of its members; and war gives no right which is not necessary to the gaining of its object. These principles are not those of Grotius: they are not based on the authority of poets, but derived from the nature of reality and based on reason.

The right of conquest has no foundation other than the right of the strongest. If war does not give the conqueror the right to massacre the conquered peoples, the right to enslave them cannot be based upon a right which does not exist. No one has a right to kill an enemy except when he cannot make him a slave, and the right to enslave him cannot therefore be derived from the right to kill him. It is accordingly an unfair exchange to make him buy at the price of his liberty his life, over which the victor holds no right. Is it not clear that there is a vicious circle in founding the right of life and death on the right of slavery, and the right of slavery on the right of life and death?

Even if we assume this terrible right to kill everybody, I maintain that a slave made in war, or a conquered people, is under no obligation to a master, except to obey him as far as he is compelled to do so. By taking an equivalent for his life, the victor has not done him a favour; instead of killing him without profit, he has "killed him usefully." So far then is he from acquiring over him any authority in addition to that of force, that the state of war continues to subsist between them: their mutual relation is the effect of it, and the usage of the right of war does not imply a treaty of peace. A convention has indeed been made; but this convention, so far from destroying the state of war, presupposes its continuance.

So, from whatever aspect we regard the question, the right of slavery is null and void, not only as being illegitimate, but also because it is absurd and meaningless. The words *slave* and *right* contradict each other, and are mutually exclusive. It will always be equally foolish for a man to say to a man or

In sum...

to a people: "I make with you a convention wholly at your expense and wholly to my advantage; I shall keep it as long as I like, and you will keep it as long as I like."

5. That We Must Always Go Back to a First Convention

210

Even if I granted all that I have been refuting, the friends of despotism would be no better off. There will always be a great difference between subduing a multitude and ruling a society. Even if scattered individuals were successively enslaved by one man, however numerous they might be, I still see no more than a master and his slaves, and certainly not a people and its ruler; I see what may be termed an aggregation, but not an association; there is as yet neither public good nor body politic. The man in question, even if he has enslaved half the world, is still only an individual; his interest, apart from that of others, is still a purely private interest. If this same man comes to die, his empire, after him, remains scattered and without unity, as an oak falls and dissolves into a heap of ashes when the fire has consumed it.

220

A people, says Grotius, can give itself to a king. Then, according to Grotius, a people is a people before it gives itself. The gift is itself a civil act, and implies public deliberation. It would be better, before examining the act by which a people gives itself to a king, to examine that by which it has become a people; for this act, being necessarily prior to the other, is the true foundation of society.

How does the US become a people before giving itself to govt. leadership?

Indeed, if there were no prior convention, where, unless the election were unanimous, would be the obligation on the minority to submit to the choice of the majority? How have a hundred men who wish for a master the right to vote on behalf of ten who do not? The law of majority voting is itself something established by convention, and presupposes unanimity, on one occasion at least.

6. The Social Compact

when they decided to go w/ majority rule — can this be binding on future generations

230

I suppose men to have reached the point at which the obstacles in the way of their preservation in the state of nature show their power of resistance to be greater than the resources at the disposal of each individual for his maintenance in that state. That primitive condition can then subsist no longer; and the human race would perish unless it changed its manner of existence.

But, as men cannot engender new forces, but only unite and direct existing ones, they have no other means of preserving themselves than the formation, by aggregation, of a sum of forces great enough to overcome the resistance. These they have to bring into play by means of a single motive power, and cause to act in concert.

240

This sum of forces can arise only where several persons come together: but, as the force and liberty of each man are the chief instruments of his self-preservation, how can he pledge them without harming his own interests, and neglecting the care he owes to himself? This difficulty, in its bearing on my present subject, may be stated in the following terms:

"The problem is to find a form of association which will defend and protect with the whole common force the person and goods of each associate, and in which each, while uniting himself with all, may still obey himself alone, and remain as free as before." This is the fundamental problem of which the *Social Contract* provides the solution.

The clauses of this contract are so determined by the nature of the act that the slightest modification would make them vain and ineffective; so that, although they have perhaps never been formally set forth, they are every-   250
where the same and everywhere tacitly admitted and recognised, until, on the violation of the social compact, each regains his original rights and resumes his natural liberty, while losing the conventional liberty in favour of which he renounced it.

These clauses, properly understood, may be reduced to one—the total alienation of each associate, together with all his rights, to the whole community; for, in the first place, as each gives himself absolutely, the conditions are the same for all; and, this being so, no one has any interest in making them burdensome to others.

Moreover, the alienation being without reserve, the union is as perfect as   260
it can be, and no associate has anything more to demand: for, if the individuals retained certain rights, as there would be no common superior to decide between them and the public, each, being on one point his own judge, would ask to be so on all; the state of nature would thus continue, and the association would necessarily become inoperative or tyrannical.

Finally, each man, in giving himself to all, gives himself to nobody; and as there is no associate over whom he does not acquire the same right as he yields others over himself, he gains an equivalent for everything he loses, and an increase of force for the preservation of what he has.

If then we discard from the social compact what is not of its essence, we   270
shall find that it reduces itself to the following terms:

"Each of us puts his person and all his power in common under the supreme direction of the general will, and, in our corporate capacity, we receive each member as an indivisible part of the whole."

At once, in place of the individual personality of each contracting party, this act of association creates a moral and collective body, composed of as many members as the assembly contains votes, and receiving from this act its unity, its common identity, its life and its will. This public person, so formed by the union of all other persons formerly took the name of *city*, and now takes that of *Republic* or *body politic*; it is called by its members *State* when passive, *Sovereign* when active, and *Power* when compared with others like itself. Those   280 who are associated in it take collectively the name of *people,* and severally are called *citizens,* as sharing in the sovereign power, and *subjects,* as being under the laws of the State. But these terms are often confused and taken one for another: it is enough to know how to distinguish them when they are being used with precision.

7. The Sovereign

This formula shows us that the act of association comprises a mutual undertaking between the public and the individuals, and that each individual, in making a contract, as we may say, with himself, is bound in a double capacity; as a member of the Sovereign he is bound to the individuals, and as a member of the State to the Sovereign. But the maxim of civil right, that no one is bound by undertakings made to himself, does not apply in this case; for there is a great difference between incurring an obligation to yourself and incurring one to a whole of which you form a part.

Attention must further be called to the fact that public deliberation, while competent to bind all the subjects to the Sovereign, because of the two different capacities in which each of them may be regarded, cannot, for the opposite reason, bind the Sovereign to itself; and that it is consequently against the nature of the body politic for the Sovereign to impose on itself a law which it cannot infringe. Being able to regard itself in only one capacity, it is in the position of an individual who makes a contract with himself; and this makes it clear that there neither is nor can be any kind of fundamental law binding on the body of the people—not even the social contract itself. This does not mean that the body politic cannot enter into undertakings with others, provided the contract is not infringed by them; for in relation to what is external to it, it becomes a simple being, an individual.

But the body politic or the Sovereign, drawing its being wholly from the sanctity of the contract, can never bind itself, even to an outsider, to do anything derogatory to the original act, for instance, to alienate any part of itself, or to submit to another Sovereign. Violation of the act by which it exists would be self-annihilation; and that which is itself nothing can create nothing.

As soon as this multitude is so united in one body, it is impossible to offend against one of the members without attacking the body, and still more to offend against the body without the members resenting it. Duty and interest therefore equally oblige the two contracting parties to give each other help; and the same men should seek to combine, in their double capacity, all the advantages dependent upon that capacity.

Again, the Sovereign, being formed wholly of the individuals who compose it, neither has nor can have any interest contrary to theirs; and consequently the sovereign power need give no guarantee to its subjects, because it is impossible for the body to wish to hurt all its members. We shall also see later on that it cannot hurt any in particular. The Sovereign, merely by virtue of what it is, is always what it should be.

This, however, is not the case with the relation of the subjects to the Sovereign, which, despite the common interest, would have no security that they would fulfil their undertakings, unless it found means to assure itself of their fidelity.

In fact, each individual, as a man, may have a particular will contrary or dissimilar to the general will which he has as a citizen. His particular interest may speak to him quite differently from the common interest: his absolute and naturally independent existence may make him look upon what he owes to the common cause as a gratuitous contribution, the loss of which will do less harm to others than the payment of it is burdensome to himself; and, regarding the moral person which constitutes the State as a *persona ficta*, because not a man, he may wish to enjoy the rights of citizenship without being ready to fulfil the duties of a subject. The continuance of such an injustice could not but prove the undoing of the body politic.

In order then that the social compact may not be an empty formula, it tacitly includes the undertaking, which alone can give force to the rest, that whoever refuses to obey the general will shall be compelled to do so by the whole body. This means nothing less than that he will be forced to be free; for this is the condition which, by giving each citizen to his country, secures him against all personal dependence. In this lies the key to the working of the political machine; this alone legitimises civil undertakings, which, without it, would be absurd, tyrannical, and liable to the most frightful abuses.

forced to be free

8. The Civil State

The passage from the state of nature to the civil state produces a very remarkable change in man, by substituting justice for instinct in his conduct, and giving his actions the morality they had formerly lacked. Then only, when the voice of duty takes the place of physical impulses and right of appetite, does man, who so far had considered only himself, find that he is forced to act on different principles, and to consult his reason before listening to his inclinations. Although, in this state, he deprives himself of some advantages which he got from nature, he gains in return others so great, his faculties are so stimulated and developed, his ideas so extended, his feelings so ennobled, and his whole soul so uplifted, that, did not the abuses of this new condition often degrade him below that which he left, he would be bound to bless continually the happy moment which took him from it for ever, and, instead of a stupid and unimaginative animal, made him an intelligent being and a man.

only abuses of civilization keep people from constantly blessing civilization

Let us draw up the whole account in terms easily commensurable. What man loses by the social contract is his natural liberty and an unlimited right to everything he tries to get and succeeds in getting; what he gains is civil liberty and the proprietorship of all he possesses. If we are to avoid mistake in weighing one against the other, we must clearly distinguish natural liberty, which is bounded only by the strength of the individual, from civil liberty, which is limited by the general will; and possession, which is merely the effect of force or the right of the first occupier, from property, which can be founded only on a positive title.

We might, over and above all this, add, to what man acquires in the civil state, moral liberty, which alone makes him truly master of himself; for the mere impulse of appetite is slavery, while obedience to a law which we prescribe to ourselves is liberty. But I have already said too much on this head, and the philosophical meaning of the word liberty does not now concern us.

9. Real Property

Each member of the community gives himself to it, at the moment of its foundation, just as he is, with all the resources at his command, including the goods he possesses. This act does not make possession, in changing hands, change its nature, and become property in the hands of the Sovereign; but, as the forces of the city are incomparably greater than those of an individual, public possession is also, in fact, stronger and more irrevocable, without being any more legitimate, at any rate from the point of view of foreigners. For the State, in relation to its members, is master of all their goods by the social contract, which, within the State, is the basis of all rights; but, in relation to other powers, it is so only by the right of the first occupier, which it holds from its members.

The right of the first occupier, though more real than the right of the strongest, becomes a real right only when the right of property has already been established. Every man has naturally a right to everything he needs; but the positive act which makes him proprietor of one thing excludes him from everything else. Having his share, he ought to keep to it, and can have no further right against the community. This is why the right of the first occupier, which in the state of nature is so weak, claims the respect of every man in civil society. In this right we are respecting not so much what belongs to another as what does not belong to ourselves.

The peculiar fact about this alienation is that, in taking over the goods of individuals, the community, so far from despoiling them, only assures them legitimate possession, and changes usurpation into a true right and enjoyment into proprietorship. Thus the possessors, being regarded as depositaries of the public good, and having their rights respected by all the members of the State and maintained against foreign aggression by all its forces, have, by a cession which benefits both the public and still more themselves, acquired, so to speak, all that they gave up. This paradox may easily be explained by the distinction between the rights which the Sovereign and the proprietor have over the same estate, as we shall see later on.

It may also happen that men begin to unite one with another before they possess anything, and that, subsequently occupying a tract of country which is enough for all, they enjoy it in common, or share it out among themselves, either equally or according to a scale fixed by the Sovereign. However the acquisition be made, the right which each individual has to his own estate is always subordinate to the right which the community has over all: without this, there would be neither stability in the social tie, nor real force in the exercise of Sovereignty.

    I shall end this chapter and this book by remarking on a fact on which the whole social system should rest: i.e., that, instead of destroying natural inequality, the fundamental compact substitutes, for such physical inequality as nature may have set up between men, an equality that is moral and legitimate, and that men, who may be unequal in strength or intelligence, become every one equal by convention and legal right.

BOOK II

1. That Sovereignty Is Inalienable

The first and most important deduction from the principles we have so far laid down is that the general will alone can direct the State according to the object for which it was instituted, i.e., the common good: for if the clashing of particular interests made the establishment of societies necessary, the agreement of these very interests made it possible. The common element in these different interests is what forms the social tie; and, were there no point of agreement between them all, no society could exist. It is solely on the basis of this common interest that every society should be governed.

3. Whether the General Will Is Fallible

It follows from what has gone before that the general will is always right and tends to the public advantage; but it does not follow that the deliberations of the people are always equally correct. Our will is always for our own good, but we do not always see what that is; the people is never corrupted, but it is often deceived, and on such occasions only does it seem to will what is bad.

    There is often a great deal of difference between the will of all and the general will; the latter considers only the common interest, while the former takes private interest into account, and is no more than a sum of particular wills: but take away from these same wills the pluses and minuses that cancel one another,[1] and the general will remains as the sum of the differences.

    If, when the people, being furnished with adequate information, held its deliberations, the citizens had no communication one with another, the grand total of the small differences would always give the general will, and the decision would always be good. But when factions arise, and partial associations are formed at the expense of the great association, the will of each of these associations becomes general in relation to its members, while it remains particular in relation to the State: it may then be said that there are no longer as many votes as there are men, but only as many as there are associations. The differences become less numerous and give a less general result. Lastly, when one of these associations is so great as to prevail over all the rest, the result is no longer a sum of small differences, but a single difference; in this case there is no longer a general will, and the opinion which prevails is purely particular.

It is therefore essential, if the general will is to be able to express itself, that there should be no partial society within the State, and that each citizen should think only his own thoughts:[2] which was indeed the sublime and unique system established by the great Lycurgus. But if there are partial societies, it is best to have as many as possible and to prevent them from being unequal, as was done by Solon, Numa and Servius. These precautions are the only ones that can guarantee that the general will shall be always enlightened, and that the people shall in no way deceive itself.

4. The Limits of the Sovereign Power

If the State is a moral person whose life is in the union of its members, and if the most important of its cares is the care for its own preservation, it must have a universal and compelling force, in order to move and dispose each part as may be most advantageous to the whole. As nature gives each man absolute power over all his members, the social compact gives the body politic absolute power over all its members also; and it is this power which, under the direction of the general will, bears, as I have said, the name of Sovereignty.

But, besides the public person, we have to consider the private persons composing it, whose life and liberty are naturally independent of it. We are bound then to distinguish clearly between the respective rights of the citizens and the Sovereign,[3] and between the duties the former have to fulfil as subjects, and the natural rights they should enjoy as men.

Each man alienates, I admit, by the social compact, only such part of his powers, goods and liberty as it is important for the community to control; but it must also be granted that the Sovereign is sole judge of what is important.

Every service a citizen can render the State he ought to render as soon as the Sovereign demands it; but the Sovereign, for its part, cannot impose upon its subjects any fetters that are useless to the community, nor can it even wish to do so; for no more by the law of reason than by the law of nature can anything occur without a cause.

The undertakings which bind us to the social body are obligatory only because they are mutual; and their nature is such that in fulfilling them we cannot work for others without working for ourselves. Why is it that the general will is always in the right, and that all continually will the happiness of each one, unless it is because there is not a man who does not think of "each" as meaning him, and consider himself in voting for all? This proves that equality of rights and the idea of justice which such equality creates originate in the preference each man gives to himself, and accordingly in the very nature of man. It proves that the general will, to be really such, must be general in its object as well as its essence; that it must both come from all and apply to all; and that it loses its natural rectitude when it is directed to some particular and determinate object, because in such a case we are judging of something foreign to us, and have no true principle of equity to guide us.   490

Indeed, as soon as a question of particular fact or right arises on a point not previously regulated by a general convention, the matter becomes contentious. It is a case in which the individuals concerned are one party, and the public the other, but in which I can see neither the law that ought to be followed nor the judge who ought to give the decision. In such a case, it would be absurd to propose to refer the question to an express decision of the general will, which can be only the conclusion reached by one of the parties and in consequence will be, for the other party, merely an external and particular will, inclined on this occasion to injustice and subject to error. Thus, just as a particular will cannot stand for the general will, the general will, in turn,   500 changes its nature, when its object is particular, and, as general, cannot pronounce on a man or a fact. When, for instance, the people of Athens nominated or displaced its rulers, decreed honours to one, and imposed penalties on another, and, by a multitude of particular decrees, exercised all the functions of government indiscriminately, it had in such cases no longer a general will in the strict sense; it was acting no longer as Sovereign, but as magistrate. This will seem contrary to current views; but I must be given time to expound my own.

It should be seen from the foregoing that what makes the will general is less the number of voters than the common interest uniting them; for, under   510 this system, each necessarily submits to the conditions he imposes on others: and this admirable agreement between interest and justice gives to the common deliberations an equitable character which at once vanishes when any particular question is discussed, in the absence of a common interest to unite and identify the ruling of the judge with that of the party.

From whatever side we approach our principle, we reach the same conclusion, that the social compact sets up among the citizens an equality of such a kind, that they all bind themselves to observe the same conditions and should therefore all enjoy the same rights. Thus, from the very nature of the compact, every act of Sovereignty, i.e., every authentic act of the general will,   520 binds or favours all the citizens equally; so that the Sovereign recognises only the body of the nation, and draws no distinctions between those of whom it is made up. What, then, strictly speaking, is an act of Sovereignty? It is not a convention between a superior and an inferior, but a convention between the body and each of its members. It is legitimate, because based on the social contract, and equitable, because common to all; useful, because it can have no other object than the general good, and stable, because guaranteed by the public force and the supreme power. So long as the subjects have to submit only to conventions of this sort, they obey no-one but their own will; and to ask how far the respective rights of the Sovereign and the citizens extend, is   530 to ask up to what point the latter can enter into undertakings with themselves, each with all, and all with each.

We can see from this that the sovereign power, absolute, sacred and inviolable as it is, does not and cannot exceed the limits of general conventions, and that every man may dispose at will of such goods and liberty as these conventions leave him; so that the Sovereign never has a right to lay more charges on one subject than on another, because, in that case, the question becomes particular, and ceases to be within its competency.

When these distinctions have once been admitted, it is seen to be so
540   untrue that there is, in the social contract, any real renunciation on the part of the individuals, that the position in which they find themselves as a result of the contract is really preferable to that in which they were before. Instead of a renunciation, they have made an advantageous exchange: instead of an uncertain and precarious way of living they have got one that is better and more secure; instead of natural independence they have got liberty, instead of the power to harm others security for themselves, and instead of their strength, which others might overcome, a right which social union makes invincible. Their very life, which they have devoted to the State, is by it constantly protected; and when they risk it in the State's defence, what
550   more are they doing than giving back what they have received from it? What are they doing that they would not do more often and with greater danger in the state of nature, in which they would inevitably have to fight battles at the peril of their lives in defence of that which is the means of their preservation? All have indeed to fight when their country needs them; but then no one has ever to fight for himself. Do we not gain something by running, on behalf of what gives us our security, only some of the risks we should have to run for ourselves, as soon as we lost it?

5. The Right of Life and Death

The question is often asked how individuals, having no right to dispose of their own lives, can transfer to the Sovereign a right which they do not possess.
560   The difficulty of answering this question seems to me to lie in its being wrongly stated. Every man has a right to risk his own life in order to preserve it. Has it ever been said that a man who throws himself out of the window to escape from a fire is guilty of suicide? Has such a crime ever been laid to the charge of him who perishes in a storm because, when he went on board, he knew of the danger?

The social treaty has for its end the preservation of the contracting parties. He who wills the end wills the means also, and the means must involve some risks, and even some losses. He who wishes to preserve his life at others' expense should also, when it is necessary, be ready to give it up for their sake. Further-
570   more, the citizen is no longer the judge of the dangers to which the law desires him to expose himself; and when the prince says to him: "It is expedient for the State that you should die," he ought to die, because it is only on that condition that he has been living in security up to the present, and because his life is no longer a mere bounty of nature, but a gift made conditionally by the State.

The death-penalty inflicted upon criminals may be looked on in much the same light: it is in order that we may not fall victims to an assassin that we consent to die if we ourselves turn assassins. In this treaty, so far from disposing of our own lives, we think only of securing them, and it is not to be assumed that any of the parties then expects to get hanged.

580

Again, every malefactor, by attacking social rights, becomes on forfeit a rebel and a traitor to his country; by violating its laws he ceases to be a member of it; he even makes war upon it. In such a case the preservation of the State is inconsistent with his own, and one or the other must perish; in putting the guilty to death, we slay not so much the citizen as an enemy. The trial and the judgment are the proofs that he has broken the social treaty, and is in consequence no longer a member of the State. Since, then, he has recognised himself to be such by living there, he must be removed by exile as a violator of the compact, or by death as a public enemy; for such an enemy is not a moral person, but merely a man; and in such a case the right of war is to kill the vanquished.

590

But, it will be said, the condemnation of a criminal is a particular act. I admit it: but such condemnation is not a function of the Sovereign; it is a right the Sovereign can confer without being able itself to exert it. All my ideas are consistent, but I cannot expound them all at once.

We may add that frequent punishments are always a sign of weakness or remissness on the part of the government. There is not a single ill-doer who could not be turned to some good. The State has no right to put to death, even for the sake of making an example, anyone whom it can leave alive without danger.

600

The right of pardoning or exempting the guilty from a penalty imposed by the law and pronounced by the judge belongs only to the authority which is superior to both judge and law, i.e., the Sovereign; each its right in this matter is far from clear, and the cases for exercising it are extremely rare. In a well-governed State, there are few punishments, not because there are many pardons, but because criminals are rare; it is when a State is in decay that the multitude of crimes is a guarantee of impunity. Under the Roman Republic, neither the Senate nor the Consuls ever attempted to pardon; even the people never did so, though it sometimes revoked its own decision. Frequent pardons mean that crime will soon need them no longer, and no one can help seeing whither that leads. But I feel my heart protesting and restraining my pen; let us leave these questions to the just man who has never offended, and would himself stand in no need of pardon.

610

6. Law

By the social compact we have given the body politic existence and life; we have now by legislation to give it movement and will. For the original act by which the body is formed and united still in no respect determines what it ought to do for its preservation.

What is well and in conformity with order is so by the nature of things and independently of human conventions. All justice comes from God, who is its
620 sole source; but if we knew how to receive so high an inspiration, we should need neither government nor laws. Doubtless, there is a universal justice emanating from reason alone; but this justice, to be admitted among us, must be mutual. Humanly speaking, in default of natural sanctions, the laws of justice are ineffective among men: they merely make for the good of the wicked and the undoing of the just, when the just man observes them towards everybody and nobody observes them towards him. Conventions and laws are therefore needed to join rights to duties and refer justice to its object. In the state of nature, where everything is common, I owe nothing to him whom I have promised nothing; I recognise as belonging to others only what is of no use to me. In
630 the state of society all rights are fixed by law, and the case becomes different.

But what, after all, is a law? As long as we remain satisfied with attaching purely metaphysical ideas to the word, we shall go on arguing without arriving at an understanding; and when we have defined a law of nature, we shall be no nearer the definition of a law of the State.

I have already said that there can be no general will directed to a particular object. Such an object must be either within or outside the State. If outside, a will which is alien to it cannot be, in relation to it, general; if within, it is part of the State, and in that case there arises a relation between whole and part which makes them two separate beings, of which the part is one, and the whole minus the part
640 the other. But the whole minus a part cannot be the whole; and while this relation persists, there can be no whole, but only two unequal parts; and it follows that the will of one is no longer in any respect general in relation to the other.

But when the whole people decrees for the whole people, it is considering only itself; and if a relation is then formed, it is between two aspects of the entire object, without there being any division of the whole. In that case the matter about which the decree is made is, like the decreeing will, general. This act is what I call a law.

When I say that the object of laws is always general, I mean that law considers subjects *en masse* and, actions in the abstract, and never a particular
650 person or action. Thus the law may indeed decree that there shall be privileges, but cannot confer them on anybody by name. It may set up several classes of citizens, and even lay down the qualifications for membership of these classes, but it cannot nominate such and such persons as belonging to them; it may establish a monarchical government and hereditary succession, but it cannot choose a king, or nominate a royal family. In a word, no function which has a particular object belongs to the legislative power.

On this view, we at once see that it can no longer be asked whose business it is to make laws, since they are acts of the general will; nor whether the prince is above the law, since he is a member of the State; nor whether the
660 law can be unjust, since no one is unjust to himself; nor how we can be both free and subject to the laws, since they are but registers of our wills.

We see further that, as the law unites universality of will with universality of object, what a man, whoever he be, commands of his own motion cannot be a law; and even what the Sovereign commands with regard to a particular matter is no nearer being a law, but is a decree, an act, not of sovereignty, but of magistracy.

I therefore give the name "Republic" to every State that is governed by laws, no matter what the form of its administration may be: for only in such a case does the public interest govern, and the *res publica* rank as a *reality*. Every legitimate government is republican;[4] what government is I will explain later on.   670

Laws are, properly speaking, only the conditions of civil association. The people, being subject to the laws, ought to be their author: the conditions of the society ought to be regulated solely by those who come together to form it. But how are they to regulate them? Is it to be by common agreement, by a sudden inspiration? Has the body politic an organ to declare its will? Who can give it the foresight to formulate and announce its acts in advance? Or how is it to announce them in the hour of need? How can a blind multitude, which often does not know what it wills, because it rarely knows what is good for it, carry out for itself so   680 great and difficult an enterprise as a system of legislation? Of itself the people wills always the good, but of itself it by no means always sees it. The general will is always in the right, but the judgment which guides it is not always enlightened. It must be got to see objects as they are, and sometimes as they ought to appear to it; it must be shown the good road it is in search of, secured from the seductive influences of individual wills, taught to see times and spaces as a series, and made to weigh the attractions of present and sensible advantages against the danger of distant and hidden evils. The individuals see the good they reject; the public wills the good it does not see. All stand equally in need of guidance. The former   690 must be compelled to bring their wills into conformity with their reason; the latter must be taught to know what it wills. If that is done, public enlightenment leads to the union of understanding and will in the social body: the parts are made to work exactly together, and the whole is raised to its highest power. This makes a legislator necessary.

ENDNOTES

1. "Every interest," says the Marquis d'Argenson, "has different principles. The agreement of two particular interests is formed by opposition to a third." He might have added that the agreement of all interests is formed by opposition to that of each. If there were no different interests, the common interest would be barely felt, as it would encounter no obstacle; all would go on of its own accord, and politics would cease to be an art.

2. "In fact," says Machiavelli, "there are some divisions that are harmful to a Republic and some that are advantageous. Those which stir up sects and parties are harmful; those attended by neither are advantageous. Since, then, the founder of a Republic cannot help enmities arising, he ought at least to prevent them from growing into sects" (*History of Florence,* Book vii).

3. Attentive readers, do not, I pray, be in a hurry to charge me with contradicting myself. The terminology made it unavoidable, considering the poverty of the language; but wait and see.

4. I understand by this word, not merely an aristocracy or a democracy, but generally any government directed by the general will, which is the law. To be legitimate, the government must be, not one with the Sovereign, but its minister. In such a case even a monarchy is a Republic. This will be made clearer in the following book.

BOOK III

4. Democracy

He who makes the law knows better than anyone else how it should be executed and interpreted. It seems then impossible to have a better constitution than that in which the executive and legislative powers are united; but this very fact renders the government in certain respects inadequate, because
720 things which should be distinguished are confounded, and the prince and the Sovereign, being the same person, form, so to speak, no more than a government without government.

It is not good for him who makes the laws to execute them, or for the body of the people to turn its attention away from a general standpoint and devote it to particular objects. Nothing is more dangerous than the influence of private interests in public affairs, and the abuse of the laws by the government is a less evil than the corruption of the legislator, which is the inevitable sequel to a particular standpoint. In such a case, the State being altered in substance, all reformation becomes impossible, a people that would never
730 misuse governmental powers would never misuse independence; a people that would always govern well would not need to be governed.

If we take the term in the strict sense, there never has been a real democracy, and there never will be. It is against the natural order for the many to govern and the few to be governed. It is unimaginable that the people should remain continually assembled to devote their time to public affairs, and it is clear that they cannot set up commissions for that purpose without the form of administration being changed.

In fact, I can confidently lay down as a principle that, when the functions of government are shared by several tribunals, the less numerous sooner or
740 later acquire the greatest authority, if only because they are in a position to expedite affairs, and power thus naturally comes into their hands.

Besides, how many conditions that are difficult to unite does such a government presuppose! First, a very small State, where the people can readily be got together and where each citizen can with ease know all the rest; secondly, great simplicity of manners, to prevent business from multiplying and raising thorny problems; next, a large measure of equality in rank and fortune, without which equality of rights and authority cannot long subsist; lastly, little or no luxury—for luxury either comes of riches or makes them necessary; it corrupts at once rich and poor, the rich by possession and the poor by covetousness; it sells the country to softness and vanity, and takes away from the State all its citizens, to make them slaves one to another, and one and all to public opinion.

This is why a famous writer has made virtue the fundamental principle of Republics; all these conditions could not exist without virtue. But, for want of the necessary distinctions, that great thinker was often inexact, and sometimes obscure, and did not see that, the sovereign authority being everywhere the same, the same principle should be found in every well-constituted State, in a greater or less degree, it is true, according to the form of the government.

It may be added that there is no government so subject to civil wars and intestine agitations as democratic or popular government, because there is none which has so strong and continual a tendency to change to another form, or which demands more vigilance and courage for its maintenance as it is. Under such a constitution above all, the citizen should arm himself with strength and constancy, and say, every day of his life, what a virtuous Count Palatine[1] said in the Diet of Poland: *Malo periculosam libertatem quam quietum servitium.*[2]

Were there a people of gods, their government would be democratic. So perfect a government is not for men.

11. The Death of the Body Politic

Such is the natural and inevitable tendency of the best constituted governments. If Sparta and Rome perished, what State can hope to endure for ever? If we would set up a long-lived form of government, let us not even dream of making it eternal. If we are to succeed, we must not attempt the impossible, or flatter ourselves that we are endowing the work of man with a stability of which human conditions do not permit.

The body politic, as well as the human body, begins to die as soon as it is born, and carries in itself the causes of its destruction. But both may have a constitution that is more or less robust and suited to preserve them a longer or a shorter time. The constitution of man is the work of nature; that of the State the work of art. It is not in men's power to prolong their own lives; but it is for them to prolong as much as possible the life of the State, by giving it the best possible constitution. The best constituted State will have an end;

750

760

770

780

but it will end later than any other, unless some unforeseen accident brings about its untimely destruction.

The life-principle of the body politic lies in the sovereign authority. The legislative power is the heart of the State; the executive power is its brain, which causes the movement of all the parts. The brain may become paralysed and the individual still live. A man may remain an imbecile and live; but as soon as the heart ceases to perform its functions, the animal is dead.

790   The State subsists by means not of the laws, but of the legislative power. Yesterday's law is not binding to-day; but silence is taken for tacit consent, and the Sovereign is held to confirm incessantly the laws it does not abrogate as it might. All that it has once declared itself to will it wills always, unless it revokes its declaration.

Why then is so much respect paid to old laws? For this very reason. We must believe that nothing but the excellence of old acts of will can have preserved them so long: if the Sovereign had not recognised them as throughout salutary, it would have revoked them a thousand times. This is why, so far from growing weak, the laws continually gain new strength in any well con-
800   stituted State; the precedent of antiquity makes them daily more venerable: while wherever the laws grow weak as they become old, this proves that there is no longer a legislative power, and that the State is dead.

12. How the Sovereign Authority Maintains Itself

The Sovereign, having no force other than the legislative power, acts only by means of the laws; and the laws being solely the authentic acts of the general will, the Sovereign cannot act save when the people is assembled. The people in assembly, I shall be told, is a mere chimera. It is so to-day, but two thousand years ago it was not so. Has man's nature changed?

The bounds of possibility, in moral matters, are less narrow than we imagine: it is our weaknesses, our vices and our prejudices that confine them. Base
810   souls have no belief in great men; vile slaves smile in mockery at the name of liberty.

Let us judge of what can be done by what has been done. I shall say nothing of the Republics of ancient Greece; but the Roman Republic was, to my mind, a great State, and the town of Rome a great town. The last census showed that there were in Rome four hundred thousand citizens capable of bearing arms, and the last computation of the population of the Empire showed over four million citizens, excluding subjects, foreigners, women, children and slaves.

What difficulties might not be supposed to stand in the way of the fre-
820   quent assemblage of the vast population of this capital and its neighbour-hood. Yet few weeks passed without the Roman people being in assembly, and even being so several times. It exercised not only the rights of Sovereignty, but also a part of those of government. It dealt with certain matters, and judged certain cases, and this whole people was found in the public meeting-place hardly less often as magistrates than as citizens.

If we went back to the earliest history of nations, we should find that most ancient governments, even those of monarchical form, such as the Macedonian and the Frankish, had similar councils. In any case, the one incontestable fact I have given is an answer to all difficulties; it is good logic to reason from the actual to the possible.

830

15. Deputies or Representatives

As soon as public service ceases to be the chief business of the citizens, and they would rather serve with their money than with their persons, the State is not far from its fall. When it is necessary to march out to war, they pay troops and stay at home: when it is necessary to meet in council, they name deputies and stay at home. By reason of idleness and money, they end by having soldiers to enslave their country and representatives to sell it.

It is through the hustle of commerce and the arts, through the greedy self-interest of profit, and through softness and love of amenities that personal services are replaced by money payments. Men surrender a part of their profits in order to have time to increase them at leisure. Make gifts of money, and you will not be long without chains. The word *finance* is a slavish word, unknown in the city-state. In a country that is truly free, the citizens do everything with their own arms and nothing by means of money; so far from paying to be exempted from their duties, they would even pay for the privilege of fulfilling them themselves. I am far from taking the common view: I hold enforced labour to be less opposed to liberty than taxes.

840

The better the constitution of a State is, the more do public affairs encroach on private in the minds of the citizens. Private affairs are even of much less importance, because the aggregate of the common happiness furnishes a greater proportion of that of each individual, so that there is less for him to seek in particular cares. In a well-ordered city every man flies to the assemblies: under a bad government no one cares to stir a step to get to them, because no one is interested in what happens there, because it is foreseen that the general will will not prevail, and lastly because domestic cares are all-absorbing. Good laws lead to the making of better ones; bad ones bring about worse. As soon as any man says of the affairs of the State *What does it matter to me?* the State may be given up for lost.

850

The lukewarmness of patriotism, the activity of private interest, the vastness of States, conquest and the abuse of government suggested the method of having deputies or representatives of the people in the national assemblies. These are what, in some countries, men have presumed to call the Third Estate. Thus the individual interest of two orders is put first and second; the public interest occupies only the third place.

860

Sovereignty, for the same reason as makes it inalienable, cannot be represented; it lies essentially in the general will, and will does not admit of representation: it is either the same, or other; there is no intermediate possibility. The deputies of the people, therefore, are not and cannot be its representatives: they are merely its stewards, and can carry through no definitive acts.

Every law the people has not ratified in person is null and void—is, in fact,
not a law. The people of England regards itself as free; but it is grossly mistaken; it is free only during the election of members of parliament. As soon as they are elected, slavery overtakes it, and it is nothing. The use it makes of the short moments of liberty it enjoys shows indeed that it deserves to lose them.

The idea of representation is modern; it comes to us from feudal government, from that iniquitous and absurd system which degrades humanity and dishonours the name of man. In ancient republics and even in monarchies, the people never had representatives; the word itself was unknown. It is very singular that in Rome, where the tribunes were so sacrosanct, it was never even imagined that they could usurp the functions of the people, and that in the midst of so great a multitude they never attempted to pass on their own authority a single plebiscitum. We can, however, form an idea of the difficulties caused sometimes by the people being so numerous, from what happened in the time of the Gracchi, when some of the citizens had to cast their votes from the roofs of buildings.

Where right and liberty are everything, disadvantages count for nothing. Among this wise people everything was given its just value, its lictors were allowed to do what its tribunes would never have dared to attempt; for it had no fear that its lictors would try to represent it.

To explain, however, in what way the tribunes did sometimes represent it, it is enough to conceive how the government represents the Sovereign. Law being purely the declaration of the general will, it is clear that, in the exercise of the legislative power, the people cannot be represented; but in that of the executive power, which is only the force that is applied to give the law effect, it both can and should be represented. We thus see that if we looked closely into the matter we should find that very few nations have any laws. However that may be, it is certain that the tribunes, possessing no executive power, could never represent the Roman people by right of the powers entrusted to them, but only by usurping those of the senate.

In Greece, all that the people had to do, it did for itself; it was constantly assembled in the public square. The Greeks lived in a mild climate; they had no natural greed; slaves did their work for them; their great concern was with liberty. Lacking the same advantages, how can you preserve the same rights? Your severer climates add to your needs;[6] for half the year your public squares are uninhabitable; the flatness of your languages unfits them for being heard in the open air; you sacrifice more for profit than for liberty, and fear slavery less than poverty.

What then? Is liberty maintained only by the help of slavery? It may be so. Extremes meet. Everything that is not in the course of nature has its disadvantages, civil society most of all. There are some unhappy circumstances in which we can only keep our liberty at others' expense, and where the citizen can be perfectly free only when the slave is most a slave. Such was the case with Sparta. As for you, modern peoples, you have no slaves, but you are slaves yourselves; you pay for their liberty with your own. It is in vain that you boast of this preference; I find in it more cowardice than humanity.

I do not mean by all this that it is necessary to have slaves, or that the right of slavery is legitimate: I am merely giving the reasons why modern peoples, believing themselves to be free, have representatives, while ancient peoples had none. In any case, the moment a people allows itself to be represented, it is no longer free: it no longer exists.

All things considered, I do not see that it is possible henceforth for the Sovereign to preserve among us the exercise of its rights, unless the city is very   920 small. But if it is very small, it will be conquered? No. I will show later on how the external strength of a great people[7] may be combined with the convenient polity and good order of a small State.

16. That the Institution of Government Is Not a Contract

The legislative power once well established, the next thing is to establish similarly the executive power; for this latter, which operates only by particular acts, not being of the essence of the former, is naturally separate from it. Were it possible for the Sovereign, as such, to possess the executive power, right and fact would be so confounded that no one could tell what was law and what was not; and the body politic, thus disfigured, would soon fall a prey to the violence it was instituted to prevent.   930

As the citizens, by the social contract, are all equal, all can prescribe what all should do, but no one has a right to demand that another shall do what he does not do himself. It is strictly this right, which is indispensable for giving the body politic life and movement, that the Sovereign, in instituting the government, confers upon the prince.

It has been held that this act of establishment was a contract between the people and the rulers it sets over itself,—a contract in which conditions were laid down between the two parties binding the one to command and the other to obey. It will be admitted, I am sure, that this is an odd kind of contract to enter into. But let us see if this view can be upheld.   940

First, the supreme authority can no more be modified than it can be alienated; to limit it is to destroy it. It is absurd and contradictory for the Sovereign to set a superior over itself; to bind itself to obey a master would be to return to absolute liberty.

Moreover, it is clear that this contract between the people and such and such persons would be a particular act; and from this it follows that it can be neither a law nor an act of Sovereignty, and that consequently it would be illegitimate.

It is plain too that the contracting parties in relation to each other would be under the law of nature alone and wholly without guarantees of their   950 mutual undertakings, a position wholly at variance with the civil state. He who has force at his command being always in a position to control execution, it would come to the same thing if the name "contract" were given to the act of one man who said to another: "I give you all my goods, on condition that you give me back as much of them as you please."

There is only one contract in the State, and that is the act of association, which in itself excludes the existence of a second. It is impossible to conceive of any public contract that would not be a violation of the first.

BOOK IV

1. That the General Will Is Indestructible

960

As long as several men in assembly regard themselves as a single body, they have only a single will which is concerned with their common preservation and general well-being. In this case, all the springs of the State are vigorous and simple and its rules clear and luminous; there are no embroilments or conflicts of interests; the common good is everywhere clearly apparent, and only good sense is needed to perceive it. Peace, unity and equality are the enemies of political subtleties. Men who are upright and simple are difficult to deceive because of their simplicity; lures and ingenious pretexts fail to impose upon them, and they are not even subtle enough to be dupes. When, among the happiest people in the world, bands of peasants are seen regulating affairs of State under an oak, and always acting wisely, can we help scorning the

970

ingenious methods of other nations, which make themselves illustrious and wretched with so much art and mystery?

A State so governed needs very few laws; and, as it becomes necessary to issue new ones, the necessity is universally seen. The first man to propose them merely says what all have already felt, and there is no question of factions or intrigues or eloquence in order to secure the passage into law of what every one has already decided to do, as soon as he is sure that the rest will act with him.

Theorists are led into error because, seeing only States that have been from the beginning wrongly constituted, they are struck by the impossibility

980

of applying such a policy to them. They make great game of all the absurdities a clever rascal or an insinuating speaker might get the people of Paris or London to believe. They do not know that Cromwell would have been put to "the bells" by the people of Berne, and the Duc de Beaufort on the treadmill by the Genevese.

But when the social bond begins to be relaxed and the State to grow weak, when particular interests begin to make themselves felt and the smaller societies to exercise an influence over the larger, the common interest changes and finds opponents: opinion is no longer unanimous; the general will ceases to be the will of all; contradictory views and debates arise; and the best advice

990

is not taken without question.

Finally, when the State, on the eve of ruin, maintains only a vain, illusory and formal existence, when in every heart the social bond is broken, and the meanest interest brazenly lays hold of the sacred name of "public good," the general will becomes mute: all men, guided by secret motives, no more give their views as citizens than if the State had never been; and iniquitous decrees directed solely to private interest get passed under the name of laws.

Does it follow from this that the general will is exterminated or corrupted? Not at all: it is always constant, unalterable and pure; but it is subordinated to other wills which encroach upon its sphere. Each man, in detaching his interest from the common interest, sees clearly that he cannot entirely separate them; but his share in the public mishaps seems to him negligible beside the exclusive good he aims at making his own. Apart from this particular good, he wills the general good in his own interest, as strongly as anyone else. Even in selling his vote for money, he does not extinguish in himself the general will, but only eludes it. The fault he commits is that of changing the state of the question, and answering something different from what he is asked. Instead of saying, by his vote, "It is to the advantage of the State," he says, "It is of advantage to this or that man or party that this or that view should prevail." Thus the law of public order in assemblies is not so much to maintain in them the general will as to secure that the question be always put to it, and the answer always given by it.

I could here set down many reflections on the simple right of voting in every act of Sovereignty—a right which no one can take from the citizens—and also on the right of stating views, making proposals, dividing and discussing, which the government is always most careful to leave solely to its members, but this important subject would need a treatise to itself, and it is impossible to say everything in a single work.

2. Voting

It may be seen, from the last chapter, that the way in which general business is managed may give a clear enough indication of the actual state of morals and the health of the body politic. The more concert reigns in the assemblies, that is, the nearer opinion approaches unanimity, the greater is the dominance of the general will. On the other hand, long debates, dissensions and tumult proclaim the ascendancy of particular interests and the decline of the State.

This seems less clear when two or more orders enter into the constitution, as patricians and plebeians did at Rome; for quarrels between these two orders often disturbed the comitia, even in the best days of the Republic. But the exception is rather apparent than real; for then, through the defect that is inherent in the body politic, there were, so to speak, two States in one, and what is not true of the two together is true of either separately. Indeed, even in the most stormy times, the plebiscita of the people, when the Senate did not interfere with them, always went through quietly and by large majorities. The citizens having but one interest, the people had but a single will.

At the other extremity of the circle, unanimity recurs; this is the case when the citizens, having fallen into servitude, have lost both liberty and will. Fear and flattery then change votes into acclamation; deliberation ceases, and only worship or malediction is left. Such was the vile manner in which the senate expressed its views under the Emperors. It did so sometimes with absurd precautions. Tacitus observes that, under Otho, the senators, while they heaped curses on Vitellius, contrived at the same time to make a deafening noise, in order that, should he ever become their master, he might not know what each of them had said.

On these various considerations depend the rules by which the methods of counting votes and comparing opinions should be regulated, according as the general will is more or less easy to discover, and the State more or less in its decline.

There is but one law which, from its nature, needs unanimous consent. This is the social compact; for civil association is the most voluntary of all acts. Every man being born free and his own master, no one, under any pretext whatsoever, can make any man subject without his consent. To decide that the son of a slave is born a slave is to decide that he is not born a man.

If then there are opponents when the social compact is made, their opposition does not invalidate the contract, but merely prevents them from being included in it. They are foreigners among citizens. When the State is instituted, residence constitutes consent; to dwell within its territory is to submit to the Sovereign.[1]

Apart from this primitive contract, the vote of the majority always binds all the rest. This follows from the contract itself. But it is asked how a man can be both free and forced to conform to wills that are not his own. How are the opponents at once free and subject to laws they have not agreed to?

I retort that the question is wrongly put. The citizen gives his consent to all the laws, including those which are passed in spite of his opposition, and even those which punish him when he dares to break any of them. The constant will of all the members of the State is the general will; by virtue of it they are citizens and free.[2] When in the popular assembly a law is proposed, what the people is asked is not exactly whether it approves or rejects the proposal, but whether it is in conformity with the general will, which is their will. Each man, in giving his vote, states his opinion on that point; and the general will is found by counting votes. When therefore the opinion that is contrary to my own prevails, this proves neither more nor less than that I was mistaken, and that what I thought to be the general will was not so. If my particular opinion had carried the day I should have achieved the opposite of what was my will; and it is in that case that I should not have been free.

This presupposes, indeed, that all the qualities of the general will still reside in the majority: when they cease to do so, whatever side a man may take, liberty is no longer possible.

In my earlier demonstration of how particular wills are substituted for the general will in public deliberation, I have adequately pointed out the practicable methods of avoiding this abuse; and I shall have more to say of them later on. I have also given the principles for determining the proportional number of votes for declaring that will. A difference of one vote destroys equality; a single opponent destroys unanimity; but between equality and unanimity, there are several grades of unequal division, at each of which this proportion may be fixed in accordance with the condition and the needs of the body politic.

There are two general rules that may serve to regulate this relation. First, the more grave and important the questions discussed, the nearer should the opinion that is to prevail approach unanimity. Secondly, the more the matter in hand calls for speed, the smaller the prescribed difference in the numbers of votes may be allowed to become: where an instant decision has to be reached, a majority of one vote should be enough. The first of these two rules seems more in harmony with the laws, and the second with practical affairs. In any case, it is the combination of them that gives the best proportions for determining the majority necessary.

1090

ENDNOTES

1. This should of course be understood as applying to a free State; for elsewhere family, goods, lack of a refuge, necessity, or violence may detain a man in a country against his will; and then his dwelling there no longer by itself implies his consent to the contract or to its violation.

2. At Genoa, the word *Liberty* may be read over the front of the prisons and on the chains of the galley-slaves. This application of the device is good and just. It is indeed only malefactors of all estates who prevent the citizen from being free. In the country in which all such men were in the galleys, the most perfect liberty would be enjoyed.

p. 295 Social order a sacred right, basis of other rights, but founded on conventions

p 296 Right of the strongest

p. 299 Right of slavery

p. 302 Civil right

p. 304 right of the first occupier

p. 304 right of property

NOTES

who was Stanton video

THE SOLITUDE OF SELF
Elizabeth Cady Stanton, January 18, 1892

Stanton delivered "The Solitude of Self" in 1892, at the convention at   1
which she resigned the presidency of the suffrage movement. Anthony
did not like the speech at first, but Stanton thought it "the best thing I have
ever written" and it remains one of the most moving statements of feminism
of any age.* Stanton's advanced age and her political isolation help to explain
the speech's sad, wearied tone, but her ultimate message was a triumphant
one, a powerful defense of the feminist philosophy by which she had lived
her life and made most of her political decisions.

The essence of Stanton's feminism was the belief that, ultimately, life
placed the same demands on women as on men, required the same resources   10
of them, and therefore, in justice, should provide them with the same individual rights. In this speech, however, her emphasis was shifting from individualism as a political philosophy to individualism as a psychological theory,
a description of the inner experience common to men and women. As such,
Stanton anticipated the existentialist philosophy associated with the rebirth
of feminism in our own time, and modern feminism's concern with the "personal" elements of women's experience.

The point I wish plainly to bring before you on this occasion is the individuality of each human soul; our Protestant idea, the right of individual
conscience and judgement; our republican idea, individual citizenship. In   20
discussing the rights of woman, we are to consider, first, what belongs to her
as an individual, in a world of her own, the arbiter of her own destiny, an
imaginary Robinson Crusoe, with her woman, Friday, on a solitary island.
Her rights under such circumstances are to use all her faculties for her own
safety and happiness.

Secondly, if we consider her as a citizen, as a member of a great nation,
she must have the same rights as all other members, according to the fundamental principles of our Government.

Thirdly, viewed as a woman, an equal factor in civilization, her rights and
duties are still the same—individual happiness and development.   30

Fourthly, it is only the incidental relations of life, such as mother, wife,
sister, daughter, which may involve some special duties and training. . . .

The strongest reason for giving woman all the opportunities for higher
education, for the full development of her faculties, her forces of mind and
body; for giving her the most enlarged freedom of thought and action; a
complete emancipation from all forms of bondage, of custom, dependence,
superstition; from all the crippling influences of fear—is the solitude and

Reprinted from *The Elizabeth Cady Stanton-Susan B. Anthony Reader: Correspondence, Writings, Speeches* (1992), Northeastern University Press.

*Stanton Letters, p. 280.

personal responsibility of her own individual life. The strongest reason why
we ask for woman a voice in the government under which she lives; in the
40   religion she is asked to believe; equality in social life, where she is the chief
factor; a place in the trades and professions, where she may earn her bread, is
because of her birthright to self-sovereignty; because, as an individual, she
must rely on herself. No matter how much women prefer to lean, to be protected and supported, nor how much men desire to have them do so, they
must make the voyage of life alone, and for safety in an emergency, they must
know something of the laws of navigation. To guide our own craft, we must
be captain, pilot, engineer; with chart and compass to stand at the wheel; to
watch the winds and waves, and know when to take in the sail, and to read
the signs in the firmament over all. It matters not whether the solitary voy-
50   ager is man or woman; nature, having endowed them equally, leaves them to
their own skill and judgment in the hour of danger, and, if not equal to the
occasion, alike they perish.

To appreciate the importance of fitting every human soul for independent action, think for a moment of the immeasurable solitude of self. We
come into the world alone, unlike all who have gone before us, we leave it
alone, under circumstances peculiar to ourselves. No mortal ever has been,
no mortal ever will be like the soul just launched on the sea of life. There can
never again be just such a combination of prenatal influences; never again
just such environments as make up the infancy, youth and manhood of this
60   one. Nature never repeats herself, and the possibilities of one human soul will
never be found in another. No one has ever found two blades of ribbon grass
alike, and no one will ever find two human beings alike. Seeing, then, what
must be the infinite diversity in human character, we can in a measure appreciate the loss to a nation when any large class of the people is uneducated and
unrepresented in the government.

We ask for the complete development of every individual, first, for his
own benefit and happiness. In fitting out an army, we give each soldier his
own knapsack, arms, powder, his blanket, cup, knife, fork and spoon. We
provide alike for all their individual necessities; then each man bears his own
70   burden.

Again, we ask complete individual development for the general good; for
the consensus of the competent on the whole round of human interests, on all
questions of national life; and here each man must bear his share of the general burden. It is sad to see how soon friendless children are left to bear their
own burdens, before they can analyze their feelings; before they can even tell
their joys and sorrows, they are thrown on their own resources. The great lesson that nature seems to teach us at all ages is self-dependence, self-protection,
self-support. . . .

In youth our most bitter disappointments, our brightest hopes and ambi-
80   tions, are known only to ourselves. Even our friendship and love we never
fully share with another; there is something of every passion, in every situation, we conceal. Even so in our triumphs and our defeats. . . .

We ask no sympathy from others in the anxiety and agony of a broken friendship or shattered love. When death sunders our nearest ties, alone we sit in the shadow of our affliction. Alike amid the greatest triumphs and darkest tragedies of life, we walk alone. On the divine heights of human attainment, eulogized and worshipped as a hero or saint, we stand alone. In ignorance, poverty and vice, as a pauper or criminal, alone we starve or steal; alone we suffer the sneers and rebuffs of our fellows; alone we are hunted and hounded through dark courts and alleys, in by-ways and high-ways; alone we stand in   90
the judgment seat; alone in the prison cell we lament our crimes and misfor-tunes; alone we expiate them on the gallows. In hours like these we realize the awful solitude of individual life, its pains, its penalties, its responsibilities; hours in which the youngest and most helpless are thrown on their own resources for guidance and consolation. Seeing, then, that life must ever be a march and a battle, that each soldier must be equipped for his own protection, it is the height of cruelty to rob the individual of a single natural right.

To throw obstacles in the way of a complete education is like putting out the eyes; to deny the rights of property is like cutting off the hands. To refuse political equality is to rob the ostracized of all self-respect; of credit in the   100
market place; of recompense in the world of work, of a voice in choosing those who make and administer the law, a choice in the jury before whom they are tried, and in the judge who decides their punishment. [Think of] . . . woman's position! Robbed of her natural rights, handicapped by law and custom at every turn, yet compelled to fight her own battles, and in the emer-gencies of life to fall back on herself for protection. . . .

The young wife and mother, at the head of some establishment, with a kind husband to shield her from the adverse winds of life, with wealth, for-tune and position, has a certain harbor of safety, secure against the ordinary ills of life. But to manage a household, have a desirable influence in society,   110
keep her friends and the affections of her husband, train her children and ser-vants well, she must have rare common sense, wisdom, diplomacy, and a knowledge of human nature. To do all this, she needs the cardinal virtues and the strong points of character that the most successful statesman possesses. An uneducated woman trained to dependence, with no resources in herself, must make a failure of any position in life. But society says women do not need a knowledge of the world, the liberal training that experience in public life must give, all the advantages of collegiate education; but when for the lack of all this, the woman's happiness is wrecked, alone she bears her humiliation; and the solitude of the weak and the ignorant is indeed pitiable. In the wild chase   120
for the prizes of life, they are ground to powder.

In age, when the pleasures of youth are passed, children grown up, mar-ried and gone, the hurry and bustle of life in a measure over, when the hands are weary of active service, when the old arm chair and the fireside are the cho-sen resorts, then men and women alike must fall back on their own resources. If they cannot find companionship in books, if they have no interest in the vital questions of the hour, no interest in watching the consummation of reforms with which they might have been identified, they soon pass into their dotage. The more fully the faculties of the mind are developed and kept in use, 130   the longer the period of vigor and active interest in all around us continues. If, from a life-long participation in public affairs, a woman feels responsible for the laws regulating our system of education, the discipline of our jails and prisons, the sanitary condition of our private homes, public buildings and thoroughfares, an interest in commerce, finance, our foreign relations, in any or all these questions, her solitude will at least be respectable, and she will not be driven to gossip or scandal for entertainment.

The chief reason for opening to every soul the doors to the whole round of human duties and pleasures is the individual development thus attained, the resources thus provided under all circumstances to mitigate the solitude 140   that at times must come to everyone.

. . . Inasmuch, then, as woman shares equally the joys and sorrows of time and eternity, is it not the height of presumption in man to propose to represent her at the ballot box and the throne of grace, to do her voting in the state, her praying in the church, and to assume the position of high priest at the family altar?

Nothing strengthens the judgment and quickens the conscience like individual responsibility. Nothing adds such dignity to character as the recognition of one's self-sovereignty; the right to an equal place, everywhere conceded—a place earned by personal merit, not an artificial attainment by inheritance, 150   wealth, family and position. Conceding, then, that the responsibilities of life rest equally on man and woman, that their destiny is the same, they need the same preparation for time and eternity. The talk of sheltering woman from the fierce storms of life is the sheerest mockery, for they beat on her from every point of the compass, just as they do on man, and with more fatal results, for he has been trained to protect himself, to resist, and to conquer. Such are the facts in human experience, the responsibilities of individual sovereignty. Rich and poor, intelligent and ignorant, wise and foolish, virtuous and vicious, man and woman; it is ever the same, each soul must depend wholly on itself.

Whatever the theories may be of woman's dependence on man, in the 160   supreme moments of her life, he cannot bear her burdens. Alone she goes to the gates of death to give life to every man that is born into the world; no one can share her fears, no one can mitigate her pangs; and if her sorrow is greater than she can bear, alone she passes beyond the gates into the vast unknown.

From the mountain-tops of Judea long ago, a heavenly voice bade his disciples, "Bear ye one another's burdens"; but humanity has not yet risen to that point of self-sacrifice; and if ever so willing, how few the burdens are that one soul can bear for another! . . .

So it ever must be in the conflicting scenes of life, in the long, weary 170   march, each one walks alone. We may have many friends, love, kindness, sympathy and charity, to smooth our pathway in everyday life, but in the tragedies and triumphs of human experience, each mortal stands alone.

But when all artificial trammels are removed, and women are recognized as individuals, responsible for their own environments, thoroughly educated for all positions in life they may be called to fill; with all the resources in themselves that liberal thought and broad culture can give; guided by their own conscience and judgment, trained to self-protection, by a healthy development of the muscular system, and skill in the use of weapons and defence; and stimulated to self-support by a knowledge of the business world and the pleasure that pecuniary independence must ever give; when women are trained in this way, they will in a measure be fitted for those hours of solitude that come alike to all, whether prepared or otherwise. As in our extremity we must depend on ourselves, the dictates of wisdom point to complete individual development.

In talking of education, how shallow the argument that each class must be educated for the special work it proposes to do, and that all those faculties not needed in this special work must lie dormant and utterly wither for want of use, when, perhaps, these will be the very faculties needed in life's greatest emergencies! Some say, "Where is the use of drilling girls in the languages, the sciences, in law, medicine, theology. As wives, mothers, housekeepers, cooks, they need a different curriculum from boys who are to fill all positions. The chief cooks in our great hotels and ocean steamers are men. In our large cities, men run the bakeries; they make our bread, cake and pies. They manage the laundries; they are now considered our best milliners and dressmakers. Because some men fill these departments of usefulness, shall we regulate the curriculum in Harvard and Yale to their present necessities? If not, why this talk in our best colleges of a curriculum for girls who are crowding into the trades and professions, teachers in all our public schools, rapidly filling many lucrative and honorable positions in life?"

. . . Women are already the equals of men in the whole realm of thought, in art, science, literature and government. . . . The poetry and novels of the century are theirs, and they have touched the keynote of reform, in religion, politics and social life. They fill the editor's and professor's chair, plead at the bar of justice, walk the wards of the hospital, speak from the pulpit and the platform. Such is the type of womanhood that an enlightened public sentiment welcomes to-day, and such the triumph of the facts of life over the false theories of the past.

Is it, then, consistent to hold the developed woman of this day within the same narrow political limits as the dame with the spinning wheel and knitting needle occupied in the past? No, no! Machinery has taken the labors of woman as well as man on its tireless shoulders; the loom and the spinning wheel are but dreams of the past; the pen, the brush, the easel, the chisel, have taken their places, while the hopes and ambitions of women are essentially changed.

We see reason sufficient in the outer conditions of human beings for individual liberty and development, but when we consider the self-dependence of every human soul, we see the need of courage, judgment and the exercise of every faculty of mind and body, strengthened and developed by use, in woman as well as man.

220   Whatever may be said of man's protecting power in ordinary conditions, amid all the terrible disasters by land and sea, in the supreme moments of danger, alone woman must ever meet the horrors of the situation. The Angel of Death even makes no royal pathway for her. Man's love and sympathy enter only into the sunshine of our lives. In that solemn solitude of self, that links us with the immeasurable and the eternal, each soul lives alone forever. A recent writer says: "I remember once, in crossing the Atlantic, to have gone upon the deck of the ship at midnight, when a dense black cloud enveloped the sky, and the great deep was roaring madly under the lashes of demoniac winds. My feeling was not of danger or fear (which is a base surrender of the
230   immortal soul) but of utter desolation and loneliness; a little speck of life shut in by a tremendous darkness. . . ."

And yet, there is a solitude which each and every one of us has always carried with him, more inaccessible than the ice-cold mountains, more profound than the midnight sea; the solitude of self. Our inner being which we call ourself, no eye nor touch of man or angel has ever pierced. It is more hidden than the caves of the gnome; the sacred adytum of the oracle; the hidden chamber of Eleusinian mystery, for to it only omniscience is permitted to enter.

Such is individual life. Who, I ask you, can take, dare take on himself the
240   rights, the duties, the responsibilities of another human soul?

THE DEVELOPMENT OF WHITE IDENTITY
"I'M NOT ETHNIC, I'M JUST NORMAL"
Beverly Daniel Tatum

I often begin the classes and workshops I lead by asking participants to
reflect on their own social class and ethnic background in small discussion
groups. The first question I pose is one that most people of color answer
without hesitation: "What is your class and ethnic background?" White participants, however, often pause before responding. On one such occasion a
young White woman quickly described herself as middle-class but seemed
stumped as to how to describe herself ethnically. Finally, she said, "I'm just
normal!" What did she mean? She explained that she did not identify with
any particular ethnic heritage, and that she was a lot like the other people
who lived in her very homogeneous White middle-class community. But her
choice of words was telling. If she is just normal, are those who are different
from her "just abnormal"?

Like many White people, this young woman had never really considered her own racial and ethnic group membership. For her, Whiteness was
simply the unexamined norm. Because they represent the societal norm,
Whites can easily reach adulthood without thinking much about their
racial group. For example, one White teacher who was taking a professional
development course on racism with me wrote in one of her papers: "I am
thirty-five years old and I never really started thinking about race too much
until now, and that makes me feel uncomfortable. . . . I just think for some
reason I didn't know. No one taught us." There is a lot of silence about race
in White communities, and as a consequence Whites tend to think of racial
identity as something that other people have, not something that is salient
for them. But when, for whatever reason, the silence is broken, a process of
racial identity development for Whites begins to unfold.

Counseling psychologist Janet Helms has described this process of development for Whites in her book *Black and White Racial Identity Development:
Theory, Research, and Practice.* She assumes, as do I, that in a race-conscious
society, racial group membership has psychological implications. The messages we receive about assumed superiority or inferiority shape our perceptions of reality and influence our interactions with others. While the task for
people of color is to resist negative societal messages and develop an empowered sense of self in the face of a racist society, Helms says the task for Whites
is to develop a positive White identity based in reality, not on assumed superiority. In order to do that each person must become aware of his or her
Whiteness, accept it as personally and socially significant, and learn to feel

1

10

20

30

Reprinted from *Why Are All the Black Kids Sitting Together in the Cafeteria?: A Psychologist
Explains the Development of Racial Identity* (1997), by permission of Perseus Books Group.

good about it, not in the sense of a Klan member's "White pride," but in the context of a commitment to a just society.

It comes as a surprise to some White people to think about their race in
40 this way. "Of course White people feel good about being White," they say. But that is not my experience with my students or with the people who come to my workshops. Most of the White people I talk to either have not thought about their race and so don't feel anything, or have thought about it and felt guilt and shame. These feelings of guilt and shame are part of the hidden costs of racism.

How can White people achieve a healthy sense of White identity? Helms's model is instructive. For Whites, there are two major developmental tasks in this process, the abandonment of individual racism and the recognition of and opposition to institutional and cultural racism. These tasks occur over
50 six stages: *contact, disintegration, reintegration, pseudo-independent, immersion/emersion,* and *autonomy.*

ABANDONING RACISM

At the contact stage, the first step in the process, Whites pay little attention to the significance of their racial identity. As exemplified by the "I'm just normal" comment, individuals at this point of development rarely describe themselves as White. If they have lived, worked, or gone to school in predominantly White settings, they may simply think of themselves as being part of the racial norm and take this for granted without conscious consideration of their White privilege, the systematically conferred advantages they receive simply because they are White.

60 While they have been breathing the "smog" and have internalized many of the prevailing societal stereotypes of people of color, they typically are unaware of this socialization process. They often perceive themselves as colorblind, completely free of prejudice, unaware of their own assumptions about other racial groups. In addition, they usually think of racism as the prejudiced behaviors of individuals rather than as an institutionalized system of advantage benefiting Whites in subtle as well as blatant ways. Peggy McIntosh speaks for many Whites at the contact level when she writes, "I was taught to recognize racism only in individual acts of meanness by members of my group, never in invisible systems conferring unsought racial domi-
70 nance on my group from birth."

While some Whites may grow up in families where they are encouraged to embrace the ideology of White superiority (children of Klan members, for example), for many Whites this early stage of racial identity development represents the passive absorption of subtly communicated messages. Robert Carter, another racial identity researcher, illustrates this point when he quotes a forty-four-year-old White male who grew up in upstate New York, where he had limited direct contact with Blacks.

There was no one to compare ourselves to. As you would drive through other neighborhoods, I think there was a clear message of difference or even superiority. The neighborhoods were poorer, and it was probably subtle, I don't remember my parents being bigoted, although by today's standards they clearly were. I think there was probably a message of superiority. The underlying messages were subtle. No one ever came out and said, White people are this and Black people are like this. I think the underlying message is that White people are generally good and they're like us, us and them.

These messages may go unchallenged and unexamined for a long time. However, the next level, disintegration, is marked by a growing awareness of racism and White privilege as a result of personal encounters in which the social significance of race is made visible. For some White people, disintegration occurs when they develop a close friendship or a romantic relationship with a person of color. The White person then sees firsthand how racism can operate. For example, one female college student described her experiences shopping with a Puerto Rican roommate. She couldn't help noticing how her Latina friend was followed around in stores and was asked for more identification than Whites when writing checks: She also saw how her friend's Black boyfriend was frequently asked to show his college ID when he visited their residence hall, while young White men came and went without being questioned. For other White people, disintegration may result from seeing racist incidents such as the police beating of Rodney King or participating in an "unlearning racism" workshop. Certainly being in a classroom where the social consequences of racial group membership are explicitly discussed as part of the course content is likely to trigger the process.

Once the silence is broken, the cycle of racism becomes increasingly visible. For example, in my class I show a very powerful video, *Ethnic Notions,* on the dehumanizing images of African Americans in the popular culture from before the Civil War through the twentieth century. The video links the nineteenth-century caricatures of Black physical features, commonly published racial epithets, and the early cinematic portrayals of stupid but happy "darkies," menacing Black "savages," and heavyset, caretaking "mammies," to their updated forms in today's media. After seeing this film, students can't help but notice the pervasiveness of racial stereotyping on television each night. The same programs they used to find entertaining now offend them. They start to notice the racism in the everyday language of family and friends. For example, one White student reported that when she asked her roommate to get her a glass of water, the White roommate jokingly replied, "Do I look Black to you?" Although I had never heard of this expression, it was very familiar to the student. Yet, before then, she had never recognized the association of Blackness with servitude, and the assumed superiority of Whiteness being conveyed in the remark.

This new awareness is characterized by discomfort. The uncomfortable emotions of guilt, shame, and anger are often related to a new awareness of one's personal prejudices or the prejudices within one's family. The following excerpts from the journals of two White students illustrate this point:

> Today was the first class on racism. . . . Before today I didn't think I was exposed to any form of racism. Well, except for my father. He is about as prejudiced as they come.
>
> It really bothers me that stereotypes exist because it is from them that I originally became uninformed. My grandmother makes all kinds of decisions based on stereotypes—who to hire, who to help out. When I was growing up, the only Black people that I knew were adults [household help], but I admired them just as much as any other adult. When I expressed these feelings to my parents, I was always told that the Black people that I knew were the exceptions and that the rest of the race were different. I, too, was taught to be afraid.

Others' parents were silent on the subject of racism, simply accepting the status quo.

Those whose parents were actively antiracist may feel less guilt, but often still feel unprepared for addressing racism outside the family, a point highlighted by the comments of this young woman:

> Talking with other class members, I realized how exceptional my parents were. Not only were they not overtly racist but they also tried to keep society's subtle racism from reaching me. Basically I grew up believing that racism was no longer an issue and all people should be treated as equals. Unfortunately, my parents were not being very realistic as society's racism did begin to reach me. They did not teach me how to support and defend their views once I was interacting in a society without them as a buffer.

At the disintegration stage, White individuals begin to see how much their lives and the lives of people of color have been affected by racism in our society. The societal inequities they now notice directly contradict the idea of an American meritocracy, a concept that has typically been an integral part of their belief system. The cognitive dissonance that results is part of the discomfort which is experienced at this point in the process of development. Responses to this discomfort may include denying the validity of the information that is being presented, or psychologically or physically withdrawing from it. The logic is, "If I don't read about racism, talk about racism, watch those documentaries or special news programs, or spend time with those people of color, I won't have to feel uncomfortable." (In the case of my students, this is usually not an option. By the time they have to deal with these emotional responses, it is too late to drop the course.)

If the individual remains engaged, he or she can turn the discomfort into action. Once they have an awareness of the cycle of racism, many people are angered by it and want to interrupt it. Often action comes in the form of educating others—pointing out the stereotypes as they watch television, interrupting the racial jokes, writing letters to the editor, sharing articles with friends and family. Like new converts, people experiencing disintegration can be quite zealous in their efforts. A White woman in her forties who participated in an antiracist professional development course for educators described herself at this stage: 170

What it was like for me when I was taking the course [one year ago] and just afterwards, hell, because this dissonance stuff doesn't feel all that great. And trying to put it in a perspective and figure out what to do with it is very hard. . . . I was on the band wagon so I'm not going to be quiet about it. So there was dissonance everywhere. Personally, I remember going home for Thanksgiving, the first Thanksgiving [while taking the course], back to our families . . . and turning to my brother-in-law and saying, "I really don't want you to say that in front of me— I don't want to hear that joke—I am not interested." . . . At every turn it seemed like there, I was *responsible* for saying something. . . . My husband, who I think is a very good, a very liberal person, but who really hasn't been through [this], saying, "You know I think you're taking yourself too seriously here and where is your sense of humor? You have lost your sense of humor." And my saying, "It isn't funny; you don't understand, it just isn't funny to me." Not that he would ever tell a racial joke, but there were these things that would come up and he would just sort of look back and say, "I don't understand where you're coming from now." So there was a lot of dissonance. . . . I don't think anybody was too comfortable with me for a while.   180

My college students have similar experiences with family members and   190
friends. Though they want to step off the cycle of racism, the message from the surrounding White community seems to be, "Get back on!" A very poignant example of this was shared with me by a young White man from a very privileged background. He wrote:

I realized that it was possible to simply go through life totally oblivious to the entire situation or, even if one realizes it, one can totally repress it. It is easy to fade into the woodwork, run with the rest of society, and never have to deal with these problems. So many people I know from home are like this. They have simply accepted what society has taught them with little, if any, question. My father is a prime   200
example of this. . . . It has caused much friction in our relationship, and he often tells me as a father he has failed in raising me correctly. Most of my high school friends will never deal with these issues and

propagate them on to their own children. It's easy to see how the cycle continues. I don't think I could ever justify within myself simply turning my back on the problem. I finally realized that my position in all of these dominant groups gives me power to make change occur. . . .

It is an unfortunate result often though that I feel alienated from friends and family. It's often played off as a mere stage that I'm going
210   through. I obviously can't tell if it's merely a stage, but I know that they say this to take the attention off of the truth of what I'm saying. By belittling me, they take the power out of my argument. It's very depressing that being compassionate and considerate are seen as only phases that people go through. I don't want it to be a phase for me, but as obvious as this may sound, I look at my environment and often wonder how it will not be.

The social pressure from friends and acquaintances to collude, to not notice racism, can be quite powerful.

But it is very difficult to stop noticing something once it has been pointed
220   out. The conflict between noticing and not noticing generates internal tension, and there is a great desire to relieve it. Relief often comes through what Helms calls reintegration. At this stage, the previous feelings of guilt or denial may be transformed into fear and anger directed toward people of color. The logic is, "If there is a problem with racism, then you people of color must have done something to cause it. And if you would just change your behavior, the problem would go away." The elegance of this argument is that it relieves the White person of all responsibility for social change.

I am sometimes asked if it is absolutely necessary to go through this phase. Must one blame the victim? Although it is not inevitable, most White
230   people who speak up against racism will attest to the temptation they sometimes feel to slip back into collusion and silence. Because the pressure to ignore racism and to accept the socially sanctioned stereotypes is so strong, and the system of advantage so seductive, many White people get stuck in reintegration thinking. The psychological tension experienced at this stage is clearly expressed by Connie, a White woman of Italian ancestry who took my course on the psychology of racism. After reading about the stages of White identity development, she wrote:

There was a time when I never considered myself a color. I never described myself as a "White, Italian female" until I got to college and
240   noticed that people of color always described themselves by their color/race. While taking this class, I have begun to understand that being White makes a difference. I never thought about it before, but there are many privileges to being White. In my personal life, I cannot say that I have ever felt that I have had the advantage over a Black person, but I am aware that my race has the advantage.

I am feeling really guilty lately about that. I find myself thinking: "I didn't mean to be White, I really didn't mean it." I am starting to feel angry toward my race for ever using this advantage toward personal gains. But at the same time I resent the minority groups. I mean, it's not my fault that society has deemed us "superior." I don't feel any better than a Black person. But it really doesn't matter because I am a member of the dominant race. . . . I can't help it . . . and I sometimes get angry and feel like I'm being attacked.

  250

  I guess my anger toward a minority group would enter me into the next stage of Reintegration where I am once again starting to blame the victim. This is all very trying for me and it has been on my mind a lot. I really would like to be able to reach the last stage . . . where I can accept being White without hostility and anger. That is really hard to do.

"BUT I'M AN INDIVIDUAL!"

Another source of the discomfort and anger that Whites often experience in this phase stems from the frustration of being seen as a group member, rather than as an individual. People of color learn early in life that they are seen by others as members of a group. For Whites, thinking of oneself only as an individual is a legacy of White privilege. As McIntosh writes, "I can swear, or dress in second hand clothes, or not answer letters, without having people attribute these choices to the bad morals, the poverty, or the illiteracy of my race. . . . I can do well in a challenging situation without being called a credit to my race. . . . I am never asked to speak for all the people of my racial group." In short, she and other Whites are perceived as individuals most of the time.

  260

  270

  The view of oneself as an individual is very compatible with the dominant ideology of rugged individualism and the American myth of meritocracy. Understanding racism as a system of advantage that structurally benefits Whites and disadvantages people of color on the basis of group membership threatens not only beliefs about society but also beliefs about one's own life accomplishments. For example, organizational consultant Nancie Zane writes that senior White male managers "were clearly invested in the notion that their hard work, ingenuity and skills had won them their senior-level positions." As others talked about the systemic racist and sexist barriers to their own achievement, "white men heard it as a condemnation that they somehow didn't 'deserve' their position." If viewing oneself as a group member threatens one's self-definition, making the paradigm shift from individual to group member will be painful.

  280

  In the case of White men, both maleness and Whiteness are normative, so acknowledging group status may be particularly difficult. Those White women who have explored their subordinate gender identity have made at least some movement away from the notion of a strictly individual self-definition and may find it easier to grasp the significance of their racial group membership. However, as McIntosh and others have pointed out, understanding one form of oppression does not guarantee recognition of another.

Those Whites who are highly identified with a particular subordinate identity may also struggle with claiming Whiteness as a meaningful group category because they feel far from the White male norm. For example, Jewish people of European ancestry sometimes do not think of themselves as White because for them the term means White Christian. Also, in Nazi Germany, Jews were defined as a distinct, non-Aryan racial group. In the context of an anti-Jewish culture, the salient identity may be the targeted Jewish identity. However, in terms of U.S. racial ideology, Jews of European ancestry are also the beneficiaries of White racial privilege. My White Jewish students often struggle with the tension between being targeted and receiving privilege. In this case, as in others, the reality of multiple identities complicates the process of coming to terms with one particular dimension of identity. For example, one student wrote:

> I am constantly afraid that people will see my assertion of my Jewish identity as a denial of whiteness, as a way of escaping the acknowledgment of white privilege. I feel I am both part of and not part of whiteness. I am struggling to be more aware of my white privilege . . . but I will not do so at the cost of having my Jewishness erased.

Similarly, White lesbians sometimes find it hard to claim privileged status as Whites when they are so targeted by homophobia and heterosexism, often at the hands of other Whites.

These complexities notwithstanding, when White men and women begin to understand that they are viewed as members of a dominant racial group not only by other Whites but also by people of color, they are sometimes troubled, even angered, to learn that simply because of their group status they are viewed with suspicion by many people of color. "I'm an individual, view me as an individual!" For example, in a racially mixed group of educators participating in an antiracist professional development course, a Black man commented about using his "radar" to determine if the group would be a safe place for him. Many of the White people in the room, who believed that their very presence in the course was proof of their trustworthiness, were upset by the comment, initially unprepared to acknowledge the invisible legacy of racism that accompanied any and every interaction they had with people of color. The White people in the course found some comfort in reading Lois Stalvey's memoir, *The Education of a WASP,* in which she described her own responses to the ways Black people tested her trustworthiness. She writes,

I could never resent the tests as some white people have told me they
do. . . . But to me, the longest tests have always indicated the deepest
hurts. We whites would have to be naive to expect that hundreds of
years of humiliation can be forgotten the moment we wish it to be. At
times, the most poignant part of the test is that black people have
enough trust left to give it. Testing implies we might pass the test. It
is safer and easier for a black person to turn his back on us. If he does
not gamble on our sincerity, he cannot be hurt if we prove false. Testing shows an optimism I doubt I could duplicate if I were black.

Sometimes poorly organized antiracism workshops or other educational
experiences can create a scenario that places participants at risk for getting
stuck in their anger. Effective consciousness-raising about racism must also
point the way toward constructive action. When people don't have the tools
for moving forward, they tend to return to what is familiar, often becoming
more vigorous in their defense of the racial status quo than they were initially.

As we have seen, many White people experience themselves as powerless,
even in the face of privilege. But the fact is that we all have a sphere of influence, some domain in which we exercise some level of power and control.
The task for each of us, White and of color, is to identify what our own
sphere of influence is (however large or small) and to consider how it might
be used to interrupt the cycle of racism.

DEFINING A POSITIVE WHITE IDENTITY

As a White person's understanding of the complexity of institutional racism
in our society deepens, the less likely he or she is to resort to explanations
that blame the victim. Instead, deepening awareness usually leads to a commitment to unlearn one's racism, and marks the emergence of the pseudo-
independent stage.

Sometimes epitomized by the "guilty White liberal" persona, the pseudo-
independent individual has an intellectual understanding of racism as a system
of advantage, but doesn't quite know what to do about it. Self-conscious and
guilty about one's own Whiteness, the individual often desires to escape it by
associating with people of color. Ruth Frankenberg, author of *White Women,
Race Matters: The Social Construction of Whiteness,* describes the confusing emotions of this process in an autobiographical essay. "I viewed my racial privilege
as total. I remember months when I was terrified to speak in gatherings that
were primarily of color, since I feared that anything I did say would be marked
by my whiteness, my racial privilege (which in my mind meant the same)."
When her friends of color were making casual conversation—chatting about
their mothers, for example—she would worry that anything she might say
about her own mother would somehow reveal her race privilege, and by the

time she had sorted it out mentally, the topic of conversation would have changed. She writes, "In that silence, I tried to 'pass' (as what? as racially unmarked? as exceptional? as the one white girl who could 'hang'?)."

370   Similarly, a student of mine writes:

> One of the major and probably most difficult steps in identity development is obtaining or finding the consciousness of what it means to be White. I definitely remember many a time that I wished I was not White, ashamed of what I and others have done to the other racial groups in the world. . . . I wanted to pretend I was Black, live with them, celebrate their culture, and deny my Whiteness completely. Basically, I wanted to escape the responsibility that came with identifying myself as "White."

How successful these efforts to escape Whiteness via people of color will
380   be depends in part on the racial identity development of the people of color involved. Remember the Black students at the cafeteria table? If they are in the encounter or immersion/emersion stages, they are not likely to be interested in cultivating White friendships. If a White person reaches out to a Black person and is rebuffed, it may cause the White person to retreat into "blame the victim" thinking. However, even if these efforts to build interracial relationships are successful, the White individual must eventually confront the reality of his or her own Whiteness.

We all must be able to embrace who we are in terms of our racial and cultural heritage, not in terms of assumed superiority or inferiority, but as an
390   integral part of our daily experience in which we can take pride. But, as we see in these examples, for many White people who at this stage have come to understand the everyday reality of racism, Whiteness is still experienced as a source of shame rather than as a source of pride.

Recognizing the need to find a more positive self-definition is a hallmark of the next phase of White racial identity development, the immersion/emersion stage. Bob, a White male student in my racism class, clearly articulated this need.

> I'm finding that this idea of White identity is more important than I thought. Yet White identity seems very hard to pin hole. I seem to
400   have an idea and feel myself understanding what I need to do and why and then something presents itself that throws me into mass confusion. I feel that I need some resources that will help me through the process of finding White identity.

The resource Bob needs most at this point are not people of color, but other Whites who are further along in the process and can help show him the way.

It is at just this point that White individuals intensify their efforts to see their Whiteness in a positive light. Just as Cross describes the period of Black

redefinition as a time for Black people to seek new ways of thinking about Blackness, ways that take them beyond the role of victim, White people must seek new ways of thinking about Whiteness, ways that take them beyond the   410
role of victimizer.

THE SEARCH FOR WHITE ALLIES
AND THE RESTORATION OF HOPE

In fact, another role does exist. There is a history of White protest against racism, a history of Whites who have resisted the role of oppressor and who have been allies to people of color. Unfortunately these Whites are often invisible to us. While the names of active racists are easily recalled—past and present Klan leaders and Southern segregationists, for example—the names of White allies are often unknown. I have had the experience of addressing roomfuls of classroom teachers who have been unable to name even one White person who has worked against racism without some prompting from me. If they can't do it, it is likely that their students can't either.   420

Those who have studied or lived through the Civil Rights era (many of my students have not) may know the names of Viola Liuzzo, James Reeb, or Michael Schwerner, White civil rights workers who were killed for their antiracist efforts. But most people don't want to be martyrs. There is a need to know about White allies who spoke up, who worked for social change, who resisted racism and lived to tell about it. How did these White allies break free from the confines of the racist socialization they surely experienced to claim this identity for themselves? These are the voices that many White people at this stage in the process are hungry to hear.

Biographies of or autobiographies by White individuals who have been   430
engaged in antiracist activities can be very helpful. For example, there is *A Season of Justice,* the autobiography of Morris Dees, the executive director of the Southern Poverty Law Center and a vigorous anti-Klan litigator. There is *Outside the Magic Circle,* the oral history of Virginia Foster Durr, a Southern belle turned civil rights activist. And there is *The Education of a WASP,* the story of Lois Stalvey, a mother struggling to create a nonracist environment for her children. Such books can be an antidote to the feelings of isolation and loneliness that White people often feel at this point. There is comfort in knowing that others have traveled this terrain.

One of the consequences of racism in our society is that those who oppose   440
racism are often marginalized, and as a result, their stories are not readily accessed. Yet having access to these stories makes a difference to those Whites who are looking for ways to be agents of change. White people who are doing this work need to make their stories known to serve as guides for others.

In my class I try to address the lack of knowledge of White role models by providing concrete examples of such people. In addition to assigning reading material, my strategy has been to invite a local White antiracist activist, Andrea Ayvazian, to my class to speak about her own personal journey

toward an awareness of racism and her development as a White ally. Students
450   typically ask questions that reflect their fears about social isolation at this
phase of development. "Did you lose friends when you started to speak up?"
"My boyfriend makes a lot of racist comments. What can I do?" "What do
you say to your father at Thanksgiving when he tells those jokes?" These are
not just the questions of late adolescents. The mature White teachers I work
with ask the same things.

My White students, who often comment about how depressing it is to
study racism, typically say that the opportunity to talk with this ally gave
them renewed hope. Through her example, they see that the role of the ally
is not to help victims of racism, but to speak up against systems of oppres-
460   sion and to challenge other Whites to do the same. One point that Andrea
emphasizes in her speaking and writing is the idea that "allies need allies,"
others who will support their efforts to swim against the tide of cultural and
institutional racism. This point was especially helpful for one young woman
who had been struggling with feelings of isolation. She wrote:

> About being an ally, a positive role model: . . . it enhanced my positive
> feelings about the difference each individual (me!) can make. I don't
> need to feel helpless when there is so much I can do. I still can see how
> easily things can back-up and start getting depressing, but I can also see
> how it is possible to keep going strong and powerful. One of the most
470   > important points she made was the necessity of a support group/
> system; people to remind me of what I have done, why I should keep
> going, of why I'm making a difference, why I shouldn't feel helpless. I
> think our class started to help me with those issues, as soon as I started
> to let it, and now I've found similar supports in friends and family.
> They're out there, it's just finding and establishing them—it really is a
> necessity. Without support, it would be too easy to give up, burn-out,
> become helpless again. In any endeavor support is important, but
> when the forces against you are so prevalent and deep-rooted as racism
> is in this society, it is the only way to keep moving forward.

480   Participation in White consciousness-raising groups organized specifically
for the purpose of examining one's own racism are another way to "keep moving forward." At Mount Holyoke College such a group, White Women
Against Racism, was formed following the 1992 acquittal of the Los Angeles
police officers involved in the beating of Rodney King. There are similar
groups with different names operating formally and informally in local communities around the country. Support groups of this nature help to combat
the social isolation that antiracist Whites often experience, and provide places
to forge new identities.

I am sometimes asked why such groups need to be made up of Whites
490   only. To many Whites it seems inconceivable that there would be any value
in participating in all-White discussions of racism. While of course there is

value in cross-racial dialogue, all-White support groups serve a unique function. Particularly when Whites are trying to work through their feelings of guilt and shame, separate groups give White people the "space to speak with honesty and candor rarely possible in racially-mixed groups." Even when Whites feel comfortable sharing these feelings with people of color, frankly, people of color don't necessarily want to hear about it. The following comment, written by a Black woman in my class, illustrates this dilemma:

> Many times in class I feel uncomfortable when White students use the
> term Black because even if they aren't aware of it they say it with all   500
> or at least a lot of the negative connotations they've been taught goes
> along with Black. Sometimes it just causes a stinging feeling inside of
> me. Sometimes I get real tired of hearing White people talk about the
> conditions of Black people. I think it's an important thing for them
> to talk about, but still I don't always like being around when they do
> it. I also get tired of hearing them talk about how hard it is for them,
> though I understand it, and most times I am very willing to listen and
> be open, but sometimes I can't. Right now I can't.

Though a White person may need to describe the racist things a parent or spouse has said or done, to tell the story to a person of color may reopen   510
that person's wounds. Listening to those stories and problem-solving about them is a job that White people can do for each other.

It is at this stage of redefining Whiteness, immersion/emersion, that the feelings of guilt and shame start to fade. Reflecting on her own White identity development, sociologist Becky Thompson chronicles this process:

> [I understood] that I didn't have to recreate the wheel in my own life.
> I began to actively seek writing by white women who have historically
> stood up against racism—Elly Bulkin, Lillian Smith, Sara Evans,
> Angelina Grimke, Ruth Frankenberg, Helen Joseph, Melanie Kaye/
> Kantrowitz, Tillie Olsen, Minnie Bruce Pratt, Ruth Seid, Mab Seg-   520
> rest, and others.

She also realized that she needed antiracist White people in her daily life with whom she could share stories and whom she could trust to give her honest feedback. Her experience in a White antiracism group helped her to stop feeling bad because she was White. She writes, "I started seeing ways to channel my energies without trying to leave a piece of my identity behind."

The last stage, autonomy, represents the culmination of the White racial developmental process. At this point, a person incorporates the newly defined view of Whiteness as part of a personal identity. The positive feelings associated with this redefinition energize the person's efforts to confront racism and   530
oppression in daily life. Clayton Alderfer, a White man with many years of personal and professional experience, describes the thinking that characterizes

this stage. "We have a more complete awareness of ourselves and of others to the degree that we neither negate the uniqueness of each person, regardless of that person's group memberships nor deny the ever-present effects of group memberships for each individual."

While autonomy might be described as racial self-actualization, racial identity development never really ends. The person at this level is continually open to new information and new ways of thinking about racial and cultural variables. Helms describes each of the six stages as representing patterns of thinking that predominate at particular points of development. But even when active antiracist thinking predominates, there may still be particular situations that trigger old modes of responding. Whites, like people of color, continue to be works in progress.

A major benefit of this racial identity development process is increased effectiveness in multiracial settings. The White person who has worked through his or her own racial identity process has a deep understanding of racism and an appreciation and respect for the identity struggles of people of color. When we see strong, mutually respectful relationships between people of color and Whites, we are usually looking at the tangible results of both people's identity processes. If we want to promote positive cross-group relations, we need to help young White people engage in the kind of dialogue that precipitates this kind of identity development just as we need to help youth of color achieve an empowered sense of racial and ethnic identity.

Though the process of examining their racial identity can be uncomfortable and even frightening for Whites, those who persist in the struggle are rewarded with an increasingly multiracial and multicultural existence. In our still quite segregated society, this "borderland" is unfamiliar to many Whites and may be hard to envision. Becky Thompson has experienced it, and she writes: "We need to talk about what living in this borderland feels like, how we get there, what sustains us, and how we benefit from it. For me, this place of existence is tremendously exciting, invigorating, and life-affirming." Though it can also be "complicated and lonely," it is also liberating, opening doors to new communities, creating possibilities for more authentic connections with people of color, and in the process, strengthening the coalitions necessary for genuine social change.

THE UNITED STATES CONSTITUTION

PREAMBLE

We the People of the United States, in Order to form a more perfect   1
Union, establish Justice, insure domestic Tranquility, provide for the
common defense, promote the general Welfare, and secure the Blessings of
Liberty to ourselves and our Posterity, do ordain and establish this Constitution for the United States of America.

ARTICLE I.

Section 8.*

Clause 1: The Congress shall have Power To lay and collect Taxes, Duties,
  Imposts and Excises, to pay the Debts and provide for the common
  Defense and general Welfare of the United States; but all Duties,
  Imposts and Excises shall be uniform throughout the United States;

Clause 2: To borrow Money on the credit of the United States;   10

Clause 3: To regulate Commerce with foreign Nations, and among the
  several States, and with the Indian Tribes;

Clause 4: To establish an uniform Rule of Naturalization, and uniform
  Laws on the subject of Bankruptcies throughout the United States;

Clause 5: To coin Money, regulate the Value thereof, and of foreign
  Coin, and fix the Standard of Weights and Measures;

Clause 6: To provide for the Punishment of counterfeiting the Securities
  and current Coin of the United States;

Clause 7: To establish Post Offices and post Roads;

Clause 8: To promote the Progress of Science and useful Arts, by secur-   20
  ing for limited Times to Authors and Inventors the exclusive Right to
  their respective Writings and Discoveries;

Clause 9: To constitute Tribunals inferior to the supreme Court;

Clause 10: To define and punish Piracies and Felonies committed on
  the high Seas, and offenses against the Law of Nations;

Clause 11: To declare War, grant Letters of Marque and Reprisal, and
  make Rules concerning Captures on Land and Water;

Clause 12: To raise and support Armies, but no Appropriation of
  Money to that Use shall be for a longer Term than two Years;

Clause 13: To provide and maintain a Navy;   30

Clause 14: To make Rules for the Government and Regulation of the
  land and naval Forces;

Clause 15: To provide for calling forth the Militia to execute the Laws
  of the Union, suppress Insurrections and repel Invasions;

---

*We begin our nation's founding legal contract with its citizens by focusing on Section 8. Sec-
tion 8 details the responsibilities and powers of the Government. Readers can then move
directly to the "Bill of Rights"—the Amendments which grant the governed ("We, the People")
inalienable rights and certain freedoms from government power.

Clause 16: To provide for organizing, arming, and disciplining, the Militia, and for governing such Part of them as may be employed in the Service of the United States, reserving to the States respectively, the Appointment of the Officers, and the Authority of training the Militia according to the discipline prescribed by Congress;

40 Clause 17: To exercise exclusive Legislation in all Cases whatsoever, over such District (not exceeding ten Miles square) as may, by Cession of particular States, and the Acceptance of Congress, become the Seat of the Government of the United States, and to exercise like Authority over all Places purchased by the Consent of the Legislature of the State in which the Same shall be, for the Erection of Forts, Magazines, Arsenals, dock-Yards, and other needful Buildings;—And

Clause 18: To make all Laws which shall be necessary and proper for carrying into Execution the foregoing Powers, and all other Powers vested by this Constitution in the Government of the United States,

50 or in any Department or Officer thereof.

AMENDMENTS TO THE CONSTITUTION OF THE UNITED STATES

Amendment I (1791)

Congress shall make no law respecting an establishment of religion, or prohibiting the free exercise thereof; or abridging the freedom of speech, or of the press; or the right of the people peaceably to assemble, and to petition the government for a redress of grievances.

Amendment II (1791)

A well regulated militia, being necessary to the security of a free state, the right of the people to keep and bear arms, shall not be infringed.

Amendment III (1791)

No soldier shall, in time of peace be quartered in any house, without the consent of the owner, nor in time of war, but in a manner to be prescribed by law.

Amendment IV (1791)

The right of the people to be secure in their persons, houses, papers, and
60 effects, against unreasonable searches and seizures, shall not be violated, and no warrants shall issue, but upon probable cause, supported by oath or affirmation, and particularly describing the place to be searched, and the persons or things to be seized.

Amendment V (1791)

No person shall be held to answer for a capital, or otherwise infamous crime, unless on a presentment or indictment of a grand jury, except in cases arising in the land or naval forces, or in the militia, when in actual service in time of war or public danger; nor shall any person be subject for the same offense to be twice put in jeopardy of life or limb; nor shall be compelled in any criminal case to be a witness against himself, nor be deprived of life, liberty, or property, without due process of law; nor shall private property be taken for public use, without just compensation.   70

Amendment VI (1791)

In all criminal prosecutions, the accused shall enjoy the right to a speedy and public trial, by an impartial jury of the state and district wherein the crime shall have been committed, which district shall have been previously ascertained by law, and to be informed of the nature and cause of the accusation; to be confronted with the witnesses against him; to have compulsory process for obtaining witnesses in his favor, and to have the assistance of counsel for his defense.

Amendment VII (1791)

In suits at common law, where the value in controversy shall exceed twenty dollars, the right of trial by jury shall be preserved, and no fact tried by a jury, shall be otherwise reexamined in any court of the United States, than according to the rules of the common law.   80

Amendment VIII (1791)

Excessive bail shall not be required, nor excessive fines imposed, nor cruel and unusual punishments inflicted.

Amendment IX (1791)

The enumeration in the Constitution, of certain rights, shall not be constructed to deny or disparage others retained by the people.

Amendment X (1791)

The powers not delegated to the United States by the Constitution, nor prohibited by it to the states, are reserved to the states respectively, or to the people.

Amendment XI (1798)

The judicial power of the United States shall not be construed to extend to any suit in law or equity, commenced or prosecuted against one of the United States by citizens of another state, or by citizens or subjects of any foreign state.   90

Amendment XII (1804)

The electors shall meet in their respective states and vote by ballot for President and Vice-President, one of whom, at least, shall not be an inhabitant of the same state with themselves; they shall name in their ballots the person voted for as President, and in distinct ballots the person voted for as Vice-President, and they shall make distinct lists of all persons voted for as President, and of all persons voted for as Vice-President, and of the number of
100 votes for each, which lists they shall sign and certify, and transmit sealed to the seat of the government of the United States, directed to the President of the Senate;—The President of the Senate shall, in the presence of the Senate and House of Representatives, open all the certificates and the votes shall then be counted;—the person having the greatest number of votes for President, shall be the President, if such number be a majority of the whole number of electors appointed; and if no person have such majority, then from the persons having the highest numbers not exceeding three on the list of those voted for as President, the House of Representatives shall choose immediately, by ballot, the President. But in choosing the President, the votes shall
110 be taken by states, the representation from each state having one vote; a quorum for this purpose shall consist of a member or members from two-thirds of the states, and a majority of all the states shall be necessary to a choice. And if the House of Representatives shall not choose a President whenever the right of choice shall devolve upon them, before the fourth day of March next following, then the Vice-President shall act as President, as in the case of the death or other constitutional disability of the President. The person having the greatest number of votes as Vice-President, shall be the Vice-President, if such number be a majority of the whole number of electors appointed, and if no person have a majority, then from the two highest num-
120 bers on the list, the Senate shall choose the Vice-President; a quorum for the purpose shall consist of two-thirds of the whole number of Senators, and a majority of the whole number shall be necessary to a choice. But no person constitutionally ineligible to the office of President shall be eligible to that of Vice-President of the United States.

Amendment XIII (1865)

Section 1.

Neither slavery nor involuntary servitude, except as a punishment for crime whereof the party shall have been duly convicted, shall exist within the United States, or any place subject to their jurisdiction.

Section 2.

Congress shall have power to enforce this article by appropriate legislation.

Amendment XIV (1868)

Section 1.

All persons born or naturalized in the United States, and subject to the juris- diction thereof, are citizens of the United States and of the state wherein they   130 reside. No state shall make or enforce any law which shall abridge the privi- leges or immunities of citizens of the United States; nor shall any state deprive any person of life, liberty, or property, without due process of law; nor deny to any person within its jurisdiction the equal protection of the laws.

Section 2.

Representatives shall be apportioned among the several states according to their respective numbers, counting the whole number of persons in each state, excluding Indians not taxed. But when the right to vote at any election for the choice of electors for President and Vice President of the United States, Repre- sentatives in Congress, the executive and judicial officers of a state, or the mem- bers of the legislature thereof, is denied to any of the male inhabitants of such   140 state, being twenty-one years of age, and citizens of the United States, or in any way abridged, except for participation in rebellion, or other crime, the basis of representation therein shall be reduced in the proportion which the number of such male citizens shall bear to the whole number of male citizens twenty-one years of age in such state.

Section 3.

No person shall be a Senator or Representative in Congress, or elector of Pres- ident and Vice President, or hold any office, civil or military, under the United States, or under any state, who, having previously taken an oath, as a member of Congress, or as an officer of the United States, or as a member of any state legislature, or as an executive or judicial officer of any state, to support the   150 Constitution of the United States, shall have engaged in insurrection or rebel- lion against the same, or given aid or comfort to the enemies thereof. But Congress may by a vote of two-thirds of each House, remove such disability.

Section 4.

The validity of the public debt of the United States, authorized by law, including debts incurred for payment of pensions and bounties for services in suppressing insurrection or rebellion, shall not be questioned. But neither the United States nor any state shall assume or pay any debt or obligation incurred in aid of insurrection or rebellion against the United States, or any claim for the loss or emancipation of any slave; but all such debts, obligations and claims shall be held illegal and void.   160

Section 5.

The Congress shall have power to enforce, by appropriate legislation, the provisions of this article.

Amendment XV (1870)
Section 1.

The right of citizens of the United States to vote shall not be denied or abridged by the United States or by any state on account of race, color, or previous condition of servitude.

Section 2.

The Congress shall have power to enforce this article by appropriate legislation.

Amendment XVI (1913)

The Congress shall have power to lay and collect taxes on incomes, from whatever source derived, without apportionment among the several states, and without regard to any census of enumeration.

Amendment XVII (1913)

170 The Senate of the United States shall be composed of two Senators from each state, elected by the people therefore, for six years; and each Senator shall have one vote. The electors in each state shall have the qualifications requisite for electors of the most numerous branch of the state legislatures.

When vacancies happen in the representation of any state in the Senate, the executive authority of such state shall issue writs of election to fill such vacancies: Provided, that the legislature of any state may empower the executive thereof to make temporary appointments until the people fill the vacancies by election as the legislature may direct.

This amendment shall not be so construed as to affect the election or term
180 of any Senator chosen before it becomes valid as part of the Constitution.

Amendment XVIII (1919)
Section 1.

After one year from the ratification of this article the manufacture, sale, or transportation of intoxicating liquors within, the importation thereof into, or the exportation thereof from the United States and all territory subject to the jurisdiction thereof for beverage purposes is hereby prohibited.

Section 2.

The Congress and the several states shall have concurrent power to enforce this article by appropriate legislation.

Section 3.

This article shall be inoperative unless it shall have been ratified as an amendment to the Constitution by the legislatures of the several states, as provided in the Constitution, within seven years from the date of the submission hereof to the states by the Congress.

190

Amendment XIX (1920)

The right of citizens of the United States to vote shall not be denied or abridged by the United States or by any state on account of sex.

Congress shall have power to enforce this article by appropriate legislation.

Amendment XX (1933)
Section 1.

The terms of the President and Vice President shall end at noon on the 20th day of January, and the terms of Senators and Representatives at noon on the 3d day of January, of the years in which such terms would have ended if this article had not been ratified; and the terms of their successors shall then begin.

Section 2.

The Congress shall assemble at least once in every year, and such meeting shall begin at noon on the 3d day of January, unless they shall by law appoint a different day.

200

Section 3.

If, at the time fixed for the beginning of the term of the President, the President elect shall have died, the Vice President elect shall become President. If a President shall not have been chosen before the time fixed for the beginning of his term, or if the President elect shall have failed to qualify, then the Vice President elect shall act as President until a President shall have qualified; and the congress may by law provide for the case wherein neither a President elect nor a Vice President elect shall have qualified, declaring who shall then act as President, or the manner in which one who is to act shall be selected, and such person shall act accordingly until a President or Vice President shall have qualified.

Section 4.

210   The Congress may by law provide for the case of the death of any of the persons from whom the House of Representatives may choose a President whenever the right of choice shall have devolved upon them, and for the case of the death of any of the persons from whom the Senate may choose a Vice President whenever the right of choice shall have devolved upon them.

Section 5.

Sections 1 and 2 shall take effect on the 15th day of October following the ratification of this article.

Section 6.

This article shall be inoperative unless it shall have been ratified as an amendment to the Constitution by the legislatures of three-fourths of the several states within seven years from the date of its submission.

Amendment XXI (1933)

Section 1.

220   The eighteenth article of amendment to the Constitution of the United States is hereby repealed.

Section 2.

The transportation or importation into any state, territory, or possession of the United States for delivery or use therein of intoxicating liquors, in violation of the laws thereof, is hereby prohibited.

Section 3.

This article shall be inoperative unless it shall have been ratified as an amendment to the Constitution by conventions in the several states, as provided in the Constitution, within seven years from the date of the submission hereof to the states by the Congress.

Amendment XXII (1951)

Section 1.

No person shall be elected to the office of the President more than twice, and
230   no person who has held the office of President, or acted as President, for more than two years of a term to which some other person was elected Pres-

ident shall be elected to the office of the President more than once. But this article shall not apply to any person holding the office of President when this article was proposed by the Congress, and shall not prevent any person who may be holding the office of President, or acting as President, during the term within which this article becomes operative from holding the office of President or acting as President during the remainder of such term.

Section 2.

This article shall be inoperative unless it shall have been ratified as an amendment to the Constitution by the legislatures of three-fourths of the several states within seven years from the date of its submission to the states by the   240
Congress.

Amendment XXIII (1961)
Section 1.

The District constituting the seat of government of the United States shall appoint in such manner as the Congress may direct:

A number of electors of President and Vice President equal to the whole number of Senators and Representatives in Congress to which the District would be entitled if it were a state, but in no event more than the least populous state; they shall be in addition to those appointed by the states, but they shall be considered, for the purposes of the election of President and Vice President, to be electors appointed by a state; and they shall meet in the District and perform such duties as provided by the twelfth article of amendment.   250

Section 2.

The Congress shall have power to enforce this article by appropriate legislation.

Amendment XXIV (1964)
Section 1.

The right of citizens of the United States to vote in any primary or other election for President or Vice President, for electors for President or Vice President, or for Senator or Representative in Congress, shall not be denied or abridged by the United States or any state by reason of failure to pay any poll tax or other tax.

Section 2.

The Congress shall have power to enforce this article by appropriate legislation.

Amendment XXV (1967)

Section 1.

In case of the removal of the President from office or of his death or resignation, the Vice President shall become President.

Section 2.

260   Whenever there is a vacancy in the office of the Vice President, the President shall nominate a Vice President who shall take office upon confirmation by a majority vote of both Houses of Congress.

Section 3.

Whenever the President transmits to the President pro tempore of the Senate and the Speaker of the House of Representatives his written declaration that he is unable to discharge the powers and duties of his office, and until he transmits to them a written declaration to the contrary, such powers and duties shall be discharged by the Vice President as Acting President.

Section 4.

Whenever the Vice President and a majority of either the principal officers of the executive departments or of such other body as Congress may by law pro-
270   vide, transmit to the President pro tempore of the Senate and the Speaker of the House of Representatives their written declaration that the President is unable to discharge the powers and duties of his office, the Vice President shall immediately assume the powers and duties of the office as Acting President.

Thereafter, when the President transmits to the President pro tempore of the Senate and the Speaker of the House of Representatives his written declaration that no inability exists, he shall resume the powers and duties of his office unless the Vice President and a majority of either the principal officers of the executive department or of such other body as Congress may by law provide, transmit within four days to the President pro tempore of the Sen-
280   ate and the Speaker of the House of Representatives their written declaration that the President is unable to discharge the powers and duties of his office. Thereupon Congress shall decide the issue, assembling within forty-eight hours for that purpose if not in session. If the Congress, within twenty-one days after receipt of the latter written declaration, or, if Congress is not in session, within twenty-one days after Congress is required to assemble, determines by two-thirds vote of both Houses that the President is unable to discharge the powers and duties of his office, the Vice President shall continue to discharge the same as Acting President; otherwise, the President shall resume the powers and duties of his office.

Amendment XXVI (1971)

Section 1.

The right of citizens of the United States, who are 18 years of age or older,   290
to vote, shall not be denied or abridged by the United States or any state on
account of age.

Section 2.

The Congress shall have the power to enforce this article by appropriate
legislation.

Amendment XXVII (1992)

No law varying the compensation for the services of the Senators and Representatives shall take effect until an election of Representatives shall have
intervened.

THE COUNTRY OF THE BLIND
H. G. Wells

Three hundred miles and more from Chimborazo, one hundred from the
snows of Cotopaxi, in the wildest wastes of Ecuador's Andes, there lies
that mysterious mountain valley, cut off from the world of men, the Country of the Blind. Long years ago that valley lay so far open to the world that
men might come at last through frightful gorges and over an icy pass into its
equable meadows; and thither indeed men came, a family or so of Peruvian
half-breeds fleeing from the lust and tyranny of an evil Spanish ruler. Then
came the stupendous outbreak of Mindobamba, when it was night in Quito
for seventeen days, and the water was boiling at Yaguachi and all the fish
floating dying even as far as Guayaquil; everywhere along the Pacific slopes   10
there were landslips and swift thawings and sudden floods, and one whole
side of the old Arauca crest slipped and came down in thunder, and cut off
the Country of the Blind for ever from the exploring feet of men. But one of
these early settlers had chanced to be on the hither side of the gorges when
the world had so terribly shaken itself, and he perforce had to forget his wife
and his child and all the friends and possessions he had left up there, and start
life over again in the lower world. He started it again but ill, blindness overtook him, and he died of punishment in the mines; but the story he told
begot a legend that lingers along the length of the Cordilleras of the Andes
to this day.   20

He told of his reason for venturing back from that fastness, into which
he had first been carried lashed to a llama, beside a vast bale of gear, when
he was a child. The valley, he said, had in it all that the heart of man could
desire—sweet water, pasture, and even climate, slopes of rich brown soil with
tangles of a shrub that bore an excellent fruit, and on one side great hanging
forests of pine that held the avalanches high. Far overhead, on three sides,
vast cliffs of grey-green rock were capped by cliffs of ice; but the glacier
stream came not to them but flowed away by the farther slopes, and only
now and then huge ice masses fell on the valley side. In this valley it neither
rained nor snowed, but the abundant springs gave a rich green pasture, that   30
irrigation would spread over all the valley space. The settlers did well indeed
there. Their beasts did well and multiplied, and but one thing marred their
happiness. Yet it was enough to mar it greatly. A strange disease had come
upon them, and had made all the children born to them there—and, indeed,
several older children also—blind. It was to seek some charm or antidote
against this plague of blindness that he had with fatigue and danger and difficulty returned down the gorge. In those days, in such cases, men did not
think of germs and infections but of sins; and it seemed to him that the reason of this affliction must lie in the negligence of these priestless immigrants
to set up a shrine so soon as they entered the valley. He wanted a shrine—a   40

handsome, cheap, effectual shrine—to be erected in the valley; he wanted relics and such-like potent things of faith, blessed objects and mysterious medals and prayers. In his wallet he had a bar of native silver for which he would not account; he insisted there was none in the valley with something of the insistence of an inexpert liar. They had all clubbed their money and ornaments together, having little need for such treasure up there, he said, to buy them holy help against their ill. I figure this dim-eyed young mountaineer, sunburnt, gaunt, and anxious, hat-brim clutched feverishly, a man all unused to the ways of the lower world, telling this story to some keen-
50   eyed, attentive priest before the great convulsion; I can picture him presently seeking to return with pious and infallible remedies against that trouble, and the infinite dismay with which he must have faced the tumbled vastness where the gorge had once come out. But the rest of his story of mischances is lost to me, save that I know of his evil death after several years. Poor stray from that remoteness! The stream that had once made the gorge now bursts from the mouth of a rocky cave, and the legend his poor, ill-told story set going developed into the legend of a race of blind men somewhere "over there" one may still hear to-day.

And amidst the little population of that now isolated and forgotten val-
60   ley the disease ran its course. The old became groping and purblind, the young saw but dimly, and the children that were born to them saw never at all. But life was very easy in that snow-rimmed basin, lost to all the world, with neither thorns nor briars, with no evil insects nor any beasts save the gentle breed of llamas they had lugged and thrust and followed up the beds of the shrunken rivers in the gorges up which they had come. The seeing had become purblind so gradually that they scarcely noted their loss. They guided the sightless youngsters hither and thither until they knew the whole valley marvellously, and when at last sight died out among them the race lived on. They had even time to adapt themselves to the control of fire, which they
70   made carefully in stoves of stone. They were a simple strain of people at the first, unlettered, only slightly touched with the Spanish civilisation, but with something of a tradition of the arts of old Peru and of its lost philosophy. Generation followed generation. They forgot many things; they devised many things. Their tradition of the greater world they came from became mythical in colour and uncertain. In all things save sight they were strong and able; and presently the chance of birth and heredity sent one who had an original mind and who could talk and persuade among them, and then afterwards another. These two passed, leaving their effects, and the little community grew in numbers and in understanding, and met and settled social and
80   economic problems that arose. Generation followed generation. Generation followed generation. There came a time when a child was born who was fifteen generations from that ancestor who went out of the valley with a bar of silver to seek God's aid, and who never returned. Thereabouts it chanced that a man came into this community from the outer world. And this is the story of that man.

He was a mountaineer from the country near Quito, a man who had been down to the sea and had seen the world, a reader of books in an original way, an acute and enterprising man, and he was taken on by a party of Englishmen who had come out to Ecuador to climb mountains, to replace one of their three Swiss guides who had fallen ill. He climbed here and he climbed there, and then came the attempt on Parascotopetl, the Matterhorn of the Andes, in which he was lost to the outer world. The story of the accident has been written a dozen times. Pointer's narrative is the best. He tells how the party worked their difficult and almost vertical way up to the very foot of the last and greatest precipice, and how they built a night shelter amidst the snow upon a little shelf of rock, and, with a touch of real dramatic power, how presently they found Nunez had gone from them. They shouted, and there was no reply; shouted and whistled, and for the rest of that night they slept no more.

As the morning broke they saw the traces of his fall. It seems impossible he could have uttered a sound. He had slipped eastward towards the unknown side of the mountain; far below he had struck a steep slope of snow, and ploughed his way down it in the midst of a snow avalanche. His track went straight to the edge of a frightful precipice, and beyond that everything was hidden. Far, far below, and hazy with distance, they could see trees rising out of a narrow, shut-in valley—the lost Country of the Blind. But they did not know it was the lost Country of the Blind, nor distinguish it in any way from any other narrow streak of upland valley. Unnerved by the disaster, they abandoned their attempt in the afternoon, and Pointer was called away to the war before he could make another attack. To this day Parascotopetl lifts an unconquered crest, and Pointer's shelter crumbles unvisited amidst the snows.

And the man who fell survived.

At the end of the slope he fell a thousand feet, and came down in the midst of a cloud of snow upon a snow slope even steeper than the one above. Down this he was whirled, stunned and insensible, but without a bone broken in his body; and then at last came to gentler slopes, and at last rolled out and lay still, buried amidst a softening heap of the white masses that had accompanied and saved him. He came to himself with a dim fancy that he was ill in bed; then realised his position with a mountaineer's intelligence, and worked himself loose and, after a rest or so, out until he saw the stars. He rested flat upon his chest for a space, wondering where he was and what had happened to him. He explored his limbs, and discovered that several of his buttons were gone and his coat turned over his head. His knife had gone from his pocket, and his hat was lost, though he had tied it under his chin. He recalled that he had been looking for loose stones to raise his piece of the shelter wall. His ice-axe had disappeared.

He decided he must have fallen, and looked up to see, exaggerated by the ghastly light of the rising moon, the tremendous flight he had taken. For a while he lay, gazing blankly at that vast pale cliff towering above, rising moment by moment out of a subsiding tide of darkness. Its phantasmal,

mysterious beauty held him for a space, and then he was seized with a parox-
ysm of sobbing laughter. . . .

After a great interval of time he became aware that he was near the lower
edge of the snow. Below, down what was now a moonlit and practicable
slope, he saw the dark and broken appearance of rock-strewn turf. He struggled to his feet, aching in every joint and limb, got down painfully from the
heaped loose snow about him, went downward until he was on the turf, and
there dropped rather than lay beside a boulder, drank deep from the flask in
his inner pocket, and instantly fell asleep. . . .

140   He was awakened by the singing of birds in the trees far below.

He sat up and perceived he was on a little alp at the foot of a vast
precipice, that was grooved by the gully down which he and his snow had
come. Over against him another wall of rock reared itself against the sky. The
gorge between these precipices ran east and west and was full of the morning
sunlight, which lit to the westward the mass of fallen mountain that closed
the descending gorge. Below him it seemed there was a precipice equally
steep, but behind the snow in the gully he found a sort of chimney-cleft drip-
ping with snow-water down which a desperate man might venture. He found
it easier than it seemed, and came at last to another desolate alp, and then
150   after a rock climb of no particular difficulty to a steep slope of trees. He took
his bearings and turned his face up the gorge, for he saw it opened out above
upon green meadows, among which he now glimpsed quite distinctly a cluster of stone huts of unfamiliar fashion. At times his progress was like clam-
bering along the face of a wall, and after a time the rising sun ceased to strike
along the gorge, the voices of the singing birds died away, and the air grew
cold and dark above him. But the distant valley with its houses was all the
brighter for that. He came presently to talus, and among the rocks he
noted—for he was an observant man—an unfamiliar fern that seemed to
clutch out of the crevices with intense green hands. He picked a frond or so
160   and gnawed its stalk and found it helpful.

About midday he came at last out of the throat of the gorge into the plain
and the sunlight. He was stiff and weary; he sat down in the shadow of a
rock, filled up his flask with water from a spring and drank it down, and
remained for a time resting before he went on to the houses.

They were very strange to his eyes, and indeed the whole aspect of that
valley became, as he regarded it, queerer and more unfamiliar. The greater
part of its surface was lush green meadow, starred with many beautiful flowers, irrigated with extraordinary care, and bearing evidence of systematic
cropping piece by piece. High up and ringing the valley about was a wall, and
170   what appeared to be a circumferential water-channel, from which the little
trickles of water that fed the meadow plants came, and on the higher slopes
above this flocks of llamas cropped the scanty herbage. Sheds, apparently
shelters or feeding-places for the llamas, stood against the boundary wall here
and there. The irrigation streams ran together into a main channel down the
centre of the valley, and this was enclosed on either side by a wall breast high.

This gave a singularly urban quality to this secluded place, a quality that was greatly enhanced by the fact that a number of paths paved with black and white stones, and each with a curious little kerb at the side, ran hither and thither in an orderly manner. The houses of the central village were quite unlike the casual and higgledy-piggledy agglomeration of the mountain villages he knew; they stood in a continuous row on either side of a central street of astonishing cleanness; here and there their parti-coloured façade was pierced by a door, and not a solitary window broke their even frontage. They were parti-coloured with extraordinary irregularity; smeared with a sort of plaster that was sometimes grey, sometimes drab, sometimes slate-coloured or dark brown; and it was the sight of this wild plastering first brought the word "blind" into the thoughts of the explorer. "The good man who did that," he thought, "must have been as blind as a bat."

He descended a steep place, and so came to the wall and channel that ran about the valley, near where the latter spouted out its surplus contents into the deeps of the gorge in a thin and wavering thread of cascade. He could now see a number of men and women resting on piled heaps of grass, as if taking a siesta, in the remoter part of the meadow, and nearer the village a number of recumbent children, and then nearer at hand three men carrying pails on yokes along a little path that ran from the encircling wall towards the houses. These latter were clad in garments of llama cloth and boots and belts of leather, and they wore caps of cloth with back and ear flaps. They followed one another in single file, walking slowly and yawning as they walked, like men who have been up all night. There was something so reassuringly prosperous and respectable in their bearing that after a moment's hesitation Nunez stood forward as conspicuously as possible upon his rock, and gave vent to a mighty shout that echoed round the valley.

The three men stopped, and moved their heads as though they were looking about them. They turned their faces this way and that, and Nunez gesticulated with freedom. But they did not appear to see him for all his gestures, and after a time, directing themselves towards the mountains far away to the right, they shouted as if in answer. Nunez bawled again, and then once more, and as he gestured ineffectually the word "blind" came up to the top of his thoughts. "The fools must be blind," he said.

When at last, after much shouting and wrath, Nunez crossed the stream by a little bridge, came through a gate in the wall, and approached them, he was sure that they were blind. He was sure that this was the Country of the Blind of which the legends told. Conviction had sprung upon him, and a sense of great and rather enviable adventure. The three stood side by side, not looking at him, but with their ears directed towards him, judging him by his unfamiliar steps. They stood close together like men a little afraid, and he could see their eyelids closed and sunken, as though the very balls beneath had shrunk away. There was an expression near awe on their faces.

"A man," one said, in hardly recognisable Spanish—"a man it is—a man or a spirit—coming down from the rocks."

But Nunez advanced with the confident steps of a youth who enters upon life. All the old stories of the lost valley and the Country of the Blind had come back to his mind, and through his thoughts ran this old proverb, as if it were a refrain—

"In the Country of the Blind the One-eyed Man is King."

"In the Country of the Blind the One-eyed Man is King."

And very civilly he gave them greeting. He talked to them and used his eyes.

"Where does he come from, brother Pedro?" asked one.

230   "Down out of the rocks."

"Over the mountains I come," said Nunez, "out of the country beyond there—where men can see. From near Bogota, where there are a hundred thousands of people, and where the city passes out of sight."

"Sight?" muttered Pedro. "Sight?"

"He comes," said the second blind man, "out of the rocks."

The cloth of their coats Nunez saw was curiously fashioned, each with a different sort of stitching.

They startled him by a simultaneous movement towards him, each with a hand outstretched. He stepped back from the advance of these spread fingers.

240   "Come hither," said the third blind man, following his motion and clutching him neatly.

And they held Nunez and felt him over, saying no word further until they had done so.

"Carefully," he cried, with a finger in his eye, and found they thought that organ, with its fluttering lids, a queer thing in him. They went over it again.

"A strange creature, Correa," said the one called Pedro. "Feel the coarseness of his hair. Like a llama's hair."

"Rough he is as the rocks that begot him," said Correa, investigating Nunez's unshaven chin with a soft and slightly moist hand. "Perhaps he will

250   grow finer." Nunez struggled a little under their examination, but they gripped him firm.

"Carefully," he said again.

"He speaks," said the third man. "Certainly he is a man."

"Ugh!" said Pedro, at the roughness of his coat.

"And you have come into the world?" asked Pedro.

"*Out* of the world. Over mountains and glaciers; right over above there, halfway to the sun. Out of the great big world that goes down, twelve days' journey to the sea."

They scarcely seemed to heed him. "Our fathers have told us men may be

260   made by the forces of Nature," said Correa. "It is the warmth of things and moisture, and rottenness—rottenness."

"Let us lead him to the elders," said Pedro.

"Shout first," said Correa, "lest the children be afraid. This is a marvellous occasion."

So they shouted, and Pedro went first and took Nunez by the hand to lead him to the houses.

He drew his hand away. "I can see," he said.

"See?" said Correa.

"Yes, see," said Nunez, turning towards him, and stumbled against Pedro's pail.   270

"His senses are still imperfect," said the third blind man. "He stumbles, and talks unmeaning words. Lead him by the hand."

"As you will," said Nunez, and was led along, laughing.

It seemed they knew nothing of sight.

Well, all in good time he would teach them.

He heard people shouting, and saw a number of figures gathering together in the middle roadway of the village.

He found it taxed his nerve and patience more than he had anticipated, that first encounter with the population of the Country of the Blind. The place seemed larger as he drew near to it, and the smeared plasterings queerer,   280 and a crowd of children and men and women (the women and girls, he was pleased to note, had some of them quite sweet faces, for all that their eyes were shut and sunken) came about him, holding on to him, touching him with soft, sensitive hands, smelling at him, and listening at every word he spoke. Some of the maidens and children, however, kept aloof as if afraid, and indeed his voice seemed coarse and rude beside their softer notes. They mobbed him. His three guides kept close to him with an effect of proprietorship, and said again and again, "A wild man out of the rocks."

"Bogota," he said. "Bogota. Over the mountain crests."

"A wild man—using wild words," said Pedro. "Did you hear that—   290 *Bogota?* His mind is hardly formed yet. He has only the beginnings of speech."

A little boy nipped his hand. "Bogota!" he said mockingly.

"Ay! A city to your village. I come from the great world—where men have eyes and see."

"His name's Bogota," they said.

"He stumbled," said Correa; "stumbled twice as we came hither."

"Bring him to the elders."

And they thrust him suddenly through a doorway into a room as black as pitch, save at the end there faintly glowed a fire. The crowd closed in behind him and shut out all but the faintest glimmer of day, and before he could   300 arrest himself he had fallen headlong over the feet of a seated man. His arm, outflung, struck the face of someone else as he went down; he felt the soft impact of features and heard a cry of anger, and for a moment he struggled against a number of hands that clutched him. It was a one-sided fight. An inkling of the situation came to him, and he lay quiet.

"I fell down," he said; "I couldn't see in this pitchy darkness."

There was a pause as if the unseen persons about him tried to understand his words. Then the voice of Correa said: "He is but newly formed. He stumbles as he walks and mingles words that mean nothing with his speech."

310   Others also said things about him that he heard or understood imperfectly. "May I sit up?" he asked, in a pause. "I will not struggle against you again." They consulted and let him rise.

    The voice of an older man began to question him, and Nunez found himself trying to explain the great world out of which he had fallen, and the sky and mountains and sight and such-like marvels, to these elders who sat in darkness in the Country of the Blind. And they would believe and understand nothing whatever he told them, a thing quite outside his expectation. They would not even understand many of his words. For fourteen genera-
320 tions these people had been blind and cut off from all the seeing world; the names for all the things of sight had faded and changed; the story of the outer world was faded and changed to a child's story; and they had ceased to concern themselves with anything beyond the rocky slopes above their circling wall. Blind men of genius had arisen among them and questioned the shreds of belief and tradition they had brought with them from their seeing days, and had dismissed all these things as idle fancies, and replaced them with new and saner explanations. Much of their imagination had shrivelled with their eyes, and they had made for themselves new imaginations with their ever more sensitive, ears and finger-tips. Slowly Nunez realised this; that his expectation of wonder and reverence at his origin and his gifts was not to be
330 borne out; and after his poor attempt to explain sight to them had been set aside as the confused version of a new-made being describing the marvels of his incoherent sensations, he subsided, a little dashed, into listening to their instruction. And the eldest of the blind men explained to him life and philosophy and religion, how that the world (meaning their valley) had been first an empty hollow in the rocks, and then had come, first, inanimate things without the gift of touch, and llamas and a few other creatures that had little sense, and then men, and at last angels, whom one could hear singing and making fluttering sounds, but whom no one could touch at all, which puzzled Nunez greatly until he thought of the birds.

340   He went on to tell Nunez how this time had been divided into the warm and the cold, which are the blind equivalents of day and night, and how it was good to sleep in the warm and work during the cold, so that now, but for his advent, the whole town of the blind would have been asleep. He said Nunez must have been specially created to learn and serve the wisdom they had acquired, and for that all his mental incoherency and stumbling behaviour he must have courage, and do his best to learn, and at that all the people in the doorway murmured encouragingly. He said the night—for the blind call their day night—was now far gone, and it behoved every one to go back to sleep. He asked Nunez if he knew how to sleep, and Nunez said he
350 did, but that before sleep he wanted food.

    They brought him food—llama's milk in a bowl, and rough salted bread—and led him into a lonely place to eat out of their hearing, and afterwards to slumber until the chill of the mountain evening roused them to begin their day again. But Nunez slumbered not at all.

Instead, he sat up in the place where they had left him, resting his limbs and turning the unanticipated circumstances of his arrival over and over in his mind.

Every now and then he laughed, sometimes with amusement, and sometimes with indignation.

"Unformed mind!" he said. "Got no senses yet! They little know they've been insulting their heaven-sent king and master. I see I must bring them to reason. Let me think—let me think."

He was still thinking when the sun set.

Nunez had an eye for all beautiful things, and it seemed to him that the glow upon the snowfields and glaciers that rose about the valley on every side was the most beautiful thing he had ever seen. His eyes went from that inaccessible glory to the village and irrigated fields, fast sinking into the twilight, and suddenly a wave of emotion took him, and he thanked God from the bottom of his heart that the power of sight had been given him.

He heard a voice calling to him from out of the village.

"Ya ho there, Bogota! Come hither!"

At that he stood up smiling. He would show these people once and for all what sight would do for a man. They would seek him, but not find him.

"You move not, Bogota," said the voice.

He laughed noiselessly, and made two stealthy steps aside from the path.

"Trample not on the grass, Bogota; that is not allowed."

Nunez had scarcely heard the sound he made himself. He stopped amazed.

The owner of the voice came running up the piebald path towards him.

He stepped back into the pathway. "Here I am," he said.

"Why did you not come when I called you?" said the blind man. "Must you be led like a child? Cannot you hear the path as you walk?"

Nunez laughed. "I can see it," he said.

"There is no such word as *see*," said the blind man, after a pause. "Cease this folly, and follow the sound of my feet."

Nunez followed, a little annoyed.

"My time will come," he said.

"You'll learn," the blind man answered. "There is much to learn in the world."

"Has no one told you, 'In the Country of the Blind the One-eyed Man is King'?"

"What is blind?" asked the blind man carelessly over his shoulder.

Four days passed, and the fifth found the King of the Blind still incognito, as a clumsy and useless stranger among his subjects.

It was, he found, much more difficult to proclaim himself than he had supposed, and in the meantime, while he meditated his *coup d'état*, he did what he was told and learned the manners and customs of the Country of the Blind. He found working and going about at night a particularly irksome thing, and he decided that that should be the first thing he would change.

400   They led a simple, laborious life, these people, with all the elements of virtue and happiness, as these things can be understood by men. They toiled, but not oppressively; they had food and clothing sufficient for their needs; they had days and seasons of rest; they made much of music and singing, and there was love among them, and little children.

It was marvellous with what confidence and precision they went about their ordered world. Everything, you see, had been made to fit their needs; each of the radiating paths of the valley area had a constant angle to the others, and was distinguished by a special notch upon its kerbing; all obstacles and irregularities of path or meadow had long since been cleared away; all 410   their methods and procedure arose naturally from their special needs. Their senses had become marvellously acute; they could hear and judge the slightest gesture of a man a dozen paces away—could hear the very beating of his heart. Intonation had long replaced expression with them, and touches gesture, and their work with hoe and spade and fork was as free and confident as garden work can be. Their sense of smell was extraordinarily fine; they could distinguish individual differences as readily as a dog can, and they went about the tending of the llamas, who lived among the rocks above and came to the wall for food and shelter, with ease and confidence. It was only when at last Nunez sought to assert himself that he found how easy and confident 420   their movements could be.

He rebelled only after he had tried persuasion.

He tried at first on several occasions to tell them of sight. "Look you here, you people," he said. "There are things you do not understand in me."

Once or twice one or two of them attended to him; they sat with faces downcast and ears turned intelligently towards him, and he did his best to tell them what it was to see. Among his hearers was a girl, with eyelids less red and sunken than the others, so that one could almost fancy she was hiding eyes, whom especially he hoped to persuade. He spoke of the beauties of sight, of watching the mountains, of the sky and the sunrise, and they heard 430   him with amused incredulity that presently became condemnatory. They told him there were indeed no mountains at all, but that the end of the rocks where the llamas grazed was indeed the end of the world; thence sprang a cavernous roof of the universe, from which the dew and the avalanches fell; and when he maintained stoutly the world had neither end nor roof such as they supposed, they said his thoughts were wicked. So far as he could describe sky and clouds and stars to them it seemed to them a hideous void, a terrible blankness in the place of the smooth roof to things in which they believed—it was an article of faith with them that the cavern roof was exquisitely smooth to the touch. He saw that in some manner he shocked them, 440   and gave up that aspect of the matter altogether, and tried to show them the practical value of sight. One morning he saw Pedro in the path called Seventeen and coming towards the central houses, but still too far off for hearing or scent, and he told them as much. "In a little while," he prophesied, "Pedro will be here." An old man remarked that Pedro had no business on path Seventeen, and then, as if in confirmation, that individual as he drew near turned and went transversely into path Ten, and so back with nimble paces towards the outer wall. They mocked Nunez when Pedro did not arrive, and afterwards, when he asked Pedro questions to clear his character, Pedro denied and outfaced him, and was afterwards hostile to him.

Then he induced them to let him go a long way up the sloping meadows   450
towards the wall with one complacent individual, and to him he promised to describe all that happened among the houses. He noted certain goings and comings, but the things that really seemed to signify to these people happened inside of or behind the windowless houses—the only things they took note of to test him by—and of these he could see or tell nothing; and it was after the failure of this attempt, and the ridicule they could not repress, that he resorted to force. He thought of seizing a spade and suddenly smiting one or two of them to earth, and so in fair combat showing the advantage of eyes. He went so far with that resolution as to seize his spade, and then he discovered a new thing about himself, and that was that it was impossible for him   460
to hit a blind man in cold blood.

He hesitated, and found them all aware that he snatched up the spade. They stood alert, with their heads on one side, and bent ears towards him for what he would do next.

"Put that spade down," said one, and he felt a sort of helpless horror. He came near obedience.

Then he thrust one backwards against a house wall, and fled past him and out of the village.

He went athwart one of their meadows, leaving a track of trampled grass behind his feet, and presently sat down by the side of one of their ways. He   470
felt something of the buoyancy that comes to all men in the beginning of a fight, but more perplexity. He began to realize that you cannot even fight happily with creatures who stand upon a different mental basis to yourself. Far away he saw a number of men carrying spades and sticks come out of the street of houses, and advance in a spreading line along the several paths towards him. They advanced slowly, speaking frequently to one another, and ever and again the whole cordon would halt and sniff the air and listen.

The first time they did this Nunez laughed. But afterwards he did not laugh.

One struck his trail in the meadow grass, and came stooping and feeling   480
his way along it.

For five minutes he watched the slow extension of the cordon, and then his vague disposition to do something forthwith became frantic. He stood up, went a pace or so towards the circumferential wall, turned, and went back a little way. There they all stood in a crescent, still and listening.

He also stood still, gripping his spade very tightly in both hands. Should he charge them?

The pulse in his ears ran into the rhythm of "In the Country of the Blind the One-eyed Man is King!"

490   Should he charge them?

He looked back at the high and unclimbable wall behind—unclimbable because of its smooth plastering, but withal pierced with many little doors, and at the approaching line of seekers. Behind these, others were now coming out of the street of houses.

Should he charge them?

"Bogota!" called one. "Bogota! where are you?"

He gripped his spade still tighter, and advanced down the meadows towards the place of habitations, and directly he moved they converged upon him. "I'll hit them if they touch me," he swore; "by Heaven, I will. I'll hit."
500   He called aloud, "Look here, I'm going to do what I like in this valley. Do you hear? I'm going to do what I like and go where I like!"

They were moving in upon him quickly, groping, yet moving rapidly. It was like playing blind man's buff, with everyone blindfolded except one. "Get hold of him!" cried one. He found himself in the arc of a loose curve of pursuers. He felt suddenly he must be active and resolute.

"You don't understand," he cried in a voice that was meant to be great and resolute, and which broke. "You are blind, and I can see. Leave me alone!"

"Bogota! Put down that spade, and come off the grass!"

The last order, grotesque in its urban familiarity, produced a gust of anger.
510   "I'll hurt you," he said, sobbing with emotion. "By Heaven, I'll hurt you. Leave me alone!"

He began to run, not knowing clearly where to run. He ran from the nearest blind man, because it was a horror to hit him. He stopped, and then made a dash to escape from their closing ranks. He made for where a gap was wide, and the men on either side, with a quick perception of the approach of his paces, rushed in on one another. He sprang forward, and then saw he must be caught, and *swish!* the spade had struck. He felt the soft thud of hand and arm, and the man was down with a yell of pain, and he was through.

Through! And then he was close to the street of houses again, and blind
520   men, whirling spades and stakes, were running with a sort of reasoned swiftness hither and thither.

He heard steps behind him just in time, and found a tall man rushing forward and swiping at the sound of him. He lost his nerve, hurled his spade a yard wide at his antagonist, and whirled about and fled, fairly yelling as he dodged another.

He was panic-stricken. He ran furiously to and fro, dodging when there was no need to dodge, and in his anxiety to see on every side of him at once, stumbling. For a moment, he was down and they heard his fall. Far away in the circumferential wall a little doorway looked like heaven, and he set off in
530   a wild rush for it. He did not even look round at his pursuers until it was gained, and he had stumbled across the bridge, clambered a little way among the rocks, to the surprise and dismay of a young llama, who went leaping out of sight, and lay down sobbing for breath.

And so his *coup d'état* came to an end.

He stayed outside the wall of the valley of the Blind for two nights and days without food or shelter, and meditated upon the unexpected. During these meditations he repeated very frequently and always with a profounder note of derision the exploded proverb: "In the Country of the Blind the One-eyed Man is King." He thought chiefly of ways of fighting and conquering these people, and it grew clear that for him no practicable way was possible. He had no weapons, and now it would be hard to get one. 540

The canker of civilisation had got to him even in Bogota, and he could not find it in himself to go down and assassinate a blind man. Of course, if he did that, he might then dictate terms on the threat of assassinating them all. But—sooner or later he must sleep! . . .

He tried also to find food among the pine trees, to be comfortable under pine boughs while the frost fell at night, and—with less confidence—to catch a llama by artifice in order to try to kill it—perhaps by hammering it with a stone—and so finally, perhaps, to eat some of it. But the llamas had a doubt of him and regarded him with distrustful brown eyes, and spat when he drew 550 near. Fear came on him the second day and fits of shivering. Finally he crawled down to the wall of the Country of the Blind and tried to make terms. He crawled along by the stream, shouting, until two blind men came out to the gate and talked to him.

"I was mad," he said. "But I was only newly made."

They said that was better.

He told them he was wiser now, and repented of all he had done.

Then he wept without intention, for he was very weak and ill now, and they took that as a favourable sign.

They asked him if he still thought he could *"see."* 560

"No," he said. "That was folly. The word means nothing—less than nothing!"

They asked him what was overhead.

"About ten times ten the height of a man there is a roof above the world—of rock—and very, very smooth." . . . He burst again into hysterical tears. "Before you ask me any more, give me some food or I shall die."

He expected dire punishments, but these blind people were capable of toleration. They regarded his rebellion as but one more proof of his general idiocy and inferiority; and after they had whipped him they appointed him to do the simplest and heaviest work they had for anyone to do, and he, see- 570 ing no other way of living, did submissively what he was told.

He was ill for some days, and they nursed him kindly. That refined his submission. But they insisted on his lying in the dark, and that was a great misery. And blind philosophers came and talked to him of the wicked levity of his mind, and reproved him so impressively for his doubts about the lid of rock that covered their cosmic casserole that he almost doubted whether indeed he was not the victim of hallucination in not seeing it overhead.

So Nunez became a citizen of the Country of the Blind, and these people ceased to be a generalised people and became individualities and familiar to

580   him, while the world beyond the mountains became more and more remote
and unreal. There was Yacob, his master, a kindly man when not annoyed;
there was Pedro, Yacob's nephew; and there was Medina-saroté, who was the
youngest daughter of Yacob. She was little esteemed in the world of the blind,
because she had a clear-cut face, and lacked that satisfying, glossy smoothness
that is the blind man's ideal of feminine beauty; but Nunez thought her beautiful at first, and presently the most beautiful thing in the whole creation.
Her closed eyelids were not sunken and red after the common way of the valley, but lay as though they might open again at any moment; and she had
long eyelashes, which were considered a grave disfigurement. And her voice
590   was strong, and did not satisfy the acute hearing of the valley swains. So that
she had no lover.

There came a time when Nunez thought that, could he win her, he would
be resigned to live in the valley for all the rest of his days.

He watched her; he sought opportunities of doing her little services, and
presently he found that she observed him. Once at a rest-day gathering they
sat side by side in the dim starlight, and the music was sweet. His hand came
upon hers and he dared to clasp it. Then very tenderly she returned his pressure. And one day, as they were at their meal in the darkness, he felt her hand
very softly seeking him, and as it chanced the fire leaped then and he saw the
600   tenderness of her face.

He sought to speak to her.

He went to her one day when she was sitting in the summer moonlight
spinning. The light made her a thing of silver and mystery. He sat down at
her feet and told her he loved her, and told her how beautiful she seemed to
him. He had a lover's voice, he spoke with a tender reverence that came near
to awe, and she had never before been touched by adoration. She made him
no definite answer, but it was clear his words pleased her.

After that he talked to her whenever he could take an opportunity. The
valley became the world for him, and the world beyond the mountains where
610   men lived in sunlight seemed no more than a fairy tale he would some day
pour into her ears. Very tentatively and timidly he spoke to her of sight.

Sight seemed to her the most poetical of fancies, and she listened to his
description of the stars and the mountains and her own sweet white-lit
beauty as though it was a guilty indulgence. She did not believe, she could
only half understand, but she was mysteriously delighted, and it seemed to
him that she completely understood.

His love lost its awe and took courage. Presently he was for demanding
her of Yacob and the elders in marriage, but she became fearful and delayed.
And it was one of her elder sisters who first told Yacob that Medina-saroté
620   and Nunez were in love.

There was from the first very great opposition to the marriage of Nunez
and Medina-saroté; not so much because they valued her as because they held
him as a being apart, an idiot, incompetent thing below the permissible level
of a man. Her sisters opposed it bitterly as bringing discredit on them all; and

old Yacob, though he had formed a sort of liking for his clumsy, obedient serf, shook his head and said the thing could not be. The young men were all angry at the idea of corrupting the race, and one went so far as to revile and strike Nunez. He struck back. Then for the first time he found an advantage in seeing, even by twilight, and after that fight was over no one was disposed to raise a hand against him. But they still found his marriage impossible.   630

Old Yacob had a tenderness for his last little daughter, and was grieved to have her weep upon his shoulder.

"You see, my dear, he's an idiot. He has delusions; he can't do anything right."

"I know," wept Medina-saroté. "But he's better than he was. He's getting better. And he's strong, dear father, and kind—stronger and kinder than any other man in the world. And he loves me—and, father, I love him."

Old Yacob was greatly distressed to find her inconsolable, and, besides— what made it more distressing—he liked Nunez for many things. So he went and sat in the windowless council-chamber with the other elders and   640 watched the trend of the talk, and said, at the proper time, "He's better than he was. Very likely, some day, we shall find him as sane as ourselves."

Then afterwards one of the elders, who thought deeply, had an idea. He was the great doctor among these people, their medicine-man, and he had a very philosophical and inventive mind, and the idea of curing Nunez of his peculiarities appealed to him. One day when Yacob was present he returned to the topic of Nunez.

"I have examined Bogota," he said, "and the case is clearer to me. I think very probably he might be cured."

"That is what I have always hoped," said old Yacob.   650

"His brain is affected," said the blind doctor.

The elders murmured assent.

"Now, *what* affects it?"

"Ah!" said old Yacob.

"*This,*" said the doctor, answering his own question. "Those queer things that are called the eyes, and which exist to make an agreeable soft depression in the face, are diseased, in the case of Bogota, in such a way as to affect his brain. They are greatly distended, he has eyelashes, and his eyelids move, and consequently his brain is in a state of constant irritation and destruction."

"Yes?" said old Yacob. "Yes?"   660

"And I think I may say with reasonable certainty that, in order to cure him completely, all that we need do is a simple and easy surgical operation— namely, to remove these irritant bodies."

"And then he will be sane?"

"Then he will be perfectly sane, and a quite admirable citizen."

"Thank Heaven for science!" said old Yacob, and went forth at once to tell Nunez of his happy hopes.

But Nunez's manner of receiving the good news struck him as being cold and disappointing.

670   "One might think," he said, "from the tone you take, that you did not care for my daughter."

It was Medina-saroté who persuaded Nunez to face the blind surgeons.

"*You* do not want me," he said, "to lose my gift of sight?"

She shook her head.

"My world is sight."

Her head drooped lower.

"There are the beautiful things, the beautiful little things—the flowers, the lichens among the rocks, the lightness and softness on a piece of fur, the far sky with its drifting down of clouds, the sunsets and the stars. And there

680   is *you*. For you alone it is good to have sight, to see your sweet, serene face, your kindly lips, your dear, beautiful hands folded together. . . . It is these eyes of mine you won, these eyes that hold me to you, that these idiots seek. Instead, I must touch you, hear you, and never see you again. I must come under that roof of rock and stone and darkness, that horrible roof under which your imagination stoops. . . . No; you would not have me do that?"

A disagreeable doubt had arisen in him. He stopped, and left the thing a question.

"I wish," she said, "sometimes———" She paused.

"Yes?" said he, a little apprehensively.

690   "I wish sometimes—you would not talk like that."

"Like what?"

"I know it's pretty—it's your imagination. I love it, but *now*———"

He felt cold. "*Now?*" he said faintly.

She sat quite still.

"You mean—you think—I should be better, better perhaps———"

He was realising things very swiftly. He felt anger, indeed, anger at the dull course of fate, but also sympathy for her lack of understanding—a sympathy near akin to pity.

"*Dear,*" he said, and he could see by her whiteness how intensely her spirit

700   pressed against the things she could not say. He put his arms about her, he kissed her ear, and they sat for a time in silence.

"If I were to consent to this?" he said at last, in a voice that was very gentle.

She flung her arms about him, weeping wildly. "Oh, if you would," she sobbed, "if only you would!"

For a week before the operation that was to raise him from his servitude and inferiority to the level of a blind citizen, Nunez knew nothing of sleep, and all through the warm sunlit hours, while the others slumbered happily, he sat brooding or wandered aimlessly, trying to bring his mind to bear on

710   his dilemma. He had given his answer, he had given his consent, and still he was not sure. And at last work-time was over, the sun rose in splendour over the golden crests, and his last day of vision began for him. He had a few minutes with Medina-saroté before she went apart to sleep.

"To-morrow," he said, "I shall see no more."

"Dear heart!" she answered, and pressed his hands with all her strength.

"They will hurt you but little," she said; "and you are going through this pain—you are going through it, dear lover, for *me*. . . . Dear, if a woman's heart and life can do it, I will repay you. My dearest one, my dearest with the tender voice, I will repay."

He was drenched in pity for himself and her.   720

He held her in his arms, and pressed his lips to hers, and looked on her sweet face for the last time. "Good-bye!" he whispered at that dear sight, "good-bye!"

And then in silence he turned away from her.

She could hear his slow retreating footsteps, and something in the rhythm of them threw her into a passion of weeping.

He had fully meant to go to a lonely place where the meadows were beautiful with white narcissus, and there remain until the hour of his sacrifice should come, but as he went he lifted up his eyes and saw the morning, the morning like an angel in golden armour, marching down the steeps. . . .   730

It seemed to him that before this splendour he, and this blind world in the valley, and his love, and all, were no more than a pit of sin.

He did not turn aside as he had meant to do, but went on, and passed through the wall of the circumference and out upon the rocks, and his eyes were always upon the sunlit ice and snow.

He saw their infinite beauty, and his imagination soared over them to the things beyond he was now to resign for ever.

He thought of that great free world he was parted from, the world that was his own, and he had a vision of those further slopes, distance beyond distance, with Bogota, a place of multitudinous stirring beauty, a glory by day,   740
a luminous mystery by night, a place of palaces and fountains and statues and white houses, lying beautifully in the middle distance. He thought how for a day or so one might come down through passes, drawing ever nearer and nearer to its busy streets and ways. He thought of the river journey, day by day, from great Bogota to the still vaster world beyond, through towns and villages, forest and desert places, the rushing river day by day, until its banks receded and the big steamers came splashing by, and one had reached the sea—the limitless sea, with its thousand islands, its thousands of islands, and its ships seen dimly far away in their incessant journeyings round and about that greater world. And there, unpent by mountains, one saw the sky—the   750
sky, not such a disc as one saw it here, but an arch of immeasurable blue, a deep of deeps in which the circling stars were floating. . . .

His eyes scrutinised the great curtain of the mountains with a keener inquiry.

For example, if one went so, up that gully and to that chimney there, then one might come out high among those stunted pines that ran round in a sort of shelf and rose still higher and higher as it passed above the gorge. And

then? That <u>talus</u> might be managed. Thence perhaps a climb might be found
to take him up to the precipice that came below the snow; and if that chim-
760   ney failed, then another farther to the east might serve his purpose better.
And then? Then one would be out upon the amber-lit snow there, and halfway up to the crest of those beautiful desolations.

He glanced back at the village, then turned right round and regarded it
steadfastly.

He thought of Medina-saroté, and she had become small and remote.

He turned again towards the mountain wall, down which the day had
come to him.

Then very circumspectly he began to climb.

When sunset came he was no longer climbing, but he was far and high.
770   He had been higher, but he was still very high. His clothes were torn, his
limbs were blood-stained, he was bruised in many places, but he lay as if he
were at his ease, and there was a smile on his face.

From where he rested the valley seemed as if it were in a pit and nearly a
mile below. Already it was dim with haze and shadow, though the mountain
summits around him were things of light and fire, and the little details of the
rocks near at hand were drenched with subtle beauty—a vein of green min-
eral piercing the grey, the flash of crystal faces here and there, a minute,
minutely beautiful orange lichen close beside his face. There were deep mysterious shadows in the gorge, blue deepening into purple, and purple into a
780   luminous darkness, and overhead was the illimitable vastness of the sky. But
he heeded these things no longer, but lay quite inactive there, smiling as if he
were satisfied merely to have escaped from the valley of the Blind in which
he had thought to be King.

The glow of the sunset passed, and the night came, and still he lay peacefully contented under the cold stars.

[1904]

A SITUATIONIST PERSPECTIVE
ON THE PSYCHOLOGY OF EVIL
UNDERSTANDING HOW GOOD PEOPLE
ARE TRANSFORMED INTO PERPETRATORS
Philip G. Zimbardo

I endorse the application of a situationist perspective to the ways in which the antisocial behavior of individuals and the violence sanctioned by nations can be best understood, treated, and prevented. This view, which has both influenced and been informed by a body of social-psychological research and theory, contrasts with the traditional perspective that explains evil behavior in dispositional terms: Internal determinants of antisocial behavior locate evil within individual predispositions—genetic "bad seeds," personality traits, psychopathological risk factors, and other organismic variables. The situationist approach is to the dispositional as public health models of disease are to medical models. Following basic principles of Lewinian theory, the situationist perspective propels external determinants of behavior to the foreground, well beyond the status as merely extenuating background circumstances. Unique to this situationist approach is the use of experimental laboratory and field research to demonstrate vital phenomena, that other approaches only analyze verbally or rely on archival or correlational data for answers. The basic paradigm presented in this chapter illustrates the relative ease with which ordinary, "good" men and women can be induced into behaving in "evil" ways by turning on or off one or another social situational variable.

I begin the chapter with a series of "oldies but goodies"—my laboratory and field studies on deindividuation, aggression, vandalism, and the Stanford prison experiment, along with a process analysis of Milgram's obedience studies, and Bandura's analysis of "moral disengagement." My analysis is extended to the evil of inaction by considering bystander failures of helping those in distress. This body of research demonstrates the underrecognized power of social situations to alter the mental representations and behavior of individuals, groups, and nations. Finally, I explore extreme instances of "evil" behavior for their dispositional or situational foundations: torturers, death-squad violence workers, and terrorist suicide bombers.

Evil can be defined as intentionally behaving, or causing others to act, in ways that demean, dehumanize, harm, destroy, or kill innocent people. This behaviorally focused definition makes the individual or group responsible for purposeful, motivated actions that have a range of negative consequences for other people. The definition excludes accidental or unintended harmful outcomes, as well as the broader, generic forms of institutional evil, such as poverty, prejudice, or destruction of the environment by agents of corporate

---

Reprinted from *The Social Psychology of Good and Evil: Understanding Our Capacity for Kindness and Cruelty*, edited by Arthur G. Miller (2005), Guilford Press.

greed. However, it does include corporate forms of wrongdoing, such as the marketing and selling of products with known disease-causing, death-dealing properties (e.g., cigarette manufacturers or other substance/drug dealers). The definition also extends beyond the proximal agent of aggression, as stud-
40 ied in research on interpersonal violence, to encompass those in distal positions of authority whose orders or plans are carried out by functionaries. Such agents include military commanders and national leaders, such as Hitler, Stalin, Mao, Pol Pot, Idi Amin, and others whom history has identified as tyrants for their complicity in the deaths of untold millions of innocent people.

History will also have to decide on the evil status of President George W. Bush's role in declaring a pre-emptive, aggressive war against Iraq in March 2003, with dubious justification, that resulted in widespread death, injury, destruction, and enduring chaos. We might also consider a simpler definition
50 of evil, proposed by my colleague, Irving Sarnoff: "Evil is knowing better but doing worse."

We live in a world cloaked in the evils of civil and international wars, of terrorism (home-grown and exported), homicides, rapes, domestic and child abuse, and countless other forms of devastation. The same human mind that creates the most beautiful works of art and extraordinary marvels of technology is equally responsible for the perversion of its own perfection. This most dynamic organ in the universe has served as a seemingly endless source of ever viler torture chambers and instruments of horror in earlier centuries, the "bestial machinery" unleashed on Chinese citizens by Japanese soldiers in
60 their rape of Nanking (see Chang, 1997), and the recent demonstration of "creative evil" in the destruction of the World Trade Center by "weaponizing" commercial airlines. We continue to ask, *why*? Why and how is it possible for such deeds to continue to occur? How can the unimaginable become so readily imagined? These are the same questions that have been asked by generations before ours.

I wish I had answers to these profound questions about human existence and human nature. Here I can offer modest versions of possible answers. My concern centers around how good, ordinary people can be recruited, induced, seduced into behaving in ways that could be classified as evil. In
70 contrast to the traditional approach of trying to identify "evil people" to account for the evil in our midst, I focus on trying to outline some of the central conditions that are involved in the transformation of good people into perpetrators of evil.

LOCATING EVIL WITHIN PARTICULAR PEOPLE: THE RUSH TO THE DISPOSITIONAL

"Who is responsible for evil in the world, given that there is an all-powerful, omniscient God who is also all-Good?" That conundrum began the intellectual scaffolding of the Inquisition in the 16th and 17th centuries in Europe.

As revealed in *Malleus Maleficarum*, the handbook of the German Inquisitors from the Roman Catholic Church, the inquiry concluded that "the Devil" was the source of all evil. However, these theologians argued the Devil works his evil through intermediaries, lesser demons, and, of course, human witches. So the hunt for evil focused on those marginalized people who looked or acted differently from ordinary people, who might qualify, under rigorous examination of conscience and torture, as "witches," and then put them to death. The victims were mostly women who could be readily exploited without sources of defense, especially when they had resources that could be confiscated. An analysis of this legacy of institutionalized violence against women is detailed by historian Anne Barstow (1994) in *Witchcraze*. Paradoxically, this early effort of the Inquisition to understand the origins of evil and develop interventions to cope with it instead fomented new forms of evil that fulfill all facets of my definition. The phenomenon of the Inquisition exemplifies the notion of simplifying the complex problem of widespread evil by identifying *individuals* who might be the guilty parties and then making them "pay" for their evil deeds.

Most traditional psychiatry as well as psychodynamic theory also locate the source of individual violence and antisocial behavior within the psyches of disturbed people, often tracing it back to early roots in unresolved infantile conflicts. Like genetic views of pathology, such psychological approaches seek to link behaviors society judges as pathological to pathological origins—be they defective genes, "bad seeds," or premorbid personality structures. However, this view overlooks the fact that the same violent outcomes can be generated by very different types of people, all of whom give no hint of evil impulses. My colleagues and I (Lee, Zimbardo, & Berthoff, 1977) interviewed and tested 19 inmates in California prisons who had all recently been convicted of homicide. Ten of these killers had a long history of violence, showed lack of impulse control (on the Minnesota Multiphasic Personality Inventory), were decidedly masculine in sexual identity, and generally extraverted. The other murderers were totally different. They had never committed any criminal offense prior to the homicide—their murders were totally unexpected, given their mild manner and gentle disposition. Their problem was an *excessive* impulse control that inhibited their expression of any feelings. Their sexual identity was feminine or androgynous, and the majority were shy. These "shy sudden murderers" killed just as violently as did the habitual criminals, and their victims died just as surely, but it would have been impossible to predict this outcome from any prior knowledge of their personalities, which were so different from the more obvious habitual criminals.

The concept of an authoritarian personality syndrome was developed by a team of psychologists (Adorno, Frenkel-Brunswick, Levinson, & Sanford, 1950) after World War II who were trying to make sense of the Holocaust and the broad appeal of fascism and Hitler. Their dispositional bias led them to focus on identifying a set of personality factors that might underlie the fascist mentality. However, they over-looked the host of processes operating at political, economic, societal, and historical levels, all of which influenced and directed so many millions of individuals into a constrained behavioral channel of hating Jews and other minority groups, while endorsing and even applauding the views and policies of their dictator.

This tendency to explain observed behavior by reference to internal dispositional factors while ignoring or minimizing the impact of situational variables has been termed the fundamental attribution error (FAE) by my colleague Lee Ross (1977). We are all subject to this dual bias of overutilizing dispositional analyses and underutilizing situational explanations when faced with ambiguous causal scenarios we want to understand. We succumb to this effect because our educational institutions, social and professional training programs, and societal agencies are all geared toward a focus on individual, dispositional orientations. Dispositional analyses are a central operating feature of cultures that are based on individualistic rather than collectivist values (see Triandis, 1994). Thus, it is individuals who are lauded with praise and fame and wealth for achievement and are honored for their uniqueness, but it is also individuals who are blamed for the ills of society. Our legal, medical, educational, and religious systems all are founded on principles of individualism.

Dispositional analyses of antisocial, or non-normative, behaviors typically include strategies for behavior modification, whereby deviant individuals learn to conform better to social norms, or facilities for excluding them from society via imprisonment, exile, or execution. Locating evil within selected individuals or groups carries with it the "social virtue" of taking society "off the hook" as blameworthy; societal structures and political decision making are exonerated from bearing any burden of the more fundamental circumstances that create racism, sexism, elitism, poverty, and marginal existence for some citizens. Furthermore, this dispositional orientation to understanding evil implies a simplistic, binary world of good people, like us, and bad people, like them. That clear-cut dichotomy is divided by a manufactured line that separates good and evil. We then take comfort in the illusion that such a line constrains crossovers in either direction. We could never imagine being like *them*, of doing their unthinkable dirty deeds, and do not admit them into our company because they are so essentially different as to be unchangeable. This extreme position also means we forfeit the motivation to understand how they came to engage in what we view as evil behavior. I find it helpful to remind myself of the geopolitical analysis of the Russian novelist Alexander Solzhenitsyn, a victim of persecution by the Soviet KGB, that the line between good and evil lies in the center of every human heart.

THE TRANSFORMATION OF GOOD PEOPLE INTO AGENTS OF DESTRUCTION

My bias is admittedly more toward situational analyses of behavior and comes from my training as an experimental social psychologist as well as from having grown up in poverty, in a New York City ghetto of the South Bronx. I believe that dispositional orientations are more likely to correlate with afflu-ence: The rich want to take full credit for their success, whereas the situa-tionists hail more from the lower classes who want to explain the obvious dys-functional lifestyles of those around them in terms of external circumstances rather than internal failures. I am primarily concerned with understanding the psychological and social dynamics involved when an ordinary, "good" per-son begins to act in antisocial ways and, in the extreme, behaves destructively toward the property or person of others. I saw, firsthand, my childhood friends go through such transformations, and I wondered how and why they changed so drastically and whether I could also change like that (e.g., they were bullied, failed in school, parents fought all the time, nothing to look forward to). I was similarly fascinated with the tale of the behavioral trans-formation of Robert Louis Stevenson's good Dr. Jekyll into the murderous Mr. Hyde. What was in his chemical formula that could have such an imme-diate and profound impact? Even as a child, I wondered if there were other ways to induce such changes, since my friends did not have access to his elixir of evil before they did such bad things to other people. I would later discover that social psychology had recipes for such transformations.

Our mission is to understand better how virtually anyone could be recruited to engage in evil deeds that deprive other human beings of their dignity, humanity, and life. The dispositional analysis has the comforting side effect of enabling those who have not yet done wrong to righteously assert, "Not *me*, I am different from those kinds of people who did that evil deed!" By positing a "me-us-them" distinction, we live with the illusion of moral superiority firmly entrenched in the pluralistic ignorance that comes from not recognizing the set of situational and structural circumstances that empowered others—like ourselves—to engage in deeds that they too once thought were alien to their nature. We take false pride in believing that "I am not that kind of person."

I argue that the human mind is so marvelous that it can adapt to virtu-ally any known environmental circumstance in order to survive, to create, and to destroy, as necessary. We are not born with tendencies toward good or evil but with mental templates to do *either*. What I mean is that we have the potential to be better or worse than anyone who has existed in the past, to be more creative and more destructive, to make the world a better place or a worse place than before. It is only through the recognition that no one of us is an island, that we all share the human condition, that humility takes prece-dence over unfounded pride in acknowledging our vulnerability to situa-tional forces. If we want to develop mechanisms for combating such malev-olent transformations, then it seems essential to learn to appreciate the extent to which ordinary people can be seduced or initiated into the performance of evil deeds. We need to focus on discovering the mechanisms among the causal factors that influence so many to do so much bad, to commit so much evil throughout the globe. (See also the breadth of ideas presented by Baumeister, 1997; Darley, 1992; Staub, 1989; Waller, 2002.)

THE MILGRAM OBEDIENCE EXPERIMENTS

The most obvious power of the experimental demonstration by Stanley Milgram (1974) of blind obedience to authority lies in the unexpectedly
210 high rates of such compliance, with the majority—two-thirds—of the subjects "going all the way" in shocking a victim with apparently lethal consequences. His finding was indeed shocking to most of those who read about it or saw his movie version of the study, because it revealed that a variety of ordinary American citizens could so readily be led to engage in "electrocuting a nice stranger." But the more significant importance of his research comes from what he did after that initial classic study with Yale College undergraduates. Milgram conducted 18 experimental variations on more than a *thousand* subjects from a variety of backgrounds, ages, both genders, and all educational levels. In each of these studies he varied
220 one social-psychological variable and observed its impact on the extent of obedience to the unjust authority's pressure to continue to shock the "learner-victim." He was able to demonstrate that compliance rates of those who delivered the maximum 450 volts to the hapless victim could soar to 90% or could be reduced to less than 10% by introducing a single variable into the compliance recipe.

Milgram found that obedience was maximized when subjects first observed peers behaving obediently; it was dramatically reduced when peers rebelled or when the victim acted like a masochist asking to be shocked. What is especially interesting to me about this last result are the data Mil-
230 gram provides on the predictions of his outcome by 40 psychiatrists who were given the basic description of the classic experiment. Their average estimate of the percentage of U.S. citizens who would give the full 450 volts was fewer than 1%. Only sadists would engage in such sadistic behavior, they believed. In a sense, this is the comparison level for appreciating the enormity of Milgram's finding. These experts on human behavior were *totally* wrong because they ignored the situational determinants of behavior in the procedural description of the experiment and overrelied on the dispositional perspective that comes from their professional training. Their error is a classic instance of the FAE at work. In fact, in this research, the average person does
240 *not* behave like a sadist when an apparently masochistic victim encourages him or her to do so.

Milgram's intention was to provide a paradigm in which it was possible to quantify "evil" by the number of buttons a subject pushed on a shock generator, which allegedly delivered shocks to a mild-mannered confederate, playing the role of the pupil or learner, while the subject enacted the teacher role. Some of the procedures in this research paradigm that seduced many ordinary citizens to engage in evil offer parallels to compliance strategies used by "influence professionals" in real-world settings, such as salespeople, cult recruiters, and our national leaders (see Cialdini, 2001).

TEN INGREDIENTS IN THE SITUATIONIST'S RECIPE
FOR BEHAVIORAL TRANSFORMATIONS

Among the influence principles in Milgram's paradigm for getting ordinary peo-   250
ple to do things they originally believed they would not do are the following:

1. Presenting an acceptable justification, or rationale, for engaging in the
   undesirable action, such as wanting to help people improve their
   memory by judicious use of punishment strategies. In experiments
   this justification is known as the "cover story" because it is intended
   to cover up the procedures that follow, which might not make sense
   on their own. The real-world equivalent of the cover story is an ideology, such as "national security," that often provides the nice big lie
   for instituting a host of bad, illegal, and immoral policies.

2. Arranging some form of contractual obligation, verbal or written, to   260
   enact the behavior.

3. Giving participants meaningful roles to play (e.g., teacher, student)
   that carry with them previously learned positive values and response
   scripts.

4. Presenting basic rules to be followed, which seem to make sense prior
   to their actual use, but then can be arbitrarily used to justify mindless
   compliance. "Failure to respond must be treated as an error" was a Milgram rule for shock omissions as well as for false commissions. But
   then what happens when the learner complains of a heart condition,
   wants to quit, then screams, followed by a thud and silence? The   270
   learner's apparent inability to respond to the teacher's testing due to
   death or unconsciousness must be continually challenged by further
   shocks, since omission equals commission. The proceedings do not
   make sense at all: How could the teacher be helping to improve the
   memory of a learner who is incapacitated or dead? All too many participants stopped engaging in such basic, obvious critical thinking
   endeavors as their confusion and stress mounted.

5. Altering the semantics of the act and action: from hurting victims to
   helping learners by punishing them.

6. Creating opportunities for diffusion of responsibility for negative   280
   outcomes; others will be responsible, or it will not be evident that the
   actor will be held liable.

7. Starting the path toward the ultimate evil act with a small, insignificant first step (only 15 volts).

8. Increasing each level of aggression in gradual steps that do not seem
   like noticeable differences (only 30 volts).

9. Gradually changing the nature of the influence authority from
   "just" to "unjust," from reasonable and rational to unreasonable
   and irrational.

290   10. Making the "exit costs" high and the process of exiting difficult by not permitting usual forms of verbal dissent to qualify as behavioral disobedience.

Such procedures are utilized across varied influence situations, in which those in authority want others to do their bidding but know that few would engage in the "end game" final solution without first being properly prepared psychologically to do the "unthinkable." I would encourage readers to engage in the thought exercise of applying these compliance principles to the tactics used by the Bush administration to cajole Americans into endorsing the preemptive invasion of Iraq (discussed further later in the chapter).

LORD OF THE FLIES AND THE PSYCHOLOGY OF DEINDIVIDUATION

300   William Golding's (1954) Noble prize-winning novel of the transformation of good British choir boys into murderous beasts centers on the point of change in mental state and behavior that follows a change in physical appearance. Painting themselves, changing their outward appearance, made it possible for some of Golding's characters to disinhibit previously restrained impulses to kill a pig for food. Once that alien deed of killing another creature was accomplished, they could then continue on to kill, with pleasure, both animals and people alike. Was Golding describing a psychologically valid principle in his use of external appearance as catalyst to dramatic changes in internal and behavioral processes? That is the question I answered
310   with a set of experiments and field studies on the psychology of deindividuation (Zimbardo, 1970).

The basic procedure involved having young women deliver a series of painful electric shocks to each of two other young women whom they could see and hear in a one-way mirror before them. Half were randomly assigned to a condition of anonymity, or deindividuation, half to one of uniqueness, or individuation. The appearance of the four college student subjects in each deindividuation group was concealed, and they were given identifying numbers in place of their names. The comparison individuation subjects in the four-woman groups were called by their names and
320   made to feel unique. They were asked to make the same responses of shocking each of two female "victims"—all with a suitable cover story, the big lie that they never questioned.

The results were clear: Women in the deindividuation condition delivered twice as much shock to both victims as did the women in the individuated comparison condition. Moreover, the deindividuated subjects shocked both victims, the one previously rated as pleasant and the other as unpleasant, more over the course of the 20 trials, whereas the individuated subjects shocked the pleasant woman less over time than they did the unpleasant one. One important conclusion flows from this research and its various replica-

tions and extensions, some using military personnel: <u>Anything that makes</u>   330
<u>a person feel anonymous, as if no one knows who he or she is, creates the</u>
<u>potential for that person to act in evil ways—if the situation gives permission</u>
<u>for violence.</u>

HALLOWEEN DISGUISES AND AGGRESSION IN CHILDREN

Outside the laboratory, *masks* may be used to create the anonymity needed
to disinhibit typically restrained behavior. For example, people mask themselves at Carnival rituals in many Catholic countries. Children in the United
States don masks and costumes for Mardi Gras and Halloween parties.
Bringing the laboratory to the party, so to speak, Fraser (1974) arranged for
elementary school children to go to a special, experimental Halloween party
given by their teacher. There were many games to play and for each game   340
won, tokens were earned that could be exchanged for gifts at the end of the
party. Half the games were nonaggressive in nature, and half were matched
in content but involved aggression: Physical confrontations between two
children were necessary to reach the goal and win the contest. The experimental design was a within-subject (A-B-A) format: in the first phase the
games were played without costumes; then the costumes arrived and were
worn as the games continued; finally, the costumes were removed and the
games went on for the third phase (each phase lasted about an hour). The
data are striking testimony to the power of anonymity. Aggression increased
significantly as soon as the costumes were worn, more than doubling from   350
the initial base level average. When the costumes were removed, aggression
dropped back well below the initial base rate. Equally interesting was the second result: that aggression had negative instrumental consequences on winning tokens—that is, it costs money to be aggressive—but that cost did not
matter when the children were anonymous in their costumes. The least number of tokens won occurred during the costumed anonymity phase, when
aggression was highest.

CULTURAL WISDOM OF CHANGING WARRIORS' APPEARANCES

Let us leave the laboratory and the fun and games of children's parties to enter
the real world, where these issues of anonymity and violence may take on life-
and-death significance. Some societies go to war without having the young   360
male warriors change their appearance, whereas others always include ritual
transformations of appearance by painting or masking the warriors (as in *Lord
of the Flies*). Does that change in external appearance make a difference in how
warring enemies are treated? After reading my Nebraska Symposium chapter,
Harvard anthropologist John Watson (1973) posed a research question, then
went to the human area files to find the answer, then published the data:
(1) the societies that did or did not change appearance of warriors prior to
going to war; and (2) the extent to which they killed, tortured, or mutilated

370 their victims. The results are striking confirmation of the prediction that anonymity promotes destructive behavior, when permission is also given to behave in aggressive ways that are ordinarily prohibited. Of the 23 societies for which these two data sets were present, the majority (12 of 15, 80%) of societies in which warriors changed their appearance were those noted as most destructive, whereas only one of the eight societies in which the warriors did *not* change appearance before going to battle was noted as destructive. Cultural wisdom dictates that when old men want usually peaceful young men to harm and kill other young men like themselves in a war, it is easier to do so if they first change their appearance by putting on uniforms or masks or painting their faces. With that anonymity in place, out goes their usual internal 380 focus of compassion and concern for others.

THE THEORETICAL MODEL OF DEINDIVIDUATION AND BANDURA'S MODEL OF MORAL DISENGAGEMENT

The psychological mechanisms involved in getting good people to do evil are embodied in two theoretical models, the first elaborated by me (Zimbardo, 1970) and modified by input from subsequent variants on my deindividuation conceptions, notably by Diener (1980). The second is Bandura's model of moral disengagement (1998, 2003), which specifies the conditions under which anyone can be led to act immorally, even those who usually ascribe to high levels of morality.

Bandura's model outlines how it is possible to morally disengage from destructive conduct by using a set of cognitive mechanisms that alter (1) one's 390 perception of the reprehensible conduct (e.g., by engaging in moral justifications, making palliative comparisons, using euphemistic labeling for one's conduct); (2) one's sense of the detrimental effects of that conduct (e.g., by minimizing, ignoring, or misconstruing the consequences); (3) one's sense of responsibility for the link between reprehensible conduct and the detrimental effects (e.g., by displacing or diffusing responsibility); and (4) one's view of the victim (e.g., by dehumanizing him or her, attributing the blame for the outcome to the victim).

Dehumanization in Action: "Animals" by Any Other Name Are College Students

A remarkable experiment by Bandura, Underwood, and Fromson (1975) reveals how easy it is to induce intelligent college students to accept a dehu- 400 manizing label of other people and then to act aggressively based on that stereotyped term. Four participants were led to believe they were overhearing the research assistant tell the experimenter that the students from another college were present to start the study in which they were to deliver electric shocks of varying intensity to the participants (according to the dictates of a reasonable cover story). In one of the three randomly assigned conditions, the subjects overheard the assistant say to the experimenter that the other students seemed "nice"; in a second condition, they heard the other students described as "animals"; in the third group, the assistant did not label the students in the alleged other group.

The dependent variable of shock intensity clearly reflected this situational manipulation. The subjects gave the highest levels of shock to those labeled in the dehumanizing way as "animals," and their shock level increased linearly over the 10 trials. Those labeled "nice" were given the least shock, whereas the unlabelled group fell in the middle of these two extremes. Thus, a single word—*animals*—was sufficient to incite intelligent college students to treat those so labeled as if they deserved to be harmed. On the plus side, the labeling effect resulted in others being treated with greater respect if someone in authority labeled them positively. The graphed data is also of interest: On the first trial there is no difference across the three experimental treatments in the level of shock administered, but with each successive opportunity, the shock levels diverge. Those shocking the so-called "animals" shock them more and more over time, a result comparable to the escalating shock level of the deindividuated female students in my earlier study. That rise in aggressive responding over time, with practice, or with experience belies a self-reinforcing effect of aggressive or violent responding: It is experienced as increasingly pleasurable.

It must be, but what is the pleasure? sense of just deserts?

What my model adds to the mix of what is needed to get good people to engage in evil deeds is a focus on the role of cognitive controls that usually guide behavior in socially desirable and personally acceptable ways. The shift from good to evil behavior can be accomplished by knocking out these control processes, blocking them, minimizing them, or reorienting them. Doing so suspends conscience, self-awareness, sense of personal responsibility, obligation, commitment, liability, morality, and analyses in terms of costs-benefits of given actions. The two general strategies for accomplishing this objective are (1) reducing cues of social accountability of the actor (i.e., "No one knows who I am, nor cares to know"), and (2) reducing concerns for self-evaluation by the actor. The first eliminates concerns for social evaluation and social approval by conveying a sense of anonymity to the actor and diffusing personal responsibility across others in the situation. The second strategy stops self-monitoring and consistency monitoring by relying on tactics that alter states of consciousness (e.g., via drugs, arousing strong emotions or hyperintense actions, creating a highly focused present-time orientation wherein there is no concern for past or future), and by projecting responsibility outside the self and onto others.

match up with kohlberg's levels of justice

My research and that of other social psychologists (see Prentice-Dunn & Rogers, 1983) on deindividuation differs from the paradigm in Milgram's studies in that there is no authority figure present, urging the subject to obey. Rather, the situation is created in such a way that subjects act in accordance to paths made available to them, without thinking through the meaning or consequences of those actions. Their actions are not cognitively guided, as they are typically, but directed by the actions of others in proximity to them or by their strongly aroused emotional states and situationally available cues, such as the presence of weapons.

Environmental Anonymity Breeds Vandalism

It is possible for certain environments to convey a sense of anonymity on those who live in, or pass through, their midst. The people living in such environments do not have a sense of community. Vandalism and graffiti may be interpreted as an individual's attempt for public notoriety in a society that deindividuates him or her.

I conducted a simple field study to demonstrate the ecological differences between places ruled by anonymity versus those conveying a sense of community. I abandoned used but good-condition cars in the Bronx, New York City, and in Palo Alto, California, one block away from New York University and Stanford University, respectively. License plates were removed and hoods raised slightly to serve as ethological "releaser cues" for the potential vandals' attack behavior. It worked swiftly in the Bronx, as we watched and filmed from a vantage point across the street. Within 10 minutes of officially beginning this study, the first vandals surfaced. This parade of vandals continued for 2 days, by which time there was nothing of value left to strip; then they simply began destroying the remains. In 48 hours we recorded 23 separate "destructive contacts" by individuals or groups, who either took something from the abandoned vehicle or did something to wreck it. Curiously, only one of these episodes involved adolescents; the rest of the vandals were adults, many well dressed and many driving cars, so that they might qualify as, at least, lower middle class. Anonymity can make brazen vandals of us all. But what about the fate of the abandoned car in Palo Alto? Our time-lapse film revealed that no one vandalized any part of the car over a 5-day period. When we removed the car, three local residents called the police to say that an abandoned car was being stolen (the local police had been notified of our field study). That is one definition of "community," where people care about what happens on their turf, even to the person or property of strangers, with the reciprocal assumption that they would also care about them.

I now feel that any environmental or societal conditions that contribute to making some members of society feel that they are anonymous—that no one knows or cares who they are, that no one recognizes their individuality and thus their humanity—makes them potential assassins and vandals, a danger to my person and my property—and yours (Zimbardo, 1976).

THE FACES OF THE "ENEMY": PROPAGANDA IMAGES CONDITION US TO KILL ABSTRACTIONS

We need to add a few more operational principles to our arsenal of variables that trigger the commission of evil acts by men and women who are ordinarily good people. We can learn about some of these principles by considering

how nations prepare their young men (admittedly, women are now members   490
of the armed forces in many countries, but it is primarily the men who are sent
into combat zones) to engage in deadly wars, and how they prepare citizens to
support the risks of going to war, especially a war of aggression. This difficult
transformation is accomplished by a special form of cognitive conditioning.
Images of "The Enemy" are created by national propaganda to prepare the
minds of soldiers and citizens alike to hate those who fit the new category of
"your enemy." This mental conditioning is a soldier's most potent weapon, for
without it, he could probably never fire his weapon to kill another young man
in the cross-hairs of his gun sight. A fascinating account of how this "hostile
imagination" is created in the minds of soldiers and their families is presented   500
in *Faces of the Enemy* by Sam Keen (1986; see also his companion video).
Archetypal images of the enemy are created by propaganda fashioned by the
governments of most nations against those judged to be the dangerous
"them"—the outsiders who are also "our" enemies. These visual images create
a consensual societal paranoia that is focused on the enemy who would do
harm to the women, children, homes, and god of the soldier's nation, way of
life, and so forth. Keen's analysis of this propaganda on a worldwide scale
reveals that there are a select number of attributes utilized by "homo hostilis"
to invent an evil enemy in the minds of good members of righteous tribes.
The enemy is aggressive, faceless, a rapist, godless, barbarian, greedy, criminal,   510
a torturer, harbinger of death, a dehumanized animal, or just an abstraction.
Finally, there is the enemy as worthy, heroic opponent to be crushed in mortal combat—as in the video game of the same name.

Ordinary Men Murder Ordinary Men, Women, and Children: Jewish Enemies

One of the clearest illustrations of my fundamental theme of how ordinary
people can be transformed into engaging in evil deeds that are alien to their
past history and to their moral development comes from the analysis of British
historian Christopher Browning. In *Ordinary Men: Reserve Police Battalion 101
and the Final Solution in Poland* (1992) he recounts that in March 1942 about
80% of all victims of the Holocaust were still alive, but a mere 11 months later
about 80% were dead. In this short period of time, the *Endlösung* (Hitler's   520
"Final Solution") was galvanized by means of an intense wave of mass mobile
murder squads in Poland. This genocide required mobilization of a large-scale
killing machine at the same time as able-bodied soldiers were needed on the
Russian front. Since most Polish Jews lived in small towns and not the large
cities, the question that Browning raised about the German High Command
was "where had they found the manpower during this pivotal year of the war
for such an astounding logistical achievement in mass murder?" (p. xvi).

His answer came from archives of Nazi war crimes, in the form of the
activities of Reserve Battalion 101, a unit of about 500 men from Hamburg,
Germany. They were elderly family men, too old to be drafted into the army,   530
from working-class and lower middle-class backgrounds, with no military or
police experience, just raw recruits sent to Poland without warning of, or any

training in, their secret mission: the total extermination of all Jews living in
the remote villages of Poland. In just 4 months they had shot to death at
point blank range at least 38,000 Jews and had deported another 45,000 to
the concentration camp at Treblinka. Initially, their commander told them
that this was a difficult mission which must be obeyed by the battalion, but
any individual could refuse to execute these men, women, and children.
Records indicate that at first about half the men refused, letting the others
540   commit the mass murder. But over time, social modeling processes took their
toll, as did any guilt-induced persuasion by buddies who did the killing, until
by the end, up to 90% of the men in Battalion 101 had participated in the
shootings, even proudly taking photographs of their up-close and personal
slaughter of Jews.

Browning makes clear that there was no special selection of these men,
only that they were as "ordinary" as could be imagined—until they were put
into a situation in which they had "official" permission, even encourage-
ment, to act sadistically and brutishly against those arbitrarily labeled, as
"the enemy."

550   Let us go from the abstract to the personal for a moment: Imagine you
witnessed your own father shooting to death a helpless mother and her infant
child, and then imagine his answer to your question, "Why did you do it,
Daddy?"

The War on Iraq: A Spurious Creation of Evil Terrorists and Infusion of National Fears

Fast forward to our time, our nation, our citizenry, and the fears of terrorism
instilled by the destruction of the World Trade Center towers since that
unforgettable day of September 11, 2001. The initial press and official reaction was to label the perpetrators of this horrific deed as "hijackers," "murderers," "criminals." Soon the label changed to "terrorists" and their deeds
described as "evil." *Evil* became the coin of the realm, used repeatedly by the
560   media as fed by the administration, and with an ever-widening net of inclu-
siveness. Osama bin Laden, the mastermind of 9/11, was the first culprit designated as evil. But when he proved elusive, escaping from the war zone in
Afghanistan, it became necessary for the administration's war on terrorism
campaign to put a new face and a new place on terrorism. Of course, terrorism works its generation of fear and anxiety by its very facelessness and non-
local ubiquity. Several countries were labeled by our president as the "axis of
evil," with the leader of one of those countries, Iraq, designated as so evil that
he, Saddam Hussein, had to be removed from power by all means necessary.

570   A propaganda campaign was created to justify a preemptive war against
Saddam Hussein's regime by identifying the clear and imminent threat to the
national security of the United States posed by the alleged weapons of mass
destruction (WMD) this evil leader had at his disposal. Then a link was
erected between him and the terrorist networks to whom, allegedly, he would
sell or gift these WMD. Over time, many Americans began to believe the

falsehoods that Saddam Hussein was involved in the 9/11 terrorist attacks, was in complicity with Osama bin Laden, and had ready and operational an arsenal of deadly weapons that threatened U.S. security and well-being. Magazine images, newspaper accounts, and vivid TV stories contributed to the "evilization" of Saddam Hussein over the course of a year.

The vulnerability to terrorism that Americans continued to experience on deep, personal levels—in part, sustained and magnified by the administration's issuance of repeated (false) alarms of imminent terrorist attacks on the homeland—was relieved by the action of officially going to war. The public and Congress strongly supported a symmetrical war of "shock and awe"—to rid Iraq of the feared WMD and destroy Hussein's evil menace. Thus, for the first time in its history, the United States endorsed what the majority believed to be a justified aggressive war that has already cost billions of dollars, untold thousands of deaths (soldiers *and* civilians), totally destroyed a nation, weakened the United Nations, and will enmesh the United States in a prolonged, Vietnam-like, "no exit" scenario for years to come.

When no WMD were uncovered, despite the alleged best intelligence reports and aerial photos of them presented by the Secretary of State to the United Nations, collective cognitive dissonance reduction seeped in to maintain the belief that it was still a "necessary" and "good" war against evil (Festinger, 1957). After many months of an all-out, desperately intense search of every part of Iraq, American troops and intelligence forces have not unearthed a single WMD! So the original reason for going to war is being played down and is being replaced by the mantra that Iraq is the new front in our worldwide fight against terrorism, thus it is good we are in control of the destiny of Iraq. But who cares what the truth really is regarding the deceptive reasons for going to war, if the United States is now safer and the president is a commander-in-chief of decisive action—as his image crafters have carefully depicted him in the media. This national mind control experiment deserves careful documenting by unbiased social historians for the current and future generations to appreciate the power of images, words, and framing that can lead a democratic nation to support *and even relish* the unthinkable evil of an aggressive war.

The Socialization of Evil: How the "Nazi Hate Primers" Prepared and Conditioned the Minds of German Youth to Hate Jews

The second broad class of operational principles by which otherwise good people can be recruited into evil is through education/socialization processes that are sanctioned by the government in power, enacted within school programs, and supported by parents and teachers. A prime example is the way in which German children in the 1930s and 1940s were systematically indoctrinated to hate Jews, to view them as the all-purpose enemy of the new (post-World War I) German nation. Space limitations do not allow full documentation of this process, but I touch on several examples of one way in which governments are responsible for sanctioning evil.

In Germany, as the Nazi party rose to power in 1933, no target of Nazification took higher priority than the reeducation of Germany's youth. Hitler wrote: "I will have no intellectual training. Knowledge is ruin to my young men. A violently active, dominating, brutal youth—that is what I am after" (*The New Order*, 1989, pp. 101–102). To teach the youth about geography and race, special primers were created and ordered to be read starting in the first grade of elementary school (see *The New Order*, 1989). These "hate primers" were brightly colored comic books that contrasted the beautiful blond Aryans with the despicably ugly caricatured Jew. They sold in the hundreds of thousands. One was titled *Trust No Fox in the Green Meadows and No Jew on His Oath*. What is most insidious about this kind of hate conditioning is that the misinformation was presented as facts to be learned and tested upon, or from which to practice penmanship. In the copy of the *Trust No Fox* text that I reviewed, a series of cartoons illustrates all the ways in which Jews supposedly deceive Aryans, get rich and fat from dominating them, and are lascivious, mean, and without compassion for the plight of the poor and the elderly Aryans.

The final scenarios depict the retribution of Aryan children when they expel Jewish teachers and children from their school, so that "proper discipline and order" could then be taught. Initially, Jews were prohibited from community areas, like public parks, then expelled altogether from Germany. The sign in the cartoon reads, ominously, "One-way street." Indeed, it was a unidirectional street that led eventually to the death camps and crematoria that were the centerpiece of Hitler's Final Solution: the genocide of the Jews. Thus, this institutionalized evil was spread pervasively and insidiously through a perverted educational system that turned away from the types of critical thinking exercises that open students' minds to new ideas and toward thinking uncritically and close-mindedly about those targeted as the enemy of the people. By controlling education and the propaganda media, any national leader could produce the fantastic scenarios depicted in George Orwell's (1981) frightening novel *1984*.

The institutionalized evil that Orwell vividly portrays in his fictional account of state dominance over individuals goes beyond the novelist's imagination when its prophetic vision is carried into operational validity by powerful cult leaders or by agencies and departments within the current national administration of the United States. Previously I have outlined the direct parallels between the mind control strategies and tactics Orwell attributes to "The Party" and those that Reverend Jim Jones used in dominating the members of his religious/political cult, Peoples Temple (Zimbardo, 2003a). Jones orchestrated the suicide/murders of more than 900 U.S. citizens in the jungles of Guyana 25 years ago, perhaps as the grand finale of his experiment in institutionalized mind control. I learned from former members of this group that not only did Jones read *1984*, he talked about it often and even had a song commissioned by the church's singer, entitled "1984 Is Coming," that everyone had to sing at some services. I will leave it to the reader to explore the similarities between the mind control practices in *1984* and those being practiced on U.S. citizens in the past few years (see Zimbardo, 2003b).

THE STANFORD PRISON EXPERIMENT: A CRUCIBLE OF HUMAN NATURE WHERE GOOD BOYS ENCOUNTERED AN EVIL PLACE

Framing the issues we have been considering as, in essence, who wins when good boys are put in an evil place casts it as a neo-Greek tragedy scenario, wherein "the situation" stands in for the externally imposed forces of "the gods and destiny." As such, we can anticipate an outcome unfavorable to humanity. In more mundane psychological terms, this research on the Stanford prison experiment synthesized many of the processes and variables outlined earlier: those of place and person anonymity that contribute to the deindividuation of the people involved, the dehumanization of victims, giving some actors (guards) permission to control others (prisoners), and placing it all within a unique setting (the prison) that most societies throughout the world acknowledge provides some form of institutionally approved sanctions for evil through the extreme differentials in control and power fostered in prison environments.

In 1971, I designed a dramatic experiment that would extend over a 2-week period to provide our research participants with sufficient time for them to become fully engaged in their experimentally assigned roles of either guards or prisoners. Having participants live in a simulated prison setting day and night, if prisoners, or work there for long 8-hour shifts, if guards, would also allow sufficient time for situational norms to develop and patterns of social interaction to emerge, change, and crystallize. The second feature of this study was to ensure that all research participants would be as normal as possible initially, healthy both physically and mentally, and without any history of involvement in drugs or crime or violence. This baseline was essential to establish if we were to untangle the situational versus dispositional knot: What the situation elicited from this collection of similar, interchangeable young men versus what was emitted by the research participants based on the unique dispositions they brought into the experiment. The third feature of the study was the novelty of the prisoner and guard roles: Participants had no prior training in how to play the randomly assigned roles. Each subject's prior societal learning of the meaning of prisons and the behavioral scripts associated with the oppositional roles of prisoner and guard was the sole source of guidance. The fourth feature was to create an experimental setting that came as close to a *functional simulation* of the psychology of imprisonment as possible. The details of how we went about creating a mindset comparable to that of real prisoners and guards are given in several of the articles I wrote about the study (see Zimbardo, 1975; Zimbardo, Haney, Banks, & Jaffe, 1973).

Central to this mind set were the oppositional issues of power and powerlessness, dominance and submission, freedom and servitude, control and rebellion, identity and anonymity, coercive rules and restrictive roles. In general, these social-psychological constructs were operationalized by putting all subjects in appropriate uniforms, using assorted props (e.g., handcuffs, police clubs, whistles, signs on doors and halls), replacing corridor hall doors with prison bars to create prison cells, using windowless and clock-less cells that afforded no clues as to time of day, applying institutional rules that removed/ substituted individual names with numbers (prisoners) or titles for staff (Mr. Correctional Officer, Warden, Superintendent), and that gave guards control power over prisoners.

710   Subjects were recruited from among nearly 100 men between the ages of 18 and 30 who answered our advertisements in the local city newspaper. They were given a background evaluation that consisted of a battery of five psychological tests, personal history, and in-depth interviews. The 24 who were evaluated as most normal and healthiest in every respect were randomly assigned, half to the role of prisoner and half to that of guard. The student-prisoners underwent a realistic surprise arrest by officers from the Palo Alto Police Department, who cooperated with our plan. The arresting officer proceeded with a formal arrest, taking the "felons" to the police station for booking, after which each prisoner was brought to our prison in the reconstructed
720   basement of our psychology department.

The prisoner's uniform was a smock/dress with a prison ID number. The guards wore military-style uniforms and silver-reflecting sunglasses to enhance anonymity. At any one time there were nine prisoners on "the yard," three to a cell, and three guards working 8-hour shifts. Data were collected via systematic video recordings, secret audio recordings of conversations of prisoners in their cells, interviews and tests at various times during the study, postexperiment reports, and direct, concealed observations.

For a detailed chronology and fuller account of the behavioral reactions that followed, readers are referred to the above references, to Zimbardo,
730   Maslach, and Haney (1999), and to our new website: *www.prisonexp.org*. For current purposes, let me simply summarize that the negative situational forces overwhelmed the positive dispositional tendencies. The Evil Situation triumphed over the Good People. Our projected 2-week experiment had to be terminated after only 6 days because of the pathology we were witnessing. Pacifistic young men were behaving sadistically in their role as guards, inflicting humiliation and pain and suffering on other young men who had the inferior status of prisoner. Some "guards" even reported enjoying doing so. Many of the intelligent, healthy college students who were occupying the role of prisoner showed signs of "emotional breakdown" (i.e., stress disorders)
740   so extreme that five of them had to be removed from the experiment within that first week. The prisoners who adapted better to the situation were those who mindlessly followed orders and who allowed the guards to dehumanize and degrade them ever more with each passing day and night. The only personality variable that had any significant predictive value was that of *F*-scale authoritarianism: The higher the score, the more days the prisoner survived in this totally authoritarian environment.

I terminated the experiment not only because of the escalating level of violence and degradation by the guards against the prisoners that was apparent when viewing the videotapes of their interactions, but also because I was
750   made aware of the transformation that I was undergoing personally (see the

analysis by Christina Maslach of how she intervened to help bring light to that dark place and end the study; in Zimbardo et al., 1999). I had become a Prison Superintendent in addition to my role as Principal Investigator. I began to talk, walk, and act like a rigid institutional authority figure more concerned about the security of "my prison" than the needs of the young men entrusted to my care as a psychological researcher. In a sense, I consider the extent to which I was transformed to be the most profound measure of the power of this situation. We held extended debriefing sessions of guards and prisoners at the end of the study and conducted periodic checkups over many years. Fortunately, there were no lasting negative consequences of this pow-   760
erful experience.

Before moving on, I would like to share parts of a letter sent to me recently (e-mail communication, October 18, 2002) by a young psychology student, recently discharged from military service. It outlines some of the direct parallels between the aversive aspects of our simulated prison many years ago and current despicable practices still taking place in some military boot-camp training. It also points up the positive effects that research and education can have:

> I am a 19-year-old student of psychology [who watched] the slide show of your prison experiment. Not too far into it, I was almost in   770
> tears. . . . I joined the United States Marine Corps, pursuing a child-hood dream. To make a long story short, I had become the victim of repeated illegal physical and mental abuse. An investigation showed I suffered more than 40 unprovoked beatings. Eventually, as much as I fought it, I became suicidal, thus received a discharge from boot camp. . . .
> The point I am trying to make is that the manner in which your guards carried about their duties and the way that military drill instructors do is unbelievable. I was amazed at all the parallels of your guards and one particular D. I. who comes to mind. I was treated   780
> much the same way, and even worse, in some cases.
> One incident that stands out was the time, in an effort to break platoon solidarity, I was forced to sit in the middle of my squad bay (living quarters) and shout to the other recruits "If you guys would have moved faster, we wouldn't be doing this for hours," referencing every single recruit who was holding over his head a very heavy foot locker. The event was very similar to the prisoners saying #819 was a bad prisoner. After my incident, and after I was home safe some months later, all I could think about was how much I wanted to go back to show the other recruits that as much as the D. I.s told the pla-   790
> toon that I was a bad recruit, I wasn't.
> Other behaviors come to mind, like the push-ups we did for punishment, the shaved heads, not having any identity other than being addressed as, and referring to other people as, "Recruit So-and-So"—

which replicates your study. The point of it all is that even though your experiment was conducted 31 years ago, my reading the study has helped me gain an understanding I was previously unable to gain before, even after therapy and counseling. What you have demonstrated really gave me insight into something I've been dealing with for almost a year now. Although, it is certainly not an excuse for their behavior, I now can understand the rationale behind the D. I.'s actions as far as being sadistic and power hungry.

THE FAILURE OF THE SOCIAL EXPERIMENT OF THE U.S. CORRECTIONAL SYSTEM

As much joy that such personal reactions bring to someone whose vision has always been for psychological research to make a difference in people's lives, I have been saddened by the lack of impact the Stanford prison experiment has had on the correctional system in the United States. When Craig Haney and I recently did a retrospective analysis of our study, with contrasting views of U.S. and California correctional policies over the past 30 years, our conclusions were disheartening (Haney & Zimbardo, 1998). Prisons continue to be failed social experiments that rely on a dispositional model of punishment and isolation of offenders. Gone is any sense of the modifiable situational determinants of crime or of basic rehabilitation practices that might reduce persistently high rates of recidivism. The United States is now the prison center of the universe, with more than 2 million citizens incarcerated, *greater than any other nation*, and growing. Our analysis revealed that prison conditions had significantly worsened in the decades since our study, as a consequence of the politicization of prisons, with politicians, prosecutors, DAs, and other officials taking a hard line on crime as a means of currying favor of an electorate made fearful of crime by media exaggerations. Misguided policies about sentencing for crack cocaine use and sale and the "Three Strikes" rulings have put a disproportionally large number of African American and Hispanic men behind bars for long sentences. There are now more African American men wasting away in the nation's prison system than fulfilling their potentials in our higher educational system.

THE EVIL OF INACTION

Our usual take on evil focuses on violent, destructive actions, but *non*action can also become a form of evil, when assistance, dissent, and disobedience are needed. Social psychologists heeded the alarm when the infamous Kitty Genovese case made national headlines. As she was being stalked, stabbed, and eventually murdered, 39 people in a housing complex heard her screams and did nothing to help. It seemed obvious that this was a prime example of the callousness of New Yorkers, as many media accounts reported. A counter to this dispositional analysis came in the form of a series of classic studies by

Latané and Darley (1970) on bystander intervention. One key finding was that people are less likely to help when they are in a group, when they perceive that others are available who could help, than when those people are alone. The presence of others diffuses the sense of personal responsibility of any individual.

A powerful demonstration of the failure to help strangers in distress was staged by Darley and Batson (1973). Imagine you are a theology student on your way to deliver the sermon of the Good Samaritan in order to have it videotaped for a psychology study on effective communication. Further imagine that as you are heading from the psychology department to the video taping center, you pass a stranger huddled up in an alley in dire distress. Are there any conditions that you could conceive that would not make you stop to be that Good Samaritan? What about "time press"? Would it make a difference to you if you were late for your date to give that sermon? I bet you would like to believe it would not make a difference, that you would stop and help no matter what the circumstances. Right? Remember, you are a theology student, thinking about helping a stranger in distress, which is amply rewarded in the Biblical tale.

The researchers randomly assigned students of the Princeton Theological Seminary to three conditions that varied in how much time they thought they had between receiving their assignment from the researchers and getting to the communication department to tape their Good Samaritan speeches. The conclusion: Do not be a victim in distress when people are late and in a hurry, because 90% of them are likely to pass you by, giving you no help at all! The more time the seminarians believed they had, the more likely they were to stop and help. So the situational variable of *time press* accounted for the major variance in extending or withholding help, without any need to resort to dispositional explanations about theology students being callous or cynical or indifferent, as Kitty Genovese's nonhelpers were assumed to be—another instance of the FAE, one that needs to be reversed.

840

850

860

THE WORST OF THE APPLES IN THE EVIL BARREL: TORTURERS AND EXECUTIONERS?

There is little debate but that the systematic torture by men and women of their fellow men and women represents one of the darkest sides of human nature. Surely, my colleagues and I reasoned, here was a place where dispositional evil would be manifest among torturers who did their dirty deeds daily, for years, in Brazil as policemen sanctioned by the government to extract confessions through torturing so-called enemies of the state. We began by focusing solely on the torturers, trying to understand both their psyches and the ways they were shaped by their circumstances, but we had to expand our analytical net to capture their comrades-in-arms who chose, or were assigned to, another branch of violence work—death-squad executioners. They shared a "common enemy": men, women, and children who, though citizens of

870

their state, even neighbors, were declared by "the authorities" to be threats to the country's national security. Some had to be eliminated efficiently, whereas those who might hold secret information had to be made to yield it up and confess to their treason.

In carrying out this mission, these torturers could rely, in part, on the "creative evil" embodied in the torture devices and techniques that had been refined over centuries since the Inquisition by officials of The Church and, later, of the National State. But our current-day torturers added a measure of improvisation to accommodate the particular resistances and resiliencies of the enemy standing before them, claiming innocence, refusing to acknowledge their culpability, or not succumbing to intimidation. It took time and emerging insights into exploitable human weaknesses for these torturers to become adept at their craft, in contrast to the task of the death-squad executioners, who, wearing hoods for anonymity and sporting good guns and group support, could dispatch their duty to country swiftly and impersonally. For the torturer, it could never be "just business." Torture always involves a personal relationship, essential for understanding what kind of torture to employ, what intensity of torture to use on this person at this time: wrong kind or too little, no confession; too much, and the victim dies before confessing. In either case, the torturer fails to deliver the goods. Learning to select the right kind and degree of torture that yields up the desired information makes rewards abound and praise flow from the superiors.

What kind of men could do such deeds? Did they need to rely on sadistic impulses and a history of sociopathic life experiences to rip and tear flesh of fellow beings day in and day out for years on end? Were these violence workers a breed apart from the rest of humanity—bad seeds, bad tree trunks, bad flowers? Or, is it conceivable that they were programmed to carry out their deplorable deeds by means of some identifiable and replicable training processes? Could a set of external conditions—that is, situational variables— that contributed to the making of these torturers and killers be identified? If their evil deeds were not traceable to inner defects but attributable to outer forces acting upon them—the political, economic, social, historical, and experiential components of their police training—then we might be able to generalize, across cultures and settings, those principles responsible for this remarkable transformation. Martha Huggins, Mika Haritos-Fatouros, and I interviewed several dozen of these violence workers in depth and recently published a summary of our methods and findings (Huggins, Haritos-Fatouros, & Zimbardo, 2002). Mika had done a similar, earlier study of torturers trained by the Greek military junta, and our results were largely congruent with hers (Haritos-Fatouros, 2003).

We learned that sadists are *selected out* of the training process by trainers because they are not controllable, get off on the pleasure of inflicting pain, and thus do not sustain the focus on the goal of confession extraction. From all the evidence we could muster, these violence workers were not unusual or deviant in any way prior to practicing this new role, nor were there any per-

sisting deviant tendencies or pathologies among any of them in the years following their work as torturers and executioners. Their transformation was   920
entirely understandable as a consequence of (1) the training they were given
to play this new role, (2) group camaraderie, (3) acceptance of the national
security ideology, and (4) the belief in socialist-communists as enemies of
their state. They were also influenced by being made to feel special—above
and better than peers in public service—by the secrecy of their duties and by
the constant pressure to produce desired results regardless of fatigue or personal problems. We report many detailed case studies that document the
ordinariness of these men engaged in the most heinous of deeds, sanctioned
by their government at that time in history, but reproducible at this time in
any nation whose obsession with national security and fears of terrorism per-   930   *Prophetic*
mit suspension of basic individual freedoms.

SUICIDE BOMBERS: SENSELESS FANATICS OR MARTYRS FOR A CAUSE?

Not surprisingly, what holds true for the Brazilian violence workers is comparable to the nature of the transformation of young Palestinians from students to suicide bombers killing Israelis. Recent media accounts converge on
the findings from more systematic analyses of the process of becoming a suicidal killer (see Atran, 2003; Bennet, 2003; Hoffman, 2003; Merari, 1990,
2002; Myer, 2003). There have been more than 95 suicide bombings by
Palestinians against Israelis since September, 2000. Originally, and most frequently, the bombers were young men, but recently a half dozen women have
joined the ranks of suicidal bombers. What has been declared as senseless,   940
mindless murder by those attacked and by outside observers is anything but
to those intimately involved. It was mistakenly believed that it was poor, desperate, socially isolated, illiterate young people with no career and no future
who adopted this fatalistic role. That stereotype has been shattered by the
actual portraits of these young men and women, many of whom were students with hopes for a better future, intelligent and attractive youth, connected with their family and community.

Ariel Merari, an Israeli psychologist who has studied this phenomenon for
many years, outlines the common steps on the path to these explosive deaths.
Senior members of an extremist group first identify particular young people   950
who appear to have an intense patriotic fervor, based on their declarations at
public rallies against Israel or their support of some Islamic cause or Palestin-
ian action. These individuals are invited to discuss how serious they are in
their love of their country and their hatred of Israel. They are then asked to
commit to being trained in how to put their hatred into action. Those who
make the commitment are put into a small group of three to five similar youth
who are at varying stages of "progress" toward becoming agents of death. They
learn the tricks of the trade from elders: bomb making, disguise, selecting and
timing targets. Then they publicize their private commitment by making a

960 videotape on which they declare themselves to be "living martyrs" for Islam and for the love of Allah. In one hand they hold the Koran, a rifle in the other, their head-band declaring their new status. This video binds them to the final deed, since it is sent home to the family of the recruit before they execute the final plan. The recruits also realize that not only will they earn a place beside Allah, but their relatives will also be entitled to a high place in heaven because of their martyrdom. A sizable financial incentive is bestowed on their family as a gift for their sacrifice.

Their photo is emblazoned on posters that will be put on walls everywhere in the community the moment they succeed in their mission. They
970 will be immortalized as inspirational models. To stifle concerns about the pain from wounds inflicted by exploding nails and other bomb parts, they are told that before the first drop of their blood touches the ground, they will already be seated at the side of Allah, feeling no pain, only pleasure. An ultimate incentive for the young males is the promise of heavenly bliss with scores of virgins in the next life. They become heroes and heroines, modeling self-sacrifice to the next cadre of young suicide bombers.

We can see that this program utilizes a variety of social-psychological and motivational principles in turning collective hatred and general frenzy into a dedicated, seriously calculated program of indoctrination and training for
980 individuals to become youthful "living martyrs." It is neither mindless nor senseless, only a very different mind set and with different sensibilities than we have been used to witnessing among young adults in our country. A recent television program on female suicide bombers went so far as to describe them in terms more akin to the girl next door than to alien fanatics. Indeed, that very normalcy is what is so frightening about the emergence of this new social phenomena—that so many intelligent young people could be persuaded to envision and welcome their lives ending in a suicidal explosive blast.

To counteract the powerful tactics of these recruiting agents requires the provision of meaningful, life-affirming alternatives to this next generation. It
990 requires new national leadership that is willing and able to explore every negotiating strategy that could lead to peace instead of death. It requires these young people across national boundaries to openly share their values, their education, and their resources and to explore their commonalities, not highlight their differences. The suicide, the murder, of any young person is a gash in the fabric of the human connection that we elders from every nation must unite to prevent. To encourage the sacrifice of youth for the sake of advancing ideologies of the old might be considered a form of evil from a more cosmic perspective that transcends local politics and expedient strategies.

CONCLUSIONS

It is a truism in psychology that personality and situations interact to gener-
1000 ate behavior, as do cultural and societal influences. However, I have tried to show in my research over the past 30 years that situations exert more power

over human actions than has been generally acknowledged by most psychologists or recognized by the general public. Along with a hardy band of experimental social psychologists, I have conducted research demonstrations designed, in part, to provide a corrective balance to the pervasive fundamental attribution error. Nevertheless, the traditional dispositional perspective continues to dominate Anglo-American psychology fueled by reliance on the individualist orientation central in our institutions of medicine, education, psychiatry, law, and religion. Acknowledging the power of situational forces does not excuse the behaviors evoked in response to their operation. Rather, it provides a knowledge base that shifts attention away from simplistic "blaming the victim" mentality and ineffective individualistic treatments designed to change the evil doer, toward more profound attempts to discover causal networks that should be modified. Sensitivity to situational determinants of behavior also affords "risk alerts" that allow us to avoid or modify prospective situations of vulnerability.

Please consider this Zimbardo homily that captures the essence of the difference between dispositional and situational orientations: "While a few bad apples might spoil the barrel (filled with good fruit/people), a barrel filled with vinegar will *always* transform sweet cucumbers into sour pickles—regardless of the best intentions, resilience, and genetic nature of those cucumbers." So, does it make more sense to spend our resources on attempts to identify, isolate, and destroy the few bad apples or to learn how vinegar works so that we can teach cucumbers how to avoid undesirable vinegar barrels?

My situational sermon has several related dimensions. First, we should be aware that a range of apparently simple situational factors can impact our behavior more compellingly than we would expect or predict. The research outlined here, along with that of my colleagues presented in this volume, points to the influential force of numerous variables: role playing, rules, presence of others, emergent group norms, group identity, uniforms, anonymity, social modeling, authority presence, symbols of power, time pressures, semantic framing, stereotypical images and labels, among others.

Second, the situationist approach redefines heroism. When the majority of ordinary people can be overcome by such pressures toward compliance and conformity, the minority who resist should be considered *heroic*. Acknowledging the special nature of this resistance means that we should learn from their example by studying *how* they have been able to rise above such compelling pressures. That suggestion is coupled with another that encourages the development of an essential but ignored domain of psychology—heroes and heroism.

Third, the situationist approach should, in my view, encourage us all to share a profound sense of personal humility when trying to understand those "unthinkable," "unimaginable," "senseless" acts of evil. Instead of immediately embracing the high moral ground that distances us good folks from those bad ones and gives short shrift to analyses of causal factors in the situations that form the context of the evil acts, the situational approach gives all

others the benefit of "attributional charity." This means that any deed, for good or evil, that any human being has ever performed or committed, you and I could also perform or commit—given the same situational forces. If so,
1050 it becomes imperative to constrain our immediate moral outrage that seeks vengeance against wrongdoers and turn our efforts toward uncovering the causal factors that could have led them in that aberrant direction.

The obvious current instantiation of these principles is the rush to characterize terrorists and suicide bombers as "evil" people, instead of working to understand the nature of the psychological, social, economic, and political conditions that have fostered such generalized hatred of an enemy nation, including our own, that young people are willing to sacrifice their lives and murder other human beings. The "war on terrorism" can never be won solely by the current administration's plans to find and destroy terrorists—since any
1060 individual, anywhere, at any time, can become an active terrorist. It is only by understanding the *situational determinants of terrorism* that programs can be developed to win the hearts and minds of potential terrorists away from destruction and toward creation—not a simple task, but an essential one that requires implementation of social-psychological perspectives and methods in a comprehensive, long-term plan of attitude, value, and behavior change.

REFERENCES

Adorno, T. W., Frenkel-Brunswick, E., Levenson, D. J., & Sanford, R. N. (1950). *The authoritarian personality.* New York: Harper & Row.

Atran, S. (2003, May 5), Who wants to be a martyr? *The New York Times,* p. A23.

Bandura, A. (1998). Mechanisms of moral disengagement. In W. Reich (Ed.), *Origins of terrorism: Psychologies, ideologies, theologies, states of mind* (pp. 161–191). New York: Cambridge University Press.

Bandura, A. (2003). The role of selective moral disengagement in terrorism and counterterrorism. In F. M. Mogahaddam & A. J. Marsella (Eds.), *Understanding terrorism* (pp. 121–150). Washington, DC: American Psychological Association.

Bandura, A., Underwood, B., & Fromson, M. E. (1975). Disinhibition of aggression through diffusion of responsibility and dehumanization of victims. *Journal of Personality and Social Psychology, 9,* 253–269.

Barstow, A. L. (1994). *Witchcraze: A new history of the European witch hunts.* New York: HarperCollins.

Baumeister, R. F. (1997). *Evil: Inside human cruelty and violence.* New York: Freeman.

Bennett, J. (2003, May 30). A scholar of English who clung to the veil. *The New York Times,* pp. A1, A14.

Browning, C. R. (1992). *Ordinary men: Reserve police battalion 101 and the final solution in Poland.* New York: HarperPerennial.

Chang, I. (1997). *The rape of Nanking: The forgotten holocaust of World War II.* New York: Basic Books.

Cialdini, R. B. (2001). *Influence: Science and practice* (4th ed.). Boston: Allyn & Bacon.

Dailey, J. M. (1992). Social organization for the production of evil. *Psychological Inquiry 3*, 199–218.

Darley, J. M., & Batson, D. (1973). From Jerusalem to Jericho: A study of situational and dispositional variables in helping behavior. *Journal of Personality and Social Psychology, 27*, 100–108.

Diener, E. (1980). Deindividuation: The absence of self-awareness and self-regulation in group members. In P. B. Paulus (Ed.), *The psychology of group influence* (pp. 209–243). Hillsdale, NJ: Erlbaum.

Festinger, L. (1957). *A theory of cognitive dissonance.* Palo Alto, CA: Stanford University Press.

Fraser, S. C. (1974). *Deindividuation: Effects of anonymity on aggression in children.* Unpublished manuscript, University of Southern California, Los Angeles.

Golding, W. (1954). *Lord of the flies.* New York: Capricorn Books.

Haney, C., & Zimbardo, P. G. (1998). The past and future of U.S. prison policy: Twenty-five years after the Stanford Prison Experiment. *American Psychologist, 53*, 709–727.

Haritos-Fatouros, M. (2002). *The psychological origins of institutionalized torture.* London: Routledge.

Hoffman, B. (2003, June). The logic of suicide terrorism. *The Atlantic Monthly*, 40–47.

Huggins, M., Haritos-Fatouros, M., & Zimbardo, P. G. (2002). *Violence workers: Police torturers and murderers reconstruct Brazilian atrocities.* Berkeley: University of California Press.

Keen, S. (1986). *Faces of the enemy: Reflections of the hostile imagination.* New York: HarperCollins.

Kramer, H., & Sprenger, J. (1971). *The malleus maleficarum.* New York: Dover. (Original work published 1486)

Latané, B., & Darley, J. M. (1970). *The unresponsive bystander: Why doesn't he help?* New York: Appleton-Century-Crofts.

Lee, M., Zimbardo, P. G., & Berthof, M. (1977). Shy murderers. *Psychology Today, 11*, 69–70, 76, 148.

Merari, A. (1990). The readiness to kill and die: Suicidal terrorism in the Middle East. In W. Reich (Ed.), *Origins of terrorism: Psychologies, theologies, states of mind* (pp. 192–200). New York: Cambridge University Press.

Merari, A. (2002, October). *Suicide terrorism.* Paper presented at the First Conference of the National Center for Disaster Psychology and Terrorism, Palo Alto, CA.

Milgram, S. (1974). *Obedience to authority.* New York: Harper & Row.

Myer, G. (2003, May 30). A young man radicalized by his months in jail. *The New York Times*, pp. A1, A14.

The new order (The Third Reich). (1989). Alexandria, VA: Time Life Books.

Orwell, G. (1981). *1984*. New York: Signet.

Prentice-Dunn, S., & Rogers, R. W. (1983). Deindividuation and aggression. In R. G. Geen & E. I. Donnerstein (Eds.), *Aggression: Theoretical and empirical reviews—issues in research* (Vol. 2, pp. 155–171). New York: Academic Press.

Ross, L. (1977). The intuitive psychologist and his shortcomings. In L. Berkowitz (Ed.), *Advances in experimental social psychology* (Vol. 10, pp. 173–220). New York: Academic Press.

Staub, E. (1989). *The roots of evil: The origins of genocide and other group violence.* New York: Cambridge University Press.

Waller, J. (2002). *Becoming evil: How ordinary people commit genocide and mass killing.* New York: Oxford University Press.

Watson, R. I., Jr. (1973). Investigation into deindividuation using a cross-cultural survey technique. *Journal of Personality and Social Psychology, 25,* 342–345.

Zimbardo, P. G. (1970). The human choice: Individuation, reason, and order versus deindividuation, impulse, and chaos. In W. J. Arnold & D. Levine (Eds.), *1969 Nebraska Symposium on Motivation* (pp. 237–307). Lincoln: University of Nebraska Press.

Zimbardo, P. G. (1975). On transforming experimental research into advocacy for social change. In M. Deutsch & H. Hornstein (Eds.), *Applying social psychology: implications for research, practice, and training* (pp. 33–66). Hillsdale, NJ: Erlbaum.

Zimbardo, P. G. (1976). Making sense of senseless vandalism. In E. P. Hollander & R. G. Hunt (Eds.), *Current perspectives in social psychology* (4th ed., pp. 129–134). Oxford, UK: Oxford University Press.

Zimbardo, P. G. (2003a). Mind control in Orwell's *1984*: Fictional concepts become operational realities in Jim Jones' jungle experiment. In M. Nussbaum, J. Goldsmith, & A. Gleason (Eds.), *1984: Orwell and our future.* Princeton: Princeton University Press.

Zimbardo, P. G. (2003b). Phantom menace: Is Washington terrorizing us more than Al Qaeda? *Psychology Today, 36,* pp. 34–36.

Zimbardo, P. G., Haney, C., Banks, C., & Jaffe, D. (1973, April 8). The mind is a formidable jailer: A Pirandellian prison. *The New York Times Magazine*, pp. 38 ff.

Zimbardo, P. G., Maslach, C., & Haney, C. (1999). Reflections on the Stanford Prison Experiment: Genesis, transformation, consequences. In T. Blass (Ed.), *Obedience to authority: Current perspectives on the Milgram Paradigm* (pp. 193–237). Mahwah, NJ: Erlbaum.

NOTES

NOTES